THE CONCEPT OF FORM IN THE TWENTIETH CENTURY

THE CONCEPT OF FORM
IN THE TWENTIETH CENTURY

Martin J. Buss

SHEFFIELD PHOENIX PRESS

2008

Copyright © 2008 Sheffield Phoenix Press

Published by Sheffield Phoenix Press
Department of Biblical Studies, University of Sheffield
Sheffield S10 2TN

www.sheffieldphoenix.com

A CIP catalogue record for this book
is available from the British Library

Typeset by CA Typesetting Ltd
Printed on acid-free paper by Lightning Source UK Ltd, Milton Keynes

ISBN-13 978-1-906055-51-6

CONTENTS

PREFACE

The present study is the outgrowth of a long-term concern with the notion of 'form', as the theoretical aspect of what is called 'form criticism'. In pursuing this interest, I found that ideas of form emerging during the last hundred years have a character different from earlier ideas. Specifically, they exhibit a concern with relationality, an intellectual orientation that is closely connected with corresponding social (including religious) ideals. The prominence of relational perspectives became clear through an acquaintance with a number of disciplines, for their theoretical similarities becomes especially apparent when they are observed together. Detailed relational applications made by individual disciplines are not pursued in the present work, however. Instead, the focus is on theoretical issues as they operate across disciplines and in society.

My analysis has benefited from discussions with quite a few colleagues in various fields. To cite all of them is impossible. Special thanks, however, go to Thomas Flynn, Hans Ineichen, and Matthias Jung in philosophy and Alvin Boskoff in sociology for careful readings of a good part of the manuscript at some time. Furthermore, I have been aided by the following associates, who have made both technical and thoughtful contributions: Michael Turner, Phillip Michael Sherman, Charles H. Kirschner, Yury Sukhodolsky, Mark Roncace, Alexander Diaz-Williamson, Kareem Khalifa, Sharon E. Rye, Peter Trudinger, Oyebisi Olatoye, Tamara Yates, Cristina Kendall, Shemanne Davis, Amy Parker, Autumn Woods, James Johnson, Philip R. Webb, and especially my long-term senior associate Nickie M. Stipe. Emory's College and Graduate School provided financial and organizational support. Among members of my family, my daughters Mary Aileen and Jeanne aided me with research and editing, my sons Samuel and Jonathan provided advice on logic and complexity theory, and, above all, my wife Nancy contributed loving support and careful reading.

INTRODUCTION

When we want to grasp something intellectually, we can say that we seek to apprehend its 'form' or pattern. Such an apprehension is different from physically encountering an object. For instance, if a rock strikes me down, no intellectual processing is required. However, if I contemplate the possibility of being struck by a rock, or if I reflect on having been struck, I consider the 'form' (or characteristics) of the rock, the 'form' (or nature) of being struck, my own 'form', and probably some causal form (or 'law'). In short, 'form'—at least as that word is used in the present study—is what is available to the intellect.

Although a rough meaning of that word is now in place, it is necessary to note that specific views of form have varied considerably in history. The present study explores views current during the period from about 1875 CE to the present, focusing especially on a 'relational' view of form, which combines generality with particularity.

Pragmatically, intellectual apprehensions of form are correlated with social and personal processes that involve what can be called 'freedom'. Just as there are different conceptions of form, so there are different ideals of freedom. In particular, the relational view of form is connected with an 'interactive' view of freedom, which includes both negative freedom 'from' and positive freedom 'to'.

The outlook of the period covered was not monolithic; rather, there were moderate divergences within the relational/interactive perspective and sharper ones between alternative views. Some attention will therefore be given to conflicts and accommodations between them.

Part I

THE RISE AND NATURE OF AN EXPLICITLY
RELATIONAL AND INTERACTIVE PERSPECTIVE

Chapter 1

MAJOR VIEWS OF FORM AND FREEDOM IN WESTERN HISTORY

In order to understand the special nature of relational conceptions of form and of associated views of freedom, as they were developed in the twentieth century, it is necessary to look at antecedents to them. The present chapter will accordingly consider relevant views that were prominent at different times in the so-called 'West'. (The specific data of the survey are fairly well known to specialists in the relevant fields and thus not heavily documented.)

As will be seen, views of form and freedom are closely interwoven. In fact, theoretical formulations in philosophy have arisen in close conjunction with corresponding social orientations, not just—as Hegel thought[1]—as belated reflections of them. This shows that in human life theory and praxis are intimately connected.

1. Four Major Views of Form

Three views of form can be contrasted with a relational conception: classical Platonism, Aristotelianism, and particularism.[2] Since classical Platonism and Aristotle's views are well known even by non-specialists, they can be treated quite briefly. Particularism is less widely known, however, and represents a group of opinions rather than a single one, so that it requires more detailed attention.

Classical Platonism, the version of Plato's thought considered here, is set forth by the figure of Socrates in the *Republic*. It views form as an ideal realm, which is in some sense more real than ordinary objects. For such objects, the realm of form provides models. This way of thinking downgrades particularity in favor of ideal forms.

Differently, Aristotle (at least as traditionally interpreted in Artistotelianism) thought of form as a unified combination of properties, called 'essence',

---

1. *Grundlinien des Philosophie des Rechts*, 1821, preface (near end).

2. In a comparable way to the present work, Pepper in 1942 delineated four 'world hypotheses'; however, he treated Platonism and Aristotelianism as two parts of one hypothesis and separated internal from external relationality. He gave only cursory attention to social contexts.

which an object shares with others of the same type. This essential character stands in contrast to the accidental features which the object also exhibits.[3] For instance, according to this concept, in a white horse the presence of four legs is essential (part of its 'form'), but whiteness is accidental.

Aristotle held that neither general forms nor particulars are real apart from each other. He thus considered the two sides to be of approximately equal significance, although he did not join them in the way relational theory came to do.

In contrast to Plato's and Aristotle's views stands a particularist outlook, which accepts only particularity, or at least gives priority to particulars. Early examples of particularism appeared in ancient Greece, but they were preserved only in fragmentary texts and second-hand reports, so that we are uncertain about their exact shape.

After an extended hiatus, particularism emerged as an undercurrent in Western Europe in the twelfth century CE. Described as the *via moderna*, it became increasingly prominent in Europe from c. 1300 on. In fact, in the fairly cautious words of Theodor Adorno, 'all philosophies of origin in modern times arose under nominalist [that is, particularist] auspices' (1956: 40).

From the European Middle Ages on, particularism became known as 'nominalism', for it holds that general terms are only 'nomina' (names or mental images) for similar objects and do not refer to something general in reality. 'Nominalism' was also the name of a logical system that is only loosely connected with particularism. However, for the sake of stylistic variety, 'nominalism' will be used, as in commonly done, as a synonym of 'particularism', when there is reference to this from the fourteenth century on. Specifically, nominalism holds that forms do not indicate patterns 'prior to' objects (contra Plato) or patterns 'in' objects (contra Aristotle). Rather, they are construed 'after' objects, as reflections upon objects or simply as convenient terms for them.

Since nominalism recognizes no patterns inherent in objects, the word 'form' comes to designate an agglomeration, an 'aggregate of all accidents, for which we give the matter a new name' (Hobbes 1840: 309 [1682]).[4] What this means is that nominalists envision a huge number of particular objects that are in principle unrelated to each other, and each object has a set of properties, none of which are repeated anywhere else (if they were repeated, they would be 'general'). In this view, order exists only if a god somehow holds things together. Without a god, there is only chaos.

3. E.g., *Metaphysics*, 1033b; *On Generation and Corruption*, 355b, 336a. (Aristotle himself was ambiguous, however, for he described essence as given in a definition; if 'essence' refers merely to what is indicated by the definition, then there is no difficulty with that concept.)
4. Similarly already Ockham, in the fourteenth century; see Buss 1999: 90.

Not surprisingly, then, and indeed usefully, particularism holds that there can be more than one appropriate classification for a given object. For instance, a white horse can be classed together with objects that have a similar color or with objects that have an organization similar enough to be also called 'horses'. Whether one chooses one classification or another depends on one's purpose.

Particularism includes many variations. These variations involve, above all, two major issues.

One issue concerns the extent to which general forms have at least a secondary kind of reality in someone's mind. Specifically, a radical version of nominalism holds that general terms are merely a matter of words and that even the mind has only vague images (thus, Alexander Bain 1870, I: 6). A more moderate version, called 'conceptualism', believes that the mind does entertain general forms. As a special case of this second option, many theistic versions hold that general forms are present in God's mind and provide standards or 'laws', which God, viewed as the grand particular, 'freely' (arbitrarily) imposes on the world.[5] Such moderate nominalism was presupposed by some of early modern science. Since any regularities that can be discovered were considered to be arbitrary (there is no rational basis for them), scientists operating within this framework held that the laws to which nature is subject need to be discovered by experimentation rather than by reason.

Particularism varies, further, in regard to the size of units that are considered primary. Units can range from the very small to the very large. For instance, the focus can be on very small units; this orientation may be called 'atomism'. Another possibility is to treat a human group, such as a nation or religious community, as an internally unified entity that does not share significantly with others; such an orientation can be called 'group particularism'. A third possibility is to view the whole universe as highly unified; this may be described as a strong holism or as 'monist universalism'.[6] In fact, each of these options was prominent at a different stage of the so-called 'Enlightenment'.

Within the Enlightenment, which is often considered to have begun in the middle of the seventeenth century CE, monist particularism arose first. It was set forth by Benedict de Spinoza (c. 1674). He accepted a long-standing definition of 'substance' as something that constitutes an independent reality and then argued—it would seem, with good reason—that there could be only one such substance, namely God, who includes everything (*Ethics*, 1.D3.P14 [1985–, I: 408, 420]).

---

5. See, e.g., Blumenberg 1966, Pt. II, section 3; cf. Schneewind 1998: 24 (on John Duns Scotus, c. 1300 CE), and, again (as a report), Griffin 2000: 115.

6. Thus, Andrea Maihofer (1998: 392) and Buss (1999: 123; cf. 280-82, 318, 345); similarly, Alvin Toffler 1980: 320; Alain Badiou 1997: 118-19.

Spinoza's view was similar to universalist ideas with a Platonist or Aristotelian base that were prominent in the early part of the seventeenth century. These included the idea that at the beginning of humanity there had been an ideal natural religion which held beliefs that are now 'common' to religions, although these differ in many other ways.[7] This universalist conception sought to overcome the religious wars that had been pervasive from the middle of the sixteenth century on. Spinoza's view was similarly universalist, but it was nominalist in its ontological framework.

An individualistic version of particularism emerged soon thereafter in the thought of John Locke. He opposed the idea that there had been a common natural religion and denied the presence of innate, and thus universal-human, moral ideas (1690, 1.3). The widely held view that the Enlightenment was universalist in outlook is thus largely in error, although it was somewhat more universalist than the Romanticism that followed it.

In fact, group particularism came next, prominent from the middle of the eighteenth century on. This involved a differential consciousness that emphasized collective change—often viewed positively as 'progress'—and 'otherness', that is, cultural diversity (see, e.g., Said 1978; Cannadine 2001: 8). Specifically, the idea that each region of the world (e.g., the 'East'), each nation, and each religion have a peculiar character (variously appreciated) became widely accepted.[8] (The political significance of such orientations will be discussed later.) Several prominent figures (including Voltaire, the important aesthetician Lord Kames, and the French revolutionary Comte de Mirabeau) held that human beings have different origins and, in that sense at least, constitute more than one species (see Richard Popkin 1987: 34-165; Anthony Pagden 1995: 175).[9] Even Immanuel Kant, whose outlook was relatively cosmopolitan, formulated an idea of four human 'races' with their specific characteristics. He considered ethical maturity to be possible only for white males (Eze 1997: 115; Bernasconi 2001).

In the nineteenth century (after the 'Enlightenment'), Georg W.F. Hegel presented a cosmic view that came close to monism by envisioning reality as a single, integrated, whole. Since he accepted the idea of progress, his universalism was not appreciative of all human beings. Rather, Hegel held

7. See P. Harrison 1990: 29, 127-64. Early proponents of this idea (such as Herbert of Cherbury, writing in 1624) stood close to Platonism. Later Matthew Tindal, who in 1730 presented a scaled-down version of this thesis (privileging Christianity and not arguing for an ideal past religion), operated with Aristotelian assumptions.

8. See Buss 1999: 121, with references for John Dryden, David Hume, Madame de Stael, Johann Herder, and others; also, Wilfred C. Smith 1962: 37-44, for the idea of a plurality of religions.

9. This idea continued well into the nineteenth century, during much of which it was reportedly the predominant 'scientific' viewpoint (Gossett 1963, chapter 4).

that the culture of his time and place (especially, of Germany) was superior to that of others; he opposed international organization.[10]

In sum, particularism comes in a number of varieties. They include radical rejections of generality along with more moderate versions that make room for generality on a secondary basis. More importantly perhaps, particularism varies in that it can focus on units of different sizes.

From the end of the nineteenth century on, however, it became apparent that particularism poses a number of intellectual problems. One problem is that something which has nothing in common with anything else cannot be understood. This point had been recognized for a long time,[11] but its implications had been ignored until it was observed, as stated by Hugh Kenner, that pure (that is, particularist) empiricism is a game where the central rule 'forbids you to understand what you are talking about' (1968: 173).

In psychology, in fact, evidence began to accumulate that perception never consists just of particulars but always utilizes general categories. The use of such categories begins on a pre-human level, for all organisms are programmed to react to certain possibilities or kinds of phenomena.[12] Thus, contrary to some theories, categories are not freshly imposed by the human mind.

Another intellectual difficulty that became apparent was how it is possible to transcend the isolation of the individual thinker. This problem became especially acute when Descartes' solution that one can count on not being deceived by God became doubtful, since the existence of God itself was in doubt. This difficulty was solved in part when a number of thinkers with a strong social sense argued that society is temporally prior to an individual human being and that even self-consciousness is social (thus, for instance, Josiah Royce 1898: 182, 201).

In any case, quite a few thinkers began to believe—this is now a fourth view—that relations are part of reality and that, in fact, form is best seen as a complex of relations. This view places particularity and generality on an equal footing. In that respect, this view resembles Aristotle's perspective. However, unlike Aristotle (as will be seen below, 4.1), a relational conception does not simply add particularity and generality to each other but rather sees them as aspects of one structure. Relations require a relative independence (and thus particularity) for the items that are related as well as a degree of connectivity (and with it a certain generality).

Since relational theory accepts generality, it is important to distinguish generality from universality. The word 'general' describes a phenomenon

10. See Buss 1999: 129.
11. There was a traditional dictum: *individuum est ineffabile*. Romantics valued this ineffability (Gadamer 1984: 24).
12. Thus already C.S. Peirce (1982–, IV: 447, 450 [1883]), in regard to the appearance of categories in animal instincts.

that is at least potentially shared by more than one object, while the word 'universal', as it is commonly used, refers to a characteristic that is shared by all members of a given group. Relational theory does accept universality, but in another way; namely, by holding that the relational net extends to all of existence. With regard to human communication, Peter Levine has described this conception as follows:

> I am likely to share certain background characteristics with many people, and these commonalities provide the grounds for our mutual understanding... Even if two people can identify no similarities in cultural background, they are likely to be able to find a third party who bridges some of the gap between them, or a chain of such people... This account never invokes the notion of a universal 'human nature' as the precondition of communication; it only assumes a complex web of differences that ultimately includes us all (1995: 191).

In short, relational theory holds that units, large or small, are neither completely independent from others nor tightly knit internally. Rather, all complexes have within them relations that introduce some divergence, and all are involved in outward relations that both connect and differentiate. Details concerning this outlook will occupy much of the present volume.

We have seen, then, four different conceptions of form: (1) form as ideal and more truly real than ordinary objects, (2) form as the 'essence' (basic structure) of objects, (3) form as a bundle of 'accidents' for which there is no rationale (although the bundle can be tightly unified), and (4) form as a complex of relations.

2. Political Aspects of the Different Views of Form

The different views of form that have been outlined each have characteristic political associations. In other words, they have a social side.

An association between politics and intellectual views of form was apparent in ancient Greece. There, emphasis on an ideal generality was connected with the aristocracy, while a particularist outlook was associated especially with the middle stratum of society. Specifically, Plato was socially elitist, although he presented some egalitarian ideas.[13] By contrast, particularists of various kinds gravitated toward relatively democratic or privatistic organizations. Among them stood Democritus, who accepted regularity in the world (perhaps even determinism, which would reflect a kind of monism) and supported democratic politics for males who were not slaves. Relatively more freewheeling was Epicurus, who highlighted deviations from regularity and enjoyed a voluntary friendship circle.

---

13. Cf. Buss 1999: 35. Plato is reported to have had an aristocratic family background.

Aristotle's position occupied a space between Platonism and particularism not only in theory but also in terms of social policy. In line with his acceptance of both generality and particularity, he favored a society in which aristocrats and the middle stratum have a balance of power.

Less clearly related to a social level was the tradition of Stoicism, which has not yet been mentioned since, unlike Platonism and Aristotelianism, it did not directly address questions of 'form'. Intellectually, Stoicism joined a particularist view of objects with a belief in an inclusive universal reason. Ethically, it pursued both private and social ideals in the Hellenistic and Roman empires. Its universalist inclusivism was probably in good part due to the cosmopolitan background after Alexander the Great's establishment of an empire; its founder, Zeno, had a father with a West-Semitic name and never became a citizen of Athens, although he lived there.[14]

Apparently no Greek philosophy championed specifically lower-class interests. Insofar as there was concern for those who are suffering, it was attributed in Greece to 'God' (or 'the gods' collectively).[15] Within philosophy, such representation of deity was made by the Greek-speaking Stoic Cleanthes (*Hymn to Zeus*) and the Roman Stoic Epictetus (*Discourses*, 1.13). In fact, Stoics included lower-class persons in their concern.[16]

The connection of the different views of form with social organization becomes even clearer when one observes what happened during succeeding millennia. Until the twelfth century CE, and less pervasively until the seventeenth, variations of Platonism formed a major component of culture in a society that was ruled from the top. Aristotelianism flourished during the twelfth century and continued for several centuries after that, as feudalism gradually gave way to an influential role for 'burghers' (the early 'bourgeoisie'); it was thus prominent in a hybrid (partly aristocratic, partly bourgeois)

---

14. Zeno's native language was not Greek; his father's name, Mnaseas, is thought to reflect either Manasseh or Menahem, both of which appear in the Bible (Pohlenz 1948: 22, 25). Albert Goedeckemeyer said that Zeno had 'a Jewish father' (1941: 11), but that assessment may well be too specific. In any case, Zeno and later Stoics were deeply indebted to ancient Near Eastern traditions, which included the religious theme that kings should be concerned with those who are otherwise neglected. That theme was radicalized and partially democratized in biblical religion, which expresses sympathy for the oppressed (as Friedrich Nietzsche, Friedrich Engels, and Slavoj Žižek [2003: 6] have seen, each in their own way).

15. Thus, Plato, *Laws*, 927; Alcidamus, according to a scholion on Aristotle's *Rhetoric*, 1373b.

16. Cynics, who were in some ways associated with Stoicism, despised social status and were at least somewhat popular with common people. However, their works are not well preserved, and one can only wonder how much active support was provided to persons at the lower end of society.

social situation, in line with Aristotle's recommendation.[17] Moving behind it, nominalism accompanied the rise of the middle class, first as an undercurrent (when independent cities began to form)[18] and then with increasing influence until the nineteenth century, while the largely urban middle class became more and more powerful. Relational theory arose later in conjunction with an inclusive social policy. Stoicism was more flexible socially and played a role throughout.[19]

It is true, one needs to be careful with this kind of sociological analysis. First of all, one should not think of clearly circumscribed 'classes'—high, middle, or low. Secondly, one should not expect rigid correlations between politics and ideas about forms.[20] However, the association of different views of form with different social structures does not appear to be accidental. Good reasons for these connections can be given.

Platonic theory supports aristocratic rule for two reasons: (1) Such a theory highlights commonality rather than separateness and emphasizes tradition, which expresses commonality with the past; for instance, aristocracy grants status on the basis of descent, which represents biological tradition. (2) Platonic theory looks up to an ideal form that stands 'above' ordinary beings, just as aristocracy grants a higher status to some persons in their very being.

In contrast, particularism inherently favors, and thus is readily favored by, the middle class.[21] Middle-class persons rely heavily on achieved status; that is, they make their way in society on the basis of competition and voluntary agreements. Unlike aristocrats, middle-class persons derive only limited advantages from tradition. Furthermore, they have little reason for solidarity with persons who stand at the lower end of the societal spectrum and indeed have less reason to be concerned with them than do those who as rulers have responsibility for the whole society. Consequently, both in ancient Greece and in 'modern' Europe, they have had relatively little concern for social welfare.

The association of relational philosophy with attention to persons who stand at the lower end of the socioeconomic scale and with persons who

17. See Buss 1999: 71, 84-86. Universities were themselves a socially hybrid phenomenon. Aristotelian philosophy (conveyed through a Muslim medium) became influential for Jewish thinking in the twelfth century and for Christian thinking from the thirteenth century on.

18. Thus, also, Günther Mensching (1992: 130).

19. Cf. now Strange and Zupko 2004.

20. Randall Collins (1998: 8) was right in saying that one cannot (firmly) predict someone's outlook from that person's social position, but the fact that there is no rigid connection between political structure and philosophical ideas does not mean that there is no connection at all.

21. By 'middle-class', I mean a position that is neither high nor low in a given society.

are marginal in other ways is described in later chapters. It is worth noting here, however, that some elements of a relational view were anticipated by Stoics, who were inclusive in their orientation.[22]

3. *Notions of Freedom*

The connection between theoretical conceptions of form and practical social orientations becomes explicit in ideas about freedom. After all, these ideas represent theoretical notions that deal with pragmatic issues.

There are different kinds of freedom.[23] They are present in every kind of society, but the relative emphasis upon them varies from society to society and from one view of form—Platonic, Aristotelian, particularist, or relational—to another (see table 1.1, positioned at the end of the present chapter).

Internal Freedom, With Positive and Negative Sides
In classic philosophical and religious works, 'freedom' was often equated with a morally good life. For instance, Socrates was cited by Xenophon (*Memorabilia*, 4.5.3) as saying that freedom means 'to do what is best'. Following Socrates in his own way, Plato held that 'virtue represents the character of the free', while vice is slavish (*Alcibiades*, 135c). Zeno, the Stoic, is reported to have made the same point (Diogenes Laertius 7.33), which was also emphasized by his followers. Along a similar line, classical Christian and Jewish statements expressed the conviction that one's 'true' life is moral or spiritual.[24]

This freedom can be called 'internal', as long as it is understood not as private but as involving the sense of being part of a larger reality. In fact, according to Plato, Zeno, Jews, and Christians (among others), internal freedom is linked with an orientation to an eternal or infinite reality that includes or is supportive of all beings (thus also C. Taylor 1989: 120-24 for Plato's view of the 'soul'). Peter Singer (Jewish by heritage) stated such a vision in a nonreligious way:[25]

---

22. On relational elements in Stoicism, see below, 3.1.

23. Surveys of themes of freedom include Spaeman 1972; Parent 1983; Coreth 1985; Blasche 1995; Hirschmann 2003: 1-74.

24. Thus, Paul in Rom. 7:22–8:2; Gal. 5:13. According to the Mishnah (c. 200 CE), a 'free' person (who is 'exalted') is one who is occupied with the study of the Law (*Avot* 6:2). Buddhist liberation (valued by Claude Lévi-Strauss 1955: 476) and various kinds of spiritual liberation (Wilber 1998: 211-13) also belong primarily to this internal kind of freedom.

25. Citing this passage does not, of course, imply approval of all of Singer's specific proposals.

> Reason provides us with the capacity to recognise that each of us is simply one being among others, all of whom have wants and needs that matter to them... Can that insight ever overcome the pull of other elements in our evolved nature that act against the idea of an impartial concern for all of our fellow humans, or, better still, for all sentient beings? (2000: 62-63)

Piaget has given the name 'decentering' to such perspective taking (1945, *passim*). Decentering, as he used the term, refers not to the abandonment of a center but to the adoption of an imaginary center of vision outside oneself. For instance, we can imagine how an object appears from a location other than the one we now occupy. Adopting such an imaginary center of vision, human beings look at themselves, as it were, from the outside. In fact, this is what we mean by self-awareness. Decentering, or self-transcendence, is thus integrally connected with selfhood. As the statement by Singer indicates, a self-aware and thus self-critical consciousness seeks 'a value that transcends individual likings and dislikings' (R.T. Allen 1998: 165). Consequently, this freedom accepts generality as a concern for the common good.

Inner freedom has a positive side, since it is freedom 'for' the larger good, but it also has a negative aspect, since self-awareness includes self-critique. Such a critique can constitute a re-examination of previously-held opinions. More frequently, awareness engages in impulse control (Grigsby and Stevens 2000: 223, 259) and thus avoids domination by bodily drives. Describing the goal of self-critique in the ancient world, Michel Foucault observed that, by fulfilling it, one is not a 'slave to one's self and to one's appetites' (1984a: 103, 105).

Restraint of the body is indeed a part of internal freedom, but it has not operated with the same force at all times and under all conditions. Rather, it has appeared with special force in aristocratically-ruled societies. For instance, in ancient Greece, rule over bodily passions was a model trait, qualifying a person for rule over society.[26] More importantly, in a hierarchically ruled society, internal freedom—sometimes expressed through sexual asceticism—has often been the only freedom available to those who are not socially elite. Through an inward conquest of 'lower' forces they could see themselves as true masters, in contrast to what they experienced in the external world (Davis 1975: 42).

However, internal freedom, especially in a positive (non-ascetic) form, is also valued in other kinds of society. For instance, persons in hunting and gathering societies regularly value dreams, report spiritual journeys, and believe that all beings are animated with an inner life. European middle-class society often joined commercial materialism with a personalist, even privatist, outlook. In any case, conscious internality is characteristic of human beings.

26. See, e.g., Foucault 1983a: 235.

During the last hundred years, the ideal of internal freedom remained important. For instance, Margaret Walker—an African American woman—said about her life in a world with continued external restrictions, 'I have learned from the difficult exigencies of life that freedom is a philosophical state of mind and existence' (1997: 3 [1980]).[27] Ecstatic forms of religion were widespread from early in the twentieth century on, especially, at first, in the US at the lower end of the social order. An inner freedom that positively values the body together with the spirit became a common theme among relatively educated persons (see below, 2.2, 3, 4; 5.5; 8.2).

As indicated, philosophy has long favored internal freedom (although not always with a self-transcending orientation). Philosophers, to be sure, constitute only a small portion of humanity. For many, perhaps for most, human beings, religion is the vehicle within which they find or express such internal freedom as they experience. A fine example of such an experience, however, has been furnished by Bertrand Russell, who was not conventionally religious.[28] In 1901, he experienced 'a sort of mystic illumination', which lasted 'for a time'. He described its beginning as follows:

> We found Mrs Whitehead undergoing an unusually severe bout of pain. She seemed cut off from everyone and everything by walls of agony, and the sense of solitude of each human soul suddenly overwhelmed me… Within five minutes I went through some such reflections as the following: the loneliness of the human soul is unendurable; nothing can penetrate it except the highest intensity of the sort of love that religious teachers have preached; whatever does not spring from this motive is harmful, or at least useless; it follows that war is wrong, that a public school education [that is, an elite private education] is abominable, that the use of force is to be deprecated, and that in human relations one should penetrate to the core of loneliness in each person and speak to that… At the end of those five minutes, I had become a completely different person… Having been an imperialist, I became a pro-Boer and a pacifist… I found myself filled with semi-mystical feelings about beauty, with an intense interest in children (1967–69, I: 145-46).[29]

27. The positive aspect of internal freedom is sometimes simply called 'positive freedom' (thus, Isaiah Berlin [1958] and, earlier, Kant [1910–, IV: 446]). Berlin also called it simply 'inner'; contra misunderstandings of him (which are still widespread), Berlin emphasized in 1993 that he did *not* reject this kind of freedom, although he had a problem with the conceptualization of external-positive freedom (see below, n. 44).

28. Russell was raised in an agnostic context but had (already prior to 1901) an interest in pantheistic mysticism (Monk 1996: 67). In regard to organized religion, he presented strong condemnations of Christianity (1957 [1927]) and of 'all the great religions' (1957: v), along with partial appreciation (1957: 110 [1903]; 1935, Chap. 10; 1945: 495; 1946: 11; 2002: 287 [1957]).

29. Besides Russell's autobiography, see Monk 1996 and Russell 2002.

Not many people have dramatic experiences such as Russell did, and, when they do, the specific content varies greatly. Yet internal freedom should be recognized as a significant aspect of the human life.

External Negative Freedom, Emphasized in 'Modern' Culture

A different, although common, notion of freedom refers to an absence of restraint by others, such as by social authorities. This can be called 'external negative', since its primary emphasis is on freedom 'from' external forces.[30]

This was the freedom implied in the social outlook of early Greek particularists (Democritus, Epicurus). It was described by Aristotle as an important value in a 'democratic' state, for which he had partial sympathy (*Politics*, 1317b). Since this freedom did not apply to slaves (at the bottom of the social order) and also was not an aristocratic ideal, it can be described as middle-class. In Athens, however, it did not apply to women.

External negative freedom became the watchword of 'modern' society in Europe as the middle class became dominant; indeed, it was emphasized one-sidedly, although not exclusively. It was associated in modern Europe with nominalism in the following ways:

First of all, nominalism does not accept any intrinsic order in reality. An implication of this assumption is that ethics and other values are in theory arbitrary. Nominalists held that both God and human beings are free to make decisions without being bound by anything; they are not even bound by their own natures, since (contra Aristotle) no intrinsic natures or essences are recognized. Another way of saying this is that values and faith are separated from fact and reason. This separation means that thinking ('reason') is ideally free from emotion (it can be 'objective') and that emotions are prized when they are free from rationality, as was done by the Romantics around 1800 CE.

As was mentioned (in section 1), most Christian nominalists held that general laws of the universe arise secondarily as a result of God's free will. Similarly, they believed that God has provided moral laws for human actions. These two kinds of law are different in that humans have freedom to choose whether or not they will obey the laws applying to them. It is true, violations of moral laws may have certain consequences, but divine forgiveness can ameliorate them, since God wants human beings to follow the divine laws voluntarily, out of love. In other words, the idea is that God and human beings have and should have freedom. The rest of reality, however, can legitimately be subjugated. When the nonhuman world is overpowered,

---

30. Locke: freedom is the power to do as one (preferentially) wills (1690, 2.21.15, 21). Voltaire: 'liberty...is...the power of doing what I want' ('Of Liberty', 1764 [1879: 580]).

human beings are free from it (not dominated by it). Power over nature became an overt theme with the nominalist Francis Bacon (*Novum organum*, 1620, 1.129).

Secondly, negative freedom enters into particularist notions because a lack of intrinsic connectivity implies the possibility of change, that is, freedom from the past. This point is implicit in the fact that nominalism was known from early on as the 'modern' way. However, an attitude that values the new (the 'modern') more than the old—and thus believes in 'progress'—did not actually become pronounced until about 1700 CE, in conjunction with a turn away from a theological perspective. This was a conscious turn toward the future, involving a struggle between supporting the 'ancients' and favoring the 'moderns'. Thirdly, when particularism focuses on individuals or on groups, it supports competition. Indeed, competitive self-assertion was emphasized in the 'modern' period.[31]

On the individual level, self-interest—in contrast to benevolence, that is, concern for others—came to be described from the seventeenth century on as the main (or even only) human motivation. An early instance of the championing of self-interest was Grotius's defense of practices by the Dutch East India Company (1995: 9 [1609]). Indeed, there is reason to agree with P. Kropotkin's judgment that objections to mutual aid were made after the Middle Ages by persons who wished 'to increase their own wealth and their own powers' (1902, Introduction).

'Self-love' emerged expressly as a theme a little before 1700 CE (Schneewind 1998: 350, 404-28) and was highlighted in the mid-eighteenth century Scottish circle that included Hume, Adam Smith, and the aesthetician Lord Kames (cf. Buss 1999: 130-31). Aristotle had already supported self-love, but only for the 'good' person (*Nicomachean Ethics*, 1169a). Without this restriction, Hume regarded self-interest as the basis of justice (1739, 3.2.2).[32] Skeptical of benevolence, Smith said that what prompts us to high virtue is not 'the love of our neighbor', but 'the love of what is honorable and noble, of the grandeur and dignity, superiority of our own characters' (1761 [2nd ed. of 1759], 3.3). Without much attention even to moral nobility, Smith based his theoretical construction of capitalism on self-love (1776, 1.2).

Aware of this movement of thought, Darwin noted that 'with increased experience and reason...the self-regarding virtues, such as temperance,

---

31. Thus, rightly, Hans Blumenberg (1966, Pt. II).

32. Both Hume and, even more, Adam Smith used the word 'sympathy', but they meant by this not care for another but rather emotional or mental resonance. When positive, this resonance leads to imitation and when negative to contempt; in general, it leads to seeking approval, including self-approval. See, e.g., A. Smith 1759, 1.1, 3, and Sugden 2002. 'Pity and compassion' are mentioned as a special kind of sympathy [1.1.1.1, 5; cf. 7.3.1.4] but are not given much attention.

chastity, etc. ...come to be highly esteemed'; this view stands in contrast with the outlook of the more socially oriented 'savages' (1871, I: 165). Kant based ethics on pride in one's supersensuous ('rational') existence and furnished a detailed description of ethics more in terms of duties to oneself—such as honesty and avoidance of 'self-pollution' (sexual or otherwise)—than in terms of duties to others.[33]

Self-assertion meant an emphasis on 'reason' in intellectual matters. Reason was previously considered as something to which one was subject, but it came to mean primarily self-confident thinking that is not dominated by anyone else.[34] This was often called 'free' thinking (e.g., by Anthony Collins in 1713). Later, Romantics thought that even 'reason' is excessively restrictive, since it implies disciplined thought.

Beyond the human individual, nominalism supported nationalism (with or without a king) from the fourteenth century on.[35] For instance, Latin as a common intellectual language for much of Europe gradually gave way to the use of local languages even for academic purposes, especially by the eighteenth century. National independence was formally recognized in the Peace of Westphalia of 1648, which specified that one nation was not to interfere with the internal affairs of another. This idea was contrary to the earlier conceptions of European countries as local entities within the Christian world, overseen by the papacy (Flood 1998: 24).

Freedom for individuals within a nation was associated with republican forms of government. In republics, political freedom was usually moderate and frequently associated with religion (see Skinner 1998). It could even allow for the rule of kings. In fact, kings and the urban middle class (the 'bourgeoisie') often arrived at common cause against the landed aristocracy.

A relative degree of freedom within a nation did not lead to a championing of freedom for human beings outside that nation. Rather, self-assertion was exerted in the conquest or enslavement of others. Beliefs in differences between 'races' or—according to some secular views—between several

---

33. See *Kritik der praktischen Vernunft*, 1788: 158, and *Metaphysik der Sitten*, 1797 (1910, VI: 417-74).

34. Thus also Dupré (2004: 338). The idea of nonauthoritarian thinking was present in Niccolò Machiavelli's *Discourses on Livy* (1551, 1.58.1: it is 'not...a mistake to defend any opinion through arguments without using either authority or force') and in Herbert of Cherbury's *De Veritate* (1624, chapter 6: 'I refer the Reader to his own faculties for proof' [1937: 154]). John Toland was one who called such a process 'reason', in contrast to 'a lazy Reliance upon Authority' (1696, 1.4). Similarly, Thomas Paine declared, in *The Age of Reason* (1794, chapter 1), that 'my own mind is my own church'.

35. Already thus for Ockham, in support of his prince against the pope (Buss 1999: 89).

human species justified such subjugations.[36] In fact, claiming freedom for oneself but not for others is not uncommon. A ready association of political liberty at home with expansion abroad was already observed by Sallust in regard to Rome (c. 40 BCE) and in more general terms by Machiavelli (c. 1520 CE).[37] The English and (beginning a little later) the US empires similarly had a republican base.[38]

Yet it should be seen that in modern times nominalism was, for the most part, moderate or impure (mixed with other perspectives). Perhaps most importantly, the idea of 'natural law' played a role, although it was now often stated in terms of 'natural rights', which had a more individualistic orientation.

Early (including Stoic) notions concerning natural law were thus continued, although more-or-less religious persons thought of natural law or rights as a general arrangement by God, distinct from a special revelation.[39] Along this view, the American 'Declaration of Independence' (1776) declared that 'all men are created equal' and 'that they are endowed by their Creator with certain inalienable Rights'.

Soon after this, to be sure, the idea of natural law began to wane. For instance, the French 'Declaration of the Rights of Man and of the Citizen' (1789) loosened the connection of rights with God and even with humanity as such. Although it made its proclamation 'under the auspices of the Supreme Being' and spoke of 'natural rights', it emphatically asserted that all 'sovereignty' and 'authority' resides in the 'Nation'. The notion of 'natural rights' was thus still used in order to oppose special privilege for some, but it was modified by an emphasis on citizenship in a nation.

Several decades later, the strongly nominalist Jeremy Bentham made the 'discovery' that liberty is an entirely 'negative' notion (Long 1977: 54)—this was clearly a new idea for him—and said that 'there are...no such things as natural rights' in distinction from 'legal' rights, which are adopted as a matter of choice (1843, II: 500 [1816]). In Germany, the 'historical school' of law, which began in the nineteenth century, substituted the idea of historical development for that of natural law.

However, before the decline of the idea of natural law became pronounced, that idea, together with the ideology of national and individual freedom and other factors that were less ideological, played a role in the

36. See above, section 1, on group particularism.
37. Sallust, *The War with Cataline*; Machiavelli, *Discourses*, 1.5.
38. Some Spaniards and others had second thoughts about the validity of empire, in part on the basis of non-nominalist thinking, but this point requires further investigation; opposition to slavery was connected with such questionings (see below, nn. 40 and 41).
39. Grotius still expressed this position in terms that were not nominalist (*On the Law of War and Peace*, 1625, 1.1.10 [ed. 1995]). Hobbes (*Leviathan*, 1651: 148 [Chap. 26]) presented a nominalist version.

abolition of slavery.[40] Much of sixteenth-century opposition to at least some forms of slavery by followers of Thomas Aquinas (extending earlier Roman Catholic rejections) had been based on a theory of natural law. Their critique became influential in western Europe and eventually in the US.[41] This critique was linked at least in part with the bias of biblically-based religion toward the 'poor', as was implicitly recognized by Adam Smith.[42] The abolition of slavery was one of the great achievements of the modern period, but it did not come about as a consequence of pure nominalism. In fact, no period has been monolithic in its orientation.

In sum, 'moderns', emphasizing particularity, championed several versions of negative freedom: from reason or feeling (when focusing on one or the other of these), from nonhuman nature (which is to be conquered), from intellectual authorities (including religious ones), from empires (insofar as they rule over one's own nation), from the past in general, and more specifically from past feudal arrangements (in favor of republicanism and capitalism). Nevertheless, during the period from the sixteenth to nineteenth centuries, various concepts were formulated to restrict or moderate this negative freedom from restraint. They included the following: an acceptance of royal authority (Bodin, Hobbes)[43] and some elements of natural law.

At the end of the nineteenth century, however, a major turn took place. One line (to be discussed in Chapter 6) moved toward a more radically negative freedom; another, toward external positive freedom.

External Positive Freedom

Near the year 1900 CE, as modernity came into full flower, many became aware of its problematic side. These problems included: a glorification of

---

40. For data and discussions, see Skinner 1978: 155-70; Davis 2001: 205-15; Stark 2003: 359-60. (Bentham's unpublished moderate opposition to slavery had a prudential base [1843, I: 344-46].)

41. Some relevant Roman Catholic data appear in Panzer 1996 (although one-sidedly so) and in a broader context (together with a consideration of other factors) in J. Wilson 1993: 208-9. 'Natural' law, right, or justice (within a broadly religious frame) was important for major leaders in the antislavery movement: Charles Montesquieu in 1748; Francis Hutcheson in 1755 (to the extent that he went in this direction); George Wallace in 1760; G.T.F. Raynal in 1770; Thomas Jefferson in 1770.

42. Smith, however, thought that members of the clergy opposed slavery for self-interested reasons, since persons at the lower end of society were their primary clientele (1978: 187–89 [1762 MS, III: 118-22]). Like most major philosophers of his time other than Hutcheson (his teacher), Smith did not oppose slavery, although he saw problems associated with it both for slaves and for masters; he did not expect abolition to occur because he thought that human beings like to dominate others (see 1759, 7.2.1.3/28; 1776, 3.2.12).

43. Hobbes believed that an acceptance of royal authority is voluntary, but then cannot be revoked; Locke, in contrast, thought that revocation is legitimate.

conflict (including conquest), misery for those not in a good position to compete (acute, as a result of the Industrial Revolution), alienation from nature (expressed in an attitude of domination over it), and an undue depreciation of the past together with an unrealistic optimism toward the future. The basic challenge, then, was how to avoid or limit these features (which all seemed to arise from a one-sided particularism) while retaining the valued aspects of modernity. Modern features continued to be accepted, including republican forms of government (valuing both individuals and local groupings), efficiency in economics (aided by competition), empirical science, a readiness for change (such as in the role of the sexes), and an appreciation for individual and group diversities. In short, the conviction that both particularity and generality are needed and that both separability and connectivity need to be recognized grew and became widespread at the end of the nineteenth century.

Accordingly, a new meaning for 'freedom' obtained currency. In the new sense, the word 'freedom' refers to the opportunity of overcoming or avoiding a deprivation that restricts achievement and enjoyment; it allows for the likelihood that social interaction can help that aim. Like the negative freedom described earlier, positive freedom of this kind is external (social) rather than internal. Yet unlike the ideal of negative freedom as independence from others, it recognizes that fulfilling desires and potentials gain from interactions, even from organized societal support.[44]

Social cooperation was, of course, not new. It had been advocated and exercised for a long time in all parts of the human world. In the West, Plato set forth a dramatic version of communal organization in the *Republic* and a relatively more restrained version in the *Laws*; Aristotle described a moderate form of societal cooperation. In medieval and 'modern' societies, there were provisions for human welfare, usually under religious auspices. Yet the treatment of such provisions as a kind of 'freedom', under the auspices of organized society, was a conscious response to the strong emphasis on negative freedom that had come before.

The idea of positive freedom was anticipated by Hegel, Antonio Rosmini, and Karl Marx (in a manuscript not published until 1932).[45] It was formally

---

44. A set of three freedoms (internal, external negative, and external positive) has been discussed somewhat widely. Isaiah Berlin, however, thought that the external positive kind is 'misleadingly' called 'social freedom' (1958: 43 [cf. above, n. 27]). John Stuart Mill had outlined three freedoms, which resemble the three discussed here (although they are not identical with them): freedom of thought and expression, freedom to act according to one's taste, and freedom to associate (*On Liberty*, 1859, 'Introductory').

45. According to Rosmini, 'social freedom' obtains when there is benevolence and justice (1837, §103). Marx and Engels said that individuals obtain freedom 'in and through' their associations (*Die deutsche Ideologie*, 1845/46 MS [1957–, III: 74]).

described as a 'positive' one by T.H. Green, who championed relational thinking and was one of the prime leaders of the social-concern movement in England around 1880 (see below, 2.1). According to Green (1885–88, II: 324, 512-16), freedom means the ability of human beings to exercise their rights and to move toward fulfilling their 'possibilities' with the aid of appropriate means, including communal, such as state, action. Green focused on this kind of freedom but did not intend to deny the simultaneous operation of negative freedom, that is, freedom from coercion. Similarly, Havelock Ellis in 1895 favored 'the socialization of all material necessities of life as the only means of obtaining freedom for individual development'; however, for him this did not imply governmental action, for he was also unhappy about state activity (Grosskurth 1980: 259).

The ideal of positive freedom has continued to the present day. For instance, Robert Neville described 'social external' freedom as one that increases 'opportunity' (1974: 115). Indeed, while negative freedom—freedom from restraint—guards against the narrowing of opportunities, positive freedom increases their range. Amartya Sen, too, has spoken of 'positive' freedom in this way (2002: 11, 583-622 [cf. his studies in 1985 and 1999]). Albrecht Wellmer explained the idea as follows: 'individual freedom is a communally facilitated freedom in the sense that other people are not just the limit, but also the condition of the possibility of my freedom' (1998: 5 [1989]).[46] A number of writers have described this aspect of freedom as 'empowerment' (Brenkert 1991; Steele 1997: 204).

A Combination of Freedoms: Interactive Freedom

It may very well be that human life requires a combination of freedoms (cf. Skinner 2003: 22). In fact, it is likely that there has always been at least some degree of combination (cf. MacCallum 1967: 314), even though relative emphases on one or the other kind of freedom have varied. When the different freedoms are pursued together intentionally, their conjunction may be called 'interactive' freedom. This conjunction has its intellectual counterpart in the relational outlook, which combines commonality with divergence.

From the end of the nineteenth century on, the ideal of interactive freedom involved consideration for the marginal and downtrodden. For instance, it was connected from the beginning with feminism. Among males, both Green and Ellis were supportive of the women's movement. Women themselves (including Simone de Beauvoir [see below, 8.1], Hannah Arendt

Behind these thinkers and behind Green stood Hegel, whose monistic tendency (see below, 3.1) unduly overshadowed negative liberty.

46. Other related analyses were made by Rolf Dahrendorf (1975: 6, 93, 98), John McGowan (1991), and Whitney Pope (1999).

[1963: 25], Meili Steele [1997], and Nancy Hirschmann [2003]) have been especially prominent among those who expressly advocated a combination of freedoms.[47]

A significant feature of such a combination is that persons who are not well positioned in society work together with others who are advantaged, so that more than pure self-interest is in play. Moral freedom—sometimes risking bodily welfare—has been exercised by the downtrodden when they act idealistically on behalf of their own group and even on behalf of humanity more generally (as was done by Martin Luther King, Jr., himself partly privileged). It was also exercised by those who had benefited from earlier arrangements, when they supported interactive freedom.

Indeed, it seems that the positive and negative aspects of external freedom can be held together only if internal freedom (ethics) is put into play. Marxism's failure lay in giving inadequate attention to this aspect. Although Marx was indebted to the biblical theme that favors the oppressed, he differed from it in emphasizing action by the oppressed themselves and in rejecting the supportive ethical actions of others.[48] It is true, Marx's stress on self-assertion by the proletariat can be regarded as valuable. Indeed, an important contribution by well-located persons (including Marx and Engels!) is not just to give paternalistic aid but to support empowerment, such as in expanding the right and opportunity to vote. Marx's unwillingness to accept cross-class cooperation, however, led to despotism by at least some of his followers.

Although one can favor all of the major kinds of freedom, it does not mean that one needs to approve their specific applications. For instance, it is possible to approve of government action to enhance positive freedom in principle without agreeing with every step taken along that line. The ideal of internal freedom, too, can vary considerably, and one person's ethical commitment can be contrary to another's. In fact, some of the sharpest antagonisms arise on the basis of conflicting convictions in this regard.

4. *Summary*

The chart in Table 1 presents the major views of form and freedom in schematic form. The several patterns represent 'ideal types', in that perhaps none of them is ever exhibited in pure form. Nevertheless, they constitute fairly distinct ways of thinking and living. The most characteristic sense of freedom held by a specific orientation is italicized.

---

47. Hirschmann treated 'positive' freedom as containing both 'internal' and 'external' versions (2003: 6-10, 200-205).

48. See especially Marx and Engels 1957–, IV: 191-203 (5 September 1847).

The radically nominalist option will be addressed in Chapters 6 and 7. The relational way will be discussed throughout the current volume.

Table 1

Views of Form	Political Structure	Views of Freedom
Platonic (the general-ideal is primary)	aristocracy/elitism, including responses by various persons who live within this kind of a society	• *internal: including positive (ethical) freedom and, in varying degrees, negative freedom 'from the body'* • *external: little negative,* but sometimes positive (cooperative)
Aristotelian (the general and the particular stand next to each other, unrelated)	combination of aristocracy and middle-class orientation, such as in the High Middle Ages	• *internal: a fairly positive* kind is implied, with body and mind largely cohesive • *external: fairly positive* and *moderately negative* ('freedom from others') *for males who are not slaves*
moderately nominalist (form is primarily particular but it is also general on a secondary basis)	leaning toward a middle class orientation, such as in 'modern' Europe	• internal: varied, but sometimes moderately negative toward the body • *external: primarily negative freedom 'from others'* (including partial freedom 'from nature')
radically nominalist a. small particulars are paramount, or b. the form of a large particular (a group) is paramount	two kinds: a. anarchist (in aspiration) b. strongly nationalist or otherwise group-oriented	• internal: little interest? • *external: largely negative* 'from others' a. for oneself b. for one's group, but with a strong unity (positive freedom) within the group
relational (the general and the particular are aspects of one structure)	close-to-egalitarian inclusiveness (with an attempt to avoid marginalization, while seeking to respect variety)	• *internal*: mind and body both viewed *largely positively*, as *connected* aspects of life • *external: both negative and positive freedom, ideally for all*

Chapter 2

INTERACTIVE FREEDOM AFTER C. 1880 CE

As already indicated, a major shift took place in the 'West' at the end of the nineteenth century, as quite a few observers also noted.[1] On the negative side, a sense that the older perspective was fading led to a *fin de siècle* mood. On the positive side, there was high optimism in overlapping socialist and feminist circles, where interactive freedom was pursued intensively. To be sure, this development represented only one side of the emerging culture history; another, more problematic, side will be discussed in Chapter 6.

1. Steps Toward Interactive Freedom in Relation to Economics

Economic arrangements were one area of life in which the question of freedom became quite important. They were, in fact, at the heart of the 'social question', which agitated Western societies at the end of the nineteenth century. This question was triggered by the problems created by *laissez-faire* competition for those that stood at the lower end of the economic spectrum. Responses during the next hundred years led to the establishment of welfare states and to varying kinds of socialism.

These responses sought a positive—that is, cooperative—freedom. For instance, US president Franklin D. Roosevelt, who enhanced social welfare arrangements, spoke in 1941 of 'freedom from want' and 'freedom from fear'.[2] These are, in one sense, negative freedoms, but they do not represent freedom from other human beings. On the contrary, they gain from societal support. Given such arrangements, Gunnar Myrdal judged that 'most people have good reason to feel freer, not less free in the Welfare State' (1960: 86).

Both disadvantaged and established members of society took part in this movement. Persons at the lower end of the spectrum applied pressure

1. That a major change began to take place about 1880 has been observed by Timothy Reiss (1982), Allan Megill (1985: xiii), Norman Cantor (1988: 6-12), Nicholas Zurbrugg (1993), David Griffin *et al.* (1993), John Deely (1994), Helmut Bernsmeier (1994; cf. below, 5.3), William Everdell (1997), Christian Delacampagne (1999: xvi), and Ronald Schleifer (2000). For Toynbee's similar assessment, see below (6.3).
2. State of the Union Address (as president of the US), 6 January 1941.

through such measures as labor strikes and increasingly through the use of a right to vote. Persons at the upper end supported, at least to some extent, the right to vote and other measures that moved in an egalitarian direction. It is not surprising that self-interested reasons played a major role in this development. Nevertheless, there were also operations that expressed an inner ethical freedom.

One—although (as we will see) not the only—factor in self-transcending contributions was the presence of ideals on behalf of the poor or down-trodden that are inculcated in the sacred texts of Judaism and Christianity, which formed the primary religious basis for the cultures being consid-ered. These ideals had stimulated social services, first on a voluntary basis and then, especially in Protestant countries after the closing of monaster-ies and nunneries, in connection with governmental processes. Jews and Christians could see, as long as they were serious about their religion, that economic conditions at the end of the nineteenth century flagrantly vio-lated their ideals. Consequently, a good number of those strongly dedicated to their faith engaged in social activity, sometimes in support of the labor movement.[3]

Such efforts emanated from several segments of the religious community. A liberal Protestant version was known as the 'Social Gospel'. Theologi-cally conservative Protestants also participated in this orientation. Among them stood William Jennings Bryan, who was the US Democratic presiden-tial candidate in 1896, 1900, and 1908, and served as Woodrow Wilson's secretary of state until he resigned over the issue of war. He 'supported the cause of labor and of woman suffrage, and…opposed capitalism, capital punishment, and war' (E. Weber 1999: 189). The Catholic church moved in a similar direction. In a well-known encyclical of 1891, Pope Leo XIII expressed the hope that all groups of society would work together in 'soli-darity' and that class distinctions would be reduced. Religiously oriented Jewish socialists such as Hermann Cohen and Martin Buber also made sig-nificant contributions to this movement (see below, 3.5).

Contributions along this line were not limited to Christians and religiously affirming Jews. After all, internal freedom appears widely. For instance, the agnostic Darrow, who opposed Bryan in 1925 on the topic of biologi-cal evolution, largely agreed with him on social issues. More importantly,

3. For different phases of this process, see, e.g., H. May 1940: 161-265; Moser 1985; Ashford 1986; Misner 1991; Reeves 2000: 25-26; Fogel 2000: 124-29. Among these, Robert Fogel (an economist) indicated that in the US much of social-concern leg-islation emerged from the 'Social Gospel'. Christian socialism near 1900 CE included African American leadership (Marable 1986: 40). Cf. Stephen Mott and Ronald Sider 1999, with a late-twentieth-century position along this line that was theologically conservative. (To be sure, most of those who considered themselves Christian—like others who did not—protected primarily their own interests.)

Marxism—expressly atheist, although indebted to the Bible—provided an inspiration for many activists. Marx and Engels implied that their motivation was a desire to be on the winning side of history rather than altruism, but the fervor with which they expressed their position belied this modest self-assessment.[4] From farther afield, Confucian traditions about governmental support provided models,[5] and the religions of India contributed an emphasis on nonviolence.

The emerging era was not strictly proletarian; rather, it moved toward providing a place for all members of a society in the structures of power. Marx envisioned that a 'dictatorship of the proletariat' would be established on a temporary basis before the arrival of a 'classless society'.[6] However, the possibility of even a temporary rule of the proletariat is questionable, for one cannot rule while one is downtrodden. Aware of the organizational weakness of the proletariat, Vladimir Lenin and, after him, Joseph Stalin relied on a party elite to rule on behalf of the populace. More appropriately, in many countries workers were able to assert themselves to a considerable extent in what has been called 'mass democracies' (e.g. Preuss 1979: 340; Flora and Heidenheimer 1981: 8, 213).

Most supporters of the welfare society (not just a 'welfare state') thought of it as a combination of governmental and voluntary arrangements, including cooperatives or communes.[7] Indeed, government action grew to an extent that had perhaps never been reached before. Much of this development can be welcomed, but a strong emphasis on the state has the problem that it focuses on a large unit. If the large unit is tightly organized, it restricts the freedom of smaller entities, such as that of voluntary groups and individuals. Thus, there were repeated calls to limit or reverse the expansion of state services. For instance, although Myrdal supported the expansion of government services in some ways (especially internationally), he saw value in simplifying and reducing state controls (1960). Just what constitutes an ideal balance between state and voluntary action was a matter of debate.

The drive for a welfare society had some success. Equality in both income concentration and biological conditions (height, longevity, etc.) increased remarkably in England, Norway, and the US from the end of the

---

4. See *The Manifesto of the Communist Party*, pt. 1 (1957–, IV: 472).

5. For instance, the Confucian system of storage for agricultural products when there is an oversupply—together with the biblical account of a similar arrangement by Joseph in Egypt (Gen. 41.33-49)—inspired some US policies in the 1930s (Culver and Hyde 2000: 57).

6. Karl Marx to Joseph Weydemeyer, 5 March, 1852 (Marx and Engels 1957–, XXVIII: 508).

7. For cooperatives—after a beginning in the early part of the nineteenth century—see, e.g., Parker 1956 and Schmiedeler 1941.

nineteenth century until c. 1970 (Fogel 2000: 143-71).[8] This process stood in contrast with the fact that equality measured by biomedical data had actually decreased during the nineteenth century, when biological conditions had deteriorated, or at least failed to increase, in the lower end of the social stratum, while they had risen at the upper end.[9] In other words, capitalism had depressed or failed to raise the lot of many people, until social democracy reversed the process. (That does not mean that some form of market capitalism cannot be useful, but a competitive economy does appear to be hurtful when it operates alone.)[10]

Not only did external (including biological) conditions improve considerably, there may also have been an increase in subjective satisfaction. According to surveys at the end of the twentieth century, life satisfaction was especially high in countries that were strong both in individual freedom and in social services (see, e.g., Inglehart 1990: 26; 1997: 177; Veenhoven 1993: 50; Diener and Suh 2000).

The possibility of meaningful work aided by education or job training was an important issue, for work usually provides more happiness than does a hand-out (cf. Lane 2000: 271). Around 1800 CE, there had been 'a nearly universal condemnation' of the emerging wage labor as a form of slavery (Lasch 1991: 203), but this arrangement took hold and became widespread. As John Dewey noted, 'economic conditions still relegate many...to a servile status' (1916: 160). This problem was met in part by individuals banding together. Cooperatives, unions, 'tenure' (for faculty), a degree of job security for government employees, and, in some countries, legal support for worker participation in business governance provided some dignity in the workplace.

Specifically, a concern for increased 'self-direction' became pronounced among employees in Italy, France, and Germany, especially from the revolts of 1967 on (A. Hirsh 1981: 144, 209-11, 222; Abse 1994: 191-93). In the US, too, there were moves in this direction. For instance, in 1985 John Naisbitt reported that a 'fundamental shift' was underway in a 'movement away from the authoritarian hierarchy . . . to the new lateral structures, lattices, networks, and small teams where people manage themselves' (253).

8.   In fact, life expectancy increased and undernourishment decreased in Britain during the war years when 'sharing' was strong, even though the Gross Domestic Product declined (Sen 1999: 49-52).

9.   See Fogel 2000: 140, 161, etc. I am assuming that his scattered data can be generalized for the US and some European countries. (Fogel himself was lukewarm about the welfare state.)

10.   According to an analysis by Amartya Sen, economic success is supported by a degree of freedom from restraint (the negative version) only if it comes together with governmental expenditures for health and other kinds of national cooperation (e.g. 1999: 44, 160-69).

It should be noted that satisfaction involves more than monetary income. In fact, there was evidence that for many persons an increase in income beyond what is necessary to meet basic needs in a given society contributed little to life satisfaction.[11]

There was more room, then, for what has been called 'postmaterialism', which values more than economic welfare. This outlook values, by definition, a quality of life that is relatively free from external prescription, and thus high in negative freedom, and also high in meaningful positive freedom, internally and externally. Specifically, 'postmaterialism' includes the following values (which will be discussed more fully below): having a say at work and in the community (including government); freedom of speech; a friendly rather than an impersonal society; a preference for ideas over money; support for feminism and internationalism; an emphasis on equality and 'inner harmony'; and an increased acceptance of abortion, divorce, extramarital relations, homosexuality, and euthanasia.[12] This orientation (called 'life politics' by Anthony Giddens [1991: 209-31]) stands in contrast to so-called 'materialism', for which a better term would be 'a desire for material orderliness'. This latter orientation rises with experiences of war, inflation, or unemployment; it is apparently heavily based on fear.[13] Postmaterialism was especially prevalent in educational and cultural occupations, as may have been true for some time, but at the end of the twentieth century was growing in other occupations in some countries.

According to available data, postmaterialism was slow to progress in the US; nevertheless, it was present. Among others, Ronald Garland projected as a 'new age' the 'removing of distinctions between management and workers' (1990: 80). He called for 'transforming work', which means

11. See Inglehart 1990: 240; Richins and Rudmin 1994; LaBarbera and Gürhan 1997: 72.

12. 'Postmaterialism' represents a cluster within the values surveyed by Inglehart and others in 42 countries from c. 1970 on (Inglehart 1990: 74-75, 89, 196; Ingelhart *et al.* 1998: 10-12).

13. The following cluster of values is defined as constituting 'materialism': order in the nation, a strong defense, low inflation, high economic growth, a stable economy, fight against crime, marriage, and having children (Inglehart 1990: 74-75, 89, 239). It should be noted, however, that while 'materialism' and 'postmaterialism' form a different cluster of values, they do not constitute mutually exclusive alternatives; persons can value *both*. Analyses (summarized and freshly furnished by G. Marks 1997; cf. Abramson and Inglehart 1995: 29, 34) show that a preference for materialism over postmaterialism is related to social or economic problems experienced either currently or in the past; thus, in Europe, materialism has been higher among those who grew up prior to 1945 than among those who came later, but in the US and in Australia—both less directly affected by World War II—age differences are smaller than in Europe.

'quality work as a commitment to self' and work 'as meditation', 'as a projection of self' (with room for creativity), and 'as service' (54-57). Such work would exhibit both positive and negative external freedom, together with internal freedom. Along this line, some persons looked for work that is 'spiritually fulfilling, socially constructive, experientially driven, emotionally enriching [and] perpetually challenging' (David Brooks 2000: 134).

In some ways, postmaterialist values would be incorporated into business. Referring primarily to medium-sized and small operations, in 1995 Barbara Brandt reported an interest in what she (and others) called 'whole life economics'. This included participation or investment in businesses or operations that promote humanitarian, participatory, and environmental policies. Organizations with such aims are especially considerate of employees, have a relatively flat salary scale, may be organized as cooperatives, or may in other ways seek to empower individuals. According to Brandt's report, quite a few of the businesses following such principles were owned by women.[14] Brandt called this version of business 'postmodern' (1995: 110).

Besides supporting personal goals, economic operations by individuals and groups could be concerned with social responsibility, which expressed ethical freedom. Specifically, during the last decades of the century, some persons and organizations became interested in 'socially responsible' investing. Such investment policies seem to have had some international effects, for instance in support of political freedom in South Africa. Not just individual investors but some companies themselves—in part stirred by the Interfaith Center on Corporate Responsibility—instituted standards for social responsibility even in the US, where such a consideration has often been low (e.g. Hopkins 1999: 56-59).

In practice, to be sure, many business organizations remained or even became exploitative-individualistic (encouraged, in some cases, by global competition).[15] Perhaps largely for this reason, many persons continued to find their work unsatisfying. For instance, in group interviews after 1975, Michael Lerner 'found middle-income people deeply unhappy because they hunger to serve the common good and to contribute something with their talents and energies, yet find that their actual work gives them little opportunity to do so' (1996: 5). He observed:

14. Cf. also Barrentine 1993. A similar but more moderate program has been presented by three males writing together: Gerald Faust, Richard Lyles, and Will Phillips (1998).

15. Global competition threatened human working conditions, especially in the absence of political control, although the argument has been made that countries that supported strong worker roles actually outperformed others (D. Gordon 1996: 5, 152).

> Surrounded by people who are fanatically focused on their own success and are willing to manipulate others for the sake of their own interests, most people feel that they must participate in those same dynamics and 'do unto others before they do to me' as a necessary form of self-protection. A society dominated by this kind of 'freedom' feels profoundly unfree (95).

It is most likely that low-income workers had little opportunity for 'free' work that involves both personal creativity and a spirit of contribution, or work that at least supports dignity.

In short, one can say that there were serious struggles to develop interactive freedom in the economic realm. These struggles achieved a degree of success in terms of social support, but by no means ideal conditions.

2. Interactive Freedom in Regard to Gender, Sex, and Family

Social concerns from the end of the nineteenth century on included the equality of the sexes. This ideal had roots in the preceding modernity. For instance, it continued the theme of freedom from domination and from tradition. At the same time, however, most feminists rejected the highly self-assertive individualism of modernity (see, e.g., Jessica Benjamin 1988: 188; Jane Gallop 1988: 116). Thus, the women's movement was for the most part neither simply modernist nor simply antimodern but, rather, 'postmodern', specifically 'transmodern' (see below, Chapter 8).

One link between the women's movement and modernity was the fact that industrialization—a fruit of modernity—led to a change in women's roles. Industrialization facilitated more effective control of disease, especially through hygiene measures; it consequently led to a cut in the human death rate on some levels of society. The lower death rate for children eventually freed women from the need for almost continuous childbearing. In earlier days, childbearing had kept them, for the most part, close to home and placed them at a disadvantage in conflict (Chafetz and Dworkin 1986: 50; Bem 1993: 31; G. Lerner 1993: 276). Furthermore, changes in technology (mentioned by Hare-Mustin and Maracek 1990: 4) meant, among other things, that males were no longer especially suited for warfare, because physical strength became less important for it. Although women were not yet heavily involved in warfare, this change was important since the earlier (and in many ways continuing) association of males with warfare was probably supportive of patriarchy.

It is true, the notion of women's equality had earlier ideological roots, some of which were present in ancient Greece. Pythagoreans and Epicureans included women in their philosophical work. Cynics emphasized sexual equality even more. Zeno the Stoic reportedly placed the sexes on equal terms in his vision of an ideal community. Furthermore, according to at least some of the sacred literature of Judaism and Christianity, both sexes are in God's image (Gen. 1.27) and have religious equality (Gal. 3.28). Although none of these processes or themes had much effect on society at large in their own time, they could emerge later to support close-to-egalitarian ideals and cooperative endeavors. The relation of religious tradition to women's liberation was nevertheless highly ambiguous, for the major religious traditions, including their scriptures, had emerged in aristo-cratically ruled societies. With their transtemporal orientations, they were often resistant to change. Thus, although a drive toward sexual equality could draw on the religious theme of support for the oppressed, traditions bound to the past also inhibited equality's progress.

In any case, the new interest in social cooperation went hand-in-hand with an increase in prominent roles for women, who made early contri-butions to social reform.[16] Women were active in early-nineteenth-century abolitionism, and their involvement gave an impetus to feminism. Subse-quently, women engaged themselves on behalf of temperance, peace, prison reform, mental health reform, and other social work (Judith Anderson 1984: xiv, xvi), as well as in support of ecology (since c. 1900, see below).

The women's movement thus included a drive not only for negative free-dom—overthrowing patriarchal power—but also for positive freedom, with a concern for others who are oppressed. Inner freedom was important for this combination, especially since it positively stressed the good that can be accomplished instead of advocating self-abnegation. The philosopher Sandra Farganis accordingly argued for the presence of all three kinds of freedom in women's self-realization: rational (in other words, internal posi-tive), external negative, and external positive (1977).

Success came to the feminist movement gradually. It began in education during the nineteenth century and then continued in voting rights, work, and family attitudes. Since access to education came earlier than appointments to academic positions, women often made an intellectual impact through association with males. Especially during the decades around 1900, they did so as wives, daughters, or friends of prominent writers.[17] (It is true,

16. See, e.g., Koven and Michel 1993; Lenz and Myerhoff 1985.
17. Such contributions had taken place earlier (G. Lerner 1993: 224-26). In the nineteenth century, the views of J.S. Mill were moved in the direction of cooperation (and socialism), as well as toward sexual equality, by Harriet Taylor, who became his wife (see Kamm 1977; Pujol in Dimand *et al.* 1995: 82-102). Subsequently, the follow-ing men, among others, had feminist wives: C.S. Peirce (Melusina née Fay [see 3.2, below]); T.H. Green (Charlotte Green was active, as he was, in women's education); Havelock Ellis (he and his wife Edith, a lesbian, spoke and wrote in favor of social cooperation and peace as well as feminism); John Dewey (he learned from his wife, Alice, as well as from Jane Addams and several other women [Dearborn 1988: 52-58, 90-92; Seigfried 1996: 48, 50-51, 74, 80, 82]); Max Weber (his wife, Marianne, was a feminist). Lester Ward, a pro-feminist founder of sociology in the US, worked with the

already at that time, a good number of women published their own works, but acknowledgment of their significance was limited.)[18] In the US, the role of women in colleges and universities declined between c. 1925 and c. 1965[19]—perhaps because traditional sex roles were re-emphasized—but increased sharply thereafter.

The emerging situation lessened differences between the activities of the sexes (although it did not eliminate them altogether). On the one hand, women became more openly self-assertive.[20] On the other hand, men placed less emphasis on aggressiveness, including a traditional glorification of war, leading Robert Bly in the 1970s (1990: 2-3) to describe 'soft males' as a new kind of man. Some women writers outlined a 'feminist morality' that leads to a non-dominating 'participatory' democracy, with care and coop-eration (Nancy Hirschmann 1992: 249, 270; Virginia Held 1993). Aspects of this vision were also held by male thinkers (e.g. by Jürgen Habermas).

Together with women's liberation, there was an extensive attack on the double standard in sexual relations common in patriarchal societies. In the US during the latter half of the nineteenth century, for instance, feminists often advocated either 'social purity', which meant primarily a restriction of male sexuality, or else 'free love', which implied a loosening of restrictions on women (Hirshman and Larson 1998: 122-33).[21] In terms of restraint, around 1900 there was strong opposition to pornography and to prostitution (especially in the US) and a rise in the legal age of consent (for sexual activ-ity), which had been around the age of ten.

Attempts to restrict male sexual activity were not very successful. Instead, following the alternative route to equality, women's sexual activity became more liberal in the 1920s and again from the 1960s on. In fact, egalitar-ian feminism influenced males sufficiently so that many men who would

cooperation of his wife, Rose (C. Scott 1976: 26, 34, 39). In 1879, the notable econo-mist Alfred Marshall published, together with his wife, Mary, a book that ended with a chapter on cooperation apparently written by her (Whitaker 1975: 67); thereafter, he acknowledged the value of her continuing advice, although his support for women's intellectual role declined and he largely excluded women from economic roles outside the home (Pujol 1992: 122-26; Tullberg in Dimand *et al*. 1995: 150-93). The physicists Marie and Pierre Curie received the Nobel Prize in 1903. Historiography has enjoyed major contributions by several husband-and-wife teams taking joint credit, including Sidney and Beatrice Webb and Charles and Mary Beard. The couple Robert and Helen Lynd published a famous sociological study.

18. For economics, see Dimand *et al*. 1995; for sociology, e.g., Yeo 1996.

19. See data in W. O'Neill 1969: 93, 95; Dimand *et al*. 1995: 9-10. Cf. Seibert *et al*. 1997 (on a decline in equality outside of academia during that period).

20. For instance, Judy Wajcman reported that women in managerial roles are creat-ing 'new hybrid forms of gender identity' (1998: 166).

21. To be sure, free love was also advocated by a number of men, largely for their own benefit.

previously have insisted on marrying a virgin—thinking of a woman as an exclusive 'possession'—no longer did so after c. 1965;[22] female virginity thus lost much of its former importance.

Sexual liberation may appear to be primarily of the negative kind: freedom from constraint or imposition. But it also created new impositions, for unmarried women became newly subject to pressure to engage in sex. They were then exposed to various dangers, including unwanted pregnancy, date rape, and disease.

Still, sexual liberation was often positive, even joyous. Externally, it supported egalitarian relations between women and men, with both being treated as mature agents. Internally, it could be experienced as opening new possibilities of being.[23] In fact, in contrast to earlier ascetic or semiascetic attitudes, sexuality became celebrated, perhaps as never before.[24] Unwanted pregnancy, whether inside or outside marriage, was countered by an increase in the availability of contraceptives and, from about 1970 on, of abortion.

However, the threat of disease (including herpes and AIDS) for non-monogamous relations proved to be a serious problem, so that more restraint needed to be exercised again, as was true after the spread of syphilis in the sixteenth century. In any case, the argument was made that, instead of simply sex, what is needed is a realization of eros—an emotional sensitivity that applies to the whole being of oneself and others—and, if possible, an increase in love, a form of positive freedom.[25]

Acceptance of eros was not unrelated to economics, for one of the forces behind the material accumulation of modernity may well have been a suppression of eros, called 'innerworldy asceticism' by Max Weber. This had even led to a suspicion of the arts, because of their failure to contribute to economic success (Buss 1999: 102). In a contrary move during the 1960s, 'hippies' and others (often less extreme) came to hold that love, or at least eros, should be valued above both war and money.

About 1970, homosexual activity became more open. Two of the most important philosophers of the twentieth century, Ludwig Wittgenstein and Michel Foucault, were homosexual, although this fact was mostly unknown

22. The source for this and a number of other statements is personal observation; supporting evidence for the US can be found in Laumann *et al*. 1994: 208-13.

23. Most extremely, perhaps, Wilhelm Reich (1945: xxii): 'the core of happiness in life is *sexual* happiness'.

24. That was true also for many who wished to limit sexual relations to marriage.

25. Herbert Marcuse sought a transformation of sexuality into eros (1955, chapter 10). Love was highlighted by Erich Fromm (1956: 20), characterizing love as 'union under the conditions of preserving one's integrity, one's individuality'; Norman Brown (1966, preface), accepting the 'polymorphous' character of eros; Starhawk and Ruth Whitney (see below, 8.2); and Marianne Williamson (1992), although probably over-emphasizing 'mind'. On love in politics, see Martin Luther King, Jr. (1958: 9; 1963a) and SNCC's statement (cited below, section 3).

by the public during their life-times, especially in Wittgenstein's case. Later on, there was less need for secrecy, but the moral acceptability of homosexual activity continued to be rejected, especially, although not exclusively, by persons who adhered strongly to traditional religion.[26]

The drive to obtain acceptability meant that negative freedom (freedom from restraint) was desired especially by those who were homosexual or bisexual.[27] After a while, the one-sided emphasis on negative freedom became less pronounced, especially as acceptance of a variety of sexual orientations became more common in society.[28] Some gays and lesbians then sought societally recognized order in the form of legal unions. 'Queerness' (formerly a derogatory term for homosexuality) was at first valued as a form of protest, but then also positively in the sense of structural openness, including meaningful associations.[29] In some contexts, the word came to be connected with religious notions, such as that of 'agape' (love), interpreted as mutual acceptance of difference (W. Tierney 1997: 30, 42).[30] Thus a complex of freedoms was supported here, also.

At the same time, some heterosexuals raised questions about the institution of marriage. Beginning in the nineteenth century, there were repeated calls to abandon marriage as a patriarchal or generally oppressive institution. Not many supported such calls, but there were revisions of marriage. These included the use of contraception (and thus fewer children) and a greater acceptance of divorce, non-legal cohabitation, and single parenthood as a deliberate choice, although these steps remained controversial. Probably even more importantly, marital structure was altered through a pervasive move toward egalitarian relations between spouses.

26. In Europe and the US, more or less half of the population accepted homosexuality in the 1990s, at least moderately; elsewhere, fewer did (Inglehart *et al.* 1998, 'value 307').

27. A tradition of anarchistic homosexuality (partially Nietzschean) extended through the twentieth century (Altman 1971: 170-74, 229; E. Sedgwick 1990: 133). It included Gilles Deleuze and Félix Guattari (see below, 7.4). See also Jeffreys 1993: 121-41.

28. A survey c. 1990 indicated that homosexual partnerships came to have a stability similar to (although less than) heterosexual unions (Weinberg *et al.* 1994: 404-5)—surprising in view of strong social pressure specifically toward the stability of heterosexual unions. Angelia Wilson (1997: 104) reported that many gays and lesbians did not identify with the 'transgressive' images of homosexuals shown (for shock value?) on British TV. (On transgression in Foucault's thought, see below, 7.4.) Ian Young found the New York gay community 'in recovery' in 1995, avoiding (self-)destructive behaviors and engaging in prosocial kinds (284). Risky behavior, however, also re-emerged, with intense debate (cf. Warner 1999: 218; E. Clarke 1999: 163).

29. Thus, e.g., Eve Sedgwick (1993: 8).

30. Religiously oriented 'queers' were represented in Goss and Strongheart 1997 and Conner *et al.* 1997.

An important aspect of family life is the raising of children. This became a major focus of discussion. Especially from c. 1870 on, a 'child welfare' movement arose. It included attacks on child abuse—quite a new issue (Cravens 1987: 329-31; L. Gordon 1989). In 1902, Ellen Key, a feminist, projected that the twentieth century would be the 'century of the child'. In retrospect, this projection was too limited, but interest in the life and rights of children, including toward the end of the twentieth a very strong concern with child abuse, was indeed extensive. Only the issue of education will be treated here.

'Progressive education' employed only limited external force and sought to go beyond a passive receipt of information. A notable exponent of this theory of education was Dewey.[31] Freedom, as Dewey described it, has a negative side; this is represented by a low level of authoritarian direction and by some 'physical unconstraint of movement' in the classroom. Yet, above all, freedom has a positive side. This is constituted by 'thinking—which is personal' (1916: 352); in other words, an 'internal freedom'. Dewey knew that the ideal of reflective freedom traditionally had been associated with high society, and he sought to democratize this ideal. Not only the elite, he said, but all are 'capable of a life of reason and hence having their own ends' (1916: 305). Furthermore, in all of his work, Dewey advocated external positive freedom in the sense of cooperation and interchange. In regard to these positions, Dewey was closely and impressively paralleled by Paulo Freire.[32]

In 1963, Dewey cautioned against making education excessively unstructured, as some educators had misconstrued his program. Soon after that, to be sure, the pendulum swung in the opposite direction, as even moderately progressive education came under attack from those who wanted to subordinate education to the needs of business.

3. 'Racial' Freedom

Another major issue was the role of groups that are often called 'races', although the term 'race' is not appropriate as a biological category. Many abolitionists had not believed in the equality of races,[33] and beliefs in the

---

31. See Seigfried 2002 and below, Chapter 3.

32. According to Freire, 'liberating education consists in acts of cognition, not transferrals of information', and overcomes 'authoritarianism'; it proceeds by 'dialogue' and leads to political and other kinds of empowerment, so that the oppressed 'liberate themselves and their oppressors as well' (1993: 60, 67, 68, 26 [1970]). Freire, more than Dewey, said that liberation must come 'from the oppressed themselves', but he added to this phrase the words: 'and from those who are truly solidary with them' (1993: 27 [1970]).

33. According to K. Campbell (1989, I: 19), 'most' abolitionists still believed in racial inequality.

superiority of one's race continued well into the twentieth century in the US, as elsewhere (see Gerstle 2001 and below, 6.1). Yet there were significant moves toward equality in this respect.

Around 1900, W.E.B. DuBois produced a powerful statement on behalf of 'black folk' (1903), and egalitarian ideas also emerged among some whites. For instance, both Dewey and Jane Addams (a leading feminist) were among the founders of the National Association for the Advancement of Colored People, which merged in 1909 with an organization begun by DuBois (Bullert 1983: 35).

Opposition to racism was based on a combination of general intellectual and religious considerations and specific ethnic and political interests. A series of anthropological and psychological studies (some of them done by Jews, such as Boas) gradually undercut the idea that there are innate divergences between the 'races'. In part on the basis of these studies, many religious leaders argued against racial discrimination.[34] In fact, Reinhold Niebuhr, a prominent member of this movement, predicted in 1945 that a combination of intellectual analyses and religious dedication would be important for such a change (1957: 125-29). This judgment proved to be correct, especially if the dedication of quasireligious Marxists is taken into account.[35] Politically, the horror of Nazi Germany, a military enemy, contributed to a revulsion against racism.

From the 1950s on, a move toward black liberation in the US was partially successful. From a theoretical point of view, it is significant that this move linked love and justice in a political program. Martin Luther King, Jr., declared in *Stride Toward Freedom* (1958) that '*agape* [love] means a recognition of the fact that all life is interrelated' and 'nonviolent resistance is based on the conviction that the universe is on the side of justice' (106).[36]

34. See, for instance, scholarly lectures in a 1909 conference (C. Kellogg 1967: 20). In 1945, Reinhold Niebuhr (1957: 125), an opponent of racism since 1942 (Gerstle 2001: 192, 408), reported that 'most of our modern anthropologists assume that race bigots are ignorant of the facts of life' and referred to a *Primer on Race* issued by the Northern Baptist Convention, which stated that 'science concludes...that there is no good evidence of inborn mental differences between races'. Soon after my arrival in the US in 1947, I encountered a religious leader who urged antiracist action. Thereafter, I learned of analyses that supported the intellectual equality of African Americans.

35. For religious aspects of the movement, see Carson 1981; Findlay 1993; Ellwood 1994 (on Jews, 235). The Federal Council of Churches took an interest in this issue from 1946 on. Its successor organization, the National Council of Churches provided a context for the training of white volunteers and by assembling hundreds of ministers, priests, and rabbis to work with them.

36. A linkage of love and justice had already been urged by Niebuhr (e.g. 1957: 28 [1950]), but King went beyond him in an important way (1958: 90-107).

In a similar way, the Student Nonviolent Coordinating Committee (SNCC) set forth in 1960 the following ideal, indebted (as was King's view) not only to biblically-based faith but also to the theme of 'non-injury' derived from religions of India via Gandhi:

> We affirm the philosophical or religious ideal of nonviolence as the foundation of our purpose...and the manner of our action. Nonviolence as it grows from Judaic-Christian traditions seeks a social order of justice permeated by love. Integration of human endeavor represents the crucial first step toward such a society. Through nonviolence, courage displaces fear; love transforms hate. Acceptance dissipates prejudice; hope ends despair (Carson 1981: 23).

Thus the African American freedom movement represented a struggle not only for negative but also for positive freedom, and it reflected as well an internal freedom of dedication. In part because it received support from others who did not have strict self-interest in mind, it sparked a moral/spiritual revival.

To be sure, less emphasis on love, together with a refusal to be limited to nonviolence, was present in the 'Black Power' movement (see below, 9.3). However, in principle and often in practice, this path, too, was not individualistic.

4. The Explosion of the 1960s

Persons who participated in the black liberation movement, such as in the 'freedom rides' of 1961 or the 'Freedom Summer' of 1964, found that the experience produced 'personal liberation' in conjunction with social involvement (McAdam 1988: 132-36). The process was 'in some way utterly selfless and yet [you] found yourself' (McAdam 1988: 138; cf. Carson 1981: 38, 302). Further, a certain sexual freedom emerged. Thus the spirit of the '60s was born.

The civil rights struggle newly energized the women's movement, in part by providing an example and in part by showing what still needed to be done for the liberation of women.[37] The struggle also had a world-wide impact, so that King is identified as one of the most important figures of the twentieth century.

Indeed, the 1960s witnessed a cultural explosion of the first order, a high point that represented a culmination for many of the movements that have been mentioned.[38] It included social and political programs with interactive

---

37. A restructuring of general society was not an afterthought for black-liberation activists but was intended from the beginning (Carson 1981: 1-2, 27-28).

38. Useful data and bibliography can be found in a massive work by Marwick (1998), which, however, did not indicate how the movements of the 1960s represented the culmination of several long-term trends.

freedom in regard to race, gender, and limitations in warfare.[39] In regard to speech, it initially sought primarily freedom of expression; however, later on, speech standards (even too strict?) were erected in support of sensitivity for different racial and cultural groups and genders.

The spirit of the '60s included self-transcendence (as inner freedom) in communes, in concerns for ecology, in meditation, and in the refusal to engage in 'materialist' pursuits of comfort and individual advancement in society. For instance, Charles Reich spoke of 'transcendence, or personal liberation', 'a liberation that is both personal and communal'; it values 'openness to any and all experience' and seeks a 'vocation' (with internal motivation) rather than a 'career' designed for external success (1970: 363, 233, 368).

This attitude was described by Reich as 'consciousness III'. According to his description, this is not competitive-individualistic, like 'consciousness I', nor 'corporate' (beholden to a unit larger than the individual), labeled 'consciousness II'.[40] Rather, it acknowledges the selfhood of oneself and others. In other words, 'consciousness III' joins an internal freedom that values both spiritual experiences and the body with an external freedom that is interactive. The fact that the various facets of this outlook were inter-related was indicated by a study of persons who were more or less closely involved in it; those who had repeated 'peak experiences' had relatively little self-centered concern with social status but a relatively high altruistic involvement in social change and service (Wuthnow 1978: 99-114).

As part of the emerging interest in experience, there was an appreciation for various states of consciousness, including mystical or quasi-mystical states. Openness to Asian traditions with a mystical cast contributed to this ethos.

In short, in the words of Marianne Williamson, 'the decade of the sixties was a societal peak experience... No one who was not there can imagine the way our souls were branded' (1995: 8-9). Similarly, Nancy Nystrom—interviewed by Robert Wuthnow (1998: 56)—said that 'the social reforms of the 1960s "turned up a little flame" inside her that said she should be "part of making things right" '. According to Wuthnow, the civil rights movement contributed to 'new ways of thinking about spiritual freedom', which included listening to 'inner voices' and 'exposing oneself to alterna-tive experiences that would help one develop those voices' (60, 83).

39. Peace concerns extended older traditions of pacifism.
40. Reich's 'consciousness I' (which highlights negative freedom, that is, indepen-dence) and 'consciousness II' (which applies external positive freedom without an adequate regard for individual independence) resembled, although they were not iden-tical with, the 'inner-direction' and 'other-direction' that had been described by David Riesman *et al.* (1950), probably known to Reich.

In France, too, the revolts of 1966–68 represented 'a qualitative new experience for those who took part in them', one that can be described as 'spiritual' (Reader 1987: 17; Ross 2002: 12). Left-wing Christians had a significant role in this (Reader 1987: 17; Ross 2002: 9); for instance, a Catholic student participant was sufficiently prominent to be singled out for prosecution by the government (Cohn-Bendit 1968: 137).

Although the movements of the '60s had a spiritual dimension, this fact does not mean that they regularly either expressed or supported traditional religious commitments. It is true, in the US and in France, quite a few devoted Christians provided leadership or support. Among them stood Terry Eagleton (1966), who moved subsequently to a religious Marxism (1970: 104) and then to a nonreligious Marxism. Yet a disproportionate number of militants, at least in Berkeley on behalf of free speech, had no religious affiliation (Somers 1965: 548), and the established forms of religion experienced major defections not long after, especially in Europe and to some extent in the US.[41] Toward the end of the twentieth century, there was some resurgence of traditional religion, but it is also possible that a long-range religious change was underway.

Why did the outburst of the '60s occur when it did? There were undoubtedly many factors at work. For instance, television provided a national audience. Furthermore, a transcendence of materialism was supported by a reasonably flourishing economy and by the welfare state, both of which acted to reduce fear. In fact, the counterculture had begun already in the 1950s (Gellert 2001: 128).

In regard to politics, the spirit of the '60s had divergent effects. On the one hand, there was a temporary increase in socioeconomic concern, especially in the US, which had lagged behind Europe in this regard. On the other hand, there was a recognition, both in the US and in Europe, that government programs can dampen human initiative and creativity (e.g. Tony Blair 1998: 3-4; N. Rose 1999: 161-67). In response to this recognition, attempts were made to operate simultaneously on three levels: individual, governmental, and through voluntary associations. As stated by Carl Boggs (2000: 127), countercultural figures 'looked toward psychological and social transformation tied to epochal shifts of consciousness and lifestyles going much deeper than mere institutional struggles or contests for power'.

Even though a reaction against liberation movements set in after c. 1970 (see below, 6.1), such movements did not die out. Rather, feminism made progress (for instance, in a revision of language use in the US and in restraining sexual harassment), and a large number of academic and other writings by women started to appear. Liberation for alternative lifestyles emerged in strength. In politics, a central theme of 'inclusion' arose (T. Anderson 1995:

41. See, e.g., Fürstenberg 1994: 281; Gallup and Lindsay 1999: 10, 16, 20.

414), with a respectful recognition for all (C. Taylor 1992).[42] This theme led to a 'mainstreaming' of various kinds of physically challenged persons and to prohibitions of discrimination against older persons. An environmental concern ('ecology') became almost universal. In economics and business, too, some people sought more meaningful and ethical involvements, as has already been mentioned.

On the theoretical level, as well, idealism continued. For instance, from the late 1960s on, psychologists and students of economics and politics became interested in the phenomenon that people do not always act on the basis of individual or group egotism.[43] This observation ran counter to capitalist and 'vulgar [that is, unsophisticated] Marxist' cynicism. Among others, Williamson called on her readers to 'heal the world through the power of love' in personal relations, work, and politics (1992: 60). This was not merely a theoretical call, but included many suggestions for social justice that are both strenuous and practical (1997). After all, as she said, 'life lived for oneself alone is not liberation, but merely another form of bondage' (1992: 219).

Enthusiasts who were in line with an apocalyptic tradition long at home in the US continued to believe that a more profound and sensitive 'new age' was dawning.[44] Such an expectation was unduly optimistic. But it is possible that the awakening of the '60s will spur additional changes, just as the religious 'awakening' in the US in the early part of the nineteenth century contributed to the abolition of slavery.[45] In any case, the African American Cornel West said that 'the sixties constitute the watershed period in contemporary American intellectual life' because of 'the inclusion of Afro-Americans, Native Americans, American women, and working-class white men in significant numbers in the academy' (1989: 238).

5. *Summary*

The period from c. 1880 on witnessed moves toward a combination of negative and positive freedoms in economic arrangements, in sexual and family

42. Freire pointed out that mere inclusion was not new (1993: 55). The word 'recognition', to be sure, is ambiguous; to some political theorists it has appeared to be too weak a term.

43. Thus, an extended series of studies, from Etzioni 1988 to Sober and Wilson 1998.

44. For instance, David Spangler saw the 'form' (although not yet the actuality) of 'Limitless Love and Truth' emerging in the New Age (1976: 148). In a more or less Christian way, Ramón Stevens said that the 1960s marked 'the Christ entity's first hesitant return' to earth (1988: 335). Cf. the similar projections by Willis Harmann (1998). Alongside these 'new age' projections, much more numerous traditional ('antimodern') apocalyptic expectations were current, especially in the US.

45. See W. Strauss and Howe 1997 (following earlier discussions).

life, and in 'racial' relations. An important aspect of this was the digni-
fied inclusion of groups of persons who previously had been marginalized.
Voting rights were extended to virtually everyone, although this achievement was reached for African Americans only relatively late in the twentieth century. Women were more fully included in the public sphere.

Internal freedom—dramatized in the 1960s—played an important part
in these developments. All these freedoms had been operative prior to the
twentieth century, but to some extent there were now explicit attempts to
recognize and combine them together.

Highly destructive developments during the twentieth century will be
discussed in Chapter 6.

Chapter 3

THE EMERGENCE OF A FOCUS ON RELATIONSHIP IN WESTERN PHILOSOPHY

1. Implicit or Partial Relational Thinking Prior to c. 1860

Relational thought is old, although until recent times it has been more implicit than explicit. For instance, in biblical and Confucian writings much is said about specific relations, but relationality as such is not an object of reflection.[1] In fact, an implicitly relational perspective may well represent the basic orientation of human life.

Such an orientation appeared in the surviving fragments of early Greek philosophy. Specifically, a number of Pre-Socratic philosophers during the sixth and fifth centuries BCE focused on several kinds of relations, both positive and negative.[2] They were interested above all in the relations of conflict and eros. Anaximander said that concrete beings are constantly involved in 'unjust' conflict, which is, however, overcome by a non-concrete ultimate. Heraclitus pointed to the pervasiveness of conflict and flux, although this is framed by a universal *logos*. Parmenides, who envisioned a strong unity, may have had room only for love (eros);[3] however, Empedocles highlighted strife along with love. Other Pre-Socratics dealt with less active relations. Among these, Pythagoras treated number as basic, exhibiting both multiplicity and harmony, and Protagoras described perception as an interaction between subject and object.

---

1. Specifically, Walter Eichrodt (1933–39) presented relationality as the central organizing principle for the Hebrew Bible, with at least partial justification; Abraham Heschel (in 1936) did so for the view of God in biblical prophecy (see Buss [1999: 170]). The Hebrew Bible accepted both particularity and generality, which, together, are important for relationality (Buss 1999: 24-26).

2. These philosophers were consequently cited as predecessors by later relational thinkers, such as Francis Abbot (1885: 15).

3. Parmenides' reported statement on love appears to draw from Hesiod's *Theogony* (seventh century BCE), in which Eros is 'the most beautiful', although not the most prominent, deity.

Subsequently, a number of Greek and Hellenistic women stressed harmony and, more specifically, love. However, women remained marginal in publicly recognized philosophy.[4]

After Socrates, as philosophy became more disciplined, relationality (not just certain kinds of relations) consciously entered into Greek philosophy, although only as a subsidiary notion. Plato grappled with relational notions in his dialogues, but his consideration of relationality remained exploratory. Aristotle listed relationality as one of several metaphysical categories; in his view, however, relationality is secondary to particular or generic substance, without a reality of its own (*Categories*, 8; cf. Hood 2004: 51). The Stoics, with a nominalist ontology, were interested in the relational dispositions of particulars, not in relations as such (Colish 1985, I: 56).

An important step was taken when Christian theology, dealing reflectively with the implicitly relational perspective present in the Bible, interacted with Greek philosophy. Specifically, relationality received explicit attention in the doctrine of the Trinity, discussed extensively from c. 300 CE on. In that doctrine, relationality allowed for both diversity and commonality among the divine Persons. Thomas Aquinas described it in this way: 'So as in God there is a real relation...there must also be a real opposition... Hence there must be real distinction in God' together with unity.[5] As will be seen, the combination of distinction and unity became a central feature of relational theory.

In late-medieval nominalism, however, real relations were limited to the divine realm.[6] Outside this realm, it treated relations—like other general phenomena—as being only a matter of thought. For instance: if A is taller than B, nominalists would regard their relation as something that emerges when one thinks about A and B. Postmedieval nominalist philosophers also held that relations are only mental—'not in nature' (thus, Spinoza; similarly, Pierre Gassendi, Hobbes, and Locke).[7]

Like Aristotle, nominalists accepted relational properties (as distinct from relations) but held that they are features of particular objects, so that they each occur only once. For instance, they did not accept fatherhood as a general (repeatable) property but believed that a certain George can have the property of being the father of a particular John and that this John has the property of being a son of that George. These relational properties were assumed to be 'accidental', not part of the nature of objects.[8]

---

4. See Waithe 1987–95, I: 15, 21, 34, 83-116 on female Pythagoreans (represented by fragments) and on Diotima (reported by Plato).
5. *Summa Theologiae*, 1, q. 28, art. 3.
6. For Ockham, see, e.g., Henninger 1989: 132.
7. See, e.g., Henninger 1989: 184; Locke 1690, 2.25.8.
8. As the early Kant expressly said in 1756 (1961, II: 459).

The moderate kind of nominalism, known as 'conceptualism' (see above, 1.1), did accept the presence of general relations in someone's mind. Specifically, theists believed that relations are present in the mind of God. In this way, Gottfried Leibniz provided a relational interpretation of phenomena such as extension, motion, and space (Leclerc 1986: 39-40, 95, 149). Although individual 'monads' do not interact with each other, he held that they are set into a structure that is present in the divine mind.[9]

Georg W.F. Hegel remained within the nominalist tradition insofar as he viewed relations as mental. However, in a position that is known as 'objective Idealism', he identified spirit/mind as the basic reality, thereby treating relationality as an ultimate principle, although more implicitly than explicitly (Wall 1983; Horstmann 1984: 45, 48).

Marx, who rejected much of Hegel's Idealism, emphasized socioeconomic relations but did not escape nominalist thinking altogether. For instance, in an 1857 manuscript he said that 'relations can be established as existing only by being thought'.[10] Outside of thought, he viewed relational characteristics as inherent in objects, implying determinism (as was true for his philosophy of history on the whole).[11] More specifically, his outlook was group-particularist, emphasizing unity within the proletariat and conflict with the outside.

Marx's contemporary, Herbert Spencer, emphasized relationality, but only as a subjective phenomenon. He held that the objective world (comparable to Kant's 'thing-in-itself') is non-relational and thus unknowable (1855; 3rd edn 1880).

2. The Emergence of Formal Relational Thinking from 1860 on

After being an undercurrent or one motif among others for a long time, the theme of relationality came into the center of attention at the end of the nineteenth century and even more so thereafter.[12] This transition was

9. Leibniz, letter to Arnauld, 14 July 1686 (1879, II: 47-59); 'Monadologie', 1714 (1965: 438-83); cf., for the status of relations, *Nouveaux essais sur l'entendment humain*, 1705 (published in 1765), 2.12, 25 (basically nominalist).

10. Marx and Engels 1957-, XLII: 78. The view sketched by Carol Gould (1978) for Marx in his supposedly most clearly relational work of 1857/58 represents what Marx came close to saying, not what he actually said.

11. Cf. Ollman 1976: 29, on Marx's 'internal' relations (cf. below, 4.1, with n. 1), with reference to Spinoza, Leibniz, and Hegel as antecedents in this regard.

12. Relationality had been important for much of postmedieval science (Piaget and Garcia 1983, 1.3.2), although not yet in a fundamental way (Mackay 1930: 24). For instance, Newton considered both relatedness and motion to be extrinsic to the existing atom (Mathews 1991: 92). An excessively internal view of relations (cf. below, 4.1) was expressed by Ralph Waldo Emerson (largely Idealist): 'A man is a bundle of relations' (Essays, 1841, First Series, 1).

not an abrupt one. Rather, it made use of notions that had arisen in an Idealist context but were gradually given a 'realist' (not purely mental) interpretation.[13]

Indeed, from about 1870 on, the idea of relationality moved to the fore for a number of those who continued to accept nominalism at least in the form of Idealism. For instance, Alexander Bain argued that 'if Relation is recognized at all, it is fundamental' (1870, I: 255)—although he was still referring to categories of thought, not of reality (cf. I: 6). The neo-Hegelian T.H. Green, who stood within a kind of objective Idealism, argued in 1874 for the centrality of relationships (1885–88, I: 281; further, 1883). The practical side of his argument was shown in his formulation of positive freedom and in his support (together with his wife) of a stronger role for women (see above, 1.3; 2.2). P.F. Fitzgerald—still more clearly Idealist, holding that 'the order of thought is the order of Being'—said that 'love', the 'mutual correlativity of being' (with 'polarity'), is central to the universe (1882: 16, 85, 87, 92).

Perhaps the first realist formulation of relational theory was presented in 1860 by Catharine Beecher, a liberal Christian educator strongly interested in philosophical issues.[14] She said that 'all our experiences of mind involve the idea of the *mutual relations of minds*'; for instance, a 'mind cannot love till there is another mind to call forth such emotion' (101). This statement, by referring to minds, stood close to philosophical Idealism. Yet Beecher—in part following the realist 'common sense' philosophy of Thomas Reid (1764)—went beyond the purely mental realm. She declared that both 'unity and plurality' (important aspects of relations) are observable everywhere in nature and thus must also be seen in God (101).

An important further step was taken when Francis Abbot argued in 1864, contra Idealism, that relations are 'objective', that is, 'real'. In 1885 (114, 205), he set forth a systematic 'relationism' that was founded on 'the All-Embracing Fatherhood-and-Motherhood of God' and expressly rejected nominalism (including that of Kant).[15] For some time before then already, he had been a supporter of feminism.[16] The 'free religion' (rejecting

13. For instance, one path towards relational realism emerged from Immanuel Kant's philosophy, through an upgrading of relationship from its position as one of the four basic principles in Kant's system to the status of the central or most comprehensive one (thus, Charles Renouvier, a socialist of sorts, in 1854–64) and by viewing relationship in realist rather than idealist terms (see Hartmann 1949: 279).

14. As an educator of young women, Beecher laid groundwork for later feminism. Although she did not want women to enter directly into the political arena, she was ready to contribute intellectually to philosophy and theology.

15. Peirce, too, regarded Kant as nominalist (cf. Ochs 1998: 67).

16. For a while from 1860 on, Abbot had charge of a girls' school (Christie 1927: 11), which brought him into the same line of work as Beecher; did he perhaps know

Christianity), for which he was a major spokesperson, also sought interactive human welfare in other ways. 'Competition', he said, 'will become rivalry in cooperation, and all distinctions of race or color or sex will be swept away'; a 'congress of nations' will govern 'without infringing' on the smallest community or person (1870: 2). He thought that nineteenth-century individualism needed to be transcended and accordingly criticized 'imperialism, militarism, commercialization, and reviving barbarism' (1906, I: viii). Abbot's antinominalism contributed to C.S. Peirce's thinking, which, with some aid from medieval philosophy, had also already begun to move in this direction.[17]

The historic significance of rejection of nominalism by Abbot and Peirce becomes apparent when one notes that in 1865 J.S. Mill declared, in an extended discussion, that realism in regard to general terms (including relations) is 'no longer extant, or likely to be revived'.[18] Just when an idea is said to be hopelessly out of date, it often arises anew. Indeed, Mill himself was in the process of moving beyond an individualistic perspective, apparently under the influence of Harriet Taylor.[19]

3. *The Semiotic-Pragmatist Path*

Like other early relational thinkers, C.S. Peirce came out of a background of Idealism. However, he arrived at the position that a sign mediates between 'ideas' and 'brute actuality'.[20]

Peirce was interested, at least from 1866 on, in the 'triple relation' of a sign, or symbol. According to his analysis, as it came to be fine-tuned by 1908, a symbol has a 'ground' (an actual or possible quality, to which the sign refers), a 'correlate' (the signifying object, such as a word), and a potential 'interpretant' (an effect, a response which may be a further sign).[21] An example would be the following triplet: actual or possible fire;

---

her work? Already in 1877 he favored 'equal rights and suffrage for women' (Persons 1947: 120; cf. 132, 146). Since he stood close to Peirce, he could have known the thinking of Melusina [Fay] Peirce (see below, n. 23).

17. See Hookway 1985: 114-15. Duns Scotus was appreciated by Peirce from 1867 on, at least, although Peirce also criticized him for being excessively nominalist.

18. Chap. 17. Mill's statement, to be sure, applied only to philosophers he regarded as important.

19. See above, Chapter 2, n. 17.

20. In 1891, Peirce described 'objective idealism' as 'the one intelligible theory of the universe' (1931–58, 6.25). However, he was wary of Hegel and in 1903 described him as a 'nominalist' with 'realistic yearnings' (1931–58, 1.19). The mediating role of a sign was stated expressly in 1908, within an argument that God is the 'creator' of both ideas and brute actuality (1931–58, 6.452, 455).

21. See, for instance, Peirce, 1982–, I: 473-77; II: 52-53; 1931–58, 1.537, 542. In

the word 'fire'; and a reaction to this word, which may involve removing oneself from danger or the expression of another sign (or both). This triple analysis had been anticipated by Augustine, as Peirce may or may not have known.[22]

Peirce saw in the structure of a symbol a correspondence with the doctrine of the Trinity, which he had accepted in anticipation of marrying Melusina Fay in 1862 (1982–, I: 503 [1866]). Fay, who led Peirce from Unitarianism to Trinitarianism and apparently also conveyed to him some of her social sensitivity, had in 1859 given a feminist interpretation to the Trinity. In social terms, she advocated and for a while practiced with her husband's support 'cooperative housekeeping', in which families cook and do a number of other household processes together (as described in [Fay] Peirce 1884). She was prominent enough to serve as the first president of the Women's Parliament in 1869–77.[23] Clearly, Peirce's background, like that of Green and Abbot, included a liberal religious feminism.

Peirce nevertheless did not rely purely on a religious or social commitment in his inclination toward a triadic analysis. Rather, in manuscripts written during 1890 and 1903, he argued on mathematical grounds for triadic structure as a primitive or basic order of reality. In these, he observed that a triad cannot be derived from a more simple pattern but that more simple and more complex structures can be derived from a triadic structure by condensation or expansion (1931–58, 1.363, 347).[24]

Peirce's development of a formal logic of relations from 1870 on, following steps by Augustus De Morgan in 1860 (see on him below, 4.2), was very important for philosophy. As will be seen, relational logic involves both particularity and generality. In regard to epistemology, too, Peirce rejected particularism. He located the possibility of transcending isolated knowledge in the 'notion of a COMMUNITY, without definite limits' (1982–, II: 239 [1868]).[25]

his later view, at least, Peirce viewed firstness and thirdness as possibility and potentiality (respectively?) and secondness as actuality (see Sorrell 2004: 23-32; Short 2004). On Peirce's view of possibility, see also below, 5.3.

22. See Augustine, *De doctrina christiana*, 2.1; Peirce referred to Augustine's characterization of logic in 1865 (1982–, I: 163).

23. The Holy Spirit played the role of Mother for her, ahead of the Son (Atkinson 1984: 10; Fay Peirce 1918, II: 3-65). An echo of the feminist version of the Trinity still appeared in a notation by Charles (Peirce) in 1907 (Fisch 1982: xxxii), long after Melusina left him. (She, in turn, continued to respect him [1918, III: 99-105]). Charles's early writings were repeatedly addressed to Melusina, a fact which reflects their mental interaction. (See Fisch 1982: xxxi-xxxii; Brent 1998: 63-65; Ketner 1998: 233-85.)

24. Within the philosophical tradition, Kant's threefold categories contributed in a major way to his interest in triads (1931–58, 1.2-3), as well as to his pragmatic orientation (1931–58, 5.3).

25. See, further, below, Chapter 5, n. 42.

Peirce was aware of the connection of these concepts with social and political issues, since they transcend mere self-centeredness (1982–, II: 271 [1869], 487 [1971]; 1931–58, 2.654; 6.294; 1.17). In fact, in 1892 he indicated that his social sense arose prior to his consistent rejection of nominalism (1931–58, 6.270).

Although much of Peirce's work did not initially appear in an accessible format, the impact of his thought on later philosophy has been profound. In the US, philosophers indebted to him include William James, Josiah Royce, John Dewey, Jane Addams, Wilhelm Jerusalem, and most subsequent thinkers, such as George Mead, C.I. Lewis, Hilary Putnam, Richard Rorty, Richard Bernstein, Sandra Rosenthal, Robert Brandom, and Robert Gibbs (among those to whom reference is made below). Peirce's influence in Europe extended in varying degrees to Edmund Husserl, Ferdinand Schiller, Bertrand Russell, Ludwig Wittgenstein, Max Scheler, Martin Heidegger, Karl-Otto Apel, Jürgen Habermas, Paul Lorenzen (1987: ix), and Jacques Derrida, as will be pointed out for most of them.

The resonance that Peirce's ideas enjoyed is undoubtedly connected with the fact that they addressed issues relevant to the social and intellectual situation of the time, such as a perceived need to balance particularity with generality. On the social side, for instance, James was critical of US imperialism, called for legislation against lynching (L. Simon 1998: 303, 313), and had at least moderate sympathy with feminism.[26] Dewey's involvements in society and education have already been mentioned (above, 2.1, 2, 3). Those of a number of others will be discussed later.

Thinkers who were strongly indebted to Peirce are generally called 'pragmatist', although this designation is also applied in a broader sense. Peirce's specific version of pragmatism is appropriately called 'semiotic' because of its focus on signs. Another version of pragmatism was presented by James. For instance, he took pragmatism as a theory of truth and held that something is true *if* it works (if it is corroborated in the future) and, more specifically, if it is 'good for life' or 'useful'. In contrast, Peirce took pragmatism as a theory of meaning and held that the meaning of a sign is in *how* it works.[27] Later pragmatists tended to follow primarily either Peirce or James (cf. Rescher 2000). Those who stood closer to James leaned toward nominalism (see below for Sellars, Quine, and Rorty).

---

26. See Seigfried 1996: 30, 113-38. In a letter to Mary Calkins, 31 July 1907, James referred to her clear and incisive critical history of philosophy (1st edn, 1907) as 'a triumph also for your downtrodden sex'. (James, however, like other supporters of women's interests, was not without male chauvinism in thought or deed.)

27. See, e.g., Peirce (1931–58, 5.402 [1878]; cf. 2.330 [c. 1902]) and James (1907: 76 [Lecture II]; 1909a: v-vii—in formulations that were written after Peirce's discussion of their differences [1931–58, 5.3, 466, 494, 504, 552]).

The fact that Peirce developed a logic of relations, analyzed the triple structure of signs, considered properties to be relational,[28] envisioned a partial indeterminism,[29] and connected thought with action[30] means that he explored virtually all aspects of relational theory. He was not alone, however, in taking up a relational path. This fact indicates that a large social/intellectual change was in progress.

Other movements that reflected this change included the 'phenomenological' and the 'grammatical-dialogical', to be described next. There were also thinkers who moved in a similar direction without clearly belonging to one of these three relational lines (see below, Chapters 4 and 5).

4. *The Phenomenological Movement*

The phenomenological movement emanated from Franz Brentano, a Catholic who toward the end of the nineteenth century revived medieval considerations, largely in his teaching. He conceived of thought as a relation to an object, even though this object may not 'exist' outside thought. His views of relations fluctuated somewhat (cf. McAlister 1982: 143-55) and appear to have gained from explorations by his students, but by at least 1915 he affirmed relations as 'real' (1933: 166-76). His students included Christian von Ehrenfels, who in 1890 presented an influential formulation of *Gestalt* as a complex of relations (see below, 4.3), and Edmund Husserl, the most important figure in phenomenology from c. 1900 CE on.

In line with, and in some ways going beyond, Brentano's early thought, Husserl stressed that consciousness (including hope) is not directed inward but outward, toward something to which it is 'related' (1950–, IX: 279-80 [1927]; ET in 1981: 23). These objects of consciousness need not be actual. Rather, actuality is 'bracketed' (that is, left out of consideration), and objects of consciousness are treated as 'possibilities'. According to this view, possibilities are not 'in' thought (that would be a nominalist notion), but thought is directed toward them (see, further, below, 5.3).

Similarities between the pragmatic and the phenomenological lines were due in part to shared backgrounds, including an interest in medieval philosophy (Peirce, Brentano) and an involvement in mathematical logic (Peirce, Husserl).[31] However, their similarities were also due in part to direct interactions between them. For instance, Peirce and Husserl exchanged papers

28. See below, 5.4.

29. Real relations, as has been mentioned, require the semi-independence of the related items. See below, 4.1, 3.

30. The development of pragmatic thought, which involves more than US 'pragmatism', is sketched in Herbert Stachowiak 1986–95.

31. For the common background, see, for instance, Peirce (1982–, II: 446 [1870 letter to Jevons]) and Husserl (1950–, IX: 30 [1901]).

on logic in 1883 and 1891 (Spiegelberg 1981: 48). Furthermore, it seems that James contributed to Husserl's transition from his early thought, which had treated logic psychologically in terms of acts of thinking, to his phenomenological approach, which considered logic to be dealing with matters that one can think about.[32]

As its name implied, the phenomenological movement was strongly interested in how the world relates ('appears') to the subject. A typical point of view was that of Maurice Merleau-Ponty (a moderate Marxian): 'It is in my relation to "things" that I come to know myself' (1945: 439).

It is then understandable that an important concern was with relations between oneself and other human beings. Husserl explored intersubjectivity extensively (1950–, volumes I, XIII-XV, XVIX), and his students carried that theme further. Scheler, who favored 'solidarism', contra both capitalism and state socialism (Henckmann 1998: 156-57), highlighted sympathy and love in 1913 and later.[33] Edith Stein examined sympathy in 1917. Jean-Paul Sartre—a partial member of this movement—later described how one becomes the object of another's 'look' (1943), and Paul Ricoeur devoted a work to 'oneself as another' (1990 [cf. below, 7.5]).

Philosophers indebted at least in part to the phenomenological tradition also include Martin Heidegger, Emmanuel Levinas, Calvin Schrag, and Bernhard Waldenfels, among thinkers who will be mentioned later.

5. *The Grammatical-Dialogical Line*

Alongside the pragmatist and the phenomenological lines was a relational movement that dealt with distinctions implied by the use of the first, second, and third 'persons' of language. If primary attention is given to two voices in their reciprocal relations, this approach can be described as 'dialogical'. If speaker, addressee, and what is spoken about all enter fully into the picture, the appropriate label is 'grammatical'. This latter version was similar to Peirce's semiotic view in that it involved both a triplet and a communicational process. But, while Peirce's view centered on the nature of a sign (from 1866 on), the grammatical approach (which Peirce had explored before then) dealt with the structure of a sentence.[34]

32. See Spiegelberg (1965, I: 116) and below, Chapter 5, n. 87.
33. Scheler's view of sympathy—with care for the other—was much closer to what most of us probably mean by it than were the views of Hume and Smith, discussed above (1.3).
34. Peirce had explored the significance of the three 'persons' in 1857 and 1859, while attending college, and somewhat more fully in 1861, while courting Fay, but he had shifted his focus in 1866 to the threefold structure of a sign, apparently because the concept of a 'sign' was important in logic. See Peirce, 1982–, I: 4, 8, 15, 45-49, 530; Ketner 1998: 233-34.

The grammatical-dialogical approach was advanced by the neo-Kantian Hermann Cohen soon after the turn of the century. Cohen viewed religion (especially his own, Judaism) as strongly ethical, above all because of its concern for the poor, and favored a kind of socialism that values individuals. In discussion of ethics, aesthetics, and religion he distinguished metaphorically between the first, second, and third persons of language. The Other is the origin of the 'I' and becomes a 'you' in ethics, so that self-consciousness—which is ethical—is a union of 'I' and 'you' (1904: 201, 202, 235). This analysis stood in contrast to Kant's more 'I'-centered ethics. The impersonal 'it' becomes a 'you', Cohen said, especially when observing suffering (1919: 19). Poetry focuses more on 'I' than does ethics, but it, too, is oriented more to 'you' than to the purely descriptive 'it' (1912, II: 23).

Cohen's reference to an interaction between 'I' and 'you' brought to fruition a discussion by Friedrich Jacobi (from 1775 on), Johann Fichte (1797), Wilhelm von Humboldt (in 1827), and Ludwig Feuerbach (in 1843).[35] The contrast Cohen made between 'you' and 'it' was largely new, although it had been anticipated by James in his saying that theism 'changes the dead blank *it* of the world into a living *thou*', with whom one's 'whole' being can interact (1897: 127, similarly 27, 134).[36]

Indebted in part to his teacher Cohen, but recognizing also a more pervasive shift in thinking around the turn of the century, Ernst Cassirer surveyed the orientation toward relational thought that was gradually becoming prominent in a broad spectrum of disciplines (1910). He presented an extended discussion of 'symbolic forms' as his own contribution to philosophy (1923–29, 1942).

Cohen's orientation proved to be influential beyond the sphere of philosophy. For instance, his analysis made an impact on the Russian Mikhail Bakhtin, who posited the presence of a (metaphorical) dialogue within literature.[37]

In the US and France, Josiah Royce and Gabriel Marcel also developed grammatical-dialogical analyses. Royce—who was socially concerned,

35. See Böckenhoff 1970 and Hinrichs 1995 (according to Hinrichs, at least, these antecedents were not yet fully dialogical). Feuerbach's discussion included a reference to the doctrine of the Trinity.

36. The contrast between *you* and *it* (although not as fully developed as by others later) may be the 'discovery' credited to Cohen by Rosenzweig (1937: 296 [1921]); it reorients an analysis by Fichte (1797, §9), which was discussed by Cohen (1904: 197-235). There was also an anticipation by Humboldt in 1827 (1903-36, III: 26-27), probably not known to Cohen.

37. The impact of Cohen on Bakhtin is well attested (e.g. Clark and Holquist 1984: 59; Bocharov 1994: 1019). Specifically, Bakhtin was aware of Cohen's aesthetics and ethics, and his discussion of the 'I and the other' in MSS written in 1920–24 resembled Cohen's reflections, although he was not satisfied with them (1990: xiv, 11, 23, etc.; 1993: ix, 22, 85, 91, 100).

opposing racism in 1908—had been deeply influenced by Peirce but envisioned a different kind of triad that resembled the three grammatical persons: the object that is interpreted, the interpreter (specifically, a speaker), and the addressee (1913, II: 142). This view stimulated Marcel to make an analysis of the three 'persons' with implications for theology. Although he was then still religiously unattached, he said that God and I are 'you' to each other. Since Marcel's notes on this topic were made in 1918–20, they show that grammatical-dialogical conceptions were 'in the air' at that time. (Theodor Litt discussed the relation between 'I' and 'you' from 1924 on.)

Ebner, a Roman Catholic who was familiar with works that moved in this direction, including one by Fichte,[38] developed in an impressive way the distinction between first-, second-, and third-person speech in reflections that began to appear in print in 1921. He connected ethics with 'I' (Ebner 1963–65, II: 25, 133 [1915–16]; I: 227-28 [1921]), but held that this 'I' is correlated with 'you' (II: 79, 93, 133 [1911–14]). God was said to be an absolute 'you' that is addressed and, even more, says 'you' to a person (II: 44 [1918]; I: 96-97, 233, 248-49 [1915–17, 1921]). Neither 'I' nor 'God' is properly spoken of in the third person (I: 33, 255-56, 258; II: 27, 33, 133 [1915–17, 1921]), although it is sometimes 'convenient' to speak of God improperly in the third person (I: 259 [1921]). This analysis was reminiscent of Kant's distinction between 'pure' and 'practical' reason, but it was expressed in relational terms.

Politically, Ebner was at least moderately in support of the new social orientation, including women's rights (I: 932, 971-75). He became very influential in theology. In addition, he made an indirect impact through Buber and Wittgenstein, who became major figures in twentieth-century thought. He thus played an important role.

Buber, Jewish, advocated a decentralized kind of socialism (cf. 1962–, I: 833-1002). Indebted to James, Cohen, Ebner, and others,[39] he described reality in terms of two major relations (1923). These are the 'I–you', which is holistic (relating with one's whole being to the other as a whole being), and the 'I–it', which is partial and thus manipulative (1923: 79-83, 129-30). God, in his view, is not a partial reality, but pure 'you'. Less theistically stated, 'spirit is not in the I, but between I and you' (103).

38. In a work that Ebner had begun to read in 1915, Fichte modeled an address to God in the second person; in 1918, Ebner credited him with aiding the birth of his own thought about language (Ebner 1963–65, II: 590, 647; III: 209).

39. Buber (1962–, I: 295) acknowledged James's contribution. Buber's indebtedness to Cohen may have been in good part indirect, especially through Rosenzweig, who received stimuli both directly from Cohen and from Rosenstock-Huessy, another student of Cohen. On Ebner's impact on Buber, see Horwitz 1988: 143-60. Buber may well have known older antecedents as well; Hans Ehrenberg, a Fichte scholar, stood close to him (see n. 36 above).

Buber implied that the two relations, I–you and I–it, are distinct. It is not entirely clear, however, whether he thought that they can be experienced together.[40] He did say that 'everything else lives in the light' of an I–you relation (1923: 83). Thus the I–it is not independent of the I–you. Yet he apparently wavered in regard to the question of whether the I–you relation includes the I–it.[41] If a holistic apprehension encompasses partial ones—a view that Buber at least approached, especially after 1923[42]—the I–you and the I–it are not unconnected relations. A practical implication of this inclusive view is that the I–you relation is not esoteric. [43] However, Buber did not expressly take up such an inclusive view. In fact, Buber was criticized for his failure to adequately acknowledge the value of the I–it relation by three other Jewish philosophers: Rosenzweig, Levinas, and Walter Kaufmann.[44]

In good part under the influence of Buber, the theme of 'meeting' or dialogue became widespread. It was prominent in theology, education, rhetoric, and psychology (see Böckenhoff 1970). Philosophers who developed that theme toward the end of the twentieth century included Bernhard Waldenfels and Robert Gibbs, who were also influenced, respectively, by phenomenology and pragmatism (see below, 7.5).

6. *Connections between Relational Streams; Wittgenstein*

There arose, then, three major relational currents in philosophy: the pragmatist-semiotic, the phenomenological, and the grammatical-dialogical. The three moved independently to a considerable extent, but they expressed a common sociocultural orientation, one in which interactive freedom was important. The fact that there could be these different (although not

40. The Taoism which formed part of his background was also unclear in this regard (cf., e.g., J. Herman 1996: 63-64).

41. Buber said that, in the I-you relation, there is no need to 'forget' any 'knowledge' about the object (1923: 82), but he also declared that 'no detail as such' [*nichts Einzelnes*] is remembered about the object (84). The former statement potentially includes the 'I–it' in the 'I–you', but the latter may exclude it, although the German phrasing is slippery.

42. See W. Stevenson 1963: 193-209, with references. In my judgment, such an inclusive view is typical for biblical literature (see Buss 1999: 22, 24).

43. A view in which I-you and I-it are integrated can give a higher status to laws (including ritual ones) than was acknowledged by Buber in 1923. In 1945 (1962–, II: 215-16), Buber did affirm that laws should be immersed in the fire of spirit but not abandoned; such a position can support a Jew's following ritual law (as Buber himself did not).

44. See Rosenzweig, letter to Buber in 1922 (Buber 1973, II: 125-28); Levinas 1967 (see further below, 7.4); Kaufmann 1980: 263-69 (mentioning Rosenzweig's critique).

necessarily contradictory) formulations of relational theory indicates that an intuitive inclination toward relationality was present in society.

Even though the three major relational currents were relatively independent, there were nevertheless lines of connection between them. The associations of Wittgenstein illustrate such a connection. These various associations also shed light on the meaning of his work.

First of all, it is useful to note Wittgenstein's connection with phenomenology. The fact that there was such a connection is clear in general, even though not in its details (cf. Gier 1981). Specifically, in the *Tractatus* (completed in 1918, published in 1922 [1984: 7-83]), Wittgenstein set forth the view that the meanings of sentences represent possibilities, which form the 'logical space' within which actual reality exists (1.13). This notion of 'meaning' as 'possibility' had already appeared in Husserl's discussions of 'signs' and 'grammar' (1901 [1950–, XIX/1: 301-52]). One can wonder whether this commonality was due simply to a common background in mathematical logic (where the idea that numbers refer to objects that are either actual or possible had already played a significant role [such as in Dedekind 1888]) or whether Wittgenstein had received reports about Husserl's ideas from his teacher Gottlob Frege.[45] It is important, however, to remember that Husserl had been stimulated by Peirce and James, so that his line was not altogether independent of pragmatism.

In any case, during 1929/30 Wittgenstein pointed to the close proximity of his early thought to 'phenomenology', with its interest in possibility. At least by that time, he had occasion to receive first-hand knowledge of Husserl's work.[46]

Wittgenstein may never have rejected the idea of possibility with its intellectual cast, but from 1929/30 on, after a ten-year silence, he emphasized the practical aspect of speech. Specifically, in 1936 and later—in the *Philosophical Investigations* (completed c. 1946 [hereafter, PI; critical edition, 2001])—he described speech as part of a 'form of life'. For this second stage, a stimulus from pragmatism is clear, as has been noted before.

Although Wittgenstein did not know Peirce's writing first-hand, he had a number of indirect contacts with it. For instance, his good friend Frank Ramsey, whom Wittgenstein credited (in the preface to PI) with pointing him in a new direction, was indebted to Peirce. C.K. Ogden, another

45. For both continuity and discontinuity with Husserl's phenomenology, see statements by Wittgenstein (including still unpublished ones) cited by Kienzler 1997: 109-10, 111, 282.

46. See 'Philosophische Bemerkungen', §4 (1984, II: 51); exchange with Schlick, 30 December 1930 (1984, III: 63). Cf. especially Husserl, a 'Syllabus of a Course of Four Lectures', delivered in England in 1922 (1981: 68, 70); part of this appeared in Ogden and Richards (1923), which Wittgenstein received as a gift.

friend, also valued Peirce's work and in 1923 gave Wittgenstein a study that included a summary of some of Peirce's ideas. Lectures by Wittgenstein in 1930 clearly presupposed Russell's pragmatic view of language (1921).

Wittgenstein knew at least some work by James. However, like Russell, he was unhappy about the utilitarian pragmatism that appears in James's writings.[47] Since Peirce himself had rejected this kind of pragmatism, one might say that Wittgenstein stood closer to Peirce rather than to James, although he appears to have been unaware of that fact.[48]

Besides pragmatism, the grammatical-dialogical line had an impact on Wittgenstein's thought, due in part to the fact that one of the driving forces of his thought was religious.[49] Having a grandfather who converted from Judaism to Christianity, he had a Jewish self-identity together with an interest in (although not an acceptance of) Christian faith. His understanding of religion had a strong ethical orientation.[50] This ethical commitment was exercised by his giving away a very large inheritance and shown also in his long-term devotion to Tolstoy. In 1935, he even sought to become a laborer in Russia.

The grammatical-dialogical approach allowed Wittgenstein to have a place for ethical and religious speech. In the *Tractatus*, he had consigned ethical and religious thought to mystical silence, but from 1929 on he made a distinction between first-person and third-person statements in such a way that ethical and religious speech were identified as first-person expressions.[51] It is true that Wittgenstein did not dwell at length on the ethico-religious significance of first-person speech. That was perhaps because he thought of himself as a philosopher rather than a theologian. Instead, he discussed in detail the role of first-person speech in talk about pain ('I hurt') and vision ('I see').[52]

47. See above, n. 27, and R. Goodman 2002: 150-54.

48. Correspondences with Peirce's ideas have been noted in works listed by Nubiola (1996); they may have come anonymously via Ramsey.

49. His religious orientation has long been known, but evidence has become especially clear recently (see 1998, 2003) through the publication of MSS dating from 1936–37, although these were available earlier to some scholars.

50. For instance: 'What is good is also divine. That, strangely, summarizes my ethics' (1998: 5 [written in 1929 in code]).

51. See the exchange with Waismann, 17 December 1930 (1984, III: 117-18). Hans Sluga has seen that Wittgenstein's analysis of 'I' has a moral ground (1996: 343).

52. Statements reported by Waismann for 22 December 1929 (1984, III: 49) and written in MS 108: 8, within a few days of that time (1994, II: 135) indicate that Wittgenstein at that point thought that first-person language is optional and misleading, at least for indicating pain. The elimination of 'I' would be in line with a theory by Georg Lichtenberg more than a century earlier, apparently known to Wittgenstein through Weininger (1903, chapter 8). Wittgenstein moved away from this position from 1930 on to accept 'I'-language under appropriate conditions, which he sought to specify.

Wittgenstein did not treat the distinction between kinds of speech in surface linguistic terms. Rather, he pointed out that there is descriptive language about oneself (as 'object'); this is not strictly 'I'-speech (as 'subject') but corresponds with what an observer can say.[53] In such cases, 'I' is a synonym for 'L. W'. (if L. W. is speaking). However, Wittgenstein did not speak about 'the I'—mixing first- and third-person speech—as some other philosophers had done.[54]

Wittgenstein held that the use of 'I' as a subject—not as an object spoken about—must be understood in terms of language processes. His discussions of this thesis were rather complex, but the following observation illustrates his point: the statement 'I believe that...' is not normally a self-description but indicates a degree of affirmation. In short, the use of 'I' is not 'private' but serves a communicative function.[55]

Wittgenstein's distinction between first-person and third-person speech was similar to the one made by Ebner. Much of this similarity can be explained on the basis of a common background, but there is evidence presented elsewhere (Buss 2006: 80-81) that Wittgenstein actually knew Ebner's work, both directly and through a report by Hänsel, a Christian friend of Wittgenstein's (since about 1918) who liked Ebner's ideas.

Wittgenstein distinguished not only between first-person and third-person speech, as did some other writers, but also, like Ebner, between second-person religious speech (such as in an address to God) and third-person theological speech. Accordingly, he said in 1932/33 (1979: 32) that theology is 'grammar', meaning thereby that theology specifies the nature of religious language.[56] Along this grammatical line, he stated in 1937 that

53. 'Blue Book', early 1934 (1984, V: 106). On 'surface' grammar, cf. PI, 1.664.

54. E.g.: 'The word 'I' does not designate a person' (1993: 228 [1935]; again, PI, 1.410); here 'I' is used in a strict (not descriptive) sense. There was a certain similarity between Wittgenstein's analysis and earlier positions that had distinguished between the 'pure' or 'transcendental' 'I' (or 'subject') and the empirical 'I' (or 'object'). But earlier positions had reified the 'I' in a way that Wittgenstein did not after 1918; specifically, Kant (1787: 404; cf. Wittgenstein, PI, 1.413), Schopenhauer (known to Wittgenstein), and Husserl (1950–, XIX/1: 372 [1901]) had spoken about 'the subject' or 'the [transcendental] I' in the third person, as Wittgenstein still did in 1918 (1922, proposition 5.641, in line with earlier jottings).

55. In the 1930s, Wittgenstein went to great lengths to show that the words used in 'I'-speech are learned in a social context (e.g. PI, 1.244); they are thus not (purely) private.

56. Johann Hamann (letter to his brother, 19 February 1760) had learned from John Bengel (*Gnomon*, Preface, §14 [1742; ET 1877: 44]) a statement by Martin Luther in an unidentified context that theology is nothing other than a 'grammar of the words of the Holy Spirit' (that is, of Scripture, as Hamann said explicitly in 1762 [1949–57, II: 129]); Lüpke (1992: 232) has cited as relevant Luther 1888–, XLVIII: 203. Bengel's reference was apparently the basis for Hamann's saying that he, 'like Luther turned the

'it is one thing to speak to God and something else to speak about God' (MS 183, 174 [1979: 80]). In his own writings, Wittgenstein expressed first- and second-person speech largely in an (easily deciphered) code or in personal letters.[57]

Wittgenstein's theory of language games also drew, more than can be shown here, on a variety of other scholarly traditions, including mathematics and the human sciences (see, e.g., Buss, 2002). These traditions had also come to incorporate relational perspectives.

7. The Association of Relational Thought with Interactive Freedom

There is a clear logical connection between relational theory and interactive freedom. As will be shown in detail in Chapter 4, relational theory accepts both a degree of connectivity and a degree of separateness. The same combination holds true for interactive freedom. Positive freedom relies on connectivity; negative freedom presupposes and encourages a degree of separateness. In fact, relational thinkers inclined in practice or at least in their ideals toward interactive freedom.

Indeed, it seems that without exception relational thinkers embraced both positive and negative freedom for society. Such a combination has already been indicated for Beecher, Fay, Peirce, Abbot, Royce, James (in part), Dewey, Cohen, Scheler, Merleau-Ponty, Buber, and, implicitly, Wittgenstein, despite their variations in specific politics.

A special angle in regard to interactive freedom is equality between the sexes. Thus it is noteworthy that women made major contributions to relational thinking. They contributed to the theorizing of theoretical and social relations both in their own writings (e.g. Beecher, Fay, Addams, and Stein, who have been mentioned) and through their impact on Green,

whole of philosophy into a grammar' (letter to F. Jacobi, 27 April 1787). Hamann's statement was quoted as a motto by Fritz Mauthner, known to Wittgenstein quite early (*Tractatus*, 4.0031).

57. See especially MS 183: 144, 146, 157, 159, 162, 173, 174, 187, 197, 233, 235 (2003: 152-243). A similar tendency also appeared in other MSS written in 1929, 1937, and 1947 (1998: 4, 5, 30-39, 72), although not in some others. In 1937, Wittgenstein referred to God in private letters to Ludwig Hänsel, especially thus: 'God with you' (a concluding wish) and 'Think much on God, and it will come out right between the two of you' (2003: 302-305); this was practical second-person speech and fell in with the recipient's religious framework. The use of code for many personal matters (including, although not limited to, religious and ethical commitments)—but not for his many reflections *about* religion and ethics—extended over a long period of time. Since the code is easily broken (a = z, b = y, etc.), it probably served the purpose not so much of secrecy as of symbolizing a deeply personal form of speech; he compared his notes with precious items locked in a jewelry box (2003: 4).

Abbot, Peirce, and Dewey. Presumably (although this may not be expressly known), thinking by women also had an effect on other men who supported feminism,[58] including Mead and Russell.[59] Women's own contributions will be treated in Chapter 8.

Philosophical formulations of relational thinking interacted not only with societal processes but also with various aspects of culture. The fields of literature and other arts are largely ignored in the present study. The role of a relational perspective in a variety of scholarly disciplines has been sketched elsewhere and will not be repeated here (Minow 1990: 173-266; Buss 2007). However, the relation of philosophy to theology—a sister and often rival discipline—deserves some attention.

Theology is, like philosophy, not independent of social history. Specifically, Christian theology first pictured God largely as a Monarch, then as a great Self or as an Artisan, and after that predominantly in terms of relations, sometimes identifying God with relationality (Buss 1979: 8). These changes in thinking clearly reflect social developments, even as, conversely, social arrangements are indebted to thoughts and ideals.

In short, various kinds of often reciprocal interactions between philosophy and religious thought have taken place. In China and India, in fact, they have been closely intertwined, insofar as one can distinguish between them at all. In the West, there has been extensive interaction during the last two millennia. One of the major themes of nominalism, however, was a division between reason and faith. In line with this theme, philosophy became officially independent from theology, especially from the seventeenth century on. This independence continued in the twentieth century, but interactions between the two endeavors continued, as has already been indicated in part.[60] The interaction between philosophy and theology was

58. See further, above, Chapter 2, n. 17, and below, 8.1.

59. Mead supported feminism along with other progressive orientations (Seigfried 1996: 30, 69). Russell's mother had campaigned for women's suffrage (1967–69, I: 155), and his first wife, Alys, had social democratic and feminist interests (Ironside 1996: 24, 76-77, 182). Russell came to support women's equality as an adolescent, after reading Mill (according to his account in 1967–69, I: 155), and served as a political candidate for the Women's Suffrage Societies in 1907. Russell also had a strongly individualistic streak in his personal life, which was connected with some aspects of radical politics, including feminism. Russell did eventually become—rightly or wrongly—less 'dogmatic' on the topic of marriage, in regard to which he had been relatively libertarian (1967–69, II: 156).

60. Gadamer (1984: 30) has noted the religious background for the dialogical component. Besides individuals that have already been mentioned (such as Peirce and Green), the following had a religious orientation: Royce, James, Dewey (moving from a liberal, socially-oriented Christianity to a naturalistic kind of religion with a remarkable involvement in public life [Martin 2002]), Mead (cf. Feffer 1993: 25-79, for Dewey and Mead), Scheler (specifically, Roman Catholic before 1924), Litt (in 1938

especially strong in the grammatical-dialogical stream, but it also played a role in pragmatism and phenomenology.

Public acknowledgment of the theological connections with philosophical thought was often absent or low-key, however, often as a matter of principle. When Peirce first proposed his triadic theory of the symbol in 1866, he did not stress the importance of trinitarian ideas in his lecture, since these ideas 'may be offensive to the prejudices of some who are present'—probably with reference to agnostics and Unitarians, both well represented in his audience (1982–, I: 503). Subsequently, he wrote on more principled grounds that 'God' as a 'name' has no legitimate place in philosophy (1931–35, 8.126 [1902]).[61] Cohen did not focus on his Jewish commitment until after his retirement from his role as chair in philosophy. Only in work thereafter (1919) did he highlight the notion of 'correlation' between God and humans. Husserl thought that religion and theology—although they are very important—belong to the personal rather than the public (including philosophical) realm.[62] The grammatical-dialogical stream treated the divergence in terms of a distinction between I–you and I–it.

A distinction between public and personal dimensions, it should be noted, does not downgrade the personal. Rather, for most persons the personal aspect—where pain, joy, love, hope, and so on take place—is basic. However, as societies become larger the division of labor within them tends to increase. Still, there can be, and probably should be, fructifying

he defended the role of Christianity against German racism), Heidegger (for a while), Arendt (see Arendt and Jaspers 1985: 202 [4 March 1951]), Jaspers, Hesse, Ricoeur, Putnam (see, for instance, Blumenthal *et al.* 2000), Gibbs, and women mentioned below, 8.2, 4. (This list is, of course, not complete.) Nozick, who came to approach a relational view, presented some theological reflections to a general audience in 1989 (217-42).

61. In a partial contrast to this statement, in 1908 he published a discussion of an argument for the reality of God in a journal devoted primarily to religious thought (1931–58, 6.452-90).

62. Born to an orthodox Jewish mother and to a Jewish father who converted to Christianity, Husserl became, as has become clear, an earnest convert to Christianity after originally holding a secular outlook (see Moran 2005: 16, with references). For him, the term 'God' belonged to theology with a personal (including moral) orientation (1950–, III/1: 109-10, 351 [1913]; XXVII: 33-34 [1924]). Its philosophical counterpart is 'the Absolute' (1950–, XXVII: 33 [1924]; XV: 668-70 [1934 MS]; 1994, VII: 218 [1934 letter]). In fact, 'true philosophy is as such theology' (1994, VII: 88 [1934 letter]). These are two ways of looking at the same reality. Of the two ways, philosophy was for him preparatory for theology. As a young man, he sought 'the find the way to God and to a life of integrity by means of strict philosophical knowledge' (1994, IV: 408 [1919 letter]), and later he said that his philosophy represented a 'so-to-say atheistic way to God' (1994, VII: 88, 124 [1934 and 1935 letters]). However, he thought that theology did not belong to his public task (1994, IV: 409 [1919]).

interchanges between relatively public philosophy and relatively personal theology, as has been pointed out in different ways by Hans Blumenberg, Leo Strauss, and Jean-François Lyotard, among others.[63]

Extensive interchange is shown also by the fact that a number of traditions other than Judaism and Christianity contributed to the formulations of relational theory. Relevant ideas that were current in China and India entered into European and American awareness from the seventeenth century on, although it appears that some time was needed for an adequate recognition of their perspectives. For instance, Chinese thought focused on relations rather than on isolated substances and probably influenced Leibniz in regard to this topic (Needham 1954–2004, II). Hegel was interested in the combination of themes of unity and difference in Hinduism, even though he was partially critical of the way these themes were treated.[64] Around the year 1900 CE, international (including African) art became highly influential. Subsequently, Buber's *I and You* (1923) was influenced by Chinese Taoism.

In fact, European philosophy had never been isolated.[65] Thus, it is misleading to speak of European thought as 'Western' in an exclusive sense. However, with increasingly global communication, interaction became more extensive.

8. *Summary*

Relational thought as such was not new, but an explicit form of it emerged at the end of the nineteenth century and soon thereafter, as Western philosophy absorbed relational motifs from Jewish, Christian, and various other traditions and formulated them theoretically. Women contributed significantly to this development.

63. For Blumenberg, Christianity's influence on 'modern' philosophy lies primarily in its raising questions (1966). Differently, Lyotard said that 'the father of Western metaphysics is St. Paul' (2004: 114 [1994]). Leo Strauss pointed to a 'mutual influence of theology and philosophy', although he emphasized 'a radical opposition' between them; he held that 'the choice of philosophy is based on faith', so that faith (although of different kinds) apparently lies behind both theology and philosophy (1979: 111, 112, 118). These formulations seem to be one-sided, each in a different way.

64. See the section on India in Hegel's lectures on the philosophy of religion, 1827 (1969–, XVI: 352), and lectures on the philosophy of history, 1822–30 (1969–, XII: 180-81).

65. The Pre-socratics (with their implicitly relational themes) were in part located in Asia Minor. (In fact, one can wonder whether Xenophanes was stimulated toward monotheism by the Persians, from whom he fled.) Various Greek philosophers (especially including Zeno the Stoic) had direct or indirect contact with Africa and the Near East. In the Middle Ages, Arabic Muslim discussions contributed to Christian nominalism (Buss 1999: 87).

Three major relational lines appeared: the semiotic-pragmatist, the phenomenological, and the grammatical-dialogical. They would interweave with each other, such as in the thought of Wittgenstein. Since the three lines diverged in regard to specifics (although not necessarily in contradictory ways), one can judge that they each in their own way furnished a theoretical formulation for a deep, intuitive sense of relationality, which must have been widely present in the culture.

As an expression of this deep sense, relational thought corresponded to and was connected with the ideal of interactive freedom, as the social involvements of its exponents show. That ideal included external-positive as well as external-negative and internal freedom.

Chapter 4

THE TWO-SIDEDNESS OF RELATIONS

The present chapter and the one that follows outline characteristic themes of a relational perspective, as they appeared in more than one of the three major philosophical lines already identified, as well as outside of professional philosophy. The themes cohere reasonably well with each other, so that it is apparent that they constitute a special way of looking at the world, more pervasive than any one line. This complex (summarized at the end of Chapter 5) can be termed the 'relational' way.

1. Relationality as a Conjunction of Separateness with Connectivity and of the Particular with the General

As relations became a central issue close to the year 1900 CE, their precise nature became the subject of considerable debate. Especially important was the question of whether relations are extrinsic—in the sense of their not affecting an object's nature—or intrinsic—in the sense of their being inherent in objects.[1] The ensuing discussion showed that viewing relations either as entirely extrinsic or entirely intrinsic are both particularist. For, on the one hand, if relations are entirely extrinsic—not affecting the nature of objects—they presuppose that these small units are fully independent and that relations are secondary.[2] On the other hand, if relations are entirely intrinsic—so that an object is firmly tied to others—then a given item is part of a whole that is 'uni-fied', a large particular. In fact, F.H. Bradley, a neo-Hegelian and political conservative (Wollheim 1959: 14), argued in 1893 (ch. 13) for the intrinsic character and, therefore, the ultimate unreality of relations; his argument was made within

---

1. To give an example: if fatherhood is extrinsic to me, I am not different by being a father; in contrast, if fatherhood is intrinsic to me, I cannot help but be one. In formal discussions of this issue, the terms 'external' and 'internal' are used, instead of the clearer 'extrinsic' and 'intrinsic'.

2. Locke, a nominalist, had spoken of relations as 'extraneous' (1690, 2.25.8; cf. Hegel, *Wissenschaft der Logik*, 1812-16, I:103, on extrinsic relationships in philosophical atomism).

a framework of a particularistic monism comparable to that of Spinoza
('the real is individual', he said).[3]

In other words, both purely extrinsic and purely intrinsic interpretations downgrade the importance of relations. An outlook that views relations as real, not merely present in thought, must hold that objects are
partially separate (relations would then be in part extrinsic) and that they
are at the same time partially linked in their being (relations are then in
part intrinsic).[4] If there are no beings that are at least semi-independent,
there is nothing to enter into a relationship, but if beings are completely
independent, they are truly not related except in an observer's mind. In
fact, the theorists that will be cited next saw that *relationality—insofar as
it is real—is a fundamental principle which simultaneously separates and
connects objects*.

The realization of this dual character of relations was not a novel
phenomenon. Rather, it was long present in Christian discussions of the
Trinity,[5] as well as in Hindu and Buddhist traditions. In early Hinduism,
positive accounts of relationality were given by Nyaya (dealing with logic
and language) and by Vaisesika—two schools that acknowledged both particularity and generality. In later Hinduism, love (a special kind of relation) was important for those (such as Ramanuja in the eleventh century)
who accepted that deity also has individuality.[6] In Buddhism, the notion of
'dependent co-arising' avoids both absolute dependence and absolute independence (see, e.g., David Kalupahana 1976: 28).

After 1880 CE, the dual structure of relations was pointed out by the
following (among others), a majority of whom will be mentioned again
later: T.H. Green (1883, §28); Russell (1897: 198); R.W. Sellars, for 'many'
relations (1922: 198); D.S. Mackay, surveying relational theory (1930:

3.   In a later, unpublished, essay, Bradley said that, since relationality involves both
disunity and unity, 'relational experience' is 'unavoidable' but (only) a 'makeshift'
(1935: 635). For Spinoza's particularist holism, see above, 1.1. Later theorists that
stressed intrinsic relations one-sidedly have often cited David Bohm, who envisioned
reality as a whole in a determinist way (thus, for example, Erroll Harris, for whom the
future was not truly open [1991: 21]). G.E. Moore (1922: 282) pointed out that theories
favoring an intrinsic character of relations actually refer to the relational qualities of
objects rather than to relations.

4.   Cf. McGilvary 1956: 227; Leisegang 1969. A number of philosophers have suggested that it is possible to regard some relations as intrinsic and others as extrinsic
(thus Duns Scotus, c. 1300 CE [1975: 106, 496], N. Hartmann [1949: 279-84], and Ferré
[1996: 336-38]); such a contrast requires a distinction between essential and accidental
characteristics and is thus, in a sense, Aristotelian (Bradley 1935: 667; Rorty 1967b).

5.   Thus, again, Joseph Ratzinger (1968: 142-43).

6.   Similarly for love, Hegel, in lectures on the philosophy of religion, 1827 (1969-,
XVII: 222).

13, 33); Simone Weil (1962: 36, 94-96 [c. 1941]);[7] Levinas (1947: 26); Buber (1962, I: 411-23 [1950]);[8] T.R.V. Murti (1955: 138, Buddhist); Julius Schaaf, saying that a relation between objects separates by connecting and connects by separating (1965: 13; 1977: 162);[9] Jean Piaget (1968: 9); Archie Bahm, with an overview of the discussion (1974: 72-76); Mary Hesse (1980: 89); Anicetus Sinaga (1981: 185); Carol Gilligan (1982: 63; 1993: xiii); Charles Hartshorne, referring to a 'mixture of dependence and independence' (1983: 164, 168); Julia Kristeva (1985, 'Credo'); Édouard Glissant (1990: 145); Edward Farley (1990: 40); Luce Irigaray (1992: 232); and Jean-François Lyotard, in a late work (1992: 48). Partial connectivity was implied in the indeterminism of Peirce and James. Specifically, in regard to love, Peirce said that it simultaneously propels into independence and draws into harmony (1931–58, 6.288 [1893]). Clearly, the dual character of relations was well known.

Because of this two-pronged character of relations, divergent formulations by A.N. Whitehead and Bertrand Russell (co-authors of *Principia mathematica*, first edn, 1910–13) were not altogether incompatible with each other, although they represented different emphases, which may also be reflected in their somewhat different politics.[10] Whitehead highlighted the intrinsic character of relations, although he recognized that extrinsic relationality is implied by the partial indeterminism that he accepted (1925: 230).[11] Differently, Russell emphasized the extrinsic character of relations in opposition to a strong holism, although he rejected unconnected atomism.[12]

---

7. Weil viewed distance as a part of love, although she associated suffering with that distance.

8. Buber here partially modified his earlier view, with more emphasis on distance. Buber was, in fact, opposed from both directions. Levinas (to whom 'otherness' was primary) objected to Buber's holding equally to union and separation in a relation (in Sydney and Beatrice Rome 1964: 24), but Marcel (with an opposite stance) criticized Buber for treating relation, which includes distance, as more primary than unity (in Schilpp and Friedman 1967: 45 [cf. Buber's response, 705]).

9. Schaaf, who in some way stood close to religious thinkers, has been influential for others who have regarded relations as central or basic (e.g. Rodolphe Gasché 1999: 5).

10. Politically, Whitehead supported social reform according to 'the moderate side of the Labour party' (see Whitehead 1941: 13; R.C. Morris 1991). Russell was more radical, in part in terms of individualism (see above, Chapter 3, n. 59).

11. Hartshorne (1983: 164) therefore regarded Whitehead's terminology as misleading. However, Whitehead may not have transcended nominalism altogether (see below, 5.3).

12. For instance, according to Russell in 1897 (190), geometry—describing relations—needs actuality, which can separate. Cf. Horstmann 1984: 188, 195.

Relations not only combine connectivity and differentiation, they also exhibit a duality of generality and particularity. Relations as such are general (for instance, having a causal effect on something else is a relation that holds true for more than one set of entities), but relations have particulars as their end terms. Accordingly, quite a few theorists—including Ernst Mach (see below, 5.4), H. Poincaré (1903, Introduction, with an argument against nominalism), R.W. Sellars (1922: 195), and Dewey (1929: 163; 1938: 270)—have held that the aim of science is the study of relations; after all, relations can appear repeatedly, although specific appearances are particular.[13]

Two somewhat different but interconnected dualities are at play in an analysis of relations: (1) a combination of partial connectivity and partial separateness,[14] and (2) a combination of generality and particularity. The first of these two dualities implies the other.

If relations are in some sense fundamental—as Peirce, among others, claimed—then these dualities do not constitute dualisms, which would presuppose unconnected dimensions. Rather, each side represents an aspect of relationality, which can be taken as 'primitive', that is, basic.

Russell recognized relational structure in the very nature of a proposition, in which something is asserted about an object. Within a proposition he held that particular and general terms (in a typical sentence the subject and the predicate) are correlates.[15] This means that the very process of saying something implies the presence of both particularity and generality. He viewed relationality, then, as representing a 'fundamental notion', which is not secondary although it has two aspects (1903, §94).

For a long time it has been recognized that only what is in some way connected and general can be understood or known intellectually. By accepting generality, relational thought allows for the possibility of intellectual knowledge. At the same time, the idea that particulars are partially independent implies that a certain mystery adheres to them.[16] Thus, relational thought accepts in principle a combination of partial knowledge and partial mystery. In causality, this combination allows for a partial indeterminism.

---

13. For antecedents to this idea, see above, Chapter 3, n. 12.

14. Ontologically, this duality applies to real relations. (Identity is not a real relation, but a logical one.) In human existence, reflexivity (a relation to oneself) involves an element of separation, or self-transcendence.

15. E.g. 1956: 4-6 (1901), 123-24 (1911), 199 (1918); Whitehead and Russell 1925–27: xix. The real 'betweenness' of relations had still been rejected by Hermann Lotze (1888, III, §9.2).

16. See variously below on Lacan, Levinas, Glissant, Bauman, and Oliver. In a late phase of his thought, Russell sought to do without particulars, since they are unknowable (1940: 122).

2. Relations in Logic and Mathematics:
Duality with Flexibility, Probability, and Indetermination

After c. 1875, the relational orientation quickly became dominant in logic, a field in which changes in intellectual orientation are often seen with special clarity. In this field, a duality of particularity and generality came to be standard.[17]

The format of post-1875 logic was thus different from both Aristotelian and nominalist logics. Aristotle's logic dealt only with general classes, each exhibiting an essence. Nominalist logic could make use of Aristotle's system, but what Aristotle had treated as classes of objects were viewed by nominalism either as collectivities—which are large particulars—or as mental concepts.[18]

In contrast to the Aristotelian and nominalist systems, relational logic simultaneously treated both particular objects and general (including theoretically possible) phenomena.[19] Symbolic logic thus introduced two kinds of symbols: one for particulars and the other for general realities. This differentiation was needed in order to deal with relations, since relations themselves are general (repeatable), while the items that are related are particular.[20] For instance, the proposition that the objects a and b stand in the relation R was often symbolized by a formula such as aRb. In the script used by this kind of formula, lower-case letters (a and b) refer to particular objects, while upper-case letters (R) refer to relations (including properties) that are 'general' (that is, repeatable).[21]

17. Thus, again, Nuel Belnap, Jr. (in Agazzi 1981: 146). That included attention to 'models', for which the term 'relational structures' has been proposed (Addison *et al.* 1965: xiii).

18. Bocheński 1956, §§12, 34, 36; Kneale 1962: 67, 303-304.

19. On possibility, see above, 3.4, and below, 5.3.

20. Thus, Peirce in 1870 (1982–, II: 365). De Morgan's foray into relational logic in 1860 had already indicated the need for such a dual set of symbols (e.g., 1966: 221, n. 2). On the basis of a common background in mathematical logic, Gottlob Frege proceeded in a way somewhat similar to that of Peirce. Specifically, he analyzed a meaning function (a kind of relation) as being both general ('continuing') and open, that is, incomplete without the particular to which it is applied. He did so in a rough way in 1879, §9 (in this early work, much—including a distinction between specific objects and kinds of objects—remains unclear), and in more precise terms in 1891: 6. The later formulation may perhaps have been sharpened through an indirect knowledge of Peirce, such as through Ernst Schröder's reference to Peirce in an 1880 review of Frege's first study, which may have been clear enough so that Frege could grasp Peirce's contribution. (Incidentally, in the early part of the twentieth century, Peirce was still better known as a logician than was Frege.)

21. Relations and properties are not formally distinguished in kind; rather, properties

In the new logic, classes could be constructed from relations (also called 'functions'), but classes were no longer as important as they had been for Aristotle. One reason for the downgrading of classification was the abandonment of the belief that there is a single correct classification for every object. In the Aristotelian tradition, categorization had presupposed the idea that some properties are 'essential' for an object and form the basis for its proper classification. Without the notion of essence (which had already been rejected by nominalism), it became appropriate to examine a variety of different arrangements (Angelelli 1967: 253-54). Depending on the features of an object that are selected for attention, a given object can exhibit one form or another. Symbolic notation proved useful in handling the complex patterns into which various individuals and different kinds of relation can enter. Since objects as a rule do not fit pre-existing categories precisely, a logic for 'fuzzy sets'—sets that have partial membership—was formulated.[22]

Relational formal logic is very flexible. Just as geometry had already been opened to a variety of structures, including those that differ from Euclid's, so also logic came to analyze many different patterns. In fact, it was ready to examine relationships of any kind involving any starting point. That is, it could move from any terms or axioms to those conclusions that can be reached from them by any freely chosen procedures (thus expressly Carnap 1937: xv). In such a logic, there was room to say that something is 'not logical' only in the sense that 'one cannot move from this point by means of this step to this other point'.

'Nonstandard' logic even allowed for contradiction, although this remained controversial. A logic of this kind, known as 'paraconsistent' or 'transconsistent', could be considered useful for representing temporal processes (as the dialectics of Hegel and Engels sought to do in a non-formal way), as well as for exhibiting paradoxes (which often involve self-negation) and moral dilemmas (two contradictory states may both be valued).[23] Consideration was given to the possibility that the world itself contains contradictions (thus, Peirce in 1893 [1931–58, 4.79] and Wittgenstein in 1939–43 [1956, *passim*], and others).

---

can be treated as one-place relations (e.g. Barwise and Perry 1999: 49), or relations can be treated as properties of pairs (etc.).

22. See, e.g., Lofti Zadeh 1965 (and later); J.A. Goguen 1969: 325-73; Witold Pedrycz and Fernando Gomide 1998. Pierre Bourdieu has described the logic of action as valuably *floue*, 'fuzzy' (1980, near end). 'Fuzzy logic' is now built into machines or operations for which non-rigidity is an advantage.

23. Thus, after earlier beginnings, especially since the middle of the twentieth century. See A. Dumitriu 1977, IV: 252-53; Rescher and Brandom 1979: 57-58, with bibliography; G.H. von Wright 1986: 13; DaCosta and Carnielli 1986; Graham Priest 1987 (improved in 2006); and A.D. Irvine 1996: 33. 'Relevance logic' is a special form of this kind of logic.

In mathematics, which is closely connected with logic, a joint role for relations and particulars also became prominent from the end of the nineteenth century on.[24] A number of systems were each built on the basis of two elements. One is particular (such as point, number, set, or sphere) and the other relational (such as betweenness, successorhood, membership, or distinction [Spencer-Brown 1979]). 'Sets' (prominent from about 1880 on) were treated as collectivities or wholes, so that they play the role of units, while open 'classes' exhibit general functions (see Fraenkel and Bar-Hillel 1958: 97, 110, 120, 147).

One branch of mathematics, developed actively from the 1880s on,[25] dealt with relations between objects or events that contain an element of unpredictability and thus need to be stated in terms of probability. Probability is a special variety of the larger concept of indetermination, which includes vagueness and incongruity, for which mathematical formulations have also been furnished.[26]

In fact, it was found that there is indetermination even within mathematics. Kurt Gödel showed in 1931 (see 1940) that any logical system strong enough to contain ordinary mathematics will contain at least one true formula that cannot be proved within that system. He demonstrated this fact by displaying a formula that declares itself to be true but unprovable ('undecidable') within a given system. It should be noted that this conclusion was not skeptical; rather, it stated that there is more mathematical truth than can be proven. Similarly, from the very beginnings of computational theorizing in 1936, it was shown that answers to some mathematical questions are 'non-computable', so that some parts of mathematics are called 'random' (Chaitin 1999: 84). Thus, a lack of strict coherence was seen even in mathematics.

3. Relations in Actual Existence:
Both Reasonableness and Indeterminism

If it is true that at least some relations are actual, not merely something that one thinks about, it follows that logic and mathematics, which analyze relations in a theoretical way, are useful for describing the actualities of the world. Indeed, many studies have shown such usefulness, especially in physics.

---

24. J. Fang (1970: 63) pointed to an interest in relations that began especially with Felix Klein in 1872. The French mathematical program *Bourbaki* (see, e.g., Fang 1970) started with a relational primitive.

25. See, e.g., Stigler 1986: 265 and, for a wide interest in probability emerging about that time, Oakley 2000: 138-60. There were, of course, some prior antecedents and many later developments.

26. See Klir and Wierman 1999 and above for 'fuzzy sets'.

Although the twentieth century began with considerable skepticism about human ability to know the order of the physical world as it exists in itself,[27] later investigations sought (and found) a certain 'beauty', or reasonableness, in physical laws. For instance, Albert Einstein stressed the importance of the 'inner perfection of a theory'—so that it is not 'arbitrary'—together with its need for external support in observation (1949: 22-23).

Specifically, most of the fundamental laws of physics involve symmetries. These symmetries are not perfect, but imperfections in symmetry were also seen as important for the history of the universe. For instance, if the universe did not contain slightly more matter than antimatter (or vice versa), nothing would exist. Furthermore, the symmetries have progressively been broken in the development of the universe, so that now there are four different 'forces'. Consequently, Steven Weinberg could see a 'possible parallel between the history of the universe and its logical structure' (1993: 149).

It appears, in fact, that the constitution of the world is not highly arbitrary, although one can have a strong hunch that it is also not completely necessary in order to have a being in the world that can talk about it.[28] Such an assessment implies that nominalist empiricism went too far in doubting that realities have a reason.

A nominalist position was expressed in Hume's skepticism about causality. Instead of a causality that implies a logical connection between events, Hume accepted only regularity, a 'constant conjunction' (for instance, B always follows A). According to Hume, this regularity has no 'reason' (there is no reason why B should follow A), but it is rigid (B always follows A, other things being equal).[29] In contrast to this view, conceptions of nature from the end of the nineteenth century on have often reversed Hume's analysis. They found a certain reasonableness in reality but denied absolute regularity or full determinism.[30]

27. See below, 5.4, on Pearson.

28. Both coherence and contingency has been recognized, for instance, by David Lindley (1993: 230, 231) and Brian Greene (1999: 365-68). In a similar way, Gaston Bachelard (1934) envisioned for physics an interaction between reason and experimentation. In regard to an anthropic principle, the 'weak' version, which holds that any world that can be talked about must contain a being who does such talking, is scientifically tenable (cf. Barrow and Tipler 1986); this version allows for contingency about there being such a world.

29. At least, this is one way to read Hume (cf. analyses of his view reprinted in Tweyman 1995).

30. Partial indeterminism, even in the nonhuman realm, was shown to be compatible with science by Gustav Fechner in 1849 (see Krüger *et al.* 1987, I, and Heidelberger 1993: 123). It was affirmed from 1866 on by Peirce (1982–, I: 412, 417); following Renouvier (see on him above, Chapter 3, n. 13), at least as a matter of faith by James in 1870 (1920, I: 147-48); privately and partially in 1873 by the physicist Nicholas Maxwell (with a religious concern [cf. Brush 1983: 89]); theoretically in

A degree of indeterminacy provides for an open future and may constitute the directionality of time, which moves from what is determinate to what is not strictly so.[31] Such a future can be described by a logic that allows for multiple truth values, including one that assigns neither truth nor falsity to a situation or event. A logic of this kind was already outlined by Aristotle in connection with a discussion of tenses (*On Interpretation*, 19a) and was discussed extensively in the Middle Ages. After a subsequent period of disinterest, it received symbolic formalization from 1908 on (Bocheñski 1956, §49).

Dynamically, partial indeterminacy makes possible what can be called 'action'. 'Action' (as the term is used here) implies some effect on future events. Such an effect requires a degree of regularity in the world. At the same time, 'action' implies that a causal agent is not entirely determined by its own past; otherwise, what takes place is a passive process. The possibility that all of nature may be active came to be seriously considered (see below, 5.5).

As has been shown, neither determinism nor indeterminism can ever be proved absolutely (von Wright 1974: 136). Thus a decision in regard to whether there is 'action', as it has just been described, will always need to be in part a matter of intuitive judgment. However, twentieth-century science—influenced by such theoretical reflections as well as by observational data[32]—has provided evidence not only that physical objects are connected in their very being but also that their processes do not contradict partial indeterminism, which implies a degree of separateness.

In any case, the notion of probability combines continuity with discontinuity. In physics, such a combination appears in the duality of particles and waves. As Born pointed out in his autobiography (1968: 35), 'the idea of probability' provides a way 'for reconciling [discontinuous] particles with [continuous] waves'.

1874 by Émile Boutroux (seeking to overcome both idealism and materialism as well as dualism, within a religious orientation [1916: vi, 160, 179]); thereafter by Karl Pearson, describing the 'grammar of science' (1892: 136); and later in varying ways by others, including Henri Bergson (1934, Chap. 3 [1930]). The change took place in part because of accumulating evidence (such as in Marie Curie's work with radium [Diggins 1994: 82]) and in part because of philosophical/social concerns to unify individuality with generality, so that physical theories were not independent of such concerns. (See Jammer 1973; Brush 1983: 79-104; Fuller 1988: 248 [with reference also the earlier position of the Epicurean-inclined Gassendi in the seventeenth century].) Positions along a non-Humean and probabilistic line have included those of Nancy Cartwright (1989), Maxwell (1998), Wesley Salmon (1998), and Judea Pearl (2000), but there has been no unanimity on this subject.

31. Cf. Ilya Prigogine and Isabelle Stengers 1984: 259, holding that probability presupposes the directionality of time, rather than vice versa (but does it matter?), and Frank Arntzenius 1995: 68.

32. See below, Chapter 5, n. 47.

The same duality is presupposed by the phenomenon of communication, for this requires both connectivity and an element of novelty. For the degree of novelty involved, information theory employs the notion of probability, especially its obverse, unpredictability (see below, 5.6).

4. *Summary*

Relational themes include the following:

Relations simultaneously separate and connect. Furthermore, relations include both particularity and generality; the endpoints of relations are particular, but relations as such (without reference to specific endpoints) are general, that is, repeatable. The two sides of these dualities do not need to be added to each other artificially because they represent two aspects of a single structure.

A relational perspective provides a new logic. This logic accepts both general and particular elements. It is more flexible than earlier logic.

As a reflection of the combination of connectivity and separateness, all of reality—large or small—exhibits both reasonableness and mystery. This combination appears even in mathematics.

A combination of connectivity and separateness shows itself in the phenomenon of probability, which indicates that there are connections but that they do not need to be tight.

These themes are included in the summary presented at the end of Chapter 5.

Chapter 5

FORMS AS COMPLEXES OF RELATIONS

Chapter 4 dealt with views concerning relations, without specific attention to their combinations in what can be called 'forms'. The present chapter will examine views concerning possible and actual combinations.

1. *Structure and Gestalt; Analysis and Synthesis*

In the relational movement, a complex of relations has often been called 'form', 'structure', or 'gestalt'.[1] The meanings of these three words cannot be rigidly distinguished from each other; however, their specific uses or emphases are typically different. The word 'structure' indicates attention to how the parts of an entity relate to each other, while the word 'gestalt' refers to a whole as it emerges as a confluence of relations. The word 'form' can cover either or both of these meanings.[2]

For instance, in mathematics, the idea of 'structure' (which has been pervasive in that field since c. 1895) includes as its basic features both particular 'elements' and repeatable—in this sense, general—'relations' between elements. In this conception, two structures that contain the same relations between the elements are said to exhibit 'homomorphism'.[3] Structures that are relatively loose or varied are often called 'networks'. Graphs show how the individual points ('nodes' or 'vertices') are connected by lines.

Although not examined apart from these relations, elements are treated as having a certain independence in such structures, in that they are

---

1. Some of the major twentieth-century developments involving form or structure have been surveyed by Lancelot Whyte (1951), Gyorgy Kepes (1965), and Piaget (1968).

2. For 'form' as a system of relationships (including the emergent whole), see, e.g., Abbot 1885: 129; 1906, I: 114 (form as 'relational constitution'); Cassirer 1923–29, III: 53, 332; Merleau-Ponty 1949: 50 (the form of a system remains the same when its internal relations continue); David Pole 1983: 82. The use of 'form' for a set of relations, treated seriatim rather than as a whole and thus synonymous with 'structure', has been a regular one in mathematics and logic. However, Whyte (1954: 198) and R.S. Crane (1953: 44, 103, 185) contrasted synthetic 'form' with analytic 'structure'.

3. See, e.g., Hodges 1993: 1-2, and above, n. 1.

not simply absorbed into their relations (Detlefsen 1996: 102-104). In fact, an existing whole cannot be completely unified, for if it is true that relations both separate and connect, any complex of relations—any 'form'—must have some internal differentiation, perhaps even some internal tension.[4]

A focus on 'structure'—that is, on the relations between the parts of a whole—is analytical. Such an approach is mentally rational in the sense that the relations within the whole are examined step-by-step. In contrast, a focus on a holistic 'gestalt' is synthetic. A synthetic view can be intuitive, in the sense that the whole (a large particular) is perceived without specific attention to its components, although some awareness of the components may well be present.

Since Buber's I-it and I-you involve partial and holistic perceptions, respectively (see above, 3.5), his I-it can be described as analytical and his I-you as intuitive. Buber viewed these two perceptions as alternatives to each other. It is likely, however, that they normally operate together, even though one's primary focus at a given time will tend to be on one of the two kinds of perception.[5] Indeed, experimental psychological evidence indicates that in perception the analytic and the holistic aspects of form are not independent of each other. In a first apprehension, which is already shaped by a preconception, the object appears as a roughly shaped whole. Then, in an extremely rapid alternation between analysis and synthesis, recognition becomes more detailed, so that the analytic aspect comes to the fore (Bachmann 2000: 16-18, 29). Subsequently, attention to details will fade again when it becomes less important for a given purpose.

In any case, whether analytically or synthetically, objects are always seen 'as' something that represents a general form. This observation does not deny uniqueness. On the contrary, an object is unique not when it lacks shared characteristics but when it exhibits an abundance of them, so that no other existing object exhibits the same combination. This combination is theoretically repeatable, although it may actually occur only once and will then be unique, as is usually true for a sufficiently complex object.

In short, forms constitute 'patterns'. In the words of Susanne Langer (1937: 23), 'anything may be said to have form that follows a pattern of any sort, exhibits order, internal connection'. This conception diverged from Hobbes's view that 'form' refers to an 'aggregate of accidents' (cited above, 1.1). The internal rationale of a form need not, and perhaps should not, be tight. However, it is the genius of a relational conception that it holds rationale and contingency in tension.

---

4. See below, 7.4, for Derrida's highlighting of internal tension.
5. See above, 3.5, for critiques of Buber.

2. *Theory Formation: Coherence and Openness*

A special kind of form appears in scholarly theory. It seeks to represent actuality by means of an intellectual structure that is grasped by the human mind.

In scholarly endeavors, a central question has been whether the proper procedure is induction—moving from particular observations to generalizations—or deduction—recognizing logical connections. In 1620, Francis Bacon championed induction. This way of proceeding at least implicitly reflected the belief that reality is fundamentally particular and that regularities are arbitrary (see above, 1.1). The inductive approach was, in fact, useful for freeing science from traditional prejudgments, although scientists after Bacon did not actually proceed purely by induction (Wedberg 1982–84, II: 35-37).

Differently, in 1874—after some anticipations of his view (see Gower 1996: 109-29) and partly indebted to Peirce—the logician W.S. Jevons described deduction from a hypothesis as the proper procedure for scientific investigation.[6] According to this theory of science, deductions from a hypothesis should be tested against reality.[7]

An approximation of this hypothetico-deductive procedure was already set forth in the thirteenth century, but the nominalist Ockham rejected it on the grounds that deductive logic would limit God's arbitrary power (Losee 1972: 36). In a certain sense, Ockham's position was justified, for some of the logical assumptions that were made at that time were far from watertight, as became apparent later. Yet his belief in the incoherence of reality may have also been unwarranted.

How does one arrive at a hypothesis? Peirce said that a new theory is occasioned by a 'surprising fact', one 'contrary to what we should expect';

6. One of Jevons's arguments was that scientists had found induction problematic. (Larry Laudan [1981: 11-14] discussed such scientists but underestimated [cf. 1984: 82] the broader sociological and philosophical aspects of the change in outlook.) Jevons's logic—which was indebted to his teacher Augustus De Morgan (founder of the symbolic logic of relations and critical of Bacon) and to Peirce (known to him through public and private communication)—exhibited a divergence from particularism (1874, I: 30). Christoph Sigwart (1878) developed a conclusion similar to Jevons, which he had reached largely independently, apparently on the basis of a common background, the major elements of which were cited by Peirce (1982–, II: 219 [1868]).

7. Jevons, somewhat like William Whewell (1847), continued to use the word 'induction' for scientific procedure, but redefined it, describing it as an inverse of deduction. In fact, since the middle of the twentieth century, inductive reasoning has been revived in a rigorous form that includes deduction from a hypothesis (specifically, the likelihood of a certain event in view of a given hypothesis) as one step (Howson and Urbach 1993).

in other words, a previous assumption is contradicted.[8] This means that a hypothesis does not arise without the context of a pre-existing theory; rather, it modifies an earlier one (Peirce 1931–58, 1.74). The chain of theories goes back to implicit categories in pre-human animal perception.[9]

Twentieth-century discussions introduced extensions and refinements of such a theory-oriented conception of science. Early in the century, Pierre Duhem pointed out that all observations are inextricably linked to theories and that no theory can be strictly disproved (1906, 2.4; 2.6.3).[10] Subsequently (in 1958), Norwood Hanson discussed at length the point that any observation is itself already theory-laden. Donald Davidson even argued that an organizing 'conceptual scheme' cannot be clearly distinguished from the individual observations that are organized (1984: 183-98 [1974]).

Considerable interest was thus directed toward the question of how succeeding theories relate to one another. According to an extreme version of holism, theories are incommensurable (non-comparable) with one another, which means transitions between them are non-rational. This idea is often associated with Thomas Kuhn, although he argued for no more than a partial incommensurability of paradigms. He said that theories are 'here and there, incommensurable'; they do not quite fit together, but a lack of fit between them is 'never total' (1962: 111, 128).[11] Accordingly, he envisioned a partial non-rationality in transitions that employ 'persuasive argumentation'—a middle way between arbitrary choice and clear demonstration (93). He also recognized that a newer theory may be inclusive of an older one, at least in terms of the problems addressed (168-69).

A less holistic conception of scientific theories was furnished by Imre Lakatos (1978). His 'research programmes' do not constitute coherent paradigms but involve somewhat loose complexes of hypotheses and procedures in the hope of reaching a position beyond the one at which one begins.[12]

Mary Hesse (1980) incisively developed a comprehensive 'network' conception for science. Her conception envisioned a continuum between theory and observation (more flexible than an overall 'paradigm') and had room for both internal coherence (within a theoretical structure) and external correspondence (that is, adequacy as a description of reality). Coherence and correspondence were seen as only partial, for they involve relations that (as she recognized) involve both partial dependence and partial independence for

8. Peirce 1982–, III: 326 (1878); 1931–58, 5.189 (1903); 7.202 (1901). Cf. 1982–, I: 440 (1866).

9. Cf. above, Chapter 1, n. 12.

10. Duhem's theory was extended by Willard Quine.

11. In fact, he later became more reserved about the use of the word 'paradigm'.

12. The so-called 'structuralist' view of Joseph Sneed was also flexible (see Sneed 1971: 304, for possible continuity between theories). Paul Feyerabend (1978) was more free-wheeling.

the items that are associated with each other (89). Furthermore, her network view allowed for partial connections between older and newer theories, so that there is often continuity along with change (137).

3. *The Ontology of Form: Possibility in Conjunction with Actuality*

Although scientific theories are human creations, a relational view holds that forms, as complexes of relations, are not purely mental creations. This point then raises the question, 'What precisely is their ontological status?' Although not all relational theorists agree, quite a few hold that forms represent possibilities.

In order to understand the rationality of such a position, it must be seen that a given form may not be actual. For instance, if a certain form is called a 'unicorn', it lacks instantiation, representing only a theoretical possibility. Since, however, it might be instantiated more than once, it is (theoretically) general rather than particular.

The question then arises: 'How is possibility related to actuality?' One answer is that possibility is logically prior to actuality, being presupposed by it, for anything that exists must have been possible. In the words of literary critic Eve Tavor Bannet (1993: 122), 'the actual…is the possibility which turns out to be the case'.

Such a position was held by Peirce. He held that, in the triplet which represents the structure of reality, possibility (identified with 'form' and with 'quality', which is 'general') is 'firstness'; actuality (involving interactions, including a physical object that serves as a signal) is 'secondness'; and meaning (which includes the other two) is 'thirdness'.[13] Possibility, then, is not dependent on what is actual, although it does have a connection with actuality.

Peirce's view and similar conceptions by other relational thinkers (including that of Weissman 2000: 28) resemble Plato's by holding that forms ontologically (not necessarily temporally) precede actual objects. However, there is a major difference. Socrates in Plato's *Republic* envisioned forms as possessing the highest grade of reality, even higher than that of ordinary actuality. In contrast, the relational position of Peirce and others assigns form as possibility a 'low' grade of reality, one that does not have the effective power of actuality.[14]

13. Peirce's ideas on form were not developed in an altogether uniform way throughout his career, but see the following texts: 1982–, I: 474 ('pure form' [1866]); II: 53 ('quality or general attribute' [1867]), I: 537 ('possibility' [1903]), I: 304 ('may-be' [c. 1904]), V: 532 ('the generality of the possible' [1905]); 1976, IV: 296-97 (form 'is generality', a 'quality or character' [c. 1912]). Cf. above, 3.3.

14. Similarly, Russell attributed 'being' to all possible objects, but 'existence' only to those that are actual (1937: 449).

In order to understand Aristotle's view of this issue, it is necessary to distinguish between 'sheer' or 'hypothetical' possibility, which, according to one view, is logically prior to actuality, and 'realistic' possibility or 'potentiality', which is a power that is present in what is actual. For instance, a unicorn is only hypothetical, but the growth of a tree is a potential.

Potency—a version of potentiality, as will be seen—was important for Aristotle, who distinguished it from logical possibility.[15] He identified potency with dynamic power. He held that this is prior to actuality in the existence of a specific object, since some power has brought this object about, but that actuality is more basic than potency in reality as a whole, for, if there is no actuality, there is no source for potency (*Metaphysics*, 1071b). However, Aristotle appears to have referred to potency only if it is actualized at least at some time or other.[16] Unactualized power—which can be called 'open potentiality'—was apparently of no interest to him, nor was he interested in a hypothetical play of sheer possibilities.

Sheer possibility and open potentiality similarly have no significant role in nominalism. Nominalists share Aristotle's emphasis on actuality, although they envision it in particularist terms. For them, a form (such as that of a unicorn) is an idea in someone's mind and is thus dependent on actuality. Furthermore, form is considered to be an 'abstraction' that is 'drawn from' actuality. In addition, most theistic nominalists believe that particulars are in practice constrained by God's 'laws', which provide for regularity, so that they have difficulty conceiving of open potentialities.[17] Indeed, postmedieval nominalists, theistic or not, have typically believed in some version of determinism, so that 'what can be' readily coincided with 'what is'. For instance, according to Spinoza, the possible and the actual coincide at all times.[18] Leibniz, too, thought that possibilities are not merely hypothetical. Rather, he held that possibilities, as they subsist in God's mind, have a drive towards actuality (e.g. 1965: 176 [1686–89]). The idea of inevitable 'progress' was one version of such a view.

What Plato, Aristotle, and nominalists thus have in common is that sheer theoretical possibilities are hardly considered.[19] In fact, in much of human

15. See, e.g., Simo Knuuttila 1993: 1-44, 106.

16. In ancient Greece, this view had already been held by Diodorus Cronos (fourth century BCE). Later, it was held by Hobbes, who said that everything possible either has been actual or will be so in the future (*Elements of Philosophy*, 1 [*De corpore*], 12.4 [1655]).

17. Hent de Vries described a restrictive view of possibility as 'possibilism' (1999: 91, 104), but this term also has other meanings.

18. *Ethics*, 1, proposition 33, n. 1 (c. 1674). A similar position had been held by Neoplatonists (Aune 1967: 420). Spinoza did allow for an 'epistemic' use of the word 'possibility', namely, to indicate that one has uncertain knowledge of something.

19. Thus, also, Kearney 2001: 83 (Kearney does not seem to accept sheer possibilities himself).

culture there has been little conscious attention paid to mere possibilities. Of course, people have always had experiences that we call 'imagination', but these experiences have often been viewed as referring to some sort of spiritual reality. For instance, dreams have commonly been thought to furnish truth, and a child's imaginary playmate can be thought of as an invisible spiritual being, not one that is merely a mental projection.[20] Thus, while human beings have always taken account of possibilities, they have not always explicitly thought of them in such terms. However, around 1900 CE, a change in conception took place, one that was reflected not only in philosophy but also in the larger culture.

The fact that an important change became current even in popular thinking is shown by a development in the meaning of the word 'imagination'. Before 1900, this word (including non-English antecedents or counterparts) usually referred to the formation of mental images of realities that are actual or believed to be actual.[21] From the eighteenth century on, 'imagination' came to be treated as something that creates new constructions and insights. However, it was still thought to present truth or reality, or some aspect of it, not just hypothetical structures (see, e.g., Mary Warnock 1976; James Engell 1981). The idea of progress supported the expectation that envisioned forms would be actualities in the future.

In the twentieth century, however, the word 'imagination' (and in its German equivalent, *Einbildung*) usually came to refer to a conception of what is possible, with no commitment that it would represent past, present, or future actuality (thus, e.g., Alan White [1990]). This shift in language shows that we are dealing here with a major change in culture, one that is strongly interested in possibility.[22]

What might bring about such a change? A major reason for the change may well be social. The idea that forms stand 'above' actuality (are more real than this), had supported an aristocratic social structure. An orientation

20. In a response to one investigator, at least, children in India have been said to have, within a more-or-less religious context, not 'imaginary companions' but 'invisible' ones (Marjorie Taylor and Carlson 2000: 250).

21. See, e.g., Hobbes, *Leviathan*, 1651, ch. 2; Hume 1739, 2.2.7; Mark Akenside 1794, argument for book 1. Thus, often still in French, such as in Lacan's description of early consciousness, in which objects are still represented only by images, not yet by words. The meaning of the word 'fantasy' (or its variations) was often more playful, but not necessarily different in this respect (see James Engell 1981: 174-83).

22. Helmut Bernsmeier (1994: 202) placed a shift in focus from actuality to potentiality (rather than to sheer possibility, as I see it) in 1880, a little earlier than Walter Falk (cited by him) had done. Kearney implied a similar starting point by beginning with Husserl, for whom possibility was indeed an important category (2001: 84-99, and in earlier studies). Gilles Fauconnier and Mark Turner have called the present 'age' (without specifying a beginning point) 'the age of imagination' (2002: 3).

that emphasizes concrete actuality had been associated especially with the middle class. A focus on possibility as a realm that is less real than actuality but nevertheless crucial appears to fit a view from 'below', more radically democratic.

A number of leftists had such an outlook. For instance, Dewey said that freedom involves not rational 'insight into necessity' but 'foresight of possibility' (1922: 312), and that art, like Israelite prophecy (which employed poetry), 'insinuates possibilities' (1934: 348-49). Ernst Bloch, a Marxian, stressed possibility and described human beings as those who have much ahead of them, but not in a deterministic way: 'the way is rough and open' (1959: 284-85).[23] 'Power to the imagination' was a key wall slogan of May 1968 in Paris (Reader 1987: 6). In fact, according to Henry Allen (2000: 97), the main problem of the 1960s was that possibility was overemphasized, with insufficient attention to what is practical. Somewhat later still, the New Age thinker Ramón Stevens declared that 'your life is a series of infinite paths or *possibilities*'. He held that the outcome of human struggle is 'in no way predetermined', but can lead to either 'peace and harmony' or 'destruction' (1988: 51, 87). According to Susan Buck-Morss, the twentieth century has been driven by a 'dreamworld'; she considered this to be valuable (2000; similarly, Jay Winter 2006).

At the same time, one must consider that an interest in sheer possibility, as is expressed in literature (see M.-L. Ryan 2001), represents not only a reaching toward an ideal but often simply an escapism in which reality is ignored. Even elementary physical laws are contravened in so-called 'fantasy' literature, such as with time reversal. In moderate amounts, escape into an imagined world can provide a helpful respite from ordinary existence, but in heavy amounts it distracts one from dealing with life. If both an open social vision (cf. Doty 1998) and conscious escapism operated at the same time, this duality illustrates the moral ambiguity of historical development.

Half-merely-possible, half-actual is the 'virtual' world. Susanne Langer described artistic 'form' as presenting virtual movement (in dance), virtual space (in the visual arts), virtual time (in music), and so on (1953). In artistic form, there is indeed actual movement (in space or time), but what is presented is enjoyed for its own sake, not (at least not immediately) for its impact on the world. On the border between the actual and the possible also stand computer-generated 'virtual realities'. Indeed, some interpreters of the scene at the end of the twentieth century judged that an interest in the 'virtual' was characteristic of their time.[24]

---

23. Cornelius Castoriadis, an anarcho-syndicalist Marxian, emphasized 'imagination', meaning a creation of what is not (yet) real (thus again in 1997); he influenced the 1968 revolt in France. Peter Leonard, a 'postmodern [that is, not orthodox] Marxist', also has envisioned 'possibilities' (1997: 27).

24. See, e.g., Tina Pippin and George Aichele 1998: 4.

In any case, a repeated theme came to be that human life has possibilities. This theme was modern in the sense that it looked forward rather than backward, but it did not continue the modern sense of confidence in the direction of history.

Possibility is related to actuality at least by thought. In fact, thought can be described as a concern with what is possible. Such a view is contrary to the nominalist position that possibilities (like other general categories) are constructions 'in' or 'by' the mind, a formulation that assumes that one already knows what 'mind' is. Instead, one can take possibility as a more elementary notion than mind and characterize mind as an orientation toward possibility.[25] Most of the characterizations of the mind reported by Rorty (1979: 35) appear to be variations of this idea. Certainly, a major advantage of having a conscious mind is that it enables one to deal deliberately with what is not currently actual.[26] Human beings, at least, have a language through which such deliberation can be communicated.[27]

Incidentally, possibility is not the only modality toward which consciousness is directed. Consciousness is also concerned with value—with what is 'good' or 'bad'; in other words, with what is desired or avoided. In any case, thought considers more than simply actuality.

Indeed, one can say that what people think 'of' are possibilities, even when they are referring to something actual. As has been mentioned, a thought about an object perceives that object 'as' something. This 'as', however, is a structure that may or may not correspond closely to the features of the object being considered. Even when it is reasonably accurate, one's primary interest may well be directed not to the object as such but toward a possibility that the object presents. It may be an aesthetic form to be enjoyed, a historical memory that sets forth a possibility that may be repeated (Heidegger 1927, §74), or a scientific understanding that opens up realistic possibilities for future action.

25. Possibility is, then, more basic than conceivability (cf. recent discussions in Gendler and Hawthorne 2002). This analysis is similar to Aristotle's position (in a sense, following Plato) that a mind has no reality other than its content (*De anima*, 429), but the content is taken here to be possibility rather than actuality.

26. Similarly, Rodney Cotterill (1998: 292, 427, 434) and Amihud Gilead (1999). The orientation itself (the act of thinking, as distinct from the object of thought) is actual (thus, e.g., Mark Rowlands [1999], but Gilead fails to make this needed distinction and, perhaps for that reason [cf. 9], views possibilities as particular [9, 20]). Nonhuman primates (and other animals?), too, have such an orientation in varying degrees (e.g. Jim Grigsby and David Stevens 2000: 217-18).

27. Thus there is a long twentieth-century tradition according to which 'propositions' expressed by language refer to possible states of affairs (John Bacon 1995: 105, mentioned Frege, Alonzo Church, Carnap, and Saul Kripke as holding that view).

Such a view of form as possibility was pursued intensively by members of the movement known as 'phenomenology' (described in Chapter 3). Members of this school insisted that the mind is always directed toward something outside of itself, but they also recognized that this 'something' may not be actual. Specifically, Husserl came to conceive of forms as ideal structures which constitute possibilities and—in thought—meanings.[28] In the US, a similar view was presented by Santayana, although he regarded the word 'possibility' as open to misunderstanding since it often refers to practical potentiality (1927).

The notion of possibility can be applied to the object of mathematics. In a classically Platonic view, mathematical relations and their complexes constitute transcendent models for the actual world. In an Aristotelian perspective, they reflect the structure of actuality. For strict nominalists, mathematical forms exist only as (human) constructions. Differently, relational theorists such as Peirce (1931–58, 5.40 [1903]), Husserl (Bernet *et al.* 1989: 76-77), and, cautiously, Richard Montague (1974: 154) and Hilary Putnam (1979: 71), as well as others both somewhat earlier and also later, have held that mathematics deals with possibilities, for which human beings construct representations (see Hellman 1989; Shapiro 1997: 11, 228).

A similar observation holds true for logic. Logic is a human process, but one can ask, 'With what kind of reality does it deal?' In many ways, logic deals with relations between actual entities. That may be a valid concern, but a major logical tradition from the middle of the twentieth century on deals with hypothetical structures, which can be called 'possible states of affairs'.[29] For instance, a number of logicians (most famously, Saul Kripke [1959]) dealt with what they called 'possible worlds'. The image of 'possible worlds' may be problematic, since it may be excessively comprehensive in scope, but possibility also enters into some kinds of logic that do not speak of 'worlds' but, for instance, of hypothetical 'states'.[30]

To be sure, many of those who used this kind of language did not concern themselves with the ontological status of possibility, treating formulations

28. Husserl 1950–, I: 234 (1900: general truths express possibility); XIX: 352 (1901); V: 26, 29 (1912); XV: 382-83 (1931). According to Heidegger, phenomenology holds that 'possibility stands higher [= is more important?] than actuality' (1927, §7, c).

29. See Buss 1979: 36, 41; Ruth Ronen 1994: 22-24; Charles Chihara 1998. The notion of possibility was a problem for the nominalistically inclined Quine (1960: 245-46); however, in 1963 (21), Quine developed the notion of a 'virtual' class, which is not far from embodying the notion of possibility.

30. Thus, treatments of 'states' that can be either actual or merely possible (reported in Greg Restall 2000: 341), and ideas of 'constructability', which apply to something that can be constructed theoretically, not necessarily by a human being (Chihara 1998: 308).

that use the notion of possibility primarily as a convenient way of saying something (as is mentioned by Doležel 1998: 13). Yet, in a sense, this lack of ontological commitment is implied in the notion of sheer or hypothetical possibility.

In any case, both mathematics and logic came to be considered by many to be the study of patterns as possibilities apart from their concrete embodiments. These disciplines could thus be thought of as engaged in an analysis of pure form.[31]

Of course, it should be emphasized that possibility is only one side of reality. Another very important side is constituted by particular actualities. These include a person one loves, any being to whom one responds, and endless others. Relational theory takes both sides into account.

A significant theoretical issue is whether the admission of possibility as well as actuality complicates ontology. As is well known, nominalists have claimed that they simplify ontology by eliminating the category of generality and with it (as we have seen) the notion of possibility. However, if nominalists admit the notion of 'property', they must assume not only a huge number of independent objects but an even larger number of particular properties, with every object having its own characteristics.[32] This is hardly a simple ontology, unless one believes in a great particular (God) who creates and holds everything together by free choice.

In contrast, a theory that admits possibility as an elementary notion provides a very elegant ontology—'elegant' in the sense that it contains great variety with relatively few primitive terms.[33] To begin with (as was seen earlier), if relationship is a basic notion, then both particularity and generality (including possibility and relations) are aspects of it. As a next step, if forms are constituted by bundles of relations, various forms, including purely hypothetical ones, can be built up out of a small number of primitive relations. (The relation of similarity/dissimilarity can be considered to be especially elementary.)[34] The way in which complex forms arise out

31. Thus, Robert Grassmann (*Die Formenlehre oder Mathematik*, 1872), Russell (1897: 137), Wilhelm Buhrkamp (1927: 240), Whitehead (1941: 677, with relevance for the Good), Roland Omnès (1999: 84). Logic had, for some time, been characterized as dealing with form, or relations, within mental apprehension (e.g. by Kant [1787: 34, 322] and Hegel).

32. See the report by G.F. Stout (1930: 386). This position is taken again by Arda Denkel (1996: 154). Cf. Cynthia Macdonald (1998: 347, n. 1); the 'trope' theory described there represents a half-way point between nominalism and realism for properties.

33. Possibility has been taken as 'primitive' (not defined in terms of more basic elements) by a range of philosophers from Peirce (see above) to Stephen McLeod (2001: 87).

34. See Stout 1930: 388; Russell 1940: 436; A.D. Woozley 1949: 98, 101.

of a small number of elementary structures has been shown in mathematics, although different systems exhibit this process in somewhat divergent ways. Similarly, ordinary logic is built up on the basis of a small number of undefined symbols. Logics of time and duty proceed in a comparable way.

What can be done is to link such analyses of possibility with examinations of the actual world. A move in this direction was made by Rudolf Carnap, who constructed a logical picture of the world with attention to elementary relations (1928). In fact, recent physics makes considerable use of the notion of possibility (see, for instance, Dainton 2001: 330). Possibility and actuality are, then, closely intertwined, although they do not need to be rigidly associated. For instance, according to one interpretation of quantum theory, quantum states are possibilities that are actualized by a measuring process (see Barr 2003: 229-32; similarly, Berkovitz and Hemmo 2005).

Indeed, Ruth Barcan Marcus, an important modal logician, has already indicated that the notion of possibility can combine simplicity with plenitude or variety (1993: 199).[35] Aesthetically, of course, the greatest good consists in the recognition of a rich structure that exhibits a certain coherence.

Nevertheless, it should be noted that modal theorists do not agree with each other in regard to the ontological status of their subject matter. Nominalists who have difficulty with real possibilities (these being general) either take possibilities as fictive forms that exist only in someone's mind as that person's creation (e.g. Brian McHale 1987: xi, 34) or view alternative worlds as equally real, although only one of them is 'ours' (David Lewis 1986). Others—including D.M. Armstrong, who stood close to Aristotle (1978: 77)—have given priority to actuality and treated possibilities as combinatory constructions of more simple forms that actually exist (1986).[36] Certainly, the human mind can form an image—a mental 'form'—only by means of a combination of actually existing phenomena.[37] However, it should be remembered that there are in actuality no straight lines or perfect circles.

Whitehead's view of possibility was somewhat unclear about its ontological foundation. He regarded 'forms', which he called 'eternal objects', to be 'possibilities' (1926: 119), and he envisioned God to be an 'actual entity' that acts as a 'repository' for them (1929: 73), so that actuality appears to be more basic. Yet, for Whitehead, 'creativity' was an ultimate even beyond

35. There is a lively debate about how much Kripke learned from her. Kripke accepted 'essences', but in a way that does not appear to be Aristotelian (see below, Chapter 6, n. 28).

36. Jon Barwise's and John Perry's 'situation semantics' (leaning toward Aristotelianism) assumes that 'abstract situations' (which may or may not be actual) presuppose actuality (1999: xlviii, 8).

37. Thus, e.g., Wittgenstein in 1933 (1958: 31).

actuality. Did he perhaps imply that possibility has its own ground in creativity, alongside actuality?

4. *The Relativity of Forms:*
The Relation of the Observed to the Observer

Having dealt with forms as possibilities, we can now turn to forms that appear in actuality. As has long been acknowledged, particulars contain an element of mystery. One cannot say anything about this mystery, except to acknowledge it.[38] Yet particulars enter into relationships, including relations with observers, and one can speak about these relations.

Which elements of an object will be given attention and thus which relations will enter into the form that is perceived is a matter that depends on the interest of the observer. This means that objects have forms not in themselves but in relation to observers. Different forms can thus all be true for the same object, so that relativity and truth do not exclude each other.

Moves Toward Non-skeptical Relativity

Protagoras (5th century BCE) already exhibited a perspectival outlook. He said that 'the human being is the measure of all things' and pointed to the relativity of perceptions. This statement has appeared to some to be skeptical, but, as represented in Plato's *Protagoras*, he apparently only emphasized the relation between subject and object.[39]

Later, nominalism took a step toward recognizing relativity by holding that observers construct labels ('names') for objects. This shift even appeared visually, for when nominalism became a significant force in the latter part of the Middle Ages, art came to employ so-called 'perspective'; that is, objects were pictured in their individuality as they would appear to a particular onlooker.[40] In literary criticism, a similar awareness was present during the time of nominalism's dominance. For instance, in 1742 Chladenius said that narratives always present a special perspective (*Sehe-Punckt*) of an event (Buss 1999: 119).

In contrast, much of twentieth-century art—often called 'abstract'—was oriented less toward the particular actuality of an object and also less toward

---

38. See above, Chapter 4, n. 16, for Russell on this.

39. In fact, Plato presented Protagoras not as an ethical 'relativist' in the sense that he denied that some social attitudes are 'wiser' or 'better' than others, but as one who said that all ethical judgments are necessarily relative to a given society (Plato, *Theaetetus*, 167; cf. his *Protagoras*).

40. An earlier use of perspective in art had been criticized by Plato (Panofsky 1991: 72), so that its absence in much of art before the fourteenth century was in part deliberate.

the view of an individual observer. This new art, which began at the end of the nineteenth century in conjunction with the fading of nominalism, was in good part inspired by Asian, Aztec, Polynesian, and African traditions. Jean Gebser has called it 'integral' (although not necessarily unified) and 'aspectival' (without a particular perspective) or 'multiperspectival' (1985: 4, 24, 42, 256). For instance, in a painting by Picasso in 1926, several sides of a human figure are shown simultaneously. This change shows a transition from an individualist orientation to a social one.

In science, similarly, moves to emphasize relationality stood in connection with socially oriented perspectives. Such a move was made (especially from 1883 on) by Mach, an advocate of cooperative socialism who combined the study of physics and psychology with a strong philosophical interest (see Blackmore 1972). He treated science as the most economical way of describing the relations of perceived phenomena. Indeed, like the neo-Kantian Karl Pearson [1892]), Mach avoided theories about objects beyond what is perceived—perhaps one-sidedly so, since constructive theories do play a useful role.[41] However, his explorations stimulated relational positions in both physics and psychology.

Perhaps more adequately, Peirce combined objectivity and subjectivity in a non-individualistic way. In his view, everything is 'relative to the mind [broadly conceived]', but 'independent of what you and I or any finite number…may think about' (1982–, II: 238-39 [1868]; III: 274 [1878]). In other words, there is no unrelated 'thing-in-itself', but the reality of an object is not tied to an individual observer. Specifically, Peirce defined the properties of an object relationally as follows:

> In what does behavior exist except that if a substance of a certain kind should be exposed to an agency of a certain kind, a certain sensible result *would* ensue, according to our experience hitherto. [Indeed,] nothing else than this can be so much as *meant* by saying that an object possesses a certain character (1931–58, 5.457 [1905, emphasis his]).

Peirce defined not only meaning but also truth relationally, in a way that was neither strictly objective (unrelated to the mind) nor subjective in a particularist sense. He said in 1906: 'truth's independence of individual opinions is due (so far as there is any 'truth') to its being the result to which sufficient inquiry *would* ultimately lead' (1931–58, 5.494 [1906]). Note the words 'sufficient' and 'would'; they indicate a theoretical limit, as that appears in mathematics.[42] (In a somewhat similar way, Nietzsche said

---

41. In fact, Lenin, who was unhappy about Mach's moderate socialism, criticized Mach and his followers because of their emphasis on what is perceived in 1902 (see 1929).

42. In 1868, Peirce had said that the real is 'that which, sooner or later, information and reasoning would finally result in'. That was a questionable statement, still

that the more perspectives one considers, the closer one approaches truth, although one never reaches it (1967–, VI/2: 383 ['Genealogy of Morals', 1887, §12]).

In response to skeptical positions, José Ortega y Gasset sought to overcome a contrast between objectivity and subjectivity by placing individuals into a larger context. Arguing that the self and things belong together, he proposed the formula 'I = I and my circumstance' (1914).[43] He agreed that reality does not have a shape independent of a point of view but held that such a view, a 'perspective', is itself a 'component' of reality (1923: 149, 152). He believed that 'God's view' is not external to individual perspectives but rather the union of these perspectives, so that human beings are 'the visual organs of divinity'—the word 'God' being 'a symbol of the *torrente vital*' (1923: 158). Holding that every perspective reveals a side of reality (1916–21, I, first essay), he declared that perspectives are 'all equally true and authentic'; 'false alone is the perspective that claims to be the only one' (1923: 152).

Relativity in Physics from Early in the Twentieth Century on

Relational reflections received support in physics. Examples included Einstein's theory of 'relativity' in 1905 (stimulated by Mach and Poincarè), Bohr's 'complementary' vision of particles and waves, and Werner Heisenberg's 'uncertainty' principle. All of these connected properties with processes of observation or registration.[44]

Lying behind these principles (Höffding 1901: 31)[45] and supported by further investigation (Herbert 1985: 211-45; Richard Morris 1987: 212-26) was the view that objects have definite properties only in interaction with each other. In this way, many came to consider the notion of 'primary' (non-relational) qualities to be no longer useful (Cassirer 1910: 407; Jammer 1966: 381; Leclerc 1986: 306, 308). For instance, the qualities that Locke had considered to be non-relational (including extension and motion or rest) appeared no longer to be independent characteristics. Objects were instead

caught in nominalism (see Murphey 1961: 171); it makes a prediction of what will actually happen (similarly also 1982–, III: 273-74 [1878]; 1931–58, 7.78 [time of writing uncertain]). However, in 1906 Peirce arrived at a more defensible (although still debatable) position, cited here.

43. This stands in the work's initial address to the reader.

44. Bohr made the relational character of his view especially clear in 1935 (697). According to Heisenberg (1958: 137) and some others, a conscious observation by a human being is not necessary, but some sort of registration is needed, such as— according to Maxwell (1998: 248)—an interaction that creates or destroys a particle. However, the question of whether (human) consciousness plays an essential role remains debated.

45. Höffding knew the work of James but created his own relational path.

said to have 'propensities'.[46] For example, an object will seem red to certain persons under certain conditions or register a certain weight on a scale, and quantum phenomena appear under certain observational conditions (cf. Richard Healey 1995: 58). By actualizing such propensities, the observer is a 'participator' in the universe (Wheeler 1994: 25).

A presupposition of all these theories is that objects are not fully separate. In the words of Arthur Eddington (1939: 110), while the older notion of particular 'substance' implied resistance to interference, that of 'form [as a system of relations] plays into [the] hands [of an] observer'.

It should be noted that the physical theories mentioned did not prove the correctness of a relational outlook. Rather, they reflected, in part at least, the philosophical and social perspective of the theorist.[47] It is true, the theories were not arbitrary in the sense that they were simply imposed on experimental data. However, without the availability of certain philosophical perspectives, observational data would presumably have been given a different interpretation. In fact, even today there is disagreement about these basic issues.[48]

Still, it should be noted that the theme of relativity does not imply skepticism. For example, Einstein's theory did not reject the possibility of knowledge but only asserted that reality and truth are relational.[49]

The Sociology of Knowledge

A similar kind of relativity also played a considerable role in sociology. About 1930, Karl Mannheim presented an influential sociology of knowledge that was indebted to Marxism and pragmatism, as well as neo-Kantianism.[50] He called his approach 'relationism' in order to distinguish

46. Thus, Dewey (1929: 266; 1938: 128-29) and C.I. Lewis (1970: 344 [1954]).

47. Erwin Schrödinger, who adhered to a Vedanta-influenced monistic idealism (Goonatilake 1998: 42), already raised the issue of a similarity between his view of physics and current 'social, ethical and cultural' concerns (1924: 724). Indeed, both Bohr and Heisenberg drew on a broad intellectual (including religious) background for their interpretations (see Brooke 1991 for a bibliography of discussions; also Cushing 1994).

48. Alternative interpretations can be given for quantum data; thus a particular interpretation is in part determined by one's deep philosophical-social predilection.

49. Cf. Rudolf Eisler 1922: 546 ('objective relativism' as a synonym for relationism); Arthur Murphy 1963: 49-78. Nonskeptical relativism has been described, for instance, by Peter Novick (1988: 167) and by Lorraine Code (1991). Incidentally, Einstein did not accept the so-called 'relationist' theory of space and time, which views space and time as derivative from matter. Rather, he viewed space-time as an independent reality, with which material objects interact. This view may well keep relations from being absorbed into objects; it allows for causal indeterminism and has room for a world history. (For a discussion of this open issue, see Dainton 2001: 301-34.)

50. Scheler, who stimulated Mannheim's position, pointed out that the 'form' of

it from both absolutism and skepticism, which, he said, constitute two alternatives within a non-relational frame of mind. In place of the word 'perspective', he used the term 'aspect structure'. He interpreted this as the way in which something is mentally 'construed' by the perceiver without its being arbitrary (1931: 662). At the same time, rejecting Kant's idea that space and time are frames furnished by the mind, he observed that the categories of human perception change over time (1929: 38 [1936, 2.5]). Such variability allowed for the possibility that the categories of perception are affected by the reality observed, rather than merely imposed.

Furthermore, the fact that comprehension has a subjective dimension does not mean that it is individualistic. Mannheim believed that human experience leads to an enlargement of one's perception. That is, it is not 'subjective' in a narrow sense, although it is 'subjective' in the sense of 'human' or 'experiential' (1931: 672, 674). Contra an individualistic interpretation, he considered that the very recognition of the particularity of one's own view implies a certain transcendence, or 'neutralization', of it (1931: 674). It is then possible to have a 'scientific critical self-awareness' (1936, 1.4).[51]

Soon after Mannheim's writing, Nazism used the idea of the relativity of knowledge to justify the dismissal of Jewish scholars, since they did not represent 'Aryan science'. Similarly, in the 1930s and 1940s, Russians improperly rejected certain biological views as 'bourgeois' (Joravsky 1970: 68).

Explicitly avoiding Nazi theory, the sociologist Robert Merton outlined an ideal form of science. Central components of this are 'universalism' (non-exclusivism), 'communism' (shared intellectual property), 'disinterestedness', and 'organized skepticism'. For him these ideals were 'moral'—not based on technical efficiency (1949: 309-14). Merton's view of science was thus not 'objective' in the sense of 'neutral'. In fact, his evaluation of Mannheim's sociology of knowledge was, on the whole, appreciative (247-64).

Karl Popper, of Jewish descent, was also deeply affected by the horror of Nazism. In a work written during the war years, he favored 'objectivity'. However, he described this as 'social' or 'intersubjective' (1945, II: 205).

---

apprehension is partially conditioned by social structure; he had received a strong impact from James, in part via the pragmatist philosopher Jerusalem (Stikkers 1980: 24). Neo-Kantianism played a major role early in the twentieth century in stressing the role of the observer. It was 'idealist', although not without realist elements.

51. In 1929, Mannheim referred to the intelligentsia as a relatively classless or class-inclusive group, which provides a high degree of impartiality. In 1931, this notion (wisely) disappeared. In later writings (including Chapter 1 of 1936 and some MSS not published by him), he continued to show an interest in the special roles of intellectuals, with much better nuances. The change after 1929 has not been widely noted, but Mannheim was in part responsible for that oversight, since he did not see to it that his work was adequately revised in the English version (1936).

He said that ' "knowledge" and "will" are...always inseparable' and that scientists always have an 'interest' (1945: 210).[52] In regard to the nature of properties, Popper supported the 'relational theory' that properties are 'dispositions' or 'propensities' (1982: 159, 206, 209 [1951–56]).

The reaction against Nazism and Stalinism did not produce a simple objectivism. Yet it undoubtedly contributed to the fact that interest in the sociology of knowledge declined sharply after World War II, at least in the US (Ben-David 1990: 426).

Interactionist visions did continue, especially on the European continent. For instance, indebted to both Marx and Husserl, Enzo Paci set forth what he called 'relationism'. According to this, 'we always experience... particular multiplicities...we live in some perspectives, in some aspects of the world', but—contra isolating interpretations—we 'realize that in every partial thing...a universal horizon is potentially present... This horizon of the world is *always* present *in us*, even if it is never fully conquered' (1972: 59-60, 77 [1963]).

A well-known theoretical reflection concerning the human side of science was presented by Habermas (1968b). In conversation with theories by Peirce, Dilthey, and Marx, he argued that 'knowledge' is connected with 'interest'.

Non-skeptical Relativity after 1970 CE
Following the upheavals of the 1960s, interactive views of scientific knowledge gained new ground. They were pursued in detailed studies and in theoretical constructions.

In regard to detail, a large number of historical/sociological studies investigated how scientific investigations and theory formations are actually carried out. Three major clusters of such investigations were appropriately described by Deborah Heath as 'steadfastly relational' (1997: 144). Among them stood, in her words, 'French and British actor-network theory' (such as that of Bruno Latour),[53] 'British sociology of scientific knowledge' (especially that of David Bloor [see below]), and, centered in the US, 'pragmatist and symbolic interactionist approaches'. Studies along these lines did not deny some sort of truth to scientific observation, but pointed out that observations and theories have a historical, human character.[54] A non-skeptical

---

52. In making this point (in a chapter on the sociology of knowledge), he went beyond Mannheim's early, relatively cautious, view published in 1929.

53. Latour described networks with both friendly interaction and controversy (1987).

54. Theorists with an interactive view included James Perlman (1995), Jürgen Mittelstrass (1995: 96: 'perspectives' have 'validity' of some sort), and Latour (1999: 85: his study of science 'does not want to divide internalist [evidence-based] from externalist [society-based] accounts').

outlook was true even for Bloor's 'strong programme', which emphasized the social side of science and mathematics. Allowing room for the nonhuman aspect of science, he agreed that 'things have the power to stimulate our sense organs' (1999: 91). The 'social constructivism' of mathematics delineated by Paul Ernest held mathematics (as an endeavor) to be contingent but not arbitrary (1998: 248).

On the theoretical side, Hilary Putnam developed a view which he at first called 'internal realism' and later 'pragmatic realism'. According to this, there is reality, but it always appears within a framework and is described differently depending on one's starting point (1981, etc.). Voicing an interactionist understanding, he said that 'the mind and the world jointly make up the mind and the world' (1981: xi). Like others, he envisioned the 'properties' of objects as existing not 'in themselves' but relationally in terms of what they 'cause' or bring about in interactions (1979: 315). He insisted that 'realism [an apprehension of the world outside oneself] is *not* incompatible with conceptual relativity' (1987: 17). In short, Putnam recognized relativity but was not skeptical. He rejected skeptical relativism in morals as well as in other knowledge. The fact that he was Jewish probably drew additional (deserved) attention to the horror of Hitler's actions (1979: xii-xiii; 1981: 168).

After about 1980, several observers furnished detailed contributions to this discussion.[55] They were not neutral, skeptical, or individualistic.

For instance, Mary Belenky and her associates espoused 'general relativity', a position that 'understands that answers to all questions vary depending on the context in which they are asked and on the frame of reference of the context in which it is embedded'. Stressing interaction, they spoke of being 'responsive to situation and context' and affirmed a 'relationship between the knower and the known' (1986: 138, 143).

Donna Haraway rejected both skeptical 'relativism' and 'totalization' and affirmed 'relationism' instead. She spoke of 'situated knowledges', which represent 'partial perspectives' (1988: 584).[56] In her view, such perspectives are indeed 'rational, objective', that is, with 'a no-nonsense commitment to faithful accounts of a "real" world'; yet they exhibit 'radical historical contingency' (579, 584). One criterion for the value of such a perspective is that it goes counter to 'domination' (585).

---

55. See elsewhere in the present volume for Hesse, E. Keller, Longino, Nelson, Code, and Hayles.

56. Haraway called her position 'nominalist' (1992: 88; 1997: 268), but it represents a kind of relational nominalism (see below, 6.3, on Sellars). Having been strongly influenced by Whitehead and Peirce (1999: 21), she emphasized relationality (e.g. 1990: 193; 1997: 268, 270; 1999: 156) and disavowed 'relativism' (1999: 59, 160). For the term 'relationism', see her interview in Schneider 2005: 141. See on her also below, 8.4.

The sociologist and philosopher Dorothy Smith took account of the fact that human beings have the ability 'to take a perspective', that is, to imagine how something looks to someone else. When several perspectives are in play, they can be coordinated. Thus she said that

> divergent perspectives are coordinated in the social act of referring... Rather than undermining the very possibility of truth being told, it is pre-cisely the multiplicity of experience and perspectives among people that is the necessary condition of truth (1999: 128).

Smith located a basis for coordination in the very fact that 'referring' is a 'dialogic' process in which one person speaks to another (1999: 127). This process involves three kinds of relations: (1) the relation between speaker and addressee; (2) the relation between a subject and an object perceived and spoken about (33, etc.); and (3) relations within the world talked about, which are the primary object of science, just as a map indicates relations between geographical sites, not the sites as such (130).[57]

Varieties of Constructivism

Toward the end of the twentieth century, it was said repeatedly that knowl-edge and ethics are 'constructed'. Such statements were ambiguous. If they meant that any judgment represents an interaction between subject and object, they were relational.[58] Insofar as they held that judgments are simply particular and arbitrary, they were skeptical or nihilist. Skeptical construc-tionism undermines itself and was thus rejected by moderate constuctiv-ists, such as Judith Butler (1993: 8, 94; cf. below, 8.4), Marilyn Friedman (2006), and James Giles (2006).

A useful distinction was offered by Ian Hacking. He said, 'Perhaps it is the idea of quarks, rather than quarks, which is the social construction' (1999: 30). Similarly, Mary Belenky et al. described 'knowledge' (not 'truth') as 'constructed' (1986: 131). In fact, a strong constructivism is radi-cally nominalist rather than relational.[59]

57. For the view that science deals with relations, see above, 4.1.

58. Hayles has proposed a 'constrained constructivism'; this (she said) involves a 'dynamic interplay between us and the world' (1993: 42). Similarly moderate were Spretnak (1991: 5) and Elizabeth Grosz (1994: 190), on the constructivism of gender. Incidentally, the 'radical constructivism' of Ernst von Glasersfeld was not really 'radical', for, as he pointed out, constructions must 'fit' the environment to survive (with Piaget [in Paul Watzlawick 1984: 17-40]). More thoroughly constructive was Heinz von Foerster, but he favored choosing the equation 'reality = community' over solipsism (in Watzlawick 1984: 60 [1973]; is this really a free choice unconstrained by experience?). Overviews of several varieties of constructivism, varying in degrees of skepticism, have been offered by Peter Janich (1996) and Ian Hacking (1999).

59. For constructivism, von Glasersfeld (see the preceding note) identified Giam-battista Vico and Kant (two outstanding 'moderns') among his antecedents.

5. *Form in Both Human and Nonhuman Reality:*
Directionality, Systems Theory

Relational Form as a Principle Uniting Human and Nonhuman Phenomena

Since views concerning physical phenomena have been discussed, it is now useful to look at what happened in the discipline of psychology. In this field, a movement early in the century highlighted the phenomenon of gestalt in perception.

The idea of 'gestalt' stood in contrast to a nominalist theory known as 'associationism'. Associationism held that (1) primary perception is of particulars and (2) that general ideas and perceptions of complexes are formed through mental operations that 'associate' individual sense data with one another (cf. Rapaport 1974). In opposition to such a theory, Mach (1886: 40, 125) and James (1890, I: 245, 548; 1909b: 279-80) argued that human beings perceive relationships and patterns immediately, not just secondarily. Evidence available at that time and later pointed in that direction, although it should be recognized that the relevant data can also be explained on the basis of a nominalist philosophy.[60] In any case, it was seen that organisms perceive relations, not just isolated phenomena. The reason is that organisms actively scan their environment, so that particular phenomena are encountered not as separate bits, but in terms of 'relational patterns' encountered in the scanning process (Wigger 1998: 68).

Giving expression to the new point of view, Mach noted that a melody appears to remain 'the same' when it is transposed, since the relations between its elements remain constant even though the individual elements change. Mach's observation was developed further by von Ehrenfels in an 1890 paper on *Gestalt* (cf. D. Murray 1995: 15); this work became well known in German culture and stimulated the work of a number of psychologists after 1910.

Gestalt psychologists believed that there is no fundamental break between mind and matter. Like Mach and other psychologists, they attempted to integrate psychological with physical reality, such as by referring to 'fields', as they had become known in physics. They sought to effect a 'new unification of nature and life' (Koffka 1935: 684).

---

60. Early experimental data of which the new outlook made use included especially those stated in 'Weber's Law', which deals with differences in the intensity of stimuli sufficient for recognition. These data could be interpreted within an associationist position by viewing the mental 'apperception' of relations as different from sensory perception (as was done by Wilhelm Wundt in 1863 and later [1908: 631-33], with Kant [1787: 134-35]; cf. Richard Lowry 1982: 207); thus the data as such, without a broader philosophical change, did not by themselves force a new view.

In fact, form as a system of relations became widely viewed as a principle that unites the various sciences and arts. Those who said so included Hermann Friedmann (1930: 405), Ernst Cassirer (1942, Chapter 4), Günther Müller (1968: 246 [1943]), Lancelot Whyte (1951), Heinrich Rombach (1965–66, II: 469), and G.S. Rousseau (1972).

It is true, the contrast between the humanities and the physical sciences, which had been made earlier by a number of German historians,[61] continued to find defenders. They regarded individuality as characteristic of human phenomena and generality as applicable to nonhuman phenomena. Participants in this debate were conscious of the fact that it had political overtones. Members on both sides of the debate recognized that a belief that human and other beings—and thus the sciences that deal with them—are not fundamentally distinct was connected with socialism (see Ernst Bernheim 1908, preface).

Between extreme positions there were, of course, many intermediate ones. One of these was outlined carefully by Dilthey.[62] He argued that the humanities have a peculiar character, in that they involve an empathetic 'understanding' which participates in the mental structures that are studied, including values and goals (1921–, V: 172, 206-17 [1894]). For such an understanding, he looked for 'structural connections', in other words, relationships (1921–, V: 215, etc.). In contrast, he believed—one may think, erroneously so—that the human mind is 'separated' from objects observed in the natural sciences, unable to extend empathy toward them (VII: 92 [1910]). For the nonhuman sciences, he acknowledged instead what (following Droysen) he called 'explanation', which places occurrences into the framework of general laws. Unlike some other theorists, however, he recognized that generality plays a role not only in the natural sciences but also in the humanities (1921–, V: 258, 265; Makkreel 1975: 112, 240-42, 349). He observed, for instance, that only commonality creates the possibility of mutual understanding (1921–, VII: 141-47).

Although no agreement was reached on this theoretical question, the general trend was toward breaking down a division between mind and matter (cf. Lovejoy 1930; Russell 1945: 833). Proposals for unifying the two forms of reality had been established earlier,[63] but previous proposals had frequently taken either mind or matter to be primary and had accordingly

61. Including especially Johann Droysen in 1868 (K. Hübner 1978: 304; M. Ermarth 1978: 243).
62. Wilhelm Windelband and Heinrich Rickert must also be reckoned among those developing intermediate positions; their distinction between generalizing and particularizing studies cut across subject matter. (On this, as well as on Dilthey's evolving thought, see Plantinga 1980: 25-27, etc.)
63. Thus, Spinoza (seventeenth century), a Jew, and Joseph Priestley (1777), a Unitarian.

propounded either 'idealism' or 'materialism'. However, when the focus shifted from substance (whether mental or material) to relations or organization, the question of whether something is mental or material began to evaporate.

In psychology, a union of flesh and spirit was implied in the appreciation for sexuality exhibited in the writings of Sigmund Freud, Havelock Ellis, and others.[64] It has even been suggested that the body was the central focus of twentieth-century philosophy (Appelbaum 1986: 3). Concern for the body was usually positive, so that freedom from domination by bodily urges was no longer important for a sense of internal freedom.

The orientations of groups not controlled by the spirit of European modernity, such as Native Americans, were often called upon as models for a sense of community with nature (e.g. Dorothy Lee 1959: 163). One can also wonder whether it is accidental that so many of the psychologists who drew together the human and the nonhuman, including Freud and most of his circle and many of the Gestalt psychologists (beginning with their leader Max Wertheimer), were Jews. In contrast, among Christians, a mind-body split had become widely current. As Christian thinkers sought to overcome this split, they often pointed out that Israelite-Jewish tradition, as it was represented in the Bible, had not separated matter from spirit. The approach that connected mind with matter was thus interactive even in drawing together different religious and cultural traditions.

Inside and Outside Views as Complementary

A central issue in twentieth-century discussions revolved around the difference between an inside and an outside view of another being. An inside view seeks to understand the other empathetically in terms of the other's perceptions, thoughts, and desires, while an outside view observes the other as it appears within one's own perceptions.

An inside view of human beings is aided by the fact that they often express the inner aspect of their life (beliefs, hopes, desires) in words, so that an observer has some evidence for how they see things. However, even when a person puts something into words, an observer must still deduce from such audible data the thoughts and feelings of the person who is observed. One cannot look directly inside another's mind. Rather, one always looks at the other from the outside and only imputes an inside.

An important question, then, is whether one also can impute an inside to nonhuman beings. If an empathetic view is taken of all processes, one

---

64. Sexuality received considerable valorization in Russian circles near 1900 CE, partly within a Trinitarian theory envisioning the Spirit as Divine Mother (B. Rosenthal 1975: 29, 81-83, 106-12). An extensive work on love (i.e., sexuality) had already been produced by the Italian Paolo Mantegazza in 1872, 1877 and 1885 (1935: xii). Among well-known later writers along this line stood Norman Brown (1966).

can attribute to each of them a goal, or *telos*, even if only on an 'as-if' basis (the object acts 'as if' it had a certain aim). In fact, if beings are thought of as 'active', it is necessary to impute to them some sort of goal-directedness that expresses their dynamic form. Whitehead made such an attribution, holding that beings have as their goal self-creation (1929: 108, 320, 380). In his later years, Husserl considered the possibility that teleology (goal-directedness) is the 'form of all forms'; it is grounded in God and appears in all of existence, but 'wakes up' (becomes conscious) in human beings (1950–, XV: 378-86 [1931 MS]).

Dynamic form does not imply a movement toward a predetermined goal. On the contrary, what was called 'action' above (4.3) presupposes a combination of predictability and unpredictability. Action, thus defined, must then always appear externally as an indeterministic process.

The legitimacy of an inside view has been controversial in the sciences. Major theorists of science, however, have noted that outside and inside formulations of a process are equivalent for descriptive purposes (thus, Max Planck [1949: 330], Ernest Nagel [1961: 403], and Ernst Mayr [1974: 113]; similarly, Werner Heisenberg [1969, ch. 17]).[65] As they see it, the two kinds of description can each be translated into the other, so that neither is more scientific than the other; however, one kind may be more convenient than the other in a given context. For instance, many processes observed in physics and other sciences are most conveniently described in quasi-teleological formulations (such as, in physics: 'shortest distance' or 'least action'; in biology: an animal 'foraging for food').[66] The mathematical notion of 'function', used by Mach for expressing correlations between phenomena (not necessarily based on causality), was neutral in regard to this issue.

Aside from the question of which kind of formulation is more convenient or otherwise useful, a choice between them can also be affected by one's attitude toward an object. Should one treat it with respect or attempt to manipulate it? An inside view can express respect for the object by attributing to it a movement of its own,[67] while an outside view readily justifies exploitation of the object for one's purposes by treating its self-directedness as unimportant. To be sure, the correlation of the two views with either respect or exploitation is not rigid, for an outside view can be appreciative and an inside view (recognizing the directedness of another being) can be

65. Cf. G.E.M. Anscombe (1957: 23) for human processes. Charles Taylor (1964: 15) defended natural teleology against philosophical atomism.

66. The concept of 'least action' arose, after early antecedents, in the seventeenth century and has remained as an overarching theory in physics, although it was not necessarily taken in terms of a purpose (see Barrow and Tipler 1986: 148-52; Hildebrandt and Tromba 1996: 301). For (quasi-) teleological conceptions in the life sciences from the 1940s to the 1990s, see Lowell Nissen 1997.

67. Thus, e.g., Brian Goodwin (1994: 231-36).

manipulative. Nevertheless, a rough correlation of an external view with a desire for manipulation is clearly observable in history, as follows.

Internal views of all objects, including nonhuman ones (attributing to them movement with a goal), was common in the Western world, as elsewhere, before the seventeenth century. Animate and inanimate beings were certainly manipulated, but that was not the only attitude taken. Then the theme of human mastery over nature came to the fore. Nominalism, which believed in the separateness of beings and in the passive nature of non-humans, supported this attitude of mastery. In 1620, Francis Bacon—who insisted that 'nothing exists in nature except individual bodies which exhibit pure individual acts in accordance with law'—said that the notion of a 'final cause...distorts the sciences except in the case of human actions'. He held forth the possibility of human rule over nature through knowledge of the laws of objects.[68] Even more than Bacon, Isaac Newton (in 1704), Robert Boyle (in 1744), and Kant (in 1786) denied 'activity' to natural (nondivine, nonhuman) processes.[69] Industrial development, supported by such an attitude, indeed enhanced human mastery of the environment.

At the end of the nineteenth century, the attitude changed, at least to some extent, with a concern that was already called 'ecological'. A 'conservation' (of nature) movement emerged with strong input from women (Merchant 1996). One wing of this movement was associated since the end of the nineteenth century with social-democratic interests (Engel 1983: 75-76). Another ('conservative') wing emphasized an ordered whole (Bramwell 1989).[70] To be sure, many who expressed ecological interests were not concerned with the nonhuman world for its own sake, but stressed the interrelatedness of humanity and its environment for humanity's sake.

Max Scheler—to give one example—criticized the capitalist desire to dominate 'Mother Nature' and called instead for a recognition of the intrinsic worth of plants and animals (1923, A.7).[71] Such a partial 're-enchantment of the world' (Morris Berman 1981) also appeared on the intellectual level.[72] For instance, according to Ivor Leclerc (1986: 148-53, 191), physics has

68. *Novum organum*, aphorisms 2, 52. However, Bacon retained the idea of inherent motions, which he described in terms of 'desires', between which there is conflict (aphorism 48).

69. See Evelyn Keller 1992: 61; Kant 1910–, IV: 544.

70. In Germany at the beginning of the twentieth century, for instance, both fascists and Jews were oriented toward nature (Harrington 1996).

71. In a continuation and intensification of concerns since the eighteenth century (Kean 1998), animal rights were given legal status by the British Cruelty to Animals Act of 1876, by Nazi laws against anthropocentrism (see Ferry 1992), by the US Animal Welfare Act of 1970, and even more powerfully in some other places (Page 1999).

72. See, further, Chalmers 1996: 297; 1997: 418-19.

shown that entities are dynamically related to each other, so that they must be thought of as active in a significant way. Frederick Ferré—like Leclerc, indebted to Whitehead—described matter not as 'dead' but as composed of 'dynamic events' (1998: 273). The philosopher of science Nancy Cartwright, too, spoke of the 'capacities', 'powers', or 'tendencies' of objects which 'try' to do certain things (1999: 29, 49, 66, 91).

Consequently, 'listening' to the other came to be a way of expressing empathy even in the nonhuman sciences. Evelyn Keller, who advocated 'eros' in contrast to exploitative aggression, reported that the biologist Barbara McClintock asked that one 'listen to what the material has to tell you', as one who has empathy with the object studied or 'feeling for the organism' (1985: 126, 138, 164, 165). Similarly, the biological theorists Ilya Prigogine and Isabelle Stengers said that 'nature speaks with a thousand voices, and we have only begun to listen' (1984: 77), so that a 'dialogue' takes place (Stengers 1997: 35). Although the word 'hermeneutics' has traditionally been used only for the elucidation of human expressions, Don Ihde advocated more broadly a 'postmodern [that is, relational] hermeneutics of things' that seeks 'ways to give *voices* to the things' (1999: 151 [emphasis in original]).

More obviously still, listening plays a role in ethics. Along this line, Rita Manning said that 'those who have had a relationship with animals, with the earth, become, through these relationships, aware of the sacredness of the earth', whereas 'exploiters are not truly relating to the natural world' (1992: 133). She then made this challenge: 'Choosing a style of life requires an understanding of your proper role in the universe and deciding what to do in concrete situations requires reflecting upon that larger commitment and carefully listening to the creatures who are with you in that concrete situation' (1992: 133-34).

Such listening implies, of course, that one recognizes or imputes an inside, a 'voice', to the other. Ethics is then based on reality (it is not arbitrary), but it takes account of an aspect of reality that cannot be apprehended by looking only at its outside. Otherwise stated, ethics belongs to the sphere of dialogue; it concerns an I-you relation.

Systems Theory
A comprehensive model for the forms of actual objects, both animate and inanimate, was furnished by 'systems theory', which began as an official enterprise in 1928 with the Austrian Ludwig von Bertalanffy but was well developed only after 1945.[73] Its program analyzed relational patterns as they appear in dynamic structures of various kinds.[74]

73. From 1954 on, after some intermediate stops, Bertalanffy worked in the US.
74. See Lars Skyttner 1996 and Yaneer Bar-Yam 1997 for more on this topic.

The theory characterized a system as a whole between whose parts there are extensive mutual interactions. For some, the word 'system' may call forth an image of something that is mechanical, rigid, static, closed to the outside, and absolute, but such an image was far from Bertalanffy's mind. On the contrary, he opposed mechanism, valued individuality and freedom, gave attention especially to dynamic and externally open systems, and acknowledged perspectivism, that is, relativity in one's perception of systems (e.g. 1968: 39, 45, 52, 78, 239-48 [1945–55]). He envisioned that wholes have emergent characteristics but do not swallow up their parts. Systems theory, then, furnished a useful framework for understanding a wide variety of phenomena by avoiding both an assumption of small independent units and a tight or mysterious holism.

One of the major features of the systems view was that it discovered parallels between operations on many different levels of existence—including the inanimate, the organic, and the human. Yet Bertalanffy was also concerned that the special character of human beings be realized for the sake of an appropriate ethics (e.g. 1968: 52 [1955]).

One of the processes of interest to Bertalanffy came to be called 'teleonomy'. This term refers to an operation that provides directionality for the organization of a system but does not imply a conscious (or even subconscious) purpose.

Important for a teleonomic process is 'feedback', of which there are two kinds:[75] 'Negative' feedback stabilizes a system. It sends out an indication that a deviation is taking place and triggers a step to counteract that deviation. 'Positive' feedback, in contrast, amplifies a process; that is, it leads to a repetition of what has just been done. By itself, positive feedback can create a problem, for if amplification involves only a part of the system, the resulting expansion of this part changes the pattern of the system as a whole.[76] In order to maintain an organization, negative feedback is also needed, stabilizing the system at least in some respect. Thus, the 'growth' of complex systems typically requires the operation of both positive and negative feedback.

For conscious beings, a combination of positive and negative feedback appears in the presence of pleasure and pain. In light of what has been said about positive feedback, one can distinguish pleasure—which affects only a part of one's being and enhances only that part to the possible detriment of other parts—from joy—which positively affects all or much of one's being. Pleasure can lead to new structuring, but it de-forms if it operates alone.[77]

75. Feedback was described by Arturo Rosenblueth, Norbert Wiener, and Julian Bigelow in 1943.

76. See D.L. DeAngelis *et al.* 1986.

77. On the applicability of feedback conceptions to emotions, cf. Nico Frijda 1986: 367-68.

Another major concern for systems theory involves boundaries and subsystems. If a large number of units are interconnected in several ways, behavior readily becomes excessively chaotic. Any well-functioning system consequently requires a boundary to divide the items that are strongly interconnected within the system from those that are outside it. This boundary does not need to be sharp but can be fuzzy.[78] Furthermore, a reasonably large system needs to have subsystems, each with its own boundary. In line with this principle, most beings exhibit the phenomenon of organizational levels. Structures of a 'higher' level contain the smaller units of a 'lower' one (a molecule includes atoms, and so forth). However, there can also be overlapping systems. Human beings, especially, can participate in several different organizational complexes simultaneously or in succession.

In the long-range history of systems, as this has been discussed, crucial roles are played by 'attractors' and 'catastrophes'. An attractor is a condition or form, the 'neighbors' of which tend to propel a given system back to that condition or form. (For instance, if a ball lies at the bottom of an indentation, a small movement of the ball up one side of the indentation will probably be followed by its return to the bottom.) Such an 'attracting' condition or form is relatively stable. If, however, some process propels a system sufficiently far away from a state so that it does not return to it, there will be a significant change, a 'catastrophe' (Thom 1972).[79] Unless a system then disintegrates, it will probably reach another reasonably stable state, which is maintained through attraction. In society, such a change constitutes a violent or peaceful revolution; in science, it means a conceptual shift.

In all phases of the history of a system, thus described, indeterminism is present in varying amounts. Indeed, a degree of indeterminacy is valuable for a system for many reasons, including the variable nature of its environment. A flexible, even somewhat unpredictable, system can deal with environmental variability more effectively than can a rigid one (e.g. Katsenelinboigen 1997). Accordingly, an important issue is an optimal balance between order and chaos, called the 'edge of organization' (Marion 1999).

One notable feature of systems theory is that, in the words of Ervin Laszlo, 'it can give us both factual and normative knowledge' (1972: 120). The reason for this combination of fact and norm is that the processes that are described by systems theory—including feedback (modeling pain and pleasure) and various kinds of interactions within and outside a circle—have relevance for ethics. It is true that descriptive analyses cannot simply be identified with ethical judgments, but in practice description and judgment cannot be separated. Specifically, Laszlo believed that systems theory

---

78. See Herbert Simon 1962; Peter Blau 1974: 300.
79. René Thom 1980 placed this analysis explicitly within systems theory.

'tells us that all systems have value and intrinsic worth' since they are 'goal-oriented, self-maintaining, and self-creating expressions of nature's penchant for order' (1972: 118). This statement, to be sure, values order one-sidedly.

Differently, Bertalanffy pointed to issues of both order and freedom, as they are described in systems theory (1968). Dealing with relations between parts and wholes, Sunny Auyang observed that 'crude models unable to handle the complexity [with which he dealt] conceptually sacrifice either the individual or the system' (1998: x).

Such ethical reflections do not support pure optimism. For instance, Wiener was aware that the systems processes he described have 'great possibilities for good and for evil' (1948: 38). Human history has amply demonstrated both.

6. *Communication*

A dynamic form of relationality appears in communication, which overcomes distance without obliterating distinctions. Most obviously, communication furnishes a bridge between its source and its recipient. Furthermore, its structure overcomes a dichotomy between matter and mind.

As has already been mentioned, two different analyses recognized a triple structure in communication. According to Peirce, a sign involves a 'ground', the physical signal itself, and an 'interpretant'. According to a grammatical-dialogical conception (including Peirce's in early sketches), communication is 'from A to B about C'.

In addition to Peirce, others were interested in signs around 1900 CE.[80] Among these, the physicist Hermann von Helmholtz presented the view that experience furnishes 'signs of'—not images comparable to—reality (1879).[81] He thus rejected a crude theory of correspondence between words and things, even while he affirmed that words 'refer' to something. Gustav Teichmüller argued in great detail that science expresses 'semiotic knowledge', showing that science involves human communicational structures (1882). Victoria, Lady Welby, developed a theory of meaning with major emphasis on context and purpose (1896, etc.), furnishing an important

80. Donald Lowe noted a move in interest from 'positive fact' to 'sign' during the early part of the twentieth century (1982: 123). Andreas Kamlah described it as a shift from operating with 'visualizable models' to operating with 'symbols' (e.g. 1983: 241).

81. Wittgenstein's early interest in language was stimulated by Heinrich Hertz, who was indebted to Helmholtz in his understanding of science as a system of signs. If Wittgenstein had followed Helmholtz directly, he would presumably have been less ready to describe language as a 'picture' (*Bild*) of the world, as he did until the spring of 1930 at least (1980: 1).

beginning point for twentieth-century discussions (Schmitz 1985: xii-xlvi; Walther 1989: 310-11). Husserl dealt with signs in 1901 (see above, 3.6).

This new interest in signs affected concepts of human existence, according to more than one observer. Julia Kristeva reached the conclusion that, from the end of the nineteenth century on, the human subject was seen as a 'signifying process' (1974a, 4.5). John Peters similarly held that 'only since the late nineteenth century have we defined ourselves in terms of our ability to *communicate* with one another' (1999: 1, 174, emphasis his).

The analysis of signs did have important antecedents. Reflections about signs date back at least to Aristotle and played an important role in Christian thought, holding that both the words of Scripture and the physical world are signs pointing to God.[82] For strict nominalism (which did not admit even general ideas), the uses of actual words were crucial (cf. Lakoff 1987: xii-xiii). In fact, nominalism's interest in words contributed to Peirce's theory of signs. This does not represent 'an irony' (as Joseph Brent thought [1998: 48]); rather, it shows that relational theory has incorporated elements of preceding perspectives.[83]

A rather superficial concern with signs, focusing on their visible form, appeared in two early-twentieth-century movements both called 'formalist': one in mathematics, the other in literary criticism.[84] At first, these two movements were not interested in the referential aspect of signs. It was soon pointed out, however, that, in line with the triadic theory of signs, an object (such as a numeral in mathematics or a printed word in literature) is not a sign unless it points beyond itself. In response to such criticism, the two movements evolved into less one-sided approaches, acknowledging that the structures studied refer to something.

In fact, in a more or less comprehensive way, language became a central interest in philosophy. 'Formal' symbolic logic (using artificial symbols) blossomed from about 1900 CE on, with a primary emphasis on syntactics—that is, on the relations between the symbols. 'Ordinary language analysis'—examining language as it is commonly used—was influential from the 1930s on, especially in the English-speaking world. It focused primarily

82. For aspects of the history of semiotics, see Copleston 1946–63 ('sign', etc., in the indices); Deely *et al.* 1986.

83. To some extent influenced by this tradition, but going beyond it, Leibniz advocated an artificial language to express logical relations; although his program remained largely unpublished in his own lifetime, presumably since it ran counter to some common assumptions, it led to the development of symbolic logic, which mushroomed in the latter part of the nineteenth century (see Alonzo Church 1936).

84. The chief name in mathematical formalism was David Hilbert; although this endeavor foundered in a sense, it led to much valuable insight. A literary formalism appeared in Russia during the 1920s; it provided a significant stimulus for future work, although needing modification and supplementation.

on semantics (thought or reference) and pragmatics (use). Another line of interest in semantics devoted extensive attention to the use of various kinds of symbols (Cassirer, S. Langer,[85] Jaspers, Ricoeur, and others).

The story of this 'linguistic turn' has been previously told (and does not need to be repeated here).[86] It is appropriate, however, to mention a discussion concerning the extent to which language is inherently more than an individual affair. Locke had propounded the view that words properly express only the speaker's own thoughts (1690, 3.2.2-5). In contrast, James and others argued that the thought and expression of two or more persons can have 'the same' content—for instance, a number.[87] Furthermore, Dewey (1925: 187), as well as the later Wittgenstein, insisted that language is social in its very structure.

Toward the end of the twentieth century, a skeptical view of language with a nominalist base questioned whether what is said actually refers to some reality outside speech (see below, 7.2). In response, Hilary Putnam—explicitly rejecting nominalism (1971)—argued that an adequate conception of language needs to consider, besides the individual speaker, 'other people and the world' (1975: 271). Along similar lines, the pragmatist Donald Davidson stated that both 'objectivity' (knowledge of objects) and 'communication' rest on 'the triangle that, by relating speaker, interpreter, and the world, determines the content of thought and speech', and that communication presupposes a common physical, not merely linguistic, world (1990: 325; cf. 1984: 201 [1977]).

In fact, the notion of communication could be taken as a central category for ethics. A number of thinkers were directly or indirectly stimulated by Peirce to adopt such a way.[88] Habermas, among them, presented the ideal of 'public and unrestricted discussion free of mastery' (1968a: 98, 163-64).

85. See her works published from 1923 on (listed in 1942: 21-22).

86. See Rorty 1967a; Dallmayr 1984 (including references to varied political aspects of the development); Soames 2003.

87. This reflection by James appears to have had a significant impact on Husserl (see above, 3.4). An apprehension of the 'same' reality came to be important in Husserl's notion of 'intersubjectivity' (cf. D. Carr 1987: 61).

88. Peirce had spoken of 'unlimited community' (1982–, III: 285 [1878]). For Royce, this involved the whole world as a community of interpretation (1913, II: 324). G.H. Mead, who supported social cooperation, described 'universal discourse' as the 'formal ideal of communication' (1934: 327 [1927 lecture]). Fred Scott, also in the pragmatic tradition, favored 'untrammeled communication' (1922: 470). Jaspers (whose connection with the Peircean tradition is unclear) called for 'unconditional' (1932, II: 183 [6.1.3, end]), 'limitless' (1935, ch. 3; 1948: 133, etc.), and 'unrestricted' communication (1958: 43). Apel referred to 'unlimited community' (1968: 164). Habermas followed this line with modifications, giving attention both to social stratification, which 'suppresses' communication, and to psychological distortion, as treated by Freud (1968b: 82, 279). He gave credit to G.H. Mead for a 'paradigm shift' (1970; 1981: 2).

For this purpose, he set truly 'communicative' reason, which aims at freely reached agreement or 'consensus', in contrast with goal-oriented speaking and acting, which is instrumental (1985: 344, 378). For instance, he distinguished between the state of being 'convinced' as a result of free communication and the state where one 'agrees to' something as a result of manipulation (1968a: 163; 1981, I, ch. 3; 1985: 352).[89]

Habermas's conception was inspiring, but it had significant problems, as others recognized. For instance, his ideal of 'unrestricted communication' is problematic, partly because it is unduly idealistic and partly because communication can be inappropriate or excessive. Furthermore, consensus is not desirable if it means that individuality and thus the possibility of disagreement is not valued, as Habermas briefly acknowledged in 1970 (260).[90] However, Habermas's ideal of seeking a free 'inner' conviction rather than an 'external' imposition (1983: 133, 144-45; cf. 1981, I: 28) guards another's freedom.

The grammatical-dialogical line viewed ethical interaction somewhat similarly in terms of a dialogue that involves listening. Thinkers along this line included Cohen, Ebner, Buber, and others who have already been discussed, as well as Levinas, Lyotard, and Gibbs, who are discussed later in Chapter 7.

Ethically more neutral (or ambivalent), the concept of 'information' was used widely from 1948 on as a measure of the 'amount' of communication, which was defined as its unpredictability.[91] That is, the informative character of a message is considered high when the message is unpredictable (what is predictable does not 'tell' one very much). Unpredictability, or 'uncertainty'—technically, 'entropy'—is thus regarded as an opportunity without which there can be no information. Since unpredictability presupposes a degree of separateness between events, the notion of information presupposes both a certain independence of objects and the possibility of bridging the gulf between them.

Information theory and other aspects of communication theory have proved to be useful in dealing with all levels of existence, including the physical, the biological, and the human.[92] A reason is that the idea of 'information', like that of a 'sign', does not focus on substances (material or mental) but on relations. Instead of being either strictly mental or strictly

---

89. German: *überzeugen* vs. *überreden* (cf. Apel 1988: 402).

90. Habermas's idea of consensus may have been influenced by Gadamer's concept of a 'fusion of horizons' in understanding (1960: 289) and by Peirce's notion of scientific agreement in the long run (see above, n. 42. Cf. Apel 1968: 164; 1973, II: 192, 207, on 'consensus'). The ideal of consensus has been criticized by Lyotard (see on him below, 7.4), Gert Ueding and Bernd Steinbrink (1986: 163), Nicholas Rescher (1993), and others.

91. See below, 10.1, 2.

92. See, e.g., Christof Wassermann *et al.* 1992 and Chalmers 1996.

material, information is constituted by arrangement and interaction. A few examples are the following: In physics, relevant phenomena are 'signals' (which are limited in speed) and the uncertainty principle (which implies an observer). In biology, internal 'messages' can be described in terms of coding theory, as they convey a certain pattern from one point to another. For human beings, aesthetic and other enjoyment is highest when they process as much unpredictable 'information' as they can handle (see below, 10.5). In short, as Gregory Chaitin (1999: 106) stated, information 'is a really revolutionary new kind of concept, and a recognition of this fact is one of the milestones of this age'.

7. Rationality and Emotion/Volition in Human Forms

In order to discuss relations between reason and emotion or volition, one must know what is meant by those words. Unfortunately, there is considerable confusion about the meaning of the word 'reason'. Most Enlightenment thinkers (and, later, Habermas) meant by 'reason' thinking that is done 'freely', that is, without automatic obedience to authority (see above, 1.3). In this case, the opposite of reason is acceptance of authority. Others identify reason with intellectual processes that are uninvolved emotionally; the opposite of this is emotionality without thought. Still others consider reason to involve a reflective consideration of the consequences or implications of a contemplated step.

Within this third conception, an important distinction needs to be made between two very different approaches (as was noted by Max Weber [1920: 265-66]).

One approach is evaluative or normative. It seeks to assess the ethical or aesthetic value of an act on the basis of its anticipated consequence or some other reflective standard. This kind of reason was predominant in classical (pre-modern) times. Another approach is instrumental; it looks for means by which to reach a goal that has been established on some other basis. Nominalism pursues this latter version on the assumption that ethical or aesthetic judgments are based on arbitrary decisions, whether by God or by human beings. In this sense, the Enlightenment figures Hutcheson and Hume held that the most fundamental human commitments are not based on rationality (Beiser 1996: 325). Kant did stress the importance of a certain kind of reason for ethics, but he considered this 'practical' (ethical) reason to be distinct from scientific reason.[93] Accordingly, with nominalism in mind, Whitehead

93. This historical development has been discussed many times, for instance by Max Horkheimer and Theodor Adorno (1944, and in later works by Horkheimer) and by Herbert Marcuse (1964: 225, 227, 235), contrasting 'instrumental' with 'critical' reasoning. Hegel, *after* the Enlightenment, did revive a more integral reason.

described the post-medieval period (including the Enlightenment) as anti-rational (1925, chapter 1), and others have identified the modern outlook in a similar way (see Dallmayr 1993: 106-107; Lash 1990: 10).

Differently, relational and comparable conceptions do not separate thinking from feeling or volition. Pragmatism,[94] 'philosophies of life' (including Bergson, Dilthey, and Simmel),[95] and 'existentialism' (which stressed thought that involves one's existence)[96] have sought to recognize a continuity of thought, action, and commitment. The notion of 'listening', already mentioned, involves an openness to the other's being and condition (such as suffering). Indeed, although the human brain apparently processes beliefs and desires to a considerable extent separately (see Nichols and Stich 2003: 159-60), they interact extensively.

One way of relating feeling and intellect is to consider how values or emotions enter into the process of thinking. In fact, will or morality has repeatedly been held to stand prior to intellectual thought in an important way. In light of the organismic heritage of humanity, such a position makes sense. Although not on the basis of biological sciences, Levinas placed the moral demand prior to knowledge (1951, etc.). Davidson held that 'charity [confidence in another] is…a condition for having a workable theory' (1984: 197) and even that 'truth rests…ultimately, on the affective attitudes' (1990: 326).

Another way to relate the two aspects is to point out that human emotions are heavily based on knowledge or on something imagined.[97] This observation, too, can point to antecedents in animal life, in which perceptions lead to emotional responses. It can then be said that ethical judgments, especially insofar as they are appropriate, are grounded in interaction with reality, just as are appropriate descriptive statements.

Many have held, in fact, that valuing and thinking are inseparably connected with each other as aspects of a single process.[98] In the words of

94. See Putnam (2002: 30). According to Rorty in an extreme statement, pragmatism holds that 'there is no epistemological difference between truth about what ought to be and truth about what is, nor any metaphysical difference between morality and science' (1982: 163). Brandom, too, has assigned to the pragmatic dimension priority in relation to thought (1994).

95. For instance, Dilthey wrote in a MS before 1880: 'there is no presuppositionless philosophy', all sciences begin in faith', i.e. with presuppositions (1921–, XIX: 49-50).

96. See below, 7.4, for a little more on existentialism.

97. E.g. Frijda 1986, with an overview of evidence and theories, old and new. Thus also Josephine Donovan (1996: 158), on sympathy, and Robert Yanal (1999: 160), for fiction.

98. Thus, among many others, Apel 1973, II: 358-435, with a reference to Peirce. Frisina (2002) discusses Whitehead, Neville, and Daniel Dennett along such a line. Paul Lorenzen treated logic 'dialogically' and thus dynamically in terms of challenge and defense (e.g. 1987).

Putnam, 'factual description and valuation can and must be *entangled*' (2002: 27; emphasis his). In short, in a fully relational view, knowledge includes value and value includes knowledge. Knowledge, then, is not neutral either in its source or in its application.[99]

If value and knowledge are indeed not separate, the question of 'natural law' arises. Although there are many different conceptions of 'natural law', all of them have in common the idea that ethics is not arbitrary but is concerned with what is fitting for human life and that the law of a state, too, should be subject to this standard. Of course, there can be much disagreement about what is fitting and how large a range of options can or should be accepted.

The currency of the idea of natural law had declined by the end of the eighteenth century, as nominalism became widely accepted (see Haakonssen 1996: 62, and above, 1.3). From the end of the nineteenth century on, however, the idea of natural law regained a degree of recognition.[100] It was already implied in the positive freedom championed by T.H. Green (see by him further 1885–88, II: 344). Perhaps more importantly, around 1900 a number of theories of law that reflected on what is good for human beings drew on the newly developing social sciences (A. Hunt 1978; Strömholm 1985: 275-81).[101]

Newer ideas concerning natural law usually held that it changes as humanity develops along with the rest of reality (e.g. Carl Friedrich 1958: 19). A synthesis of nature and history thus emerged. Thomas Aquinas already had indicated that natural law includes the possibility of variation and change in specific matters.[102] In fact, far from being rigid, the idea of natural law allows for change in ethical behavior as conditions change, unlike a belief in arbitrary eternal decrees by God that are envisioned by most religious nominalists.

One reason for sympathy toward natural-law ideas, especially in the middle of the twentieth century, lay in a revulsion toward horrors perpetrated by political systems, such as Nazism, which, in line with the 'historical school', rejected natural law. Not only did Nazi acts show a logical consequence of this rejection, but those who experienced a revulsion against them recognized that they believed in a morality which is not

99. See, for instance, Longino 1990, as well as Habermas 1968b.

100. For some of this development, at the beginning of the twentieth century and again since 1940, see Rommen 1947, Covell 1992, and George 1992. Natural law theories varied considerably.

101. Whether the Supreme Court (not just legislators) should consider natural law became controversial in the US; the Court did so in ruling against segregation by taking sociological studies into account.

102. Thomas Aquinas, *Summa theologica*, 2/2, q. 57, art. 2, in the train of somewhat obscure statements by Aristotle, *Nicomachean Ethics*, 1134b; cf. Leo Strauss 1953: 157.

simply arbitrary (e.g. Will Herberg 1976: 193 [1960]; Peter Doll 1985: 85; Novick 1988: 282-90, 627; Apel 1988: 386; Anthony Lisska 1996: 8-10, 17-55).

Appeals to natural law have often been made by oppressed people. After all, if 'might is right', then those who are oppressed are wrong. In his *Letter from Birmingham City Jail*, King appealed to the idea of 'natural law' with this explication of it: 'Any law that uplifts human personality is just. Any law that degrades human personality is unjust' (1963b: 6-7). Perhaps most of the twentieth-century freedom movements were based in good part on an idea of this sort. In particular, both racial and gender liberation were supported by extensive observations—scholarly and otherwise—which showed that past ideas about the races and the sexes were erroneous. Even many of those who had benefited from earlier arrangements were persuaded to abandon them on the basis of these observations.

A version of natural law that became widely accepted employed the term 'human rights'. This resurrected, in modified form, the idea of 'natural rights' that had fallen on hard times in the nineteenth century. It was formally adopted in the 'United Nations Declaration on Human Rights' in 1948 (B. Tierney 1997: 345).

A relational position was well expressed by Lakoff and Johnson: 'moral concepts...are not absolute, but they are also not arbitrary' (1999: 325). Similarly, Christina Traina stated that 'nature is neither determinative of nor irrelevant to ethics' (1999: 334).[103] This kind of ethics—based neither on strict determination nor on arbitrary choice—supports an interactive freedom that has room for choice while giving attention to the actualities of the world.

During the twentieth century, as earlier, the issue of an interplay between rationality and emotionality sometimes became entangled with the issue of possible differences between the sexes. According to an old stereotype, rationality is masculine and emotionality is feminine. A different judgment was made by Michèle Le Doeuff in 1989/1990; she said then (at least) that men have a greater tendency than women to be one-sided or split and thus either unemotionally rational or excessively irrational.[104] It should be noted, however, that such a divergence—insofar as it has indeed been true—is not necessarily inborn.

103. Traina, a Catholic feminist, criticized the specifics of church pronouncements, as is possible when ethics is based on 'nature' or 'custom' rather than on arbitrary divine law.

104. According to Le Doeuff, 'masculinism' (not necessarily equivalent to all men's thinking) can involve either 'total rationality' (1990: 8) or an 'irrationality' that denies community (1989, §2.13). In 1998, however, she did not repeat such a judgment but, rather, criticized the distinctions others (including E. Keller) made between men and women.

As a matter of fact, several women philosophers made major integrative contributions, linking emotion and rationality.[105] In theoretical discussions of this issue, they usually accepted rationality.[106] For instance, Cecile Jackson noted that 'when rationality is jettisoned so too is the basis of criticism' (1995: 140). For some women, to be sure, the incorporation of ethics implied a transformation of reason, one in which men, too, can then participate. For instance, in Norway in 1982, B.A. Sørensen instituted an extensive discussion of 'responsible rationality', which she set in contrast to 'technical limited rationality' (Ve 1998: 326, 333). In the US, the feminist epistemology of Hilary Rose described a 'caring rationality' (1994: 33).

Integrated perspectives, however, were not limited to women. Quite a few men also pursued a combination of emotion and knowledge. Among these stood the important psychologist James Baldwin (1915) and later in the century Martin Schiralli, who argued for a 'constructive [not nominalist] postmodernism' (1999: 150). Combinations were also offered by others in the recent and distant past.[107] Thus, the old sexual stereotype needs at least to be relativized.

Although notable attempts have thus been made to examine interactions between feeling and thought, this topic requires further exploration. To do so is perhaps one of the major tasks that lie ahead.

105. These thinkers included Welby (1896), on meaning; Edith Stein (1917), on empathy; Simone Weil (1962), on love; Lucie Olbrechts-Tyteca, on argumentation (with Chaïm Perelman, 1958); Susanne Langer, on mental phenomena as 'modes of feeling' (1967–82, I: 31); Anscombe (1957), on intention; Kristeva (1985), on love, etc.; Mary Warnock, on imagination (1976: 202); Mary Hesse (1980), Evelyn Keller (1985, 1992), and Sandra Harding (1986, 1991, 1998), on science; Martha Nussbaum, on knowledge and ethics (1990, 1995); Linda Zagzebski (1996), describing efforts to make cognitive contact with reality as a virtue; and Patricia Churchland (1998), citing research showing the role of feelings in good decision making. Alison Jaggar's discussion of the 'importance of emotion for knowledge' was also impressive (1989); as an antecedent of her position, she mentioned Plato's thesis that knowledge requires love—a point Socrates learns in the *Symposium* from Diotima, a 'wise woman'. See, further, Karen Green 1995: 9-12, 168, with references to a number of feminists holding to a union of feeling and thinking.

106. The following, among others, have explicitly accepted rationality: Susanne Langer (1937, 1953, 1967–82), Martha Nussbaum (1989: 778; 1990: ix, together with definite, although not exclusive, attention to particularity), Pauline Johnson (1994: 131), Pamela Anderson (1998), Linda Nicholson (1999: 11-13). Furthermore, Ruth Barcan Marcus has been a crucial contributor to logic (see above, section 3).

107. Other men who have pointed to a union of emotion and knowledge included Dewey (cf. Sandra Rosenthal 1986: 265-328) and, earlier, Spinoza (see Genevieve Lloyd 1984: 51 [in fact, Lloyd did not identify maleness altogether biologically]). Linda Zagzebski (1996: 52, 63, 169, 338) has pointed to Hobbes, Descartes, Peirce, James, and others as those who have seen such a union, at least in part.

8. *Summary*

According to Gilles Fauconnier and Mark Turner, 'we live in the age of the triumph of form' (2002: 3). For instance, abstract art (see above, section 4) led interpreters to speak about a discovery of 'form' in a new way (see Cheney 1924: 90). Such an assessment is true if 'form' is understood in terms of complexes of relations. Earlier periods had different concepts of form. The following *major themes* appeared in the relational tradition:

Forms can be approached analytically by giving attention to their constituent elements and relations, or synthetically by focusing on the resultant whole. A holistic vision includes an element of intuition, which is largely subconscious, whereas an analytical view is more consciously reflective.

Forms, as complexes of relations, constitute possibilities, which may or may not also be actual. Thought (including desire) is directed toward such forms.

According to many versions of relational theory, all properties are relations. Treated by themselves, then, objects do not have properties but only potentials. In any case, forms, as they are perceived, are always relative to an observer. That fact, however, does not mean that they are arbitrary, for relations are real, including the relation between the observer and the observed.

Forms can be dynamic. Systems theory explores how interacting elements can either remain stable or change. What can be called 'growth' involves a degree of stability (continuity) as well as change.

Communication is a dynamic process that has a triple structure. It presupposes differentiation, which it bridges. It has a pattern that is usefully applied to all levels of existence.

In human forms, thought and emotion interact. While they may be distinguished, they cannot be separated.

These themes hold together *a series of dualities*. They are not dualisms, in the sense that they operate independently. Rather, in each case, the two sides belong together.

In Chapter 4, it was shown that relational theories accept both sides of the following oppositions (although, on a given occasion, one or another of the two sides of a given duality may come to the fore):

partial connectedness	::	partial distance
generality	::	particularity
a degree of unpredictability	::	a degree of regularity
an element of reasonableness	::	an element of arbitrariness
some coherent understanding	::	(religious) mystery, (secular) 'fact'

According to the analysis of the present chapter, a relational conception of form also presents another group of pairs, for which it envisions mutual interaction:

holistic intuition	::	analytic rationality
possibility	::	historical actuality
the observer	::	the observed
acknowledgment of the inside	::	acknowledgment of the outside
communication	::	uncertainty
(emotion) feeling	::	thinking (reason)
(evaluative) ethics	::	(descriptive) knowledge

These relational themes were not limited to any one theoretical line within relational theory, as the following table of theorists who have been mentioned in the present work reveals. Those listed in the right-most column include some philosophers who do not fit well in one of the three columns farther left as well as specialists in different disciplines—including physics, psychology, and theology—who are mentioned in the present volume and are surveyed more fully in Buss 2007. The emptiness of some cells in the following table may be due to limitations in the presentation, since the different disciplinary traditions are not represented fully.

Relational Themes According to Major Traditions

	semiotic pragmatism	phenom-enology	grammatical -dialogical	other theorists
A conjunction of separate-ness with connectivity and of the particular with the general	X		X	X
Consequently: both coher-ence and incoherence, a combination reflected in the phenomenon of probability	X			X
Form seen both as a whole and as composed of the parts that are related to each other	X		X	X
Forms (complexes of rela-tions) viewed as possibilities	X	X		X
The relativity of forms in relation to an observer	X	X	implied	X
Forms as crossing the boundary between human and nonhuman beings	X		X	X
Communication as providing information to semi-inde-pendent beings	X	X	X	X
Interconnection between rationality and emotions in human forms	X		implied?	X

Relational theory, however, was not static. Rather, there were *historical developments* within each theme. For these, a few highlights can be presented.

Both particular and general terms entered into logic at the end of the nineteenth century, as a logic of relations was developed. Especially from the 1950s on, possibility became a major conceptual frame. During the last decades of the twentieth century (after an anticipation by Wittgenstein), 'paraconsistent' logic made room for formulas that affirm both of two contradictory states.

The relativity of knowledge was recognized from the end of the nineteenth century on in a way that was not skeptical, for it went together with an acceptance of the relativity (that is, at least partial connectivity) of being. A systematic sociology of knowledge made major strides from the 1920s on. It was applied in an extreme way by Nazis and Marxists, so that a negative reaction set in subsequently, but it re-emerged with strength in the last third of the twentieth century.

A strong interest in the theory of signs began at the end of the nineteenth century and continued thereafter. More specifically, human language became a central focus of philosophy from the 1930s on. A major breakthrough in the theory of communication came in 1948 with the construction of information theory, which showed, for instance, that unpredictability provides an opportunity. The notion of information proved to be widely applicable to human and nonhuman processes and supported earlier moves to recognize a continuity between human and other forms.

The present chapter has focused primarily on the intellectual side of a relational outlook, but a number of *practical implications* of the ideas that have been mentioned can be stated in terms of freedom. Specifically, a relational outlook fosters:

(1) A social outlook that combines common and mutual concern with degrees of independence, in other words, both positive and negative freedom in the societal realm.

(2) An attitude toward oneself that values both matter and mind, so that internal freedom accepts both body and spirit.

(3) A sense of considerable commonality with nonhuman beings, so that their freedom is also acknowledged and supported.

(4) An acceptance of both possibility and actuality; the idea of possibility supports a reach for alternative—one can hope, better ('freer')—social arrangements, with a belief that history is not determined but free to move toward various alternatives.

The fact that leading relational thinkers actually held such views in regard to praxis was indicated in Chapter 3 and from time to time in the present one.

Part II

DISPUTE ABOUT RELATIONAL/INTERACTIVE THEORY

Although relational theory and interactive freedom together represented a significant complex of ideas during the period beginning at the end of the nineteenth century, this path was not the only one pursued during that time. On the contrary, it was rivaled by several others. Thus, for an adequate picture of that period, it is necessary to present at least a sketch of the alternatives.

Chapter 6

THE MAJOR ALTERNATIVES

1. *Moves Contrary to Interactive Freedom*

Violent Group Conflict
Major horrors of the twentieth century reflected group particularism, in which a given group is treated as a large unified entity that stands in conflict with others (see above, 1.1, 3).[1] There is little negative freedom for individuals within the group, but strongly negative action toward those outside it.

In Germany, group particularism arose under the name of National Socialism.[2] This name should be taken seriously, for it focuses strongly on one nation in contrast to others and, in this case, also on 'race' as its foundation. A similar, although somewhat less virulent, version appeared in Italy under the name of 'fascism'. In the Shoah (or 'Holocaust'), Nazis destroyed Jews and others—including Poles, gypsies, communists, social democrats, and homosexuals—in order to create 'purity' within the nation and gain victory for their race. Outside the nation, Nazism engaged in conflict with other groups.

It should be noted that the destructiveness of Nazism was not due to a lack of intelligence.[3] Rather, Nazis were intelligent enough to apply a conceptual vision that excluded a meaningful commonality beyond their own circle. This fact shows that intellectual excellence is not enough to guard against catastrophic irresponsibility.

The Nazi worldview was oriented toward pure power and mastery (see below, 7.1, for Spengler's formulation of this outlook). Thus, their acts of cruelty and humiliation were deliberate.[4] Rejecting natural law, as had

1. This aspect of twentieth-century history is traced in Glover 1999 and Köhler 2000.
2. There were sociological reasons for this rise, but they are not of immediate concern here. That a strong nationalism represents a form of particularism has been pointed out also by Michael Murrmann-Kahl (1992: 173, for German thought).
3. Thus, rightly, Robert Ericksen (1985: 26). There is also little reason to think that Nazis were especially emotionally disturbed (Zillmer *et al.* 1995), whatever may have been true of Adolf Hitler.
4. See Des Pres (1976, ch. 2) for such actions. It must be seen that Nazism was not merely incidentally nasty, nor did it 'hate' (that is too positive), but it was to a large

become standard in Germany, they refused to recognize transnational justice.[5] It was ironically appropriate, then, that their leaders were eventually
tried in an international court. By deliberately degrading masses of people in
concentration camps and even more by throwing them into ovens, Nazism
may well have reached an epitome of viciousness. A reasonable explanation
for this is that National Socialism represented an extreme form of the competitive self-assertion that was embraced by high modernity.

Marxism, especially as applied by Lenin and Stalin, also exhibited an
aggressive group particularism. The collective entity it sought to represent
was not a nation (except, in part, under Stalin) but a 'class'—the proletariat,
together with its Marxist 'leaders'. Marx believed only in self-assertion
for relations between groups; Lenin and Stalin, in addition, did not allow
for freedom within the group.[6] Although Marxism contained many com-
mendable ideals (in fact, most of the proposals of the *Manifesto* of 1848
have been adopted by non-Communist countries), its practice constituted—
together with Nazism—a major horror.

It should be noted, however, that group aggressiveness was not new in the
twentieth century, nor was it limited to Nazism and Stalinism. Various kinds
of violent group conflict had for a long time caused untold sorrows. Christians had already harassed and killed Jews in large numbers. Extermination
of other tribal groups was also advocated in the Bible.[7] Furthermore, in
both world wars of the twentieth century, mass destruction of enemy civil-
ians was practiced by countries that enjoyed considerable internal freedom.
Earlier, there had been conquests, slavery, and other racially oppressive
actions, including lynchings and the denial of voting rights, which continued in the US long into the twentieth century.

extent nihilist (as I remember from readings as a child; cf. Kren and Rappoport 1994:
33, 42). Steven Katz (1994: 580) observed that the unusual character of the Shoah lies
in its open 'transcendence and inversion of all ethical and mediating norms' (to be
sure, the word 'all' is too strong).

5. The Nazi party program held to a special 'moral feeling of the German
race' (Nicolaisen 1966: 61-62); the rejection of natural law allowed mass murder
to be accepted judicially, since it was ordered by the state. See studies collected in
W. Maihofer 1962: 2, 16, 309, 323 ('The Third Reich took legal positivism [rejecting
natural law] at its word').

6. Thus also Roslyn Bologh (1990: 267). For Marx, see above, Chapter 1, n. 48;
Chapter 2, n. 4. Marx and Engels advocated antagonism between the proletariat and
the rest of society until the proletariat establishes its rule (e.g. *Manifesto*, 1848 [1957–,
IV: 481]). The similarity of Nazism with Leninism (one of its prime enemies) was
pointed out by Adolf Ehrt (1933: 36).

7. The biblical inculcations fortunately were far from what actually happened;
rabbis reinterpreted them considerably (Weinfeld 1992: 92). Wholesale destruction
was practiced in the ancient Near East prior to the Bible (P. Stern 1991), as well as in
other times and places.

Problems in the US After 1968

After about 1968, new problems arose. They emerged, coincidentally or not, soon after the assassination of King, an act that was hostile to liberation and removed a major idealistic figure.

The union of several kinds of freedom that had been approached in the 1960s fell apart to a considerable extent thereafter. Repeatedly, negative freedom led to behavior that was destructive to others, to oneself, or to both. Destruction of persons other than oneself included most notoriously the murders by the Charles Manson 'family' in 1969. Destruction of self could paradoxically take place in a turn towards the self (Boggs 2000: 178). It is true, the use of relatively mild 'dope' (which was distinguished by users from more debilitating 'drugs' [T. Miller 1991: 25]—definitions varied) helped some people to move from a materialistic order to a more or less spiritual or artistic one (especially if they graduated from using it), but it severely disoriented some. Pursuits of positive freedom sometimes failed to respect the negative freedom of individuals sufficiently, attempting to accomplish too much by force rather than by persuasion.[8]

In any case, much of society struck back harshly against the spirit of the '60s. For instance, protesting students were gunned down at Kent State and Jackson State Universities in 1970.

It is possible to understand the occurrence of the backlash to some extent, just as it is possible to give reasons for Nazism's rise. For instance, the Vietnam War (lost by the US) and the relatively high inflation after 1968 (due in part to high oil prices and exacerbated in the US by war costs) most likely contributed to the reaction, since war and inflation seem to lead to a desire for order and thus to conservatism.[9] Furthermore, one can find a reason in the rhythmic character of history. In 1951 Michael Oakeshott had already observed that outbursts of 'the politics of faith' (not necessarily religious in character) that look for 'perfection' are regularly followed by periods of relatively conservative skepticism. He was sympathetic toward the skeptical phase, but, as he noted, skepticism can be used defensively by the powerful as a means for keeping the less powerful quiet (1996: 69, 94, 111).[10]

In any case, cynicism reigned to a considerable extent in both academic and general culture.[11] It could be directed against the idealism that called

---

8. While force was certainly needed for desegregation, it was not as useful for integration. That both coercion and deliberation are needed was argued by Jane Mansbridge (1996).

9. See above (Chapter 2, n. 13).

10. See, further, below, 7.2.

11. Cynicism came to be a major topic of discussion, such as for Peter Sloterdijk (1983), Jeffrey Goldfarb (1991), and Richard Stivers (1994). The subtitle of Michael Lerner 1996 spoke of an 'age of cynicism'.

for change; it could also reflect discouragement in view of the slow change. Accordingly, during the 1980s 'some 43 percent of the American populace fit the profile of the cynic, who sees selfishness and fakery at the core of human nature' (Kanter and Mirvis 1989: 1-2). According to Harris polls, a sense of alienation from society (in this sense) rose from 29% to 67% between 1966 and 1995, and then declined a little (Humphrey Taylor 1997: 3).

In line with this cynicism, an open materialism rose in the US, as also in Great Britain (Miringoff 1999: 105, 109). Presumably as a reflection of adult values, between 1966 and 2000 US college freshmen became much more interested in becoming rich and much less interested in finding meaning in life.[12] Their teachers seemed similarly to become occupied with climbing the academic ladder in a prescribed manner. This situation may not have constituted a major change from what had gone on earlier, but a system of evaluating academic achievement on the basis of numerical data, including quantity of publication, acted to limit creativity.[13] In England, 'a kind of generalized selfishness hard to reconcile with the qualities of a truly civilized society' replaced the 'idea of a common good, which genuinely lay behind the welfarism' of preceding decades; such was the judgment of Mary Warnock, although she had in many ways supported the program of the conservative government (2000: 196). The gap between the rich and the poor grew.[14]

Even forms of nihilism appeared from the end of the 1960s on.[15] Some of them inclined toward 'transgression' or an 'outlaw' life for its own sake, placing a high value on negative freedom and to some extent supporting violence and valuing death.[16] To be sure, the rebellious outlook was often unclear in its thrust. For instance, Jeffrey Escoffier did not know whether its aim was to 'transform social norms' or to resist normality altogether (1998: 174).

12. According to reports by the Cooperative Institutional Research Program, published annually in the *Chronicle of Higher Education* (the latest one for the twentieth century in 26 January 2001, A49; reports for the years 1966–90 are tabulated in Dey *et al.* 1991). To be sure, no major decrease in expressed altruism was reported.

13. A numerical standard was mandated in England by the conservative government (M. Warnock, 2000: 186).

14. See Danziger and Gottschalk (1993). Although greater inequality did not re-emerge in every respect (Fogel 2000: 217), pay differentials (among other things) increased, even within a single business.

15. See, e.g., Rosenau 1992: 142-43; Edwards 1994: 145; A. Wilson 1997: 100; Munt 1998: 3.

16. An outlaw life was championed by contributors to Arthur and Marilouise Kroker (1993). 'Transgressions', from murder (although without approval) to religion (!), were treated with appreciation in Godwin *et al.* 1996. For death mysticism, see, e.g., Crisafulli 2000: 38, 156.

One level in which more-or-less nihilist attitudes could show themselves was that of popular culture. In addition to ordinary and idealistic music, there was some that expressed violent or otherwise deliberately shocking sentiments that were quite often misogynist, homophobic, and racist.[17] Especially near the year 2000 CE, a sense of meaninglessness was pervasive.

More serious even than cynicism and nihilism were the effects of that aspect of the backlash that called for 'law and order'. This was primarily directed, as is usually the case, not to misdeeds by the well-to-do but to transgressions by those who were not so well off. A moderate concern for order is, of course, entirely legitimate. However, an excessively sharp concern can arise in response to a perceived threat of anarchy, just as the dictatorial society in Germany during the 1930s was due in part to a fear of anarchy. To be sure, as earlier in Germany, the fear of anarchy was exaggerated and the response was unduly harsh.

Although crime statistics prior to 1973 are very unreliable (since victimization surveys were not instituted until that year), it is indeed possible that there was a rise in violence between the mid-1950s and 1973.[18] However, if an increase in violent crime did occur, it had little to do with changes that were initiated at the end of the 1960s, for children born thereafter were too young to commit such acts. In fact, after 1973 (when the first reliable statistics appear),[19] there was a 30% decrease in theft and burglary (Chambliss 1999: 3). Yet national hysteria in the US—in part with racial overtones—went beyond a moderate response to a huge increase in imprisonment, which came to be five times that of many European countries, although crime rates in the two regions were similar (D. Gordon 1996: 140-41; Chambliss 1999: 7).

This increase in incarceration was largely due to an undiscriminating (but, it appears, racially discriminatory) 'war on drugs'. In fact, more than half of US imprisonment was for drug sale or use, even for the use of relatively 'soft' drugs, such as marijuana. A reason often given for the outlawing of

17. On misogyny, see, e.g., O'Brien 1995: 122, 134, 227-28, 305; Padel 2000: 304; Bennett 2000: 45-46; on the glorification of violence, e.g., Padel 2000: 218-23; on both of these attitudes, Whiteley 2000: 14. African American 'gangsta rap' had a somewhat similar character, but it was, on the whole, more angry than nihilist, and, of course, not anti-black, although not infrequently anti-white and misogynist. Neither angry nor sexually explicit expressions are, as such, nihilist or anarchist. (The observations here made about music were aided by Nickie Stipe.)

18. If so, a cause for that rise probably lay in the fact that punishments for most crimes decreased sharply from 1950 to 1970; perhaps that decrease was too great. According to figures furnished by Reynolds 1995: 13-15, the average prison time for a reported murder or rape dropped to about half of what it had been earlier, and the average time served for robbery or burglary dropped to less than a fifth.

19. From 1973 on, randomly selected persons in the US were asked whether (and, if or how) they had been victimized during the preceding year. This type of survey is more accurate than counting cases reported to the police.

'soft' drugs was that their use would lead to the use of 'hard' ones. However, this belief was for the most part unjustified (Majoor 1998: 141), and it is likely that a more important reason for the attack on the milder drugs was a desire to oppose their tendency to undercut materialism. Unfortunately, the war on drugs itself significantly increased the murder rate (and perhaps the rate for other crimes), as had happened during Prohibition (of the sale of alcohol) earlier in the century (cf. Himmelfarb 1995: 227).

A major problem in the handling of crime was that those imprisoned were overwhelmingly nonwhite. The fact that lower-income and minority persons appear disproportionately in jails is perhaps a universal phenomenon, but in the US the situation was especially serious because of the presence of a sizable black minority, which was thus put under pressure (see Jerome Miller 1996: 49-50, 65-86). This minority continued to form a largely separate community. If whites were imprisoned at a similar rate, there might very well have been a better recognition of the horrors perpetrated, which were quite contrary to interactive sensitivity.

It is worth noting that one-sided self-centeredness (whether internal in self-absorption or external in socioeconomic drives) and a one-sided law-and-order orientation (seeking personal safety in a centralized society) both reflect varieties of particularism. They differ, of course, in the size of the unit highlighted, namely the individual or the group.

2. Divergent Aspects of Internationalization

Internationalization was an important process of the twentieth century, having both positive and negative impact. Interaction between cultures, of course, was not new, since international communication, colonization, and imperialism had proceeded for some time. Nevertheless, it reached new heights.[20] New means of communication (regular international mail, telegraph, telephone, radio, television, air travel, the World Wide Web, etc.) provided for extensive and rapid interaction. Linkage became strong enough to produce two world wars and, in response to them, transnational organizations.

Western colonialism expanded rapidly after 1875, with a carving up of Africa. After c. 1950, a reversal took place, and colonial empires were officially dismantled. Nevertheless, unofficial imperialism continued. It is true, not all aspects of 'modernizing' were deplorable; for instance, technological inventions and, repeatedly, institutions of majority-rule democracy (including new roles for women) were welcomed by many who deplored other aspects of Western (or 'Northern') influence. However, a central issue is whether such procedures were received voluntarily (allowing for negative

20. Kenneth Boulding (1964) thought that internationalization represented the central feature of the twentieth century.

freedom). In globalization various kinds of financial and political pressures were exerted, so that the dividing line between free appropriation and imposition was far from clear.[21]

Globalization yielded some advantage for efficiency in economic operations, but it also had major human costs and created pressures on the environment, as had been true in earlier phases of industrialization. Thus, to counter such detrimental aspects, steps needed to be taken to assure a 'welfare world', just as there have been provisions for welfare societies. Such a condition, however, has not yet been realized (thus also Zygmunt Bauman 2006: 96).

On the positive side of an international orientation, many westerners abandoned the idea that they occupied the top of an evolutionary ladder, with the members of other societies occupying lower rungs. One major reason for this change in outlook may have been better acquaintance with other cultures. For instance, the discovery—from 1875 on—of Paleolithic art dating well before 10,000 BCE was a surprise that met with initial disbelief, but it became accepted as showing that impressive art is not something new. Similarly, in the latter portion of the nineteenth century anthropologists discovered that many small groups without a written tradition believed in a 'high god' who plays the role of a chief deity. This fact showed that an earlier evolutionary scheme, which envisioned a development from animatism (everything has vital power) via animism (belief in spirits) and polytheism to monotheism and then to atheism was too simple. Further anthropological studies during the twentieth century reinforced a sense of the basic equality of human life. One reason for such an attitude lay in a disenchantment with modern Western life because of some of the effects of industrialization and, even more, in view of terrible wars and atrocities.

On the negative side, an open avowal of the superiority of the US appeared again at the beginning of the twenty-first century. Military action reflected this sense.

More theoretical discussions of international relations are presented in Chapter 9.

3. *The Major Alternatives as Different Responses to Modernity*

A number of developments in twentieth-century culture have been called 'postmodern'.[22] However, this term is not very useful unless one knows what is meant by 'modern'. Thus it is useful to look at this word first.

---

21. For instance, there was strong imposition through the US-dominated World Bank and International Monetary Fund. (See Catherine Caufield 1996 for a critical but balanced view of the World Bank.)

22. See M. Rose 1991: 3-20; Welsch 1993: 12-43; Bertens 1995; Cahoone 1996: 3. For Etzioni (in 1968: 15), the term 'post-modern' referred primarily to an increase in information processes after 1945.

In one of its meanings, the word refers to what is 'recent'. Accordingly, during the last one hundred years, the word has often referred to twentieth-century developments. Examples include: 'modern art', 'modern litera-ture', and 'modern mathematics'. With another, very different, meaning, the word 'modern' has a historical orientation and refers to a culture that began toward the end of the Middle Ages with its *via moderna* and reached its height in the eighteenth and nineteenth centuries.

An advantage of the historical meaning of the word 'modern' (as in Chapter 1 of the present study) lies in the fact that it captures the spirit of that time, when the 'new' increasingly came to be valued. This sense, described by Marx and Engels for the 'bourgeois' outlook, was as follows: 'constant revolutionizing of production, uninterrupted disturbances of all social relations, everlasting uncertainty and agitation... All that is solid melts into air' (*Manifesto of the Communist Party*, 1848, part 1 [1957–, IV: 465]). Similarly, Foucault stated that 'modernity is often characterized in terms of the consciousness of discontinuity of time: a break with tradition, a feeling of novelty, of vertigo in the face of the passing moment' (in Paul Rabinow 1984: 39).

If the word 'modern' is used in this sense for a period reaching its high-point in the nineteenth century, the various movements after that time can then be seen as different responses to modernity. They were thus collectively 'postmodern'. The responses were quite divergent in character, however, so that Richard Rorty could say about the term 'postmodern' that 'nobody has the foggiest idea of what it means' (1997). There were at least four very different kinds of postmodernism: antimodernism, modified modernism, transmodernism, and ultramodernism, as has already been noted in part by observers of them. For instance, according to the French social theorist Luc Ferry (1990: 312-19), there have been three major movements in relation to modernism: a rejection (returning to the old), an inclusive going beyond, and a summit (an extreme).[23]

Antimodernism; Support for Traditional Order
One reaction to the high modernity of the nineteenth century was to revive with some modifications positions that were set forth in pre-modern or early-

23. Analyses along such a line were made by the sociologist Rosenau (1992) and the demographer Ray (1997) to be cited below, and already before them by the philos-opher-theologian Griffin, who was known to Rosenau. Griffin distinguished between 'constructive' (or 'reconstructive') and 'eliminative' postmodernism (1988: x, xi). Ferry's student Bruno Latour—who specialized in the sociology of science but unfor-tunately wrote in a somewhat obscure style, as he himself admitted (1993: ix)—called the three movements, respectively, antimodern, 'nonmodern' or 'relational', and 'post-modern' (that is, radically modernist). None of these analyses, however, provided a clearly presented comprehensive picture.

modern times, for instance by Aristotle (officially accepted by the Roman Catholic church) or by the Protestant Reformers. In fact, some of those who did so were especially happy to use the word 'postmodern' for, as one of them said, they were 'no longer intimidated by modernity' (Oden 1995: 20).[24]

Strongly antimodern positions rejected major features of modern culture, including many of the conclusions of historical criticism in regard to the Bible and sometimes even the use of money.[25] Socially, antimodernism was often interested in traditional order, especially in the sexual realm; much of it was reserved toward feminism.

Antimoderns did not reject 'freedom', to be sure. Rather, they continued the theme of internal ethical/religious freedom, which had been valued in much of premodernity. Thus, they repeatedly continued a fairly negative attitude toward the body. Furthermore, insofar as they accepted authority, they were low in exercising external negative freedom, that is, they seldom supported independent thinking or behavior.

Antimodern positions are not discussed in the present volume, since they were not remarkably new. Yet their presence needs to be recognized.

Modified Modernism; Mixed Nominalist/Relational Views
Many positions modified nominalism by including relational perspectives. For example, Quine said that nominalism 'would be my position if I could make a go of it' (1985: 199; cf. 1960: 60), but he found that relational concepts were needed for his logic.

The term 'nominalism' could then be redefined so that it would at least accept relations, although not other kinds of general phenomena. This road was adopted early on by R.W. Sellers, who was nominalist in regard to general descriptive terms but accepted the reality of relations (1922: 195; 1932: 155, 171-72, 319, 358). Harty Field was quite strongly nominalist; he sought to do without 'numbers' in physics—since numbers are not purely particular and are thus a problem for nominalism—but he accepted part-whole relations (1980).

Indeed, many of the most widely discussed philosophers of the twentieth century expressed such a mixed perspective or oscillated between the alternatives.[26] Quite a few of them wrote in an obscure style, perhaps as

24. Nancey Murphy, for instance, has described 'postmodern conservative theology' (1997: 113-29). Perhaps one should place among antimoderns the more conservative neo-Aristotelians in France, Germany, and the US (see Benhabib 1990: 332-33; Tepe 1992: 80).

25. See Buss 1999: 205 (for T.S. Eliot) and Karanikas 1969: 56 (for the Agrarians in the Southern US).

26. For a closer analysis, see Chapter 7. Cf. responses to these thinkers described below, 8.4; 9.1.

a consequence of their attempting to hold disparate perspectives together. They will be discussed in Chapter 7.

Transmodernism, Including Relational Theory

Other writers moved more consistently beyond nominalism. From about 1940 on, the word 'postmodern' came to describe such a way. Except for a few anticipations, this usage of the word began with Bernard Bell in 1939. Bell rejected optimistic science, statism (which emphasizes political 'units'), major violent conflict ('no possible modern war can be compatible with [human] welfare', 1939: 175), and intellectual nihilism ('there is no truth, they would seem to say', 5). He proposed instead a sober view of reality as containing evil (ix) and, in affirmative terms, an understanding that 'reality involves not merely activity and reason but also love' (33). He advocated a love of God that leads to love of one's neighbor (49).

In subsequent years, a number of other theoreticians employed the term 'postmodern' in a similar way. For instance, John Randall, Jr., used the term to refer to a science that has room for religion, morality, and aesthetics (1944: 369). From 1964 on, it was claimed by philosophical theologians and by philosophers with a religious interest, influenced in part by Alfred North Whitehead. Among them stood John Cobb and Frederick Ferré (see Griffin *et al.* 1993: 33).

A corresponding use of the term 'postmodern' appeared in 1947 in the abridged version of early volumes of Toynbee's *Study of History*. Working with Toynbee's approval, the editor used the term 'postmodern', followed by a question mark, to describe Western culture after 1875 (1947–57, I: 39). Toynbee used the term in 1954 in a later volume of the full study (1934–61, VIII: 338), although he dated the beginning of the postmodern period slightly later, to about 1900. He characterized this period as one in which the rule of the middle class was countered by the 'rise of an industrial urban class'. That rise contributed strongly, of course, to the formation of welfare societies and thus in part transcended individualism.

The architectural theorist Charles Jencks used the term 'postmodern' similarly in 1977. He was not aware at that time that Ihab Hassan and others had introduced another meaning for the term, one that referred to an outlook that strongly values disorder. As Jencks explained later, he 'used the term to mean the opposite of' what Hassan designated, specifically, 'the end of all avant-garde extremism, the partial return to tradition and the central role of communicating with the public' (1987a: 6). He accepted and valued both historical particularity and a 'universal grammar' (1987a: 8; 1987b: 11-13; 1997: 10, 25).

In a similar way, Bruce Cole and Adelheid Gealt described 'postmodern' visual art as combining modern aspects with older features in a way that seeks to transcend the moment (1989: 323). Beyond art, the postmodernism of Charlene Spretnak wove together Buddhist, Native American, goddess-oriented, biblical, and newer religious perspectives (1991).

However, since in the 1970s the use of the word 'postmodern' became a popular way to refer to radical nominalism (see below), a number of writers adopted the term 'transmodern' for a view that includes both particularity and generality. Perhaps the first to use this word was the literary theorist Petru Dumitriu in 1965. In contrast to modernity—which he described as sometimes optimistic and sometimes splintering or nihilist—he envisioned 'a complex system of ambivalent functions and movements within a sta-tistical-probabilistic knowable world' (1965: 259). As was observed above (4.2), probability is a very important concept for relational theory.

Toward the end of the twentieth century, Enrique Dussel accordingly adopted the description 'transmodern' for his philosophy of liberation. Ini-tially (in 1976, according to his report), he had labeled his view 'postmod-ern', but he switched to the other term in order to avoid confusion (1995: 170). Dussel associated modernity with conquest and capitalism (1995: 12, 117). He urged in their stead a combination of 'alterity' (otherness) with 'solidarity, which is...analogic, syncretic...which bonds center to periph-ery, woman to man, race to race, ethnic group to ethnic group, humanity to earth, and occidental to Third World cultures' (1995: 138).

Similarly, Paul Ray used the designation 'trans-modern' in 1997 for a way of life that combines personal freedom and social concern. Comparable uses of the word by Marc Luyckx, Couze Venn, and David Turnbull to refer to postcolonial developments will be mentioned later (below, 9.2).[27]

The transmodern movement, thus named, was quite broad. Besides the relational tradition to which the present volume is devoted, it is possible to include within its compass a number of other positions, including moderate forms of Aristotelianism.[28]

On the whole, the transmodern stream was connected socially with lib-eration movements, if liberation is taken in an interactive sense, includ-ing both negative and positive aspects (freedom 'from' and freedom 'for').

27. However, Paul Vitz (1998) used the term 'transmodern' for a position that stood fairly close to the 'antimodern' stream; he referred to quite a few thinkers and artists in Europe and the US along this line. Indeed, distinctions between movements are never precise.

28. Among the transmoderns that are not specifically relational, one can locate those neo-Aristotelians who are relatively liberal (e.g., Martha Nussbaum, who, in fact, called her position 'liberal' [1999: 55-80], and probably D.M. Armstrong and Charles Taylor) and a number of others, including Robert Neville. One can also locate within transmodernism a non-Aristotelian version of essentialism, according to which the originating condition (materials, etc.) of an object is 'essential' to it, since it lies behind any future form of that object (see, e.g., Saul Kripke [1980] and Storrs McCall [1994: 245]).

In 1992, Pauline Rosenau described the following concerns as operative within what she called the 'affirmative' version of postmodernism, more or less equivalent to the relational view described in the present study: peace, ecology, feminism, spirituality (sometimes including parapsychology), and an involvement with 'the oppressed, the mentally ill, citizens with disability, the homeless, and the generally disadvantaged' (144).

Perhaps in good part because of such a vision, which reaches beyond those who had been dominant and in many ways continued to be dominant in Western society, relational thinking was prominent in writings by women and postcolonial authors (see Chapters 8 and 9, below). However, it was also present in works by Caucasian males, especially after 1980 (see 7.5).

Ultramodernism: Radical Nominalism

Another stream moved in the opposite direction—toward a radicalized nominalism. As mentioned above (1.1), moderate nominalism had accepted general patterns as secondary realities, usually thought of as arrangements ('laws') by God. Radical nominalism sought to abandon even this level of generality and instead emphasized fragmentation.

In major ways this stream extended Romantic particularism.[29] Yet it went beyond this by pushing aside not only pre-Romantic rationality but also the individual subject that was valued by Romanticism.[30] It often moved toward skepticism and even nihilism (see below, 7.2). In line with what several Marxists had said, Richard Rorty described it as an extreme form of 'bourgeois' irrationalism (1983).[31]

Since this path represented a purified nominalism (thus also Eagleton [1996: 112, 121]), it has been called 'ultramodern' or 'hypermodern' by Jencks and others.[32] Zygmunt Bauman, at a time when he was at least moderately supportive of this position, described it as 'fully developed modernity' (1992: 187; similarly, James Winders 2001: 198).

However, from about 1970 on, several literary critics, including most influentially Hassan, called this radical nominalism 'postmodern'.[33] Hassan's analysis arose out of a background in literary criticism, which had by then revived concerns with design and genre that had largely fallen into abey-

---

29. The link with Romanticism was explicit in Diane Elam 1992, which was favorable to nominalist postmodernism.

30. See below for Foucault (in 1976), Deleuze, and, by implication, skeptics discussed in 7.2.

31. For Marxists, see György Lukács (1953) and Fredric Jameson (1991: postmodernism is 'the cultural logic of late capitalism').

32. E.g. Jencks 1987a: 6; Griffin 1988: 10; Arthur Kroker and David Cook 1988: 243-90.

33. Thus, very fully, in 1982 (1987: 91).

ance during the eighteenth and nineteenth centuries.[34] That kind of literary criticism was 'modern' in the sense of 'recent'. In Hassan's usage, the word 'postmodern' then referred to what others have instead called 'ultramodern'. Incidentally, Hassan did not think that what he called 'postmodernism' represented the culture of his time (the 1970s and 1980s). Rather, he noted at the same time a 'growing spiritual unity of humanity' (1975: xvi). For his own view, he favored a critical pluralism along the lines of James with at least some faith (1987: 86, 181, etc.).

The radically nominalist stream began, like the relational, at the end of the nineteenth century. Its most important early representative was Friedrich Nietzsche. He increasingly emphasized power (a major nominalist theme) and rejected the emerging interactive outlook, including international peace organizations, egalitarianism, socialism, and feminism. Later, radical nominalists were similarly reserved or even hostile toward social democracy and feminism and sometimes toward political involvement as such. Often, they leaned toward anarchism or were ready to accept a fragmenting capitalism in fairly pure form. They were on the whole reluctant to engage in international cooperation. The freedom they valued was primarily negative. (For details, see Chapter 7.)

This perspective was by no means inherently opposed to religion. On the contrary, it could be used to support a need for faith. In fact, some traditional Christians found a point of contact with the ultramodern notion that there are no group-transcending commonalities.[35]

4. *The Relative Numerical Strength of the Major Alternatives in the US*

During the last decades of the twentieth century, quite a few surveys attempted to measure the relative strength of these different orientations in society. Some of these used the term 'post-material' roughly in the sense of 'transmodern'.[36] A useful survey by Paul Ray (1997) indicated that in 1994 the US population included three major groups.

A little over a quarter of the population in Ray's survey were '*traditionalists*'. They valued 'traditional relationships', as these might appear in a small town.

Close to half of the population adhered to '*modernism*', which, Ray said, 'emerged 450 years ago as the governing world view of the urban merchant

34. See Buss 1999: 136-39, for the downgrading of form and genre in the eighteenth and nineteenth centuries. An exception—Hegel's theory of literary forms—was not published by him.

35. MacIntyre stood along this line, as well as a good number of Protestants.

36. The category 'materialism' (see above, Chapter 2, n. 13) seems to combine what Ray will treat separately as 'traditionalism' and 'modernism'.

classes and other creators of the modern economy'. Its orientation ranked high in 'financial materialism', 'success as high priority', and 'cynicism about politics'.

A third group, constituting slightly less than a quarter of the population, were what Ray called '*Trans-Moderns*'. Members of this group ranked high in regard to 'nature as sacred', 'green values', 'ecological sustainability', 'voluntary simplicity', 'pro-feminism in work', 'altruism', 'idealism', and wanting 'to be activist'. They were relatively low in cynicism about politics.

With regard to religion, the three perspectives differed not so much in degree as in kind, although there was a considerable overlap.[37] For traditionalists—86% of whom identify with the 'religious right'—the highest reported religious orientation was 'conservative religious beliefs', most likely literalistic in regard to the Bible (53%). For modernists, the highest was constituted by 'conventional' Catholic or mainline Protestant beliefs (40%). For transmoderns, the largest figures were for a belief that 'religious mysteries exist' (53%) and for an interest in 'spiritual psychology' (40%); transmoderns, however, exhibited an especially wide spectrum of religious orientation, ranging from strongly 'conservative' religious belief (30%) to an absence of religious identification (15%).

Ray furnished a sociological analysis of the respondents. He found that traditionalists were, on the average, older and, perhaps for this reason, lower in education than others. Modernists spanned a wide range of income levels and racial identifications. At the upper end of the socioeconomic ladder, a third were free-market enthusiasts strongly supportive of present society, while two-thirds were 'more cynical and less success-oriented'. Of those who stood economically in the middle or below (about 60% of them), half strove for upward mobility (including many members of ethnic minorities), while the rest were 'alienated and cynical' workers (including especially blue-collar workers who had lost better-paying jobs).[38] Trans-moderns were mostly middle-aged, with relatively few young or old; 60% were women. Their median birth year of 1954 means that the majority were either young adults or children during the 1960s. Ray described less than half of trans-moderns as 'core' members, who tended to be located in the upper-middle class.[39]

It is possible to modify Ray's classification in the following way: If one subdivides modernists into those who are fairly cynical and those who are

37. For this aspect, see also Ray and Anderson 2000: 28, 190.

38. In Europe, the New Right drew largely on the 'less secure segments of the working class' (Inglehart *et al.* 1998: 13).

39. A similar location was noted above (2.1) for 'postmaterialists', which may largely constitute the same group.

not, one obtains, in Ray's terms, four close-to equal-size formations: traditionalists, ordinary modernists, cynical modernists, and trans-moderns. These correspond somewhat closely, although not perfectly, to the divisions that have been described on the intellectual level: antimoderns, moderate moderns, ultramoderns, and transmoderns.

It can be seen from this that, in the US, full-fledged transmoderns constituted a minority. Their educational level was relatively high, so that they were influential in public discussion. Yet they could not muster enough votes in elections to dominate the political scene. Whatever successes they had in politics came from allying with others at the lower end of the socio-economic scale, whose interests stood within the sphere of transmodern concern, while another coalition joined traditionalists with many nonpoor modernists.

5. *Summary*

The period after c. 1880 CE witnessed not only moves toward freedom but also terrible horrors. Many of them were perpetrated by movements that were group-particularist (National Socialist or Marxist-Leninist-Stalinist). In the US, there was both a free-wheeling economic self-centeredness, even nihilism, and a strong law-and-order attitude (with excessive incarceration). International interactions were ambiguous in character. Thus it would be difficult to argue that this period was, overall, 'better' than previous ones.

Within a society such as the US, major divergences existed. There were tensions between the following groups: 'antimoderns', who sought to restrain external negative freedom, especially in the sexual realm; moderate 'modernists', who were happy to continue a competitive economic system, although they supported moderate social services; 'transmoderns', who favored an active concern for human beings and for the environment together with non-economic values (such as self-direction); and 'ultra-moderns', who reveled in fragmentation and were often cynical or skeptical. These groups or movements were not rigidly separated, yet tensions between them were pronounced.

Chapter 7

STRUGGLES BETWEEN RELATIONAL THINKING AND
NOMINALISM IN THE WORK OF CAUCASIAN MALES

Different versions of nominalism were prominent among rivals to relational
theory. Some of them were quite radical. To be sure, Peirce rightly observed
that no one has ever 'set forth nominalism in an absolutely thoroughgoing
manner; and it is safe to say that no one ever will, unless it be to reduce it to
absurdity' (Peirce 1982–, II: 484 [1871]). In fact, a nominalist bent repeatedly entered into a compromise with relational theory, so that the resulting
hybrids may be described as 'mixed' positions. Such positions—including
those of Heidegger, Levinas, Lyotard, Foucault, and Derrida—require close
attention, so that one can see how they intertwined, or oscillated between,
relational and nominalist perspectives. Since it is not possible to understand
the mixed positions without considering those that are more purely nominalist, they require at least brief notice as well.

Virtually all nominalist or seminominalist theories of form were set forth
by Caucasian males. This fact was probably not due to their biological constitution as males, for, as has already been seen and will be seen further,
some Caucasian and most non-Caucasian males adopted a relational outlook.
It seems, rather, that many Caucasian males were not ready to make a sharp
break with the predominantly nominalist tradition to which they were accus-
tomed: After all, philosophers regularly gave attention to the thinkers of
the preceding three centuries, while feminism threatened their privileged
position.

1. Power-Oriented Nominalism

Power has always been highlighted one-sidedly in nominalism, since reasonableness and sensitivity to reality are rejected as bases for ethics. In this
tradition, power is readily seen as 'power-over', domination.

In theistic versions, God's power was emphasized.[1] Most theist nominalists, to be sure, held that God established general patterns on a secondary basis (see above, 1.1). Since they can be manipulated by human

---

1.   See, e.g., Dupré 1993: 123, 130. Thus, also, K. Barth (see Buss 1999: 281).

beings, there is room for human power. Human self-assertion (including 'reason'), however, came to be increasingly emphasized in high modernity (c. 1700–1900 CE); this undercut the idea of a God.

Atheism at first did not threaten a dissolution of order, for the idea of natural law still held sway (see above, 1.3). Yet that idea gradually dissolved during the nineteenth century. Non-theist nominalism had the following three options: (1) a positive affirmation that emphasizes human power; (2) skepticism; and (3) some form of negative affirmation, or 'nihilism'. Nietzsche pursued primarily the first of these three options.

Nietzsche favored neither skepticism nor nihilism as an absolute, although he is often thought to have done so. Rather, he developed a positive perspective that increasingly emphasized self-assertive power, especially in notes he did not publish.[2]

An intellectual aspect of this orientation was that Nietzsche rejected objectivity. That stance had affinity with relational theory in that it did not separate scientific knowledge from questions of value or commitment. In contrast to a relational view, however, Nietzsche based his rejection of objectivity not on a sense of connectedness but on self-assertiveness by the observer. Nietzsche already valued self-assertiveness in history writing in a moderate way, contra objectivity, in 1874 (1967–, III/1: 289-90). More strongly, he declared in 1888 that objectivity militates against 'individual interests..."egoism" ' (1967–, VI/3: 185).

With his strong emphasis on power, Nietzsche rejected the ideals of the emerging interactive outlook, including international peace organizations, egalitarianism, socialism, and feminism.[3] For instance, in 1887 he said that he opposed 'democracy, the substituting of international arbitration courts for war, an equality of rights for women, and a religion of pity' (1967–, VI/2: 421 ['Genealogy of Morals', §25]). In the last work he published (1889), Nietzsche described freedom as conflictual. In contrast to 'Christians, cows, females...and other democrats...the free human being is a *warrior*' (VI/3: 133-34 ['Twilight of the Idols', §38]). To be sure, this conception did not necessarily imply violent aggressiveness (cf. VIII/1: 221). Nor did it refer to a forcefulness that accomplishes a task in the future—an idea undercut by his theme of 'eternal recurrence' (cf. Hatab 2005: 128).

Those who claimed Nietzsche as their forerunner could adopt either individualism or a pronounced nationalism. Both of these orientations focused on units (particulars), although they are of different size.[4] Furthermore,

2. But see the statement by Nietzsche quoted above, 5.4.
3. See, e.g., Appel 1999 and Burgard 1994: 8-9, although Burgard saw things to like in Nietzsche.
4. See Aschheim 1992; Ferry and Renault 1997 (on French followers of Nietzsche, right and left both, often with authoritarian tendencies [e.g. 106; cf. 159]); and Irena Makarushka (1994, fairly individualistic).

Nietzsche fascinated many who followed him only on certain points. Among them stood racists (such as Nazis) and some feminists who valued his emphasis on self-assertion.[5]

Not devoted to interactive freedom but also not strictly racist was the following statement by Oswald Spengler in 1922, inspired, he said, by Nietzsche:[6]

> In history it is always a matter of life, of race, of the triumph of the will to power, and not of the victory of truth... World history is world judgment: it has always justified the stronger and the fuller life, sure of itself, assigning it a right to existence, independently of whether that has seemed right to a wakeful consciousness; it has always sacrificed truth and justice to power and race [although race was not defined in biological terms] and has condemned to death those human beings and those peoples for whom truth was more important than action, and justice more essential than power.[7]

This sentiment was by no means due merely to Germany's defeat in World War I. A sharp expression of this view (harking to Nietzsche, but more violent) had already been expressed by the Italian Futurists, who paved the way for fascism, in 1909: 'We want to glorify war...militarism, patriotism, the destructive gesture of the anarchists...and contempt for women... to demolish museums, libraries, fight morality' (Lichtheim 1972: 39).

Of course, Nietzsche was not the cause but, rather, an early example of radical nominalism. The fact that the various elements of his perspective, including the more extreme versions that were jotted in notes he did not publish, had major resonance implies that there was a widespread readiness for them. Indeed, Nietzsche was cited frequently. In France, he became influential at least by the 1920s, especially for Bataille, who objected to finding 'form' since this concept is insufficiently anarchic (1970–88, I: 217 [1929]).

2. *Skepticism as an Issue*

Some forms of radical nominalism inclined toward skepticism. In fact, the logician C.I. Lewis gave reason to believe that 'the only consistent nominalist is also...a skeptic' (1970: 331 [1953]). After all, if reality is

5. For feminists, see, for instance, essays made available in K. Oliver and Pearsall 1998.

6. The work (published in 1918–22) was largely written before World War I, but the conclusion (cited here) may have been added at a later stage; Spengler acknowledged indebtedness to Nietzsche in the preface to the second edition.

7. In the 1930s, in partial criticism of Hitler, Spengler said that 'race' is not to be taken in terms of a biologically pure one (cf. Felken 1988). That position was in line with Nietzsche 1967–, VI/2: 80. Yet Spengler's thesis was otherwise valued by Nazis; Hitler echoed it in 1923 (1980: 887).

fundamentally disconnected, how will one know any part of reality other than oneself? In the fifth century BCE, the atomist Democritus had already expressed some strong skepticism, since human beings are 'separated from reality' (fragments 6-8).

Similar to skepticism, although not as thoroughly negative, is questioning the ability of reason to obtain truth. Such questioning could lead to a reliance on faith or on some other kind of intuition.

Skeptical 'relativism' (holding that one view is as good as another) was a specter in Europe and the US from the end of the nineteenth century on. For instance, Francis Abbot mentioned this kind of 'relativism' as a problem already in 1885 (23); Husserl spoke of 'skeptical relativism' in 1901 (1950–, I: 118-58). In fact, during the years from 1890 to 1930, a questioning of human reason was present in the idea that science should be thought of as 'conventional hypothesis' and in a sense that reality cannot 'be conceived as an orderly system' (H.S. Hughes 1958: 109, 428, 430).

Although a 'crisis of reason' antedated World War I (Batnitzky 2000: 4; similarly, Heidegger 1950: 15), pervasive irrationalism was especially strong in Germany and Italy between the two World Wars (Gay 1968; F. Stern 1999: 49).[8] In Italy, Benito Mussolini declared that fascism is a 'super-relativist movement', although in practical rather than theoretical terms. He characterized relativism as follows: 'By equalizing ideologies, all equally fictional, the modern relativist concludes that everyone has the right to create his own and to insist on it with all the energy of which he is capable'. In adopting such a view, he said, Italian fascism is, following Nietzsche, 'a formidable creation of an individual and national "will to power" ' (1924: 374, 377). Adolph Hitler is reported to have made an even stronger statement in the early 1930s:

> We stand at the end of the age of reason.... Our revolution is not merely political or social; we stand before a huge turning-over, in moral conceptions and in the mental orientation of human beings. We end an erroneous path of humanity.... Conscience is a Jewish invention... There is no truth, either in a moral or in a scientific sense (Rauschning 1940: 210).

Whether Hitler actually made this statement cannot be verified, but the fact that the report was made in 1940 shows that such a set of ideas was available at that time.

Skepticism waxed and waned during the twentieth century. In the US, a definite skepticism was present in the field of historiography from about

---

8.   According to Forman 1971: 38, 'Spengler epitomizes…a set of attitudes, widely diffused among educated Germans, explicitly hostile to the ideology of the exact sciences' after World War I. Cynicism during this period has been described (although one-sidedly) by Sloterdijk (1983) as a background for Nazism. A study of German irrationalism, with its antecedents, was presented by György Lukács (1953).

1910 until about 1940. This was replaced by renewed confidence in objectivity, largely in reaction against both Nazism and Stalinism (cf. above, 5.4). After 1970, however, severe doubts about truthful knowledge again emerged (see Novick 1988). Expressing the sense of fragmentation that created such doubts, the relatively skeptical historian Keith Jenkins said that in '[nominalist] postmodern times, nothing connects' (1997: 10).[9]

Toward the end of the twentieth century, in fact, even unrelenting skepticism appeared in the English-speaking world. On a nominalist basis, Peter Unger proposed that 'nobody can ever *know*, or be *reasonable* or *justified* in believing much more than hardly anything, including this very thing' (1975: 247, 308 [emphasis his]).[10] That is classical 'Pyrrhonian' skepticism, which doubts even itself. (It was attributed to Pyrrho [c. 300 BCE] and espoused by Michel de Montaigne in 1580 CE [1992: 385].) Hilary Lawson, calling his view 'postmodern', similarly stated that 'if we have knowledge, it is that there can be none' (1989: xi) and that this view, too, 'is not intended to be held' (1985: 7). For Paul Mann, a Pyrrhonian path led to 'anethics', that is, 'neither ethics nor anti-ethics' (1999: 199). The fact that this path was also self-canceling was a situation that he accepted (xvi).

However, not all skepticism was radical. Some moderate forms of it were called 'irrealism' (thus, Nelson Goodman)[11] or 'antirealism'. For instance, Goodman spoke of 'worldmaking' rather than of a person's seeing the world in a certain way (1978). Antirealism was explored by Michael Dummett, a prominent theist philosopher, as well as by nontheists (see Dummett 1978: 146). A recurring question in such antirealism was whether there is a (recognizable) world 'independent' of oneself. This question is, of course, nominalist, for in a relational perspective (as well as in some others), there is no total independence.

Although nominalism readily inclines toward skepticism, the two are not strictly correlated. Theistic nominalism is normally not skeptical (since it relies on faith), and skepticism may have some other base. For instance, in ancient Greece the Platonic tradition had a skeptical phase that was facilitated by the exploratory nature of Plato's dialogues. Thus one must consider, in addition to a strictly theoretical (such as nominalist) ground, a sociological reason for skepticism.

Sociologically, it appears that skepticism is a transition phenomenon.[12] It is true that there is always some sort of transition underway. This fact may

9. However, later, in 2000, Jenkins described postmodernism in more affirmative terms.

10. Unger later changed his position considerably.

11. Thus, Nelson Goodman in 1996 (203); more cautiously, earlier (1978: x). Goodman was nominalist in logic, although not in ontology.

12. Thus, already, Franz Brentano (1926: 8-19).

account for the presence of at least mild skepticism at all times. Sharp and extended skepticism, however, appears to be associated with a major social or cultural change. One can then ask whether skepticism arises when an old view has become tired. Skepticism would then serve to prepare the way toward a newer outlook and would in this sense be creative.[13]

The suggestion that skepticism is creative, however, is contradicted by historical observation. In Western philosophy, skepticism flourished for several centuries from about 300 BCE on and was prominent again in the sixteenth and seventeenth centuries. In each case, the philosophy that became most widely accepted after the time of skepticism—Platonism and Stoicism in the first case and nominalism in the second—was formulated before that time. Thus, in these cases, skepticism did not prepare the way for something new. Rather, skepticism seems to have reflected a situation of uncertainty in view of rival positions. In some cases, it may have served as a defense against the new tide.

These considerations fit twentieth-century developments. When skepticism became prominent around 1900 CE, relational thinking was in the process of emerging. The reappearance of skepticism in the 1970s came on the heels of the idealistic upheaval of the 1960s.

3. *Nihilism and Seminihilism*

Nihilism is different from skepticism. Intellectually and emotionally, it affirms denials. However, it includes a great many positions that diverge from each other.

Donald Crosby (1988) listed the following kinds of nihilism: (1) political (opposing all social order); (2) moral, with three varieties: (a) rejecting morality as such, (b) refusing to state moral principles, (c) treating those principles that one does hold as arbitrary; (3) cosmic (denying that the cosmos has meaning); and (4) existential (holding that one's life is meaningless). Of these kinds, the third, cosmic nihilism, has become the most widely accepted. Various versions of the others began to appear in the West from the middle of the nineteenth century on.[14]

Twentieth-century nihilism (in its various forms) radicalized the nominalism of the preceding period, as Albert Camus pointed out.[15] According

---

13. This interpretation may be implied in Linda Hutcheon's view (1988: xiii, 231) that a critical questioning 'from within' leads to a new position.

14. For Mikhael Bakunin in 1842—often thought of as a beginning point for nihilism—destruction was not an end in itself, however, but a step toward creation. In Asia, something that might be called 'nihilism' had been set forth by Buddhism, which made an impact on some versions of European nihilism, more than can be shown here.

15. Camus 1951, Chaps. 2, 3; thus, also, Lyotard 1979a, ch. 10.

to Camus, nihilism logically leads to suicide or murder; in its stead, he embraced 'absurdity'. This overcomes nihilism by placing a positive value on a simultaneously yes-and-no attitude toward life ('rebellion') and by acknowledging commonality with other human beings, who share absurdity (1942; 1951, chs. 1, 5). In contrast, said Camus, the nihilist says, 'We are alone' (1951, ch. 2, end).

Most nihilists wanted the lack of meaning to be openly acknowledged. For instance, the Romanian E.M. Cioran held that 'the freedom to kill ourselves...grants us a strength and a pride to triumph over the loads which overwhelm us' (1949: 57). Accepting the absence of pre-given meaning in a different way, Fred Newman and Lois Holzman said: 'Neither life nor development require meaning... We have come to the end of meaning and development even as we must (and can) continue making meaning and developing' (1997: 163-64). Thus, like many others, they said that, although there 'is' no meaning, one can make meaning.

Other nihilists wanted to hide their perspective. For instance, Loyal Rue held that nihilism should be acknowledged by intellectual elites but hidden from others; for, although nihilism is true in its belief that 'the universe is blind and aimless', it is culturally maladaptive (1994: 3, 279). He thus advocated a 'noble lie' (5). Acknowledging indebtedness to 'Norwegian-American Lutheranism'—his cultural background—he called for 'care' for all living beings without grounding it intellectually (278).

Nevertheless, political or social nihilism became attractive on a popular level. During the second quarter of the twentieth century, heroic death mysticism—almost a worship of death—was prevalent in German culture.[16] Popular nihilism in the US has already been reported in Chapter 6.

Heidegger, a Seminihilist
Heidegger, one of the most influential thinkers of the twentieth century, believed that no one would doubt that nihilism was the 'normal condition' of humanity in his time and held, in fact, that humanity and nihilism belong together (1950: 13, 31). Yet the *nihil* ('nothing', negativity) represented for him only one side of reality; relationality formed another aspect. His thought can thus be described as seminihilist.

Heidegger was trained in Catholic theology. In 1919, he rejected Catholicism but aligned himself with Protestant thinkers. In the early 1930s, he became anti-Christian. After that, he took up a position that he described as positively and negatively post-Christian (1938/39: 415).

16. I remember this from my youth, spent as a German in China. See, for instance, Peter Gay 1968: 81, 126, 139 on right-wing students 'intoxicated with death'; 140 on suicide novels.

In *Being and Time* (1927), Heidegger presented a view of the 'ontology' of conscious (human) existence, which (in line with Fichte 1806: 77-80) he called *Dasein*, literally 'being [consciously] there'.[17] His analysis of *Dasein* was in relationally dynamic terms, including 'being in the world', 'availability' (something is 'at hand'), 'being-with', 'care' (being concerned about something), and 'calling-on'. Some of these themes were clearly drawn from religious tradition as well as from unpublished phenomenological writings by Husserl that Heidegger edited and published in 1928.

Together with these themes, Heidegger set forth a quasi-nihilist position by speaking of death not merely as the cessation of life that is to be accepted as an aspect of finitude but rather as a directional end toward which one moves, expressing a form of the death mysticism then current. In 1929, he said that *Dasein*'s 'holding itself into the Nothing' brings about both anxiety and transcendence. The positive aspect—transcendence—is constituted by a conscious relation to being, as a contrast to nonbeing, and includes a relation to self (1929: 113-15).

A noteworthy feature of *Being and Time* was that Heidegger turned the notion of 'possibility'—which in phenomenology described that toward which the mind is directed—into a central category for the directionality of (human) existence. Specifically, he described existence as a 'throwing of oneself into one's own actual possibility' (1927, §60). This possibility is not 'pre-given' but is produced in one's resolve. Existence should, then, be understood not as a (solid) 'present' (§6) but as a movement that is open, although death belongs definitively to it (§53).

Being and Time was oriented primarily toward the individual; for instance, being toward death was described in individualistic terms. However, the work was far from solipsistic, for *Dasein*'s resolve also allows for the fulfilling of possibility by others. Furthermore, Heidegger's opposition to Germany's republican organization after World War I (Safranski 1998: 292) exhibited a reluctance toward individual freedom, and *Being and Time* already referred to 'folk' as a collectivity (1927, §74).

Group particularism, however—together with the idea of a leading individual—came to the fore when Hitler came to power in 1933. In an address delivered early in 1934, Heidegger said that all parts of society are bound together 'in the one great will of the State', which is embodied in the 'overarching will' of the *Führer*. In him, the German people (*Volk*) constitute an 'emerging unity' (1934a: 232-37; cf. Faye 2005: 187-247).

To be sure, Heidegger came into conflict with some policies of the Nazi party. In theoretical terms, he pointed out that we are 'a' people, not 'the'

17. Prior to Fichte and often later, the term *Dasein* referred simply to 'existence', human or otherwise, without an implication of consciousness. The German idiom '*da sein*' often means 'being consciously present' (cf. the English 'I was there').

people (1934b: 60). This judgment contradicted a statement by Fichte, a favorite of Nazism's supporters because of his emphasis on unity and on German existence as exemplary.[18] Still, Heidegger believed in 'the inner truth and greatness' of National Socialism (which has 'nothing in common' with what then went by that name) and anticipated that Germany, as a 'metaphysical people', would provide spiritual energy in contrast to the technological orientation of Russia and the US (1976–, XL: 208, 40-41 [1935]); he continued in this belief until after the end of World War II.[19]

Indeed, from the end of 1934 on, and more definitively in 1936 (Heidegger 1946: 313), Heidegger moved beyond one-sided group particularism. In private notes he focused on the dynamics of 'being'. This theme was not altogether new, for both at the beginning and end of *Being and Time*, he had characterized *Dasein* as a form of existence that is concerned with 'being', in contrast to non-thinking beings that have no such concern. However, Heidegger now explicitly distinguished between viewing 'being' as a 'metaphysical' abstraction from ordinary beings and viewing it—as he would hereafter—as reality that underlies beings in the plural and is in contact with the realm of the 'deities' (1934/35, *passim*, at least in nuce; 1938: 428, 436 [1936]). (In unpublished manuscripts, although not in later publications, he often represented this deep reality by an old spelling, *Seyn*, which had been used by Fichte and Schelling.)

In this view, being has an engaged side, which Heidegger called the *Ereignis*, 'occurrence'.[20] *Ereignis* has its 'own' (*eigen*) character and is a singular reality, but it embraces all lesser events. As Heidegger eventually said explicitly, it constitutes a *singulare tantum*, a 'great particular' (1957: 29). Already from about 1936 on, Heidegger always spoke of the *Ereignis* in the singular.[21] Heidegger emphasized that there is a 'difference' between being and beings, but the 'occurrence' (*Ereignis*) of being has the property of 'identity'; it 'unifies' humanity and being (1957: 47, 31).

Heidegger thus stood in a tradition of monist particularism, which treats comprehensive reality as a unit (see above, 1.1). This tradition had been pursued, at least in part, by the philosophical Idealists Fichte, Schelling, and Hegel and by the mixed relational-nominalist and prominently anti-Nazi theologian Karl Barth.[22] Barth (whose work Heidegger knew) described

18. See Fichte 1808, seventh lecture; Ott 1988: 152; Sluga 1993.

19. See Bambach 2003. Heidegger supported National Socialism as a spiritual (supposedly antitechnological) movement as late as 1953, according to a letter reported by Ettinger 1995: 99.

20. The translation 'occurrence' covers the collective meaning of *Ereignis* better than does 'event', a common rendering. (*Das Ereignis*, in any case, transcends ordinary 'occurrences'; cf. Polt 2005: 385-86.)

21. Earlier uses of the word *Ereignis* by Heidegger were more informal.

22. Fichte's and Hegel's tendencies toward monism have been mentioned. For Barth

Jesus Christ as the great singular dynamic *Ereignis*, which underlies all (at least, all 'good') particular events.[23] Heidegger, to be sure, did not link the *Ereignis* with Jesus, if only because an 'ontic' (concrete, specific) item did not, in his view, belong to philosophy (1976–, IX: 47-67 [1927]).

According to Heidegger, the *Ereignis* brings God to human beings. Using terminology employed by Barth and by Rudolf Bultmann (friend of both Barth and Heidegger), Heidegger said that it 'calls' the human being, who accepts in response to such a call the rule of 'the last [that is, ultimate] god, the great quiet' (1936/37: 24-26, 31, 34).[24] However, opposing Christianity as well as ultranationalism and Idealism, Heidegger rejected what he characterized as a false transcendence that has been sought in the Christian 'God', in a 'folk', or in 'ideas'.

In Heidegger's view, being and beings have in common an involvement with time, or movement, as had already been suggested in the last sentence of *Being and Time*. In attributing movement and thus some sort of time to ultimate reality, Heidegger differed from Fichte (1806: 77-80) but agreed with other monist particularists mentioned. He viewed the fundamental movement of being, *Geschichte* (using the ordinary German word for 'history'), as the 'deep ground' for *Historie*, ordinary events as seen by an external observer.[25]

see Buss 1999: 281-82. Cunningham has identified versions of nominalist monism in Fichte, Hegel, Schelling, Heidegger, and others (including, it seems, Barth) (2002: 127, 185, 236, 250).

23. Connections with Schelling have been discussed by Seidel (1999, 2001). Barth, well known for his opposition to Nazism in the Hitler era, called Jesus Christ an *urgeschichtlich* ('protohistorical') *Ereignis* (1919: 65, 223; 1927: 43, 230, 281; 1932: 201, 343). Similarly, Rudolf Bultmann, who was influenced by Karl Barth and with whom Heidegger interacted closely during the 1920s, spoke of Jesus Christ as *Ereignis* (1926: 53, 194-95; 1958, I [1933!]: 64 [1926], 106 [1927], 134, 144 [1928]; 1958, II: 11 [1931]; and in later works mentioned in Seidel 2002.)

24. For the background of this usage of the term 'last' (ultimate), see Barth 1924: 37, 56-60 ('last' is equated with 'first' as ultimate); Bultmann 1926: 53, 110; 1958, I (1933): 49, 51 (1926, discussing Barth 1924), 106 (1927), 143-44 (1928), 165, 171 (1929); 1958, II: 11 (1931). More generally, see Coriando 1998; Philipse 1998: 189, 235.

25. Heidegger 1934/35: 144-46; 1935: 40; 1936/37: 9, 10, 78, 90, 106; 1938: 453, 493-94, 507 (1936). As soon as 1928 (274), Heidegger spoke of 'protohistory' as underlying ordinary processes. A distinction between *Geschichte* as fundamental movement (*Ursprung*, 'origin') and *Historie* as surface development was made in Barth's commentary on Romans, 1919 (7, 20, 43, 59, 75, 100, 101) and 1922 (5, 6, 117; cf. 1932: 343), with a partially Platonic, but dynamic ontology (cf. Barth 1922: vii); this work, which created a sensation, was known to Heidegger (Bambach 1995: 200; cf. Barash 2003: 129-30, 133, 153). Heidegger's distinction between *Geschichte* and *Historie* was not strongly grounded ontologically before 1936 (1919/20: 256; 1920/21: 125; 1927, §§73, 76; 1934b: 78, 90; it was somewhat more so in 1934/35: 144-47); the distinction had older roots, especially in the work of Kierkegaard (cf. Seidel 2001: 409, 413), without a monist conceptuality.

Heidegger held that the movement of being has a tragic dimension. In *Being and Time*, he had described how individuals regularly lose themselves in superficial activities; he had not thought that this process was avoidable but had asserted that the process of losing oneself is inherent in existence, something to be wrestled with rather than avoided (1927, §38). From the mid-1930s on, he described a similar process on the level of collective history. In large-scale ordinary history, he said, being is 'forgotten'. The forgetting takes place, above all, in technology and, more generally, in science and in metaphysics (1950: 343; 1954a: 37-65). Heidegger did not imply that these ways should be opposed—on the contrary, they should be accepted and pursued within their limits—but he held that their problematic character should be recognized (1959b: 24-28; 1957: 33, 51-69).

Although Heidegger had this tragic view of history, he was far from pessimistic. In fact, he repeatedly cited Friedrich Hölderlin's poetic statement, based on a religious motif, that 'where danger grows, what rescues also grows' (1949: 71, 73; 1950: 273; 1954a: 29). For participation in rescue, Heidegger rejected self-assertive striving in technology and science in favor of 'waiting' (1959b: 37 [1944/45]). This involves a calm 'letting be' of (ordinary) 'things', which is not quietude but makes possible 'the creation of works that last' (1959b: 28).

At the same time, Heidegger held that the realization-of-Being (*Ereignis*) by its very nature 'removes itself'; that is, it makes itself unreachable or questionable (1954b: 10).[26] Heidegger could symbolize this situation by crossing out the word 'being' (1950: 34). This crossing-out was not a simple negation, for he would also cross out the word 'nihil' (1950: 31). He could even equate 'being' with 'the nihil' (1938/40: 140). Being is thus complex; in fact, the 'mystery' of the nihil represents one side of the recognition even of technological objects (1959b: 26).

According to Heidegger, a connection with Being does appear in language. He saw in speech, and especially in poetry, a counter to the forgetting of Being (1938: 510; 1950: 287, 294-95; 1954a: 36; 1959a: 219). He regarded true 'thinking' as a form of poetry, different from science (1950: 303; 1954b: 9-10). To be sure, speech is based on, and returns to, silence (1938: 510; 1959a: 215-16).

Insofar as speech is relational, Heidegger participated in relational thinking. A relational outlook appeared more specifically in Heidegger's reflections on theology (1938: 439). In these reflections he participated in the grammatical-dialogical tradition by distinguishing between second-person and third-person speech.[27] He referred to God as a reality that one cannot

---

26. Similarly, for God, Barth 1932: 175, 348, 383.

27. Heidegger knew the journal Brenner from 1911 on (Kisiel 2002: 4, 26) and may thus have been familiar with Ebner's work (see above, 3.5, 6, for Ebner and

calculate or talk about (1936/37: 405; 1950: 294-95; 1957: 71). Consequently, he doubted the god of 'metaphysics', to whom, indeed, one cannot
'pray' or 'sacrifice' (1957: 70; cf. 1954a: 27).

Third-person metaphysics, an objectifying speech about ultimate reality,
was for Heidegger the key intellectual form of nihilism (1950: 32). That did
not mean for him that metaphysics should be abandoned. Rather, Heidegger
held that, just as nihilism in general cannot be overcome by human beings
in the sense of leaving it behind (1950: 31), so, too, metaphysics—which
'belongs to the nature of humanity'—cannot be avoided, although one can
make moves toward overcoming it (1954a: 71-78).

The practical significance of Heidegger's developing perspective can be
stated in terms of his views of 'freedom'. In 1927 (*Being and Time*), his
idea that *Dasein* throws itself into its own possibility contained a negative
element—freedom 'from' determination—but Heidegger spoke at the same
time both of freedom 'for' death and 'for' a call from other beings (1927,
§§53, 58, 74). In 1933, he rejected 'academic freedom' as too individualistic and equated freedom to follow one's own law with following the law of
one's people as it is expressed by its leader (1933: 113). Later, he described
'freedom' in quasi-religious terms as an openness to the reality of beings,
letting them be (1943: 186-93), with the nihil present in its mystery.

Baudrillard, Embracing Nihilism
Baudrillard has often been considered to be the nominalist postmodern *par
excellence*, although he himself has preferred the description 'ultramodern'
(Hegarty 2004: 3-5). In his post-Marxist period (after c. 1972), he described
himself as a nihilist or, at least, as a would-be nihilist, since absolute nihilism may well be impossible (1981: 231). Indeed, he thought of the culture
of his time as nihilist in that simulation has taken the place of reality.

Specifically, Baudrillard characterized the state of affairs at that time as
one that came 'after the orgy'. He described this orgy as the endpoint of
'the explosive movement of modernity, a liberation in all domains: political liberation, sexual liberation, liberation of productive forces, liberation
of destructive forces, liberation of women, liberation of the child, liberation of unconscious drives, the liberation of art' (1990: 11). Clearly, for him
these movements constituted the endpoint of modernity. What can one do
now, in 'postmodernity' (1981: 231)?[28] 'We can only simulate the orgy and
the liberation now...all the finalities of the liberation are already behind us'
(1990: 11).

Wittgenstein). However, others (including Bultmann) also rejected 'objectifying'
speech about God (Barash 2003: 140).

28. Baudrillard dated modernity to the nineteenth century (1981: 231) and the early
part of the twentieth (1989: 40).

According to his analysis, current 'simulation' takes place in technology—which, in his view (like that of Heidegger) removes one from reality—and in the spectacle of television.[29] In such simulation, non-referential language has become God, with phallic (self-assertive?) presence (1976: 305, etc.). It has eternal significance, for unlike meaning—hope for which is now lost—'appearances are immortal, invulnerable to the nihilism of meaning and nonmeaning' (1981: 236).

The reality that Baudrillard considered to have been murdered was not positive knowledge. On the contrary, what has been killed is an awareness of mystery, that is, of the fact that beings cannot be known (2000: 70-74). Nevertheless, the 'murder' that has taken place was not taken as absolute. Rather, he expressed 'radiant optimism' of the kind to which Hölderlin had referred in speaking of the correlation of danger and rescue. He believed that 'today the object wakes up and reacts, determined to keep its secret alive' in pervasive themes of indeterminacy, uncertainty, relativism, and non-realism (2000: 76, 81).

Baudrillard supported this affirmation of mystery by calling on the insight of relational theory that 'in relations between things there is always a hiatus, a distortion, a rift' so that 'at the core of every human being and everything there is...a fundamentally inaccessible secret' (2000: 71, 80). He did not, however, join this theme with its complement, that in relations there is also partial connectivity and thus partial knowledge. Instead, he said that 'our task is clear: we must make that world ever more unintelligible, ever more enigmatic' (2000: 83).

It is not surprising, then, that in politics Baudrillard favored negative rather than positive or interactive freedom. Insofar as he had a program, it was strongly conflictual. For instance, he declared that 'we will fight obscenity with its own weapons' (1983: 7). In the revolt of May 1968, he primarily valued the anarchic and rebellious side (1989: 43). He noted with dismay that subsequent culture contained the 'gentle ideologies' of 'human rights...antiracism, the antinuclear movement, and the environment' and 'rediscovered love, selflessness, togetherness, international compassion, and the individual tremolo' (1989: 43).

In regard to the role of women, Baudrillard thought, in line with a traditional stereotype, that 'femininity is the principle of uncertainty' (1979: 25). He argued that 'the women's movement' has failed to recognize that women's effective power lies in 'seduction', which 'takes from discourse its sense and turns it from its truth' (18, 77).

---

29. This idea built on Guy Debord's notion of 'spectacle'; before 1988, however, Debord was optimistic that the unreal 'spectacle' dominant in society could be overcome (Jappe 1999: 118, 133). Baudrillard argued that the Gulf War was a dramatic simulation (R.J. Lane 2000: 95-97).

In the area of social action, Baudrillard was opposed to 'sexist, racist, ethnic, or cultural discrimination'—which, he held, reflect the death of otherness—but he rejected 'politically correct' efforts to counteract victimization or disabilities. He was unhappy about a 'blackmailing into responsibility' (with the aim of preventing AIDS) and about criticisms of the death penalty, for in his view a 'refusal to risk' is 'nihilism' of the kind he rejected (1995: 182-94). In short, he was opposed not only to 'whitewashing violence'—failing to recognize its presence—but also to 'exterminating all germs' (1990: 88).[30]

Vattimo, A Faith-Based Nihilist

Vattimo also espoused nihilism, viewing Nietzsche's and Heidegger's thoughts as antecedents. Rejecting skeptical 'relativism' (1992: 38, 119), he asserted—not merely suggested as a possibility—'the senselessness of reality' (1992: 95).

In line with power-orientation, he held that reality is fundamentally one of 'force'. However, he did not argue for an ethic based on force, but held that 'once violence is uncovered, it no longer achieves its aim' (1992: 98). He believed that 'nihilism, the discovery that alleged "values" and metaphysical structures are just a play of forces', undermines hierarchies (1993: 93-94 [1980]) and that 'one of the effects of nihilism may well be to undermine the reasons by which violence is justified and nourished' (1997: 29). Consequently, nihilism leads to distancing oneself from the will to live, thereby leading to 'compassion' (1992: 102-103).

Vattimo thus adopted what Nietzsche had decried as Christian nihilism. Indeed, he believed that nihilism needs to be seen within the horizon of the Christian doctrine of Incarnation (1997: 54; 1998: 93), for this doctrine includes the idea of the 'kenosis' or self-emptying of Christ, who, according to Phil. 2:7, divested himself of divine powers to become the human being Jesus. Seeing 'the history of Being as kenotic' (1999: 39, 68), Vattimo welcomed 'postmodern' nihilism (1992: 5, 42) as a movement toward 'weak' thought, one that does not claim firm truth. While force is fundamental to reality, kenosis uncovers this fact and thereby makes it less harmful.

His view of history was, then, fairly optimistic. Although he did not think that the world had necessarily become better, he observed that 'modern anticlericalism, founded on the self-assurance of scientist and historicist reason that saw no limit to total domination, has come to an end', in Italy as well as elsewhere. He noted with approval the popularity of 'many "Christian values" [as they were identified in his country]', including humanitarianism, calls for solidarity, and condemnation of racism and war (1999:

---

30. He was critical of 'security' measures (such as 'social security'), of legislation for automobile safety, and of opposition to suicide (1976: 271, 273).

56). However, he believed—especially, although not only, because he was homosexual—that the Christian church has erred grievously in sexual matters and said that this was the reason why most of his school friends had 'abandoned religious practices' (1999: 71-73).

Like many others who refrain from strongly positive judgments, Vattimo was neither reactionary nor radical politically. Rather, he was reticent toward 'certain revolutionary excesses of the 1960s and the 1970s'. 'We believed', he said, 'that we could realize justice on earth, but now reckon that it is no longer possible and turn our hopes to God' (1999: 74, 24). His standard was 'to live in accord with one's age [i.e., time]'; he wanted to live in a way that would 'not offend my culture' (1999: 75).

Still, Vattimo has spoken of 'emancipation' (1992: 5, 7; 2004: title). Thus, his nihilism is not stark.

A striking phenomenon is that the nihilists Baudrillard and Vattimo portrayed large-scale movements, evaluated more or less optimistically. Their views were thus not altogether negative. Rather, they celebrated the downward movement that they depicted. Large-scale movements were also envisioned by Nietzsche and Heidegger, although, understandably, not by skeptics.

4. *Nominalist and Relational Perspectives in Combination or Oscillation from Mid-Century on*

Positions that incorporated both nominalist and relational elements were common during the twentieth century. During its first half, mixed positions were found in the thinking of James, Sellars, and others that have been mentioned in Chapter 6, as well as in the thinking of Heidegger, discussed in greater detail. Other combinations of the two strands appeared during the second half of the century. Since these constitute relatively recent history, they call for special attention. In order to limit the discussion to a reasonable scope, primary attention will be given to prominent French thinkers.

In France, a series of short-range fluctuations took place during the twentieth century, each lasting about fifteen years. A major reason for these fluctuations is that French culture is centered in Paris, so that rapid shifts take place as intellectuals communicate in proximity with each other (see Gutting 2001). The shifts were especially striking from the perspective of observers outside of France, since only the more startling developments— the stronger shifts—caught their attention. Of course, the impact of these movements outside the country lagged somewhat behind the alternations in France itself.

During the early part of the century three waves were dominated in turn by Boutroux (a neo-Kantian indeterminist [see above, 4.3]), Henri Bergson (who was especially concerned with the notion of time), and Alexandre Kojève (with partially Marxist lectures on Hegel), although there were also other significant figures (see above, section 1, for Bataille). The major phases after c. 1940 are known respectively as existentialism, structuralism, and poststructuralism. A new outlook began about 1980, but it did not receive a special name; less unified, it exhibited a range of perspectives that included relational and nihilist views by different thinkers. The following somewhat brief overview deals with the major movements between 1940 and 1980.

'*Existentialism*' was represented in different ways by Gabriel Marcel, Jean-Paul Sartre, Simone de Beauvoir, and Albert Camus. This orientation took center stage in France from about 1942 till the early 1950s after beginning in Germany, where Buber, Heidegger, and Jaspers set forth relevant 'philosophies of existence' (Wahl 1959).[31] Existentialists overtly focused on human existence in a personally committed (not 'objective') way; however, some were particularist while others were relational in outlook.

The most prominent particularist was Sartre. Making a sharp distinction between human and nonhuman beings, he insisted that in human beings 'existence' precedes 'essence' in the sense that there is no pre-established structure for human life (1943: 60). The idea that there is no pre-established structure of course provided powerful support for negative freedom ('do as you choose'). In fact, Sartre was at first quite individualistic.[32] His thought also included relational elements, however, in part at least under the influence of de Beauvoir.[33] For instance, his great work on 'Being and Nothingness' (1943) contained quite a few interesting relational analyses (such as, one's receiving the look of another). Nevertheless, Sartre emphasized distance and conflict (1943: 502). Accordingly, when he moved away from individualism after c. 1952, he did so in support of Marxism, which also has a nominalist/conflictual cast.

Reacting primarily against the early Sartre, '*structuralism*', the next movement, became prominent in France after about 1955.[34] Major exponents of this movement included the anthropologist Claude Lévi-Strauss (who had begun along this line a little earlier), the literary critic Roland Barthes (for a while), the language theorist A.J. Greimas (especially in 1966), and, at least in part, both the Marxist thinker Althusser and the psychoanalyst Jacques Lacan.[35]

31. Of these, Buber and Jaspers were predominantly relational in outlook (see elsewhere in the present volume and Jaspers 1935 [1973: 60]).

32. 'Hell is other people', said a character in his play *No Exit*, first produced in 1944.

33. See references in Kamber (2000: 3-4) and below, 8.1, for de Beauvoir; also, T. Flynn 1997–2005, I: 84-85, 127, 277, 285.

34. There had been various antecedents in other places, including Prague.

35. See Dosse 1991–92 on Althusser and, on the five figures mentioned, further, below.

Although structuralists had varying emphases, all of them were anti-individualistic and envisioned universal structures, including continuities between human and nonhuman beings. It was reported that Parisians went to parks and touched natural objects in order to express a new sense of community with nature.

Interest in human commonality was exemplified by the fact that Lévi-Strauss pointed to the presence of sophisticated thought in 'primitive' (that is, oral) culture. According to Lévi-Strauss, profound thinking is reflected in the 'deep' structures of myths and social procedures; this thinking has its basis in a logic that is widely shared—perhaps universal—in human culture. Two aspects of this view can indeed be welcomed: (1) an enhanced appreciation for all human forms, including those of small groups with an oral culture,[36] and (2) attention to the role of human thought instead of viewing human beings in terms of relatively unthinking behavior.

A relational aspect of Lévi-Strauss's analysis appeared in his focusing not on individual units of myths, but on the phenomenon that myths constitute 'bundles of...relations' (1958–73, I, ch. 11 [1955]). Individual motifs of myths vary widely, but relations (as distinguished from individual units) and even bundles of relations can be universal, or at least very widespread. Since the way relations are expressed varies from society to society, however, Lévi-Strauss was interested in guarding the integrity of particular cultures, each forming a peculiar whole (1958–73, II, ch. 18 [1952]).

In terms of social issues, Lévi-Strauss advocated 'respect for societies very different from ours', but at home he was interested in 'participation in the transformation of our own society' (1958–73: 368). Specifically, in the early 1930s, he was politically active as a socialist (Deliège 2004: 8). Later, in line with his interest in the role of the mind in society, he also (or especially?) supported 'internal' freedom as expressed in Buddhism (1955: 476).

A weakness of Lévi-Strauss's analyses was that they were unduly schematic and looked too hard for unified wholes. Nevertheless, the patterns he presented were not altogether rigid. Rather, one of his more famous observations was that myths seek to provide a mediation for opposing items and thus move to overcome simple contrasts.

In emphasizing the tightness of wholes, structuralists relied heavily on Ferdinand de Saussure's linguistics. Saussure rightly observed that a language forms a system, but he described the phenomenon of language one-sidedly in terms of the relations that appear within it without giving equal attention to the relations of language with the nonlinguistic world. For instance, Saussure's dictum that 'in language there are only differences without positive terms' was well-known (1916, 2.4.4). The meaning of this

---

36. This appreciation was not totally new, but it was newly stressed.

statement can be illustrated as follows: the word 'day' obtains its meaning in a given context by standing in contrast either with 'night' (meaning something like twelve hours) or with 'week' (meaning twenty-four hours). Saussure's dictum was valuable in drawing attention to the fact that word meanings operate as parts of a larger complex rather than separately. Yet it ignored the obvious fact that most words do reflect an interaction of human beings with nonhuman realities, such as the contrast between day and night. Furthermore, Saussure ignored the principle that relations require a degree of independence for items that are connected. Contra this principle, Saussure and structuralists following him made language or a text appear to be not only self-contained but also fully integrated.

These weaknesses of structuralism—excessively schematic analysis and too great an assumption of structural unity—brought about a reaction against it in 1967. Barthes made another turn then (Lavers 1982: 7), and Derrida argued for the presence of ruptures or discontinuities in an influential trilogy. Foucault moved in a similar direction about that time. Their positions are thus known as '*poststructuralism*'. The prefix 'post' does not mean simply 'after' but something like 'a step beyond'. Indeed, 'poststructuralist' positions continued some structuralist themes. For instance, the emphasis of structuralism on the continuity of human and nonhuman existence was retained. At the same time, the theme of rupture had an affinity with the thought of some existentialists, especially Sartre. Thus one can see then a spiral-like process at work, in which previous insights are not simply jettisoned.

The heyday (or early phase) of poststructuralism lasted in France until about 1980. Foucault, Derrida, and Lyotard moved thereafter toward less anarchic positions, and a number of women and men presented relational positions that gave approximately equal attention to connectivity and separateness, as will be seen.

The individual figures that will be treated in detail—Levinas, Lyotard, Derrida, and Foucault—clearly took an active part in one or more of these phases. They should thus not be seen as isolated figures.

Levinas

Born in 1906 in Lithuania, Emmanuel Levinas moved to France in 1926 and studied under Husserl and Heidegger in Germany during 1928 and 1929. He was a religiously committed Jew, although when writing as a philosopher he did not make it a point to say so.

Levinas took a major part in the dialogical tradition. Specifically, he was indebted to Buber. However, like Rosenzweig and Kaufmann (see above, 3.5), he challenged Buber's apparent disassociation of the I-you from involvement in practical matters. To bridge the dichotomy between a highly personal I-you and an impersonal I-it, he introduced the category of 'third parties'. These constitute the societal dimension, mediating between the personal and impersonal aspects of life (1963: 34 [1957]).

Levinas thought that speech is basic to human existence, which is not solitary (1951: 91-94; 1957: 251). Since he knew that 'every relation' exhibits 'a simultaneity of the distance between the terms and their union' (1961, 2.A.1), he said that 'language is a relation between separated terms' (1961, 3.B.1). Yet he emphasized the negative side of this relation by saying that 'conversation…maintains the difference between me and the other' (a 'radical' separation) without mentioning connectivity at the same time (1961, 1.A.2). He said also that there is no 'conjunction' between oneself and deity (1986: 264 [1981]). Disjunction thus took priority for him over connectivity.

Levinas's complex position is well exemplified by his giving priority to 'otherness'. In a relational way, he grounded ethics not in the self (as many moderns have done), but in the 'face' (*visage*) of the 'other', which 'speaks' to one (1951: 98; 1982: 92). In doing so, he avoided the self-centered version of nominalism, but he adopted an alternative that exists within nominalism: authoritarianism. He described the 'other' as having an 'infinite' character, as one who 'commands…as a master', to whom one 'submits' in obligation (1961, 3.B.4, 6).

In this emphasis on otherness with an authoritarian cast, Levinas stood close to Protestant mixed nominalist-relational theologians (including Søren Kierkegaard and Karl Barth) who had an impact on French philosophy from the 1920s on, such as on existentialism. Like some existentialist thinkers, including especially Levinas's teacher and friend Jean Wahl—Levinas transferred the theme of otherness from the divine to the human realm (see Moyn 2005: 12, 113-94; Wahl 1949: 53). In this way, one can understand how Levinas viewed the voice of the human other as embodying infinity and having authority, so that one has infinite responsibility for the other (1995, ch. 6 [1986]).[37]

Insisting on 'heteronomy' (the receipt of requirements from the outside) and 'inequality' in an ethical relationship, Levinas rejected Buber's conception of a reciprocal dialogue (e.g., 1957: 251; 1986: xv, 229-30 [1979]). In a stark way, he spoke of oneself as being subject to the 'persecuting hatred' of the other, who makes an overwhelming demand, and as thus being an

---

37. On Barth, cf. above, n. 22. The shared theme of heteronomous 'otherness' in Barth's and Levinas's thinking has been noted by some observers (including G. Ward [1995]). Nominalism had begun within Islam and Christianity during the latter part of the Middle Ages; differently, traditional Judaism accepted non-reasoning authority only for ritual law, not for ethics (see Buss 1999: 49-50, 70-74, 87-90, 99, 126-28, 154, 281-83, 353). Levinas thus stood in this respect closer to Protestant nominalism than he did to his own Jewish tradition.

'expiation' for the other's (persecuting) 'fault' (cf. Isaiah 53), for selfhood means having 'regard for all there is' (1974, 4.4). Paradoxically, such a conception is in danger of putting oneself above the other, whose savior one becomes.

In line with this inegalitarian view, Levinas was patriarchal in regard to the question of women's roles (1963: 46-57 [1960]). He was criticized for this reason by Luce Irigaray, who supported reciprocity (1990: 913, 917).

One issue that deeply concerned Levinas is whether there can be a holistically inclusive view. In contrast to Buber, who had described the I-you relation as holistic and therefore transrational, Levinas distinguished between 'infinity' and 'totality' in the following way: 'infinity' is encountered in the ethical relation with another; 'totality' represents a rational whole, which Western philosophy has pursued. Levinas judged that the philosophical pursuit of totality has turned out to be impossible (1961, preface; 1985).[38] Nevertheless, he attributed an appropriately inclusive apprehension to religion. 'Religion', he said, is 'the bond that is established between the same and the other without constituting a [rationally grasped] totality' (1961, 1.A.2). Commonality, then, also has a legitimate role.[39]

Highlighting the theme of 'otherness' represented Levinas's prime contribution to philosophical ethics, since prior to his time philosophy had not often been other-oriented. Although the theme remained unclear (is 'otherness' dialogical, primarily conflictual, or distancing?), it reverberated widely at the end of the twentieth century.

Lyotard

Jean-François Lyotard moved through several periods, each with rather different points of view. Early on, he combined elements of Marxism with anarchism. Partially breaking with Marxism, he supported the student-led revolt in May 1968, which the Communist Party rejected as too anarchic. After 1968—disappointed by the failure of the revolt—Lyotard moved into the proximity of nihilism until the latter 1980s.[40]

Especially for a while after 1970, Lyotard's primary emphasis was on discontinuity. One example of this emphasis was an insistence on the separateness of 'language games', specifically, on a division between description and prescription—between the 'is' and the 'ought'—a typical distinction in nominalism (1979a, §14; 1983: ix).[41] This distinction implied that there are 'no

38. In his rejection of totalization, Levinas followed the Jewish thinker Rosenzweig.

39. Furthermore, Levinas considered 'sameness' to belong to the realm of 'history' (1961, 1.A.2).

40. See J. Williams 2000: 7, 19, for details of these steps.

41. Lyotard expressly agreed with Kant in this 'dispersion of genres' (1983, excursus after §181). It is not accurate, however, to say that he followed Wittgenstein, as he

criteria' for justice, since there is no grounding for it in reality (1979b, §§1, 3, 7). In fact, for a long time Lyotard's politics were rather negative. During the 1970s and into the 1980s, he held that all forms of collective politics (1973: 307)—including parliamentary representation (1985: 563)—are oppressive.

Still, Lyotard presented two general considerations for the exercise of justice, which together potentially constitute a relational stance. One (a 'prescription of universal value') was that multiplicity itself is a norm (1979b, §7). The other stated the following basic rule of the ethical language game: justice involves listening, accepting the role of addressee (1979b, §4; 1983, §161).

With the theme of 'listening' Lyotard continued a line of thinking that ran from the Hebrew Bible to Levinas.[42] In fact, he later referred to the fact that Western philosophy is as much dependent on the biblical tradition as it is on Greek philosophy (2004: 114 [1994]). Specifically, he described Jews as bearers of the message that 'the law does not belong to us' (1993a: 162 [1990]). Nevertheless, he differed from Levinas and others by holding that 'the position of the sender [of the call to justice] must remain empty'; one should place there neither oneself nor another authority—presumably, also not the 'face' of the other (1979b, §§4, 7). The other is thus actually absent.

In regard to women's issues—a pivotal social concern—Lyotard expressed unhappiness with what was known as 'feminism', since this movement 'cannot avoid falling into…identification with virile power'. Instead of feminism, he favored a 'feminine principle', which rejects much of what is known as 'reason' (1977: 208-9). Anticipating Baudrillard on this topic, he said that 'writing is feminine if it operates by *seduction*', rather than by attempting to 'convince' someone by reasoned argument; the most powerful contribution of the 'women's struggle', he believed, lies not in political self-assertion but in a rejection of the primacy of theoretical discourse, since the 'philosophical (and political) method' is 'a male way of thinking' (1977: 213-14, 229).

In later writings, Lyotard attributed to a female voice an instruction for the mind 'to receive' (1988a: 27) and described as 'feminine' the 'openness' he favored as an aspect of 'listening' (1995: 183-89). That was in line with an extensive tradition which, at least from the latter part of the nineteenth century on, valorized a 'feminine' (receptive) way that male writers might assume.[43] From a feminist standpoint, this tradition can be regarded as progress, for it expresses a positive attitude toward women's characteristics. Yet it reflects an old stereotype, the applicability of which many now wish to avoid or limit.

---

claimed, for Wittgenstein observed differences between language games but did not assert their unrelatedness.

42. Cf. Lyotard 1983, §170, excursus, on his indebtedness to Levinas.

43. See, e.g., Alice Jardine 1985: 38, 58, 62, 188.

Best known among Lyotard's views is his thesis that the 'postmodern condition' is marked by a rejection of 'grand narratives', that is, of large, optimistic visions of human history (1979a).[44] Among the visions to be rejected are: 'the salvation of creatures through the conversion of souls', 'the dialectic of Spirit', the 'emancipation' of reason and of human labor, and an 'enrichment of all' through 'capitalist technoscience'.[45] Insofar as his thesis of the end of grand narratives did not reject all large constructions but only the idea of progress, it was not novel.

In fact, Lyotard's thesis did not represent adequately the culture of his time. For instance, Lyotard himself insisted that what he called 'postmodernism' has 'nothing to do with what is called postmodernity in the market of contemporary ideologies'; specifically, he rejected the idea that his position was paralleled by developments in architecture and literature (1988b: 202). Grand theories of history were set forth by the nihilists Baudrillard and Vattimo, who claimed the term 'postmodern' for themselves. After all, to speak about a 'postmodern' age, however, is itself a macrohistorical judgment—an optimistic one if the postmodern outlook is favored.

It is ironic, then, that Lyotard's historical assessment came to function as a metanarrative, as he soon recognized (1983, §182). It became in part a self-fulfilling prophecy. Many writers, anxious not to be out of step with their time, thought that they needed to avoid large-scale views of history. To do so, to be sure, was contrary to Lyotard's rejection of an ethics that requires one to 'bow down' before whatever is current (1979b, §5), if it was indeed true that an avoidance of metanarratives represented the current condition. Not surprisingly, Lyotard came to describe his work on the 'postmodern condition' as his 'worst book' (1995: 189).[46] Lyotard himself later projected a future history of the universe, envisioning a growth in complexity (1993b).

In assessing Lyotard's rejection of grand narratives in 1979, it is important to note that it reflected his disenchantment specifically with Marxism. By the end of the 1960s he had come to believe that there is 'no alternative to the dominance of the capitalistic arrangement' (1995: 174). During the 1980s he refused to line up with Mitterand's moderate socialism, although he supported it in some ways (J. Williams 2000: 37; Reader 1987: 139). Instead, he favored small-scale voluntary programs, which, according to his observations, have grown since the 1960s (1993b, ch. 12, end).

44. An antecedent of this idea, rejecting specifically a Marxist utopian vision, was that of the 'end of ideology', begun by Camus in 1946 (D. Bell 1988: 411-13).

45. Lyotard 1979a, Introduction, §14; 1986, ch. 2 (1984).

46. During the 1980s, Lyotard assigned different meanings to the word 'postmodern' (see 1982: 365-67; 1986: 120; 1988b: 202). Clearly he had become uncertain about his earlier thesis. In 1993 he lamented the 'postmodern affliction', which he identified with a 'foreclosure of the Other', that is, with cutting off connections (1993c: 146).

During the 1980s, Lyotard gradually became less anarchistic (Dews 1987: 219), moving toward a more relational view. In 1983 he remarked that even a mathematical formula is communicational, for it 'implies an addressor, an addressee, and their non-fortuitous (didactic) relation' (1983, §193). Subsequently, discussing the phrase 'Judeo-Christian', he gave voice to the standard relational formula: 'Our hyphen, like all marks of union, disunites what it unites' (1992: 48).

In regard to politics, he said then—in contrast to his earlier criticism of parliamentary democracy and of large operations generally—that 'in the republic [which is "indispensable"] there is a principle of universalization which relates to the function, inherent in speech, of *addressing* the other' (1993c: 139, 143). In 1991 he even co-authored a statement in support of the 'international coalition' in the Gulf War (Finkielkraut *et al.* 1991). On the theoretical level, he rejected an earlier anti-rational orientation (directed in 1974 against Marxism) and voiced support for a 'rational, consistent representation of the world' (1995: 190).

In the last year of his life he commented on, and imaginatively rewrote, Augustine's *Confessions*, a work in which he had long been interested. His commentary (1998, cut short by his death) featured God's being addressed in the second person. For Augustine, God was the source of the ethical address to which one is to listen. An address to God is then a reply to that source. Since Lyotard's commentary indicates a sympathy with Augustine's confessions, it is thus apparent that he believed that, although there is no 'god' who is 'the witness to justice and truth' (1995: 190), it is meaningful to respond to the authorless voice that addresses one.

In short, Lyotard participated in the relational tradition, although nominalism represented a prominent strain in his thought. His outlook fluctuated considerably, somewhat in line with the general movement of thought in France.

Foucault

A combination of the nominalist and relational lines also appeared in the works of Michel Foucault, who was slightly younger than Lyotard. As a highly influential figure during the last part of the twentieth century, he deserves careful attention, especially since the final movement of his thought, which can be judged to be the most appropriate one, is not well known. Important to observe is that his thought underwent major transformations.[47] The older positions were not entirely abnegated, but they were placed into a new light.

---

47. Dates of Lyotard's interviews are given, together with other bibliographic information, in Bernauer and Rasmussen 1988: 119-58. It should be noted that his transitions were multiple and sometimes gradual.

Foucault was a member of the Communist Party from 1950 to 1952 but became disillusioned by his experience in the Party and by events in Eastern Europe. This disillusionment probably contributed to his subsequent interest in irrationalism, although he had already suffered from depression earlier (James Miller 1993: 172; Macey 1993: 25-61). Trained in Freudian theory, he published works on the history of mental illness and its treatment methods. Thus psychology constituted a long-term interest for him.

From 1963 on Foucault examined several kinds of relations in turn— first, the gaze to which a person is subject (in the clinic [1963a]) and then the following three: discourse, power, and, finally, the self as such (that is, reflexivity).[48] The last three will receive attention here.

Specifically, in 1966 he analyzed *discourse* in a generally structuralist way. He described a cultural pattern as 'the ensemble of relations that can unite at a given period the discursive practices' of various disciplines or endeavors (1969, 4.6.e).

In 1971/72, after working with prisoners, Foucault's primary interest moved from discourse toward *power*. Expressly indicating this shift, he said that 'one's point of reference should not be the great model of language and signs, but that of war and battle'; historical importance lies in 'relations of power, not relations of meaning' (1976a: 121-23; 1977a: 19). He argued that power 'produces reality' (1975, 3.2, end); in particular, it creates the 'soul' ('born out of methods of punishment, supervision, and constraint'), the 'individual' (1975, 3.3; 1980: 98 [1976]).

By the end of 1978, however, Foucault came to believe that 'rather than explaining other phenomenon', 'power is that which must be explained' (1991: 148). He moved then toward what he called 'care of *self*', together with a concern with 'government' (1984a: 114). The conjunction of 'self' with 'government' was supported by Foucault's observation that in Greco-Roman tradition the mastery of self—a part of self-care—was closely associated with one's rule over society (see above, 1.3). He characterized 'government' in constructive terms as 'neither warlike nor [negatively] juridical' (1982: 221). At the same time, he saw the self in terms of a reflexive relation 'by which the individual constitutes and recognizes the self as subject' (1984b, Introduction, 1)—the self being a 'form', not a substance (1984a: 107). This relation to self, he said, is ontologically prior to relations with others (1984a: 104, 116).

An indication of Foucault's interest in a relational conception was given not only in his early interest in a 'gaze', but also in his repeated use of the term 'network' (1975, 1.1). An important aspect of the image evoked

48. Foucault himself pointed out the sequence of these topics (1984b, Introduction, §1); they are treated by Thomas Flynn (1997–2005, II: 143-74) as aspects rather than as phases of Foucault's thought.

by this term is that the nodes of a network are treated as each having a certain integrity. The relative freedom of nodes within a relation appears in Foucault's characterization of 'power' as a relation that meets resistance and thus engages freedom; he contrasted this process with 'domination' or 'violence', which is not met with resistance.[49] Thus, his notion of power was reciprocal.

However, in Foucault's thought, relational perspectives were interwoven with those he called 'nominalist' and even 'nihilist', indebted to Nietzsche. This side was especially prominent in the phases that emphasized discourse and power.[50]

One issue involved the question of truth. During the period of 1971–77, when he was privileging power and strife, Foucault gave voice to considerable skepticism. Interviews published in 1976 and 1977 gave the impression that he rejected the possibility of truth because he equated whatever goes by that name with 'claims to truth', saying that 'truth is of this world' and that 'each society has its regime of truth' (1976b: 33; similarly, 1977a: 25). (A less skeptical, although fallibilist, position would be that truth is not of this world but, rather, a limit concept, as it was for Peirce and Nietzsche—something that one can approach.) Not much later, changing his tune, Foucault said that he was concerned with 'the discourse of true and false' and its 'effect in a real to which they are linked' (1981a: 14 [c. 1978]). In 1982 he expressly rejected 'a skeptical or relativistic refusal of all verified truth' (212). Thereafter he averred that a political regime should be neither 'indifferent to truth' nor 'prescribe the truth' (1984c: 23), and, with a nice balance: 'I believe too much in the truth not to suppose that there are different truths and different ways of saying it' (1989: 314 [1984]).

Foucault also shifted his position in regard to whether one should entertain a comprehensive view. In 1968, he opposed a 'totalizing', 'global', or 'grand' history, which envisions a 'single common trajectory', such as 'the progress of reason', or even, 'the spirit of a century' (1968: 853). Similarly, in 1971 he called for a renunciation of 'theory and general discourse' (47). He took this antiholistic stance in opposition to both Marxism and psychoanalysis, albeit he attributed some heuristic value to both of them (1980: 81 [1976]). In later years, Foucault continued to reject a 'global' view, but he came to embrace generality.[51] In 1978, he insisted that the issues he dealt with

49. 1976a: 123; 1977b: 92, 95; 1982: 217, 220-21; 1984a: 108-9. Foucault was not so much interested in restraining power as in enabling those subject to power (e.g., prisoners) to resist it.

50. References to Nietzsche appeared repeatedly (although with some ambivalence: 1967: 9; 1989: 327 [1984]). A 'nominalist' inclination was stated in 1976a: 123; 1981a: 14 (1978/80).

51. Already in 1969 he advocated a loosely organized 'general history', which recognizes dispersion, instead of a 'global' one (17, 19); this idea reflected a usage, in his

were 'more truly general' than those with which Communists and Social-ists were concerned; for instance, madness is a 'general problem in every society' (1991: 152-55). Such issues as 'the power of men over women, of parents over children, of psychiatry over the population, of administration over the ways people live' involve '"transversal" struggles...not limited to one country' or 'to a particular political or economic form of government' (1982: 211).[52] Accordingly, in partial contrast with his earlier insistence on the 'local character of criticism' (1980: 81 [1976]), he said, in line with the progress of his own thought: 'One always moves backwards toward the essential. The most general things appear last' (1984c: 18).

Furthermore, Foucault varied in regard to issues of continuity and self-hood, which he saw as linked to each other. In 1969, he objected to a continuous history since it is needed for the functioning of a (structured) 'subject', which he rejected at the time (21-22). However, later he affirmed both the subject and continuous history, finding considerable relevance in Greco-Roman attitudes toward sexuality, so long as one takes into account differences in context between then and now (1984d: 40). He believed that Christianity, too—despite its problems—must be considered in founding a modern morality. Specifically, according to his analysis, the Greeks did not yet have a 'subject'; the subject, rather, arose with Christianity, in which a person is 'subject' to God (1982: 212; 1989: 330 [1984]). He held that modern psychology represents a secularization of the Christian way (1988: 49 [1982]). He did not reject this Christian and secular post-Christian line altogether, but he called for 'new forms of subjectivity' that resemble in part the Greco-Roman concern for oneself (1982: 216; 1988: 19 [1982]).

With this new appreciation for the subject (which was characteristic for French thought in general toward the end of the twentieth century [Gutting 2001: 388]), Foucault emphasized reflective thought. At an earlier point, he had blocked the possibility of questioning current culture by holding that 'knowledge' gained by 'the activity of the subject' is too weak to be either 'useful for, or resistant to, power' [1975, 1.1]. However, a little later, he judged that 'thought exists truly both beyond and within systems and structures of discourse' (1981b: 21). He explained that thinking can make 'conflicts more visible...making them more essential than simple confron-tations of interests', so that 'reform' will be possible (1981b: 34). Thinking involves not an automatic rejection of social practices but an examination and thus a questioning of their assumptions, for thought entered into them (32-33). Thinking is likely to show that social arrangements are neither 'arbi-trary' nor 'necessary' (1981a: 5-6 [1978/80]). 'Thought', thus exercised, 'is

French context, of the term 'general history' for a history more spotty than a 'total' or 'global' one (M. Dean 1994: 38).

52. The term 'transversal' was originally used in mathematics for a line that cuts across others. See Calvin Schrag 1992: 148-79.

freedom in relation to what one does, the motion by which one detaches oneself from it, establishes it as an object, and reflects on it as a problem' (in Rabinow 1984: 388 [1984]). 'Problematization'—as he came to call this process—is the 'work of modifying one's own thought and that of others'; it is 'the intellectual's reason for being' (1984c: 22).

Foucault's thinking had a practical side, which can be stated in terms of freedom. Externally, he especially valued negative freedom. For instance, on the economic front, he explored free-market 'neoliberalism' (M. Peters 2001: 13, 127). More importantly, he opposed a number of traditional restrictions on individual activity. At least early on, he valued 'transgression', which he characterized as going beyond an established limit, although not to the point of revolution (1963b: 756). In fact, he found transgression to lie at the heart of sexuality, perhaps since human sexuality is always restrained and may even be enhanced by restraint, perhaps also since his own homosexuality transgressed traditional standards.

Furthermore, especially in later years, Foucault valued internal freedom. A good part of what he said positively then focused on the 'care of the self', with self-mastery as a primarily aesthetic project (1984b, Introduction, §1; 1984c: 20). He also sought a quasi-mystical transformation. From 1975 on—reportedly until the end of his life—he used psychotropic drugs, which he told friends were 'revelatory' or, in any case, an 'intense delight' (Macey 1993: 339-40). He experimented with sadomasochism in the hope 'for a total transformation of life' (James Miller 1993: 328). Importantly, Foucault valued a negative aspect of internal freedom: readiness to move beyond one's own past, which he both practiced and advocated.[53]

Yet Foucault was weak in regard to external positive freedom. In his theory, he considered relations with others to be less basic than the relation to oneself. In regard to particular issues, he was reserved toward the welfare state (e.g. 1983b: 55), and women were largely absent from his history of sexuality (Richlin 1998). Cooperation played little role in his thought. Accordingly, Honi Haber—although she was also appreciative of Foucault—said, with some justice, that Foucault's project lacked an adequate recognition of 'subjects-in-community' (1994: 104).[54]

Derrida
A combination of the relational and nominalist lines was explicit in the writings of Jacques Derrida. Identifying Peirce and Nietzsche as symbolic of those two lines, he declared that they represent two angles between which one should not choose (1967a: 427-28).[55]

53. On this negative aspect of internal freedom, see above, 1.3, and below, 10.4.
54. For other feminist reactions, see below, 8.4.
55. Derrida studied Peirce's work at Harvard in the 1950s (Pettigrew 1995: 365).

Acknowledging an affinity with Peirce (1967c: 71), Derrida said that the 'center' of structure is not a 'thing' but a 'function', that is, a relation (1967a: 411, 497). (In fact, in mathematics, structures are not usually thought to have a center but are treated as a system of relations.) Furthermore, he located the 'origin' of an object in *différance*, a kind of negative relation, insofar as the notion of origin remains useful at all (1967a: 428).[56] With Peirce, he held that the 'sign'—which incorporates *différance* (since a signal refers to something not immediately present)—is primitive, that is, basic (1967b: 26).

In a tilt toward Nietzsche, Derrida said that 'form fascinates when one no longer has the power [French: *force*] to understand power in itself' (1967a: 11). Yet he could also say, more positively and thus in a less Nietzschean way, that *différance* is 'the formation [basis] of form' (1967c: 92).

In 1967, Derrida described his work as one that overcomes the 'logo-phonocentric' orientation of prior 'philosophy of the West, that is, of the world' (1967a: 294; 1967c: 13). In his judgment, the older orientation, for which he used the symbol of speech (it is 'logo-phonocentric'), did not sufficiently emphasize the *différance* he favored. In place of 'speech', he used the image of 'writing', for, as is well known, writing is normally less closely connected with an immediate context than is oral communication.

Since women's liberation represented one of the most important aspects of the 1968 revolt, which took place not long after he wrote his first major works, it is important to see Derrida's thought in relation to this movement. Doing so can shed light on a change in his thinking.

Derrida opposed 'phallogocentrism', that is, a centeredness on 'phallic logos', or male reasoning (1972a: xxi; 1994: 340). This did not mean, however, that he supported what he and others called 'feminism'. In France (as in the US), the word 'feminism' designated a movement that sought 'women's reproductive rights (birth control and abortion), legal rights (divorce law reform), economic rights (equal opportunity, equal pay, child-care), and protection against physical violence' (A. Hirsh 1981: 218). A negative assessment of this movement was made by Antoinette Fouque, an analyst trained by the socially conservative Lacan and leader of the movement *Psychoanalyse et politique* (*Psych et po*). *Psych et po*, which was aided by the large inheritance of one of its members (Beauvoir 1984: 232; Jenson 1996: 79), favored not political action but the mental transformation of society so that traditionally feminine characteristics would be valued more highly.[57] Clearly, Derrida stood closer to *Psych et po* with its critique of

---

In his ideas of *différance*, however, he was influenced by Saussure's less contextual analysis of language.

56. In 1972a: 12 (1968), he rejected the suitability of the notion of 'origin'.

57. See Allwood 1998: 29 (she does not make clear Fouque's relation to Derrida,

cultural phallocentrism than to political 'feminism'. In 1984, he did express some support for the political version by saying that it is 'experienced as "better" insofar as it is desired by those who practically dispose of the greatest "force" in society' (1984: 121-22). Yet this acknowledgment of the influence such feminism had gained did not represent a principled endorsement of it. In 1985, he said that 'deconstruction is certainly not feminist' (30).

Still, there is evidence that Derrida's relation to the women's movement changed to some extent around 1980. Before then, his image of 'writing' had one-sidedly highlighted a traditionally masculine (not necessarily biologically male) emphasis on disassociation (in the ancient world long-distance communication by means of writing was largely handled by males). In 1975, however, Hélène Cixous—a long-time friend, who stood between political feminism and *Psych et po*—proposed a 'both/and' logic as an alternative to Derrida's favoring of 'writing'. This dual logic would overcome (although not annihilate) the contrast between 'speech' and 'writing' and between other oppositions. In other words, Cixous had room for both connectivity (symbolized by speech) and distance (symbolized by writing). She saw in this duality a 'couple', without a hierarchical relation that sets one over the other (115-16).[58] Cixous's reflections may have contributed to Derrida's shift c. 1980 toward a more affirmative perspective.[59] In any case, in his later phase the image of 'writing' receded.

Instead of 'writing', Derrida came to favor the word 'deconstruction'. This word includes both 'de' and 'con', so that it is far from purely negative. In fact, Derrida expressly said that he did not choose between a 'negative or nihilist' operation and a positive one; rather, 'I very much love everything which I deconstruct' (1982: 119). The two sides go together, for, as he said, he could not 'conceive of a radical critique which would not ultimately be motivated by some sort of affirmation' (1984: 118). As he explained in 1988, undecidability—which he supported—is different from 'indeterminacy', since it is 'a *determinate* oscillation between possibilities' and involves 'relations of force...differences of force' (148).

but Fouque's opposition to feminism went back to at least 1973 [E. Marks and Courtivron 1980: 74-75]). See, further, Jardine 1985: 20, 182, and Duchen 1986: 32, 34, 59, 79-85. Cixous, Irigaray, and Kristeva were to some extent associated with this group (see below, 8.2).

58. Cixous was undoubtedly influenced by some earlier written or oral statements by Derrida about doubleness along with undecidability (cf. 1972b: 250), but Cixous questioned Derrida's one-sided focus on 'writing'.

59. Derrida, however, apparently did not acknowledge such an influence. In fact, Derrida rarely discussed women authors, although he repeatedly discussed the role of women. For references by Derrida to the feminine—with few references to women writers—see Jardine 1985: 62, 178-207. Derrida did analyze some of the work of Cixous in his foreword to Sellers 1994.

Questions have been raised about whether undecidability or deconstruction permits energetic positive involvement or definite opposition to
something that is judged to be evil (thus, e.g., Simon Critchley 1992: 236;
Jappe 1999: 164). Indeed, it is reported that Derrida showed 'utmost res-
ervation' during the '68 revolt (Ross 2002: 190). Yet he was active politically in many other ways, such as in taking part in the moderately socialist
government of the 1980s (Reader 1987: 97). In a dialogue published in
2001, he took account of a variety of potentially contradictory considerations concerning social policies, finessing them (Derrida and Roudinesco
2001).

Indeed, Derrida asserted that there is a positive connection between
deconstruction and ethics, specifically, that deconstruction is an 'openness
towards the other' (1984: 124). This statement was not unproblematic, for
Derrida held that the call to ethics comes from a secret part of one's self,
from 'God in me' (1992: 102). Thus, his ethics expressed a commitment that
was, after all, self-centered. Still, beyond subjectivism, Derrida affirmed
that 'there is' justice and that 'justice' in itself is not deconstructable (1990:
944). In that way, justice is different from concrete law, to which deconstruction is applicable.

One of Derrida's concerns in his last years was how to have room for universality along with particularity. He believed that 'political democracy…
cannot be disassociated' from a 'universal rationality' (1996c, §22) and that
'republican democracy' is indeed a 'universalizable model' (1996c, §11).
Further, in dealing with 'faith', without which 'there is no society', Derrida
held that religious revelations involve both singularity (unique events) and
universality. Rather than favoring one of these sides over the other, he said,
'I oscillate and I think that some other scheme must be constructed to understand the two at the same time' (in Caputo 1997: 24). He looked forward to
a 'new Enlightenment', which 'will know how to respect both singularity
and the universal' (in Caputo 1997: 123).

As a crucial instance of universality, Derrida spoke of 'messianicity',
with 'promise', as a basic structure that is present in all language and is
crucial for ethics; as such it is not identifiable with a particular 'messianism'
(1996a: 128; 1996c, §22; and in Caputo 1997: 23-24). Messianicity implies
a comprehensive historical perspective. Connecting this theme with that
of 'emancipation', Derrida said (clearly contra Lyotard 1979a), 'I have no
tolerance for those who—deconstructionist or not—are ironical with regard
to the grand discourse of emancipation' (1996b: 82).

In regard to religion, Derrida (Jewish by heritage) stood close to traditional theology but remained reserved. For instance, his view that a 'center'
is constituted by a relation rather than by a 'thing' was not unlike the conceptualization of God by a number of Jewish and Christian theologians who
have also not viewed God as an object (presumably, he was aware at least

of Buber's view along this line).[60] Expressing ambivalence, however, he simultaneously used the word 'God' and rejected its use when he said that 'the persistence of God in my life is called by other names, so that I rightly pass for an atheist' (Derrida 1991, §30; cf. Kearney 1993: 45).

More affirmatively, he related justice to the experience of the 'mystical' (1990: 947). Early on, with reference to the Bible, he spoke of 'scriptural' *différance* as a rupture in reality, even within 'God'; he related this rupture to Jewish non-self-identity (1967a: 103-4, 112), with its readiness for self-criticism. Later, he dealt with Jewish, Christian, and Muslim themes that included hospitality, compassion, forgiveness, and prayer, although without commitment to a religious outlook (e.g., 2001 [1997]; cf. Sherwood and Hart 2005).

It is clear that Derrida participated in certain elements of the relational tradition, including its both/and perspective, especially after 1980. His early emphasis on disassociation was valuable in that it furnished a counterbalance to the one-sided emphasis on unity in structuralism. Yet he apparently did not realize that relational theory had already combined connectivity with separateness, so that a 'new enlightenment' was not merely future.

Rorty

Richard Rorty, a neo-pragmatist in the US, occupied a similar position on the border between nominalism and a relational view. Like the major writers that have just been discussed, he had an audience that ranged far beyond academic philosophy.

Less of a realist than Peirce (cf. Rorty 1990: 4), but carrying further James' and Dewey's rejection of a 'spectator theory of knowledge', Rorty argued in 1979 against the view that knowledge serves as a 'mirror of nature'. This argument as such was not novel, for the 'mirror' image had been rejected from the eighteenth century on.[61] Yet Rorty was more radical than many before him, saying that 'the point of philosophy is to keep the conversation going rather than to find objective truth' (372, 377).

In 1995, however, Rorty indicated that he had moved away from this antirealism (Saatkamp 1995: 191-93). The move was aided by Davidson's reference to 'triangulation' (two observers sighting an object), a form of intersubjectivity that is based on communication. Rorty now sought to avoid not only the image of 'mirror', supporting realism, but also that of 'projection', supporting antirealism, and to escape an antithesis between those two.

60. The idea that God is not 'a being' has been standard in theology.
61. See Abrams 1953. Rorty did not mention discussions of the 'mirror' position (either critical or supportive) by Helmholtz, Mach, and Lenin (see above, 5.4).

Rorty continued to espouse 'nominalism' (1998a: 331), but his version apparently accepted relations, although not other general terms. His stress on conversation already presupposed contact with other human beings, even if not with nonhuman reality. He advocated 'solidarity' in social life (1991: 21-45 [1985, 1987]).

In practice Rorty supported the ethics that he inherited from religious tradition and from the Enlightenment. For instance, he said that aiding a 'stranger from whom all human dignity has been stripped' is a 'Jewish and Christian element in our tradition...gratefully invoked by free-loading atheists like myself' (1983: 588). For intellectuals, however, Rorty advocated a stance of irony that is 'sufficiently historicist and nominalist to have abandoned the idea that...central beliefs and desires refer back to something beyond the reach of time and chance' (1989: xv, 87). To be sure, this 'irony is of little public use', and the intellectual has little to contribute to public social discourse (1989: 94, 120). Nevertheless, he vigorously supported social democracy (1998b).

Marxians

A number of mixed nominalist-relational positions were Marxist. In fact, Marx himself exhibited such a mixed orientation (above, 3.1). However, quite a few Marxists developed it further in a contingent/relational (rather than rigid/determinist) way that has been called 'humanist' or 'dialectical' (Warren 1984). It is not possible to discuss the Marxist tradition adequately here, but reference has already been made to the view of Habermas, the background of which included both Marx and Peirce.[62] Several French figures more or less deeply indebted to Marxism deserve at least a brief notice.

Louis Althusser, who was indebted to structuralism but is usually treated as a full-fledged Marxist, participated in the dialogical tradition in his thesis that ideology 'transforms' individuals into 'subjects' by 'hailing' them as a police officer might ('hey, you') (1970: 31). This notion of 'interpellation', as he called it, was modeled on biblical ideas, although he was atheist (1970: 33-35), and resembled a statement by Ebner in 1921 (1963–65, I: 96) that God created the human being by addressing it (see above, 3.5). The notion of a subject-creating address was developed further by Foucault (see above) and Judith Butler (below, 8.4).

Gilles Deleuze and Félix Guattari combined elements of Nietzscheanism and Marxism. In 1968, near the beginning of poststructuralism, Deleuze treated 'difference' as primary. However—in part inspired by Spinoza, who played an important role in French philosophy (Schrift 2006: 78-80)—he held that the differences together constitute 'univocity' (a single voice). In

62. For other Marxists, see, e.g., Hudelson 1990.

162   *The Concept of Form in the Twentieth Century*

harmony with this view, Deleuze and Guattari envisioned a *rhizome* figure that has no focal points but only lines of connection within it and set forth the 'magical' formula 'pluralism = monism' (1980: 15, 31). Apparent opposites often do meet.

Alain Badiou combined the tradition of nominalist universalism typical of Marxism with relational elements inherent in mathematical models he used. He rejected Levinas's preferring 'difference' to 'sameness' and asserted that 'the universal is not a negation of particularity' (cf. above, 1.1); in his view, 'only what is an immanent exception is universal' (1997: 118-19). Paul (of the Christian Bible) provided him with an intellectual model for a specific event that has universal significance; however, he held that, not Christ in particular, but various events, both political and personal, raise claims to which one should be 'faithful' (1988, 1993, 1997). In short, he envisioned multiple particularist universals. For society, he rejected both non-temporal human rights and ethically indifferent cultural relativism (1993).

5. *Relational Thinking after c. 1980*

The relational outlook won new life near the end of the century, although, as has been seen, it was rivaled by skeptical and nihilist views, which often received greater attention. Since French thinkers have received special notice so far, it is appropriate to continue the story by giving attention especially to French contributions.

In 1980, the journal *Le débat* began with the stated purpose of countering the 'political irresponsibility of intellectuals', their 'obscurity of thought and style', and their insistence that 'younger scholars…follow their Masters [especially Lacan] blindly' (Pavel 1989: 18). According to Pavel (20), those participating in the opening of *Le débat* agreed 'that nihilism, antihumanism, and the critique of identity and the subject were no longer viable'. About that time, Lyotard, Foucault, and Derrida also moved toward less skeptical positions, as has been seen.

Whether specific political changes contributed to the emergence of the new outlook is difficult to say. However, the 1981 election of the moderately socialist Mitterand as president, which affirmed many of the ideals of the 1960s, may have been a sign of the time. It is true, Mitterand's social-democratic moves were partially reversed even while he was in office. Yet the issues that had been raised in the 1960s did not concern so much economic welfare as self-determination in the face of hierarchies (such as in the university and in business), the roles of the sexes, relations between the human and the nonhuman world, and matters of the human 'spirit' (in conjunction with the body).

In fact, according to Keith Reader (1987: 13), 'the dethroning of economism from its place at the centre of left-wing thought is the most pervasive and abiding legacy of May [1968]' in France. The newly emerging 'politics of subjectivity' (Reader 1987) could be cultural, academic, or religious—separately or together. For instance, poetry became strongly valued as an expression of personal freedom (Dews 1979: 168), while science was questioned especially in regard to its supposed objectivity, as has been seen for the US. At the end of the 1970s, a circle associated with the journal *Tel quel*, which had previously been oriented toward Marxism and psychoanalysis, became interested in the revival of a concern for religion then going on (Ffrench 1995: 264-67; cf. de Vries 1999). In 1983, the name of this journal was changed to *L'infini*, apparently alluding to Levinas's thought and indicating at least a partially religious interest (Sollers 1983: 5).[63]

In this new situation, a number of more or less consistently relational thinkers became prominent. The women among them (Irigaray, Cixous, Kristeva, and Le Doeuff) are discussed in Chapter 8, but significant contributions were also made by male figures, including the following: Michel Serres, Alain Finkielkraut, Jean-Luc Nancy, and Paul Ricoeur.

Serres was a student and at one time a colleague of Foucault (1992: 59). He moved to the US in 1984. Although he published more than can be discussed here, his general outlook was made accessible in an extended public conversation with his student Latour.[64] In this conversation (1992), Serres stated that he envisioned reality as 'an ensemble of relations' (180). This ensemble is large-scale, but 'the larger [something] is, the more fragile it is' (176). In other words, he supported the pursuit of large-scale visions in part since they are less firm than more limited visions. An orientation toward what is fragmentary, he said, is not radical but rather conservative; playing with the meaning of *fragment* in French—which, like 'rock' in English, can refer to a hard object of any size—he said fragments are hard, while relations are fluid (171, 176, 179).

Serres believed in a universal 'morality' (based on 'the science of relations'), although specific rules, which he called 'ethics', may be 'relative, like customs' (1992: 278-79). This universal 'moral law' is minimally to refrain from harm and maximally to 'love all global ensembles—individual, collective, living, and inert' (294). In his encounters with many people, Serres found them quite diverse, but nevertheless 'always and everywhere the same: wounded, pained, timid…vicious, cruel…arrogant…obedient…courageous…objectively pitiable' (271). In his view, indebted to Simone Weil, wisdom goes with weakness, and is present in ordinary people (270). Indeed, he said, 'the motor of history is, precisely, those who have failed [which include] the poor, the excluded, and the most miserable. I even

63. The journal was edited from then on by Philippe Sollers (Kristeva's husband), who had converted from Marxist atheism to Catholicism.
64. Latour is cited repeatedly in the present study.

believe that, among the attributes of God, theologians and philosophers have forgotten infinite weakness' (179). The inclusive orientation of a relational view—with special reference to the poor and the downtrodden generally—was thus exhibited in his perspective.

Approaching a comprehensive vision, Serres referred to God as 'the sum of relations' (1992: 291). Yet he also spoke about the 'death of God', at least in current intellectual terms (218). In any case, he held that—whatever one may believe about God—'there is nothing real but love, and no law other than the one that calls for it' (1990: 84).

Finkielkraut, too, expressed opinions that can be characterized as relational. A son of Polish Jews (his father survived Auschwitz), he was active in the French Left during 1968 and for a few years thereafter. However, he turned away from this involvement, largely because anti-Israel and even antisemitic sentiments in the Left made him reflect on his Jewishness. In regard to the position of Jews, he observed that one can get rid of other persons not only through homogenization, but also 'in the name of otherness'. That is, one can consider others so different that they are excluded and even eradicated, as was done by the Nazis (who rejected 'a universal morality') and by other, more recent, groups (1996: 69, 154), and as may be done by future antisemites (1982: 170-71). Constructively, Finkielkraut said that love is a 'paradoxical bond' that is directed toward the 'enigma', 'distance', or 'incognito' of the other (1984: 65).

Nancy was similarly relational in his outlook. In a work devoted to the topic of freedom, he insisted that singularity and relationship are not contrary to each other but rather imply each other. On the one hand, a relation occurs only in discontinuity; on the other hand, having one's own identity (*ipseity*) involves a withdrawal from complete independence (*aseity*) and 'is constituted by and as sharing' (1988: 94-95). Given this analysis, freedom 'furnishes' or 'is' relation (93-94). 'We share what divides us: the freedom of an incalculable and improbable coming of being into presence, which always places us as *ones* in the presence of *others*' (123-24). Clearly, the freedom championed by Nancy was positive (freedom 'with') without losing the negative (freedom 'from').

Nancy had a certain religious sensitivity, but he was unhappy that 'in the last few years a nauseating traffic has grown up around a supposed return of the spiritual and of the religious', for God is 'he who wishes to remain unknown' (1985, §§13, 14). He took up a position similar to that of 'dialogical' thinkers: 'God', he said, 'does not belong to the "there is" ' (1993: 236).[65] Rather, the word ' "God"…*becomes* a proper name only when it is *addressed* to that singular existent which lacks a name' (1985, §6).

65. The dialogical thinker Marcel (see above, 3.5) can easily have been known to him.

Ricoeur has for many years been well respected both in France and internationally.[66] Prior to 1980, he had taken account of the several French phases mentioned, learning from them but also keeping a certain distance from them. During the time when existentialism reigned, he focused on forms of individual human life (such as guilt) without being strongly individualistic. When structuralism was dominant, he thought that it did not give sufficient attention to the subject and to the world outside the text and that it was too static, lacking an interest in events. To balance these deficiencies, he gave attention to subjectivity, to external reference, and to temporal processes. In turn, early poststructuralism seemed to him to be excessively fragmenting.

After 1980, he made important contributions in a major work on 'Time and Narrative' (1983–85) and in a study entitled 'Oneself as Another' (1990). In the latter work, he criticized Levinas for dealing inadequately with relationality (1990: 388); however, it is possible to judge that, moving opposite Levinas, Ricoeur tied self and other too closely together by speaking of ethics in terms of self-esteem.

On the basis of a religious commitment, which he attempted to keep distinct from his philosophical analysis, Ricoeur had been a pacifist socialist before World War II. He came to reject pacifism but continued to favor a decentralized form of socialism, with 'participation in discussion at all levels' (1961).[67] In his later years, he again argued for a kind of justice that incorporates love (1991). Interactive freedom was thus an ideal for him.

Outside of the French sphere, too, many thinkers accepted relational thinking after 1980. They included moderate Marxists as well as moderate supporters of market economy.

In particular, the Marxian tradition rejected much of its one-time rigidity without accepting sheer fragmentation. For instance, Ernesto Laclau and Chantal Mouffe argued that identities such as class are 'relational' (involved in a multiplicity of relations) rather than fixed; thus there is no necessary connection between the socioeconomic position and the politics of a given person (1985: 85-86).[68] This analysis took account of the

66. Especially after his retirement in 1980, Ricoeur frequently taught outside of France, but he was highly respected in France at the end of the twentieth century, as he had been earlier (Reagan 1996: 48).

67. In 1968–70, he was on the whole in support of the aims of student rebels; however, as dean, he suffered from the rebellion (Reagan 1996: 31-38), although, according to Touraine (1971: 343), those who attacked him in 1970 were nonpolitical rowdies who took advantage of the situation.

68. This modification had already been anticipated by the 'Frankfurt School' (Adorno, Marcuse, Horkheimer, and Habermas [see on these at various points above]) and to some extent by Antonio Gramsci (not treated here). For Mouffe, see also below, 8.4.

phenomenon that intellectuals can favor radical democracy, although they are themselves not lower-class. Howard Sherman similarly advocated a 'relational' Marxism that considers groups to be 'sometimes in conflict'— not always (1995: 29, 115).

Among those who did not self-identify as Marxists, a number of social and economic theorists who had begun with a view that strongly favored negative freedom moved toward what Chris Sciabarra described as 'dialectical' positions, supporting 'total [including positive] freedom' (2000: 363-83). A prominent figure for whom this was true was Robert Nozick, who modified his earlier championing of an individualist economics. He came to recognize a 'pull' that emanates from the other, calling for respect and support (1981: 451-73; 1989: 212). In this observation, he may have been influenced by Levinas; in 1989, when addressing a general audience, he referred to Judaism in affirmative terms.

Dialogue was a repeated theme. For instance, the pragmatist Richard Bernstein supported the 'practical task of furthering the type of solidarity, participation, and mutual recognition that is founded in dialogical communities' (1983: 231). Bernhard Waldenfels—who had linked the dialogical tradition with phenomenology in 1971—discussed an interaction between order and disorder (1987) and emphasized 'responsiveness' (1997). Similarly, Robert Gibbs, who was indebted to Peirce and to an extensive Jewish tradition (including Levinas), described 'listening' as central for ethics and in this way outlined the nature of responsibility (2000).

Furthermore, David Weissman systematically presented a relational position that stood largely in the pragmatist tradition and was in part indebted to Whitehead. He argued that 'reality is constituted of relationships…and also of…free particles' (2000: 87). He held, further, that there are 'two modes of being, possibility and actuality'. These two conjunctions (relationships/ particles and possibility/actuality) are both typical of relational thinking (as discussed above, 4.1; 5.3).

As has already been seen, Hilary Putnam, Robert Brandom, and Robert Neville presented constructive positions that can be placed in the transmodern stream.[69] Not surprisingly then, a decrease of skepticism was observed near the turn of the century.

To be sure, not everyone was pleased with the decline of skepticism; rather, this decline was lamented by Michael Bérubé (2000) and Vattimo (2001: 232). However, it should be noted that Vattimo, along with Baudrillard, championed a kind of nihilism that was in its own way positive, for it asserted and celebrated an absence or a demise of knowledge.

---

69. For them, see above at various points.

6. *An Overview of the Struggle*

Clearly, the rise of explicit relational thinking in conjunction with the ideals of interactive freedom met with rivalry from the very beginning. Perhaps the sharpest alternative was presented by Nietzsche, who opposed the new social orientation and championed self-assertion, especially in notes that he did not publish. Of course, no single individual is powerful enough to determine the course of history, but some of Nietzsche's words were used to express a mood that led to Italian fascism and German Nazism.

Other philosophers espoused skepticism or nihilism. There is reason to think that skepticism and perhaps nihilism represent transition phenomena, reacting against an outlook that is in the process of emerging. Skeptical and nihilist views were, in fact, expressed primarily by Caucasian males. It is likely that their views reflected a deep sense of insecurity in view of the fact that their hegemony was being undermined.

The emerging struggle between relational theory and nominalism led to the formation of hybrid positions, in which relational and nominalist concepts were intertwined. In fact, many prominent theories were of this sort.

It is noteworthy that the three major relational lines that began near the beginning of the twentieth century continued, even though repeatedly in conjunction with other perspectives. Versions of pragmatism were developed by Habermas, Rorty, Putnam, Brandom, and Gibbs. Phenomenology formed a background for Heidegger, Levinas, Derrida, Ricoeur, and Waldenfels. Elements of the grammatical-dialogical tradition played a role in the thinking of Heidegger, Althusser, Levinas, Lyotard, Foucault, Derrida, Nancy, Waldenfels, Nozick, and Gibbs.

The struggle between relational theory and more or less skeptical nominalism did not run smoothly. In the US, skepticism was stronger in the early decades of the twentieth century and near its end than it was during the middle decades. In France, there was a series of rapid fluctuations. Between 1940 and 1980, French thought highlighted first dispersion in a certain kind of existentialism, then cohesion in structuralism, and then dispersion again in poststructuralism. To a large extent, this fluctuation exhibited a spiral character, so that reflections made in one phase were often continued by the next in modified form. After 1980, a relational outlook, which combines a degree of dispersion with a degree of cohesion, came to the fore, but nihilism was strongly represented as well.

In the various positions discussed, the word 'form' was not a prominent way of referring to an intellectual pattern. In part, this absence was due to the prominence of skeptical or nihilist orientations. It was also due in part to the fact that the term 'structure' was used in its stead, indicating a relatively rational and rigid view of wholes, to which 'poststructuralists' reacted in opposition. Sometimes, nevertheless, the word 'form' appeared.

For instance, Foucault said that the self is a 'form', a complex of relations, rather than a 'substance'. With his typical ambivalence, Derrida (in 1967, as cited above) not only downgraded 'form' in favor of 'force', but also supported form as an outcome of the *différance* he favored.

In their attitudes toward external freedom, nominalist and seminominalist positions varied in line with their intellectual components. They often valued negative freedom, but group particularists stressed a high degree of unity within a group together with hostility to those outside it.

Orientations toward internal freedom were strongly present in many writings, but they varied in character. Specifically, religious issues—which concern internal freedom as an aspect of holistic commitment—could be explored positively, negatively (with freedom from a religious tradition), or in a mixed way. Accordingly, they were addressed in different ways by Heidegger, Baudrillard, Vattimo, Sartre, Lévi-Strauss, Levinas, Derrida, Badiou, Serres, Finkielkraut, and others. The theological traditions on which these figures drew were not monolithic but included the thinking of Karl Barth, who remained in good part nominalist. In his last years, Foucault had quasi-mystical experiences and highlighted self-critique, a form of internal freedom.

Chapter 8

RELATIONAL VS. NOMINALIST APPROACHES
IN WRITINGS BY WOMEN

Women participated in the rise of formal relational thought from its very beginning and played a prominent role in its development, especially so after about 1970 CE when academic positions became more accessible to them. The reason for their prominent role in the relational line probably lies largely in the fact that relational thinking is inclusive and thus welcomes contributions by women. Hardly any women included non-relational elements in their thinking, so that it is not necessary to disentangle different theoretical lines within their work, as is done for Caucasian males in Chapter 7.

The present chapter primarily covers women who wrote in English or French. Complementing the discussions presented in Chapters 3, 4, and 5, it mentions only briefly those whose thought has already been reported.

1. *The Impact and Progress of Women's Thinking until c. 1970 CE*

Pioneers of formal relational thought included Catharine Beecher, Lady Welby, Melusina Fay Peirce, Alice Dewey, and others who have already been reported (ch. 2, n. 17; 3.2; 5.6).[1] Two other important pioneers were Jane Addams and Charlotte Gilman, although neither of them had a formal academic role.[2]

Addams, who was devoted to a Christianity of deed rather than of faith, emphasized the need for ethics to move beyond 'individual relations' to 'larger social relationships' (1902: 221). The work in which she made this statement (on *Democracy and Social Ethics*) was described by James as 'one of the great books of our time' and was used as a text by John Dewey (Seigfried 1996: 228). Another one of her studies dealt with peace (1907). Her role in the formation of the National Association for the Advancement of Colored People, already mentioned, reveals her considerable influence.

1. Harriet Taylor can also be counted as pointing in that direction.
2. The significant role of women in the turn toward relational thought has been noted by Minow in a history of sociology (1990: 173-266).

Gilman interacted closely with Dewey. She thus contributed not only through her own writing but also indirectly through her association with Dewey to a transcendence of individualism in general and to feminism in particular. For instance, she pointed out that the women's movement and the labor movement were linked (1914: 260; cf. Seigfried 1996: 235).

Major contributions along relational lines were made mid-century by Edith Stein, Simone Weil, Susanne Langer, and Hannah Arendt. Among these, Arendt valued plurality together with interaction (Hull 2002: 40-74).[3] For instance, she spoke of a 'web of relationships' and said that 'action and speech need the surrounding presence of others' (1958: 181, 188). She observed that 'we first become aware of freedom or its opposite in our intercourse with others' (1961: 148).

The work of Simone de Beauvoir was important both in general theoretical terms and with respect to the role of women. In regard to theory, she was not only influenced by her partner, Sartre, but also made an impact on his thought.[4] Indeed, she went significantly beyond his focus on negative freedom by insisting on positive freedom. She said that 'freedom can be accomplished only through the freedom of others', for individuals are 'defined only [by their] relation to the world and to other individuals'; they exist only by personal transcendence (1947, Conclusion). Having room for both separateness and connectivity, she said that an appropriate morality will allow for the possibility 'that separate existents can at the same time be tied to each other and that their singular liberties can forge laws valid for all' (1947: 25).

Beauvoir described woman as the 'second sex'. Noting that 'the category of the Other' is integral to consciousness, she said that this category is in principle a reciprocal one; however, since women have lacked a way to organize themselves, they have so far only been the 'other' for males, who are considered to be the 'subjects' or 'absolute' (1949, I, Introduction). She argued that womanhood as a gender is 'made', not 'born', yet she also believed that there will always be some differences between the sexes. In part for this reason, she advocated that women have close relations with other women so that they have their 'own existence' (1949, II, Conclusion). She was bisexual, but in recommending close relations she was probably thinking not only of those that are sexual.

Women were by no means uniform in their thinking. For instance, Ayn Rand, who had experienced Russian socialism, presented in reaction an antistatist position (e.g. 1943). Her relative individualism, however, was

---

3.   For instance, drawing on her Jewish heritage, she used the biblical account of God's creating 'male and female' to support both individuality (no two persons are the same) and community (1958: 8; 2005: 39, 61, 94).

4.   See J. Allen and J. Pilardi in Waithe 1987–95, IV: 282.

not aggressive. She opposed 'initiating physical force against others' (Gotthelf 2000: 91) and spoke of a certain literary figure's being 'free enough to feel benevolence' for his opponents (1943, Pt. 4, ch. 18). Furthermore, she emphasized the employment of shared reason. In fact, she rejected nominalism in favor of a non-Aristotelian essentialism that recognizes the nature of an object on the basis of its 'existing relationships' (1990: 7, 43, 52 [1966–67]; cf. Sciabarra 2000: 133-39). In rejecting skepticism, she stressed the 'objective' character of such a recognition.

2. *Major Relational Themes in Women's Writings after 1970* CE

From about 1970 on, women gained greater access to and better status within academia. There were then many important contributors so that it is difficult to do them justice, although several notable figures, including Mary Hesse and Dorothy Smith, have already been discussed (above, 4.3; 5.4).

Women writers were oriented so frequently toward relational thinking that this kind of thought has been considered (inaccurately) to represent a specifically female perspective. Some thinkers indeed supported a relational path especially for women,[5] but others advocated that a traditionally feminine approach of this sort be incorporated into the life of both sexes (so, e.g., Rosalind Rosenberg 1982: 246). Still others argued that relationality provides the basis for fully equal connections between women and men (e.g. Isabel Heyward 1982). Some women, to be sure, sought separation from men (e.g. Sheila Jeffreys 1993: 206). Quite a few stressed an interaction with nature, such as in 'ecofeminism', which assumes the 'interrelationship'—indeed, 'interdependence'—of all beings 'and the right of all to exist' (Josephine Donovan 1993: 208).

A duality of connectivity and differentiation within the notion of relation was affirmed frequently. For instance, Carol Gilligan said that 'we know ourselves as separate only insofar as we live in connection with others, and...we experience relationship only insofar as we differentiate other from self' (1982: 63). Julia Kristeva placed otherness at the center of love: 'It is because I am separate, forsaken, alone vis-a-vis the other that I can psychologically cross the divide that is the condition of my existence and achieve... ecstasy' (1985, 'Credo'). Luce Irigaray declared, 'You are transcendent to me' and 'what brings us together, separates us'; thus she preferred to say, 'I love to you', instead of 'I love you' (1992, title, 161, 232).

A number of writers affirmed that 'identity' and even 'autonomy' are not contrary to relations.[6] For instance, Ana Keating said that 'Identity is

---

5. Thus, the Jungian M. Esther Harding (1935: 224) and the Freudian Nancy Chodorow (1978: 169).

6. On identity, see Barbara Smith 1983: xi (distinguishing between 'autonomy',

always relational' and is, at least often, 'fluid' (1996: 39, 89). Jean Keller, who characterized autonomy in terms of an ability to represent oneself and to accomplish an intended task, gave a 'dialogical account of autonomy' (1997: 161).

Relations need not be harmonious but can be conflictual. In fact, women recognized many different kinds of relations, including different levels of positive or negative concern.

Reasonably harmonious are relations characterized by cooperation. Michelle Moody-Adams said that cooperation—not just conflict and competition—is 'in some interesting sense...."natural" ' (1998: 259). In any case, some women held that education should be 'collaborative' rather than competitive (e.g. Evelyn Ashton-Jones and Dene Thomas 1995).

Positive relations that go beyond cooperation, which may be only prudential, were characterized as 'care'. In an analysis that opened up an extensive discussion, Gilligan contrasted an ethic of justice that was based on a conception of 'equal worth' with an ethic of 'care', in which 'everyone will be responded to and included' and 'no one will be left alone or hurt' (1982: 63). This care ethic sees 'a world comprised of relationships, a world that coheres through human connection rather than through systems of rules' (29).

Aware of an earlier essay by Gilligan, Nel Noddings made care the subject of a full study in which she pointed to the place of 'receptivity, relatedness, and responsiveness' (1984: 2). She was interested in care, not merely as one person's action or attitude, but as a relationship between two (or more) persons; thus, according to her definition, caring does not take place unless the recipient recognizes it (69). Furthermore, she provided this theoretical ground: 'An ethic of caring is based on a relational ontology; that is, it takes as a basic assumption that all human beings—not just women—are defined in relation' (1989: 236-37). This definition did not imply determinism. Rather, she said, relationality involves a response that is 'at least partly under the control' of each participant in a relation (1989: 237).

Although an ethic of care stands in some tension with an ethic of justice, Seyla Benhabib wished to hold them together (1987). Making use of Habermas's emphasis on communication, she argued that 'every generalized other [an object of justice] is also a concrete other [an object of care]' (1992: 165).

which rests on strength, and 'separatism', which is based on fear); Rosi Braidotti 1991: 281-82 (referring to 'interconnected monadism' in a 'relational mode of thought'); Norwenna Griffiths 1995: 1 (speaking of 'webs of identity'); Eva Kittay 1999: xii, 2 (concerning 'interdependence' together with 'difference'). On autonomy, see Nancy Hirschmann 1992: 286 (for the development of 'a relational autonomy'); Jennifer Radden 1996: 91 ('the relational model...permits and even requires the exercise and expression of autonomy').

Love is even stronger than 'care'. Indeed, Starhawk's vision of love was all-inclusive:

> All is relationship. Perhaps the ultimate ethic of immanence is to choose to make that relationship one of love: love of self and others, ecstatic love, transforming love, delighted love for the myriad forms of life...for wind and sun...love of light and the mysterious darkness, and raging love against all that would diminish the unspeakable beauty of the world (1988: 42, 44).

For her, as for others, connectivity was not rigid: 'Without randomness in a system, there would be nothing new' (43).

Love could be seen as being directed toward the reality of a being beyond oneself. For instance, according to Iris Murdoch, 'compassion or love' is the 'faculty which is supposed to relate us to what is real and thus bring us to what is good' (1971: 66). Similarly, Marilyn Frye spoke of a 'loving eye' that acknowledges a 'reality' beyond one's interests (1983: 75). Love, however, could also be seen as going beyond reality through imagination. Doing so, Teresa de Lauretis favored love in part since it indicates the presence of 'fantasy', which is less self-centered than 'desire' (1994: 284-85).

In any case, an important question was: does a loving person know the other? Kelly Oliver argued that love requires both 'flesh' and 'language' (1997: 232). 'Flesh' is different from intellectual knowledge. In Oliver's words, the other cannot be 'known' in a full sense and so cannot be 'completely understood' (1998: 175). Beyond rational understanding, she supported a more mysterious process called 'witnessing', which includes both 'observing [the other] and testifying [about the other]' (1998: 174; 2001—'witnessing' and 'testifying' are terms with religious associations, as she mentioned).[7] Witnessing, she said, refers to 'relations with difference and otherness that are neither hostile nor assimilating but rather loving or welcoming' (1998: xii).

Ruth Whitney, who described God as 'Infinite Love', went so far as to say that 'feminism is the vision and practice of love' (1998: xii, 21). She rejected 'fusion' but described love as 'a dialogue' (25, 28). The view that people are always or basically 'selfish, power-hungry, greedy' was considered to be a patriarchal one. Instead, she thought—probably also one-sidedly—that 'both women and men are innately loving' (15, 159).

Conflictual relations were also recognized as valuable, however. For instance, Jean Baker Miller, a leading writer on women's psychology, stressed that relationality 'must encompass conflict', especially the kind of conflict that makes for 'more and better connections' and accordingly 'leads to growth' (1986: 140). 'Anger', then, is a 'part of relationships' (Miller and Surrey 1997: 200).

---

7. A similar point of view—but exaggerating the mystery, it seems—was presented by Zygmunt Bauman in 1993.

Many statements and political acts by women countered oppression by men (e.g. Marilyn Frye 1983: 1-16, 33). According to Iris Young, the 'faces' of oppression include exploitation, marginalization, powerlessness, cultural imperialism, and violence (1990: 58-63). To be sure, some writers cautioned against a one-sided image of women as victims, since doing so may picture them as unduly weak.[8] Indeed, many feminists attacked not merely the oppression of women, but sought 'freedom' from oppression for others also (Morgan 1982: xiii).

The reality of conflict raised the question of power. Some feminist philosophers of science criticized the 'centrality of dominance relations' in modern science, viewing this as a masculinist outlook.[9] Although most women writers were ready to accept the use of power, many rejected the equation of power with 'dominance' (e.g. Emmet 1953) or with 'violence' (e.g. Arendt 1970). On the whole, there was more interest in 'power-with' or in 'power-for' than in 'power-over' someone or something.[10] Such a position does not necessarily reject all violent force. Chantal Mouffe insisted that violence is sometimes needed for the emergence of democracy (1999: 190).

The various positions just mentioned did not, of course, altogether agree. Still, it is clear that—according to the formulation of Nancy Hirschmann—many of them embraced mutually modified versions of both negative and positive freedom in the social order (2003).

The relations that have been mentioned so far are external. In addition, women were interested in internal relations. In fact, the two kinds of relations overlap each other. For instance, an important feature of internal freedom (as mentioned) is ethical self-transcendence, an integral part of selfhood.

In contrast to external authority, internal apprehension played an important role in what Mary Belenky and her associates described as 'women's ways of knowing' (1986: 5). These include 'silence' and 'listening to the views of others' together with listening to 'the inner voice'. Listening to others was said to be, at its best, an 'active and demanding process' (37); in contrast, those who think that they receive all knowledge without being active themselves are likely to think of their sources as 'authorities, not friends' (39).

These authors valued both 'separate' and 'connected' knowing. 'Separate' knowing entertains doubt, recognizing 'that everyone may be wrong' (104). This doubt includes an acknowledgement that oneself may be wrong;

8. See Betty Friedan 1981: 187; Adrienne Rich 1986: 221; Chandra Mohanty 1987: 35, on roles of women internationally; Michèle Barrett 1988: v, revising an earlier position somewhat; and Amy Allen 1999, II: 18-24.

9. E.g., Lynn Nelson (1990: 212). For Evelyn Keller, see above, 5.5.

10. See Amy Allen 1999.

after all, self-criticism is part of internal freedom (see above, 1.3, and below, 10.4). 'Connected' knowing means that one is empathetic toward others and also trustful of one's own experience, so that one does not rely on authoritative pronouncements (112-13). Whether or not these 'ways' are indeed especially characteristic of women, it should be noted that their formulation represented a theoretical contribution by women.

Starhawk similarly pointed to an internal process as she distinguished between three kinds of power. Alongside 'power-over' and 'power-with', she listed 'power-from-within'. This, she said, is 'linked to the total mysteries that awaken our deepest abilities and potentials'; more specifically, power-from-within arises from a 'sense of connection' with other beings, all of whom are 'dynamic' and have 'inherent value' (1987: 9, 15).

When internal freedom reaches (or attempts to reach) all of reality, it can be called 'religious' or 'spiritual'. In fact, much of the feminism that stressed a connection with the nonhuman world—such as 'ecofeminism'— was oriented toward spirituality or the sacred.[11] For instance Carol Adams said that 'God unfolds in relationships' (1994: 195), and Gloria Anzaldúa, that 'like love, spirituality is a relational activity leading to deep bonds between people, plants, animals, and the forces of nature' (1997: vii).[12]

Spiritually oriented feminists were, on the whole, not traditional in their form of religion. For instance, some of them renewed goddess worship (e.g. Starhawk 1987: 310). Yet many feminists were also active within Jewish and Christian communities.[13] Some held that they were, in part, 'the heirs of a very strong account—a Hebrew-Christian story'—concerning the liberation of the oppressed (Elshtain 1997: 333).[14]

In France, several prominent figures connected women's issues with religion or the 'sacred'. They included Irigaray and Kristeva (already mentioned) as well as Hélène Cixous.

Irigaray argued that only the God of 'monosexed truth' is dead (1984: 133). She looked for a 'female god' to come, for without God there can be no communication or communion: 'only the divine offers us—requires—freedom'

11. E.g. Maria Mies and Vandana Shiva 1993: 16; Carol Adams 1993; cf. overviews by Mellor (1997) and H. Eaton (1998).

12. Enthusiastically inclusive works were produced in the US by Charlene Spretnak (1982, 1991), Cynthia Eller (1993), Riane Eisler (1995), Mary Daly (1998), and Gail Holland (1998). Other exponents of 'women's spirituality' were Audre Lorde, Adrienne Rich, and Alice Walker (cf. Conner *et al.* 1997: 37).

13. Major Christian feminists—only a small selection—were discussed by Ruether (1998). On Anzaldúa, see, further, below, 9.3. Martha Nussbaum identified herself as a 'liberal Jew' (1999: 21). Catholic, although not necessarily self-identified as 'feminist', were Anscombe and Hesse.

14. Jean Bethke Elshtain did go beyond traditional Christianity, chairing a task group supporting gays (1995: 53).

(1987: 74, 79-80). This freedom, she said, is simultaneously carnal and spiritual (1992: 35); it connects the microcosmic with the macrocosmic dimensions (1984: 14).

Cixous, a lesbian writer with a Jewish background, also focused on internal freedom. She said that 'the face of God'—which she identified with what she presents—'*is none other than my own face*, but seen naked'. It unveils 'the small non-truths that are needed in living under the blow of truth' (1993: 63).

Kristeva grew up in an Eastern Orthodox family in Marxist Bulgaria, entering France in 1965. Although she was 'not a believer' (1985: 35), she explored Jewish, Christian, and other religious traditions with a simultaneous focus on love and separation. Instead of supporting 'religion', she favored an acknowledgment of the 'sacred', which, she said, stands at the tensive conjunction of individual gratification and community (1998a: 43). She believed that the experience of the twentieth century had shown 'that socio-political transformation is not possible without a transformation of subjects' (1974b: 23). Accordingly, she sought both external and internal freedom: both the 'liberty of desire...for objects, knowledge and production' and the 'liberty of a retreat, in intimacy and mystical participation' (1998b: 62).

The question of how internal and external freedoms should be related was addressed by Drucilla Cornell. She emphasized the importance of an 'imaginary domain', which recognizes all human beings as members of 'the moral community of persons' (1998: 16, 23). In her view, societal laws should protect and support this 'sanctuary', but they should not attempt to shape it if genuine freedom is to obtain.

The practice of 'consciousness raising', carried out in small-group discussions about issues facing women, was in good part internal, but it had external implications. Widely pursued for several decades, it assumed that liberation requires 'self-transformation' in interaction with 'social and political transformation' (P. Allen 1970: 12-13; McLaren 2002: 155, 158). The transformation sought in such discussion largely involved increased self-assertiveness.

Furthermore, an important element in an internal focus was attention to the body. This was frequently positive (such as in The Boston Women's Health Book Collective 1984). Gloria Steinem asked, when advocating a 'revolution from within': 'How could we have let body and spirit, sexuality and spirituality be split?' (1992: 311).

3. *The Question of Women's Special Character*

Is the outlook that has just been described, then, peculiarly 'feminine' or 'female'? In other words, what differences, if any, are there between and within the sexes?

The view that there are major differences between the sexes has been called 'essentialist', but those who were accused of holding such a view did not necessarily adhere to essentialism in an Aristotelian sense, which would mean that women all share a certain set of characteristics that is absent from men.[15] However, the term could be used in a 'strategic' sense as a short-hand way of speaking on behalf of women, temporarily ignoring variations among them, as was done by Gayatri Spivak (1987: 205; 1990: 11; 1993: 4).

Irigaray did accept a certain kind of essentialism, although it is not clear what kind (1984, etc.). It is possible that she considered the difference between the sexes to constitute something like an 'ideal type' (mildly Platonic in character). In any case, that was Kristeva's position. She believed that the difference between women and men 'belongs to *metaphysics*' (1979); in other words, it is theoretical rather than empirical. The dichotomy, she said, acts to 'inscribe difference at the heart of the universal' (1996: 269).

If 'femininity' is defined in ideal (quasi-Platonic) terms, rather than as representing (in an Aristotelian way) the character of all women and only of women, it is a form of life in which males can participate. In this sense, Linda Shepherd (1993) considered the following features of 'science' to be 'feminine': feeling, receptivity, subjectivity, multiplicity, nurturing, cooperation, intuition, relatedness, social responsibility. She believed that these features also appear in men, although they are more typical of women.

Incidentally, envisioning and valuing a difference between women and men does not necessarily assume that such a difference is biologically based. What has been called 'cultural feminism' could leave that question open (cf. Echols 1989: 5-6).

In any case, to what extent relative differences (tendencies rather than essences) should be valued was a question in regard to which there were divergent opinions. Representing one side of the debate, some women hoped that differences between the sexes would become minimal. Susan Okin, for instance, has said that 'a just future would be one without gender' (1989: 171). In regard to intellectual processes, Susan Haack rejected a special 'feminist epistemology' (1998: 123).

Others accepted relative difference together with commonality. For instance, Anne Phillips valued 'sexual and other kinds of difference' and rejected the idea of a 'degendered, "neutered" individual as the basis for our aspiration'. At the same time, she supported 'an impulse toward universality: a recognition of the partial, and potentially confining, nature of all our different and specific perspectives from which we have previously viewed the world; a politics of greater generality and alliance' (1993: 71).[16]

15. Thus, rightly, e.g., Cressida Heyes (2000: 20-23).
16. Similarly, e.g., Pamela Jensen (1996: 18) and Janet Jakobsen (1998: 150, etc.).

Especially with the rise of gay/lesbian/transgender concerns, this issue moved to another level. Thus, Judith Butler asked, 'Why can't the framework for sexual difference itself move beyond binarity into multiplicity?' (2004: 197).

An expressly relational position, which rejected uniformity, was outlined by Iris Young. Instead of 'essentializing' groups, she favored 'a relational understanding of group differences', which accepts 'overlapping experiences'. 'Difference', she said, 'emerges not as a description of the attributes of a group, but as a function of the relationships between groups and the interaction of groups with institutions' (1990: 171). In a similar way, Scandinavians Anna Jónasdóttir and Drude von der Fehr sought to overcome a dichotomy between 'equality' and 'difference' through '*thinking relationally*' (1998: 4). They said that 'instead of thinking in terms of closed or discrete categories of meaning and societal facts, this view is directed at processes in which people interactively…create various kinds of social and cultural value'.

A move beyond dichotomies leads to 'both/and' thinking, which some have thought to be typical of, although not limited to, women (Tavor Bannet 1993: 88-112). According to Caroline Whitbeck (1984), this kind of thinking tones down oppositions between human groups, between spirit and matter, between private and public realms, or between the human and the divine, since it accepts both differences and commonality.

4. *The Question of Postmodernism*

Most commonly, feminists held to the version of postmodernism that has been called 'transmodern', which includes a relational view. For instance, Rosi Braidotti spoke of feminism's 'relational mode of thought' as 'the one possible new ethical system of postmodernism' (1991: 282-83). In a similar vein, bell hooks declared:

> Radical postmodernism calls attention to those shared sensibilities which cross the boundaries of class, gender, race, etc., that could be fertile ground for the construction of empathy—ties that would promote recognition of common commitments and serve as a base for solidarity and coalition (1990: 27).

Sandra Harding, too, used the word 'postmodern' with a constructive relational meaning. Like the Marxian Nancy Hartsock (1983: 231), she advocated a 'standpoint' theory: one that speaks from a certain social location without the implication that doing so vitiates a claim to truth. In fact, she held that an oppressed group (proletariat or women) has a better insight into social reality than does a ruling one, for ruling persons are blinded by the fact that the current order favors them (1998: 18). Furthermore, she held that (appropriate) values do not undermine but, rather, support science.

Specifically, 'commitments to antiauthoritarian, participatory, and emancipatory values and projects...increase the objectivity of science' (1986: 27).

A subjective element was not ruled out by Harding's position. On the contrary, a recognition of the subjective aspect 'increases the objectivity of research and decreases the 'objectivism' which hides this kind of evidence from the public' (1987: 9). 'Objectivity' here does not mean 'neutrality' (1998: 129). Harding refused to grant that a nominalist (or skeptical) view is the only one to be recognized as 'postmodern' and said instead: 'I think standpoint theory...*is* a postmodernism, and I think that feminism is a postmodernism' (in Olson and Hirsh 1995: 24; similarly, earlier, Harding 1991: 49).

It is true, Harding's position may have been unduly self-confident. More moderate versions of standpoint theory held that it is possible to acknowledge the place where one stands without becoming skeptical, but that one should not claim a privileged access to truth. For instance, Dorothy Smith, well known for 'taking up women's standpoint' within sociology, rejected the idea that 'women's experience is privileged' (1997: 393, 395 [cf. on her above, 5.4]). The Marxian ('post-Marxist') Mouffe also did 'not really see how any group can have epistemic privilege' (1999: 186).

Although women's views were thus at least moderately affirmative and for the most part relational, they were faced with the nominalist postmodernism advocated by a number of male writers (see above, 7.4). In the US, this confrontation took place especially during the 1980s as a delayed response to French thinking of the 1970s. In reporting this situation, one can distinguish between responses (1) to Lyotard, with his characterization of 'postmodernism' in 1979; (2) to Foucault and Derrida, who joined relational with nominalist ideas; and (3) to strongly fragmenting (including skeptical and nihilist) positions, often cited without attribution to an individual author.

In regard to Lyotard, the most important issue was his claim in 1979 that 'grand narratives' met a demise. Women writers who spoke to this point were largely critical of this view.

For instance, it was possible to distinguish between the secular and religious visions that Lyotard placed together. Specifically, Donna Haraway— who was part of the Catholic Left at the end of the '60s (1997: 13, 28)—said that 'universal, totalizing [secular] theory is a major mistake'. Yet, as an 'Irish Catholic', she affirmed the 'continued relevance of religion' (1990: 214-15, 223; cf. 1997: 2).

Apart from the question of religion, Braidotti reported that 'the majority of feminists have applied a healthy dose of suspicion to the melancholy discourse of the loss of legitimacies of master narratives' (1997: 219). Even Nancy Fraser and Linda Nicholson, who in many ways stood close to seminominalist thinkers, argued, 'contra Lyotard, that postmodern critiques need forswear neither large historical narratives nor analyses for societal macrostructures' and that 'postmodern feminists need not abandon large theoretical tools needed to address large political problems' (1988: 390). Similarly, Dorothy Smith said that 'we are always located in particular, actual places', but to 'repudiate master narratives defeats the essential character of inquiry' (1990: 34). Lynn Hunt went so far as to assert that 'metanarratives are the kinds of narratives that make action possible' (1990: 110).

Comprehensive visions could be accepted not in terms of strict predictability, but on a tentative basis. In this way, Miranda Fricker supported 'some form of "totality" as a *regulative ideal*' (1994: 102; similarly, 2000), and Honi Haber held that at least a 'temporal' (provisional) closure is needed, one that is subject to revision (1994: 133). Emphatically, but also cautiously, the Marxian Kathi Weeks affirmed an 'aspiration to totality' (1998: 97).

Chantal Mouffe, also Marxian, characterized the notion of 'difference' in a way which diverges from sheer unconnectedness and which includes reference to totality: 'difference is the possibility of constituting unity and totality at the same time that it provides their essential limits' (1996: 254). Going in the same direction, Victoria Bonnell and Lynn Hunt judged that 'knowledge grows by specialization and fragmentation, but understanding what that knowledge means probably requires some reintegration' (1999: 26-27).

Reactions to Foucault and Derrida were complex. Typically, women thinkers appreciated some aspects of their thinking, especially the relational strand, but rejected others, especially the nominalist/skeptical side.[17] Thus, Joan Scott, one of the more appreciative readers of Foucault, referred at one point to his 'relational' perspective (1988: 59). Elizabeth Grosz, who emphatically dismissed (nominalist) 'postmodernism', was sympathetic toward Derrida (1997).

Several specific aspects of the work of Foucault and Derrida were valued. For instance, quite a few agreed with Foucault's undermining of classical Marxism, which had focused one-sidedly on class identification. Lesbians and bisexuals, especially, appreciated Foucault's questioning of traditional attitudes toward sexuality. (That was true, for instance, for Shane Phelan [1994] and Ladelle McWhorter [1999], although they did not endorse Foucault's viewpoint altogether.) In Derrida's work, some saw a valuable challenge to established ways of thinking, one that can also warn women of positions that are too simple (e.g. Drucilla Cornell 1991; Diane Elam 1994).

---

17. A both-positive-and-negative view of Foucault was furnished, e.g., by Jana Sawicki (1991); a more sharply critical one, by Somer Brodribb (1992). Varied feminist treatments of Foucault appeared in Hekman 1996, and of Derrida in N.J. Holland 1997. The 'final Foucault' was appreciated at least in good part by contributors to Dianna Taylor and Karen Vintges 2004.

Yet most women writers saw that Foucault and Derrida were androcentric (e.g. Jana Sawicki 1991: 102-109; Ellen Feder and Emily Zakin 1997: 45) and that the skepticism of these two men, even though it was moderate, created problems for feminism.[18] Thus, both in the US and in France (Allwood 1998: 66), feminists directed definite criticism against some elements of Foucault's and Derrida's writings.

In a history of research dealing with nonhuman primates, Haraway showed that certain values and mythic structures (especially of a Judeo-Christian kind) entered into the research (1989). Yet she also distanced herself from a strongly constructionist view of science, which—along the lines of Foucault in the mid-1970s—grounded everything in 'force fields'. In her judgment this was a masculinist war-like image (1988: 577-78).[19]

Perhaps the most famous challenge is Hartsock's, especially in response to Foucault's writings during the 1960s and 1970s:

> Why is it that just at the moment when so many of us who have been silenced begin to demand the right to name ourselves, to act as subjects rather than objects of history, that just then the concept of subject becomes problematic? Just when we are forming our own theories about the world, uncertainty emerges about whether the world can be theorized. Just when we are talking about the changes we want, ideas of progress and the possibility of systematically and rationally organizing human society become dubious and suspect (1990: 163-64 [1987]).[20]

Some of the objections to these writers and to others who stood close to them focused on their exclusiveness and mystifying style. Meaghan Morris observed that this line constitutes 'largely a male debate', in which women's work is rarely cited (1988: 11, 15). hooks objected similarly: 'As a discursive practice it is dominated primarily by the voices of white male intellectuals and/or academic elites who speak to and about one another with coded familiarity' (1990: 24).

A similarly sharp critique of poststructuralists was presented by Meili Steele. She thought that they use 'terrorism' instead of dialogue in their manner of presentation, since they disavow a 'common ground' on which to base 'arguments' (1997: 29-30). In regard to content, she held that the views of Foucault and Derrida, as well as of Lyotard, 'block' the 'empowering shapes of positive liberty', such as is sought in education, through their primary appeal to 'negative freedom' (1997: 31, 204-205).

18. Derrida expressly rejected political 'feminism' of the kind favored by de Beauvoir, although he supported the women's special cultural perspective advocated by Antoinette Fouque (see above, 7.4).

19. In a similar way, Helen Longino 1990, Lynn Nelson 1990, Jane Duran 1991, and Dorothy Smith 1999 emphasized the contextual nature of knowledge without adopting skepticism.

20. Similarly, Sandra Harding (less strongly Marxist than Hartsock) in 1987: 10.

However, after these three figures moved toward more positive positions after about 1980 CE (which came to be known in the US a decade later), Hartsock modified her assessment of them. She still held that 'far from being a resource for the development of new and more inclusive social movements, [skeptical] postmodernist theories represent and express the voices of the powerful', but she also saw with appreciation that this kind of postmodernism showed that 'the destabilized voices of the powerful' were 'being forced to come to terms with the voices of the disenfranchised' (1998: 251).

A relatively positive reaction to Foucault and other French thinkers was presented by Judith Butler, a Jewish lesbian. She also adopted their difficult style.

In 1990 she discussed feminist issues in terms of Foucault's view that subjects are produced by power.[21] Her analysis favored the opinion that gender is 'constructed' rather than inborn. Unfortunately, the term 'construction' was unclear. To clarify her position, Butler pointed out in 1993 that it is not true (and that she had not intended to say) that 'everything is discursively [arbitrarily] constructed'; on the contrary, 'the debate between constructivism and essentialism misses the point of deconstruction', which avoids one-sidedness (8).

In 1993 and even more in 1997, Butler discussed Foucault's thesis (indebted to Althusser) that subjecthood arises from being addressed by a superior power. She accepted that thesis, being fully aware that a theological idea lay behind it. However, going beyond Althusser and in part beyond Foucault, she described the subject as not just passive but as 'the effect of power in recoil' (1997: 6).

In fact, Butler was not a skeptical relativist. Rather, she expressly disavowed 'a nihilistic relativism incapable of furnishing norms' and even accepted 'totalizing' as 'a site for permanent political contest' (1992: 6, 8, 17). She also rejected a then-popular 'antifoundationalism', which sought to avoid a concern with fundamental issues, and said that such a view (as also its opposite, which seeks a secure ground) engenders skepticism. Instead, she argued that 'theory posits foundations incessantly' (1992: 7).

Toward the end of the 1990s, Butler recognized, on the basis of her experience as a leader of a group dedicated to 'gay and lesbian human rights', that the idea of 'universality' does not need to be rejected altogether. She came to see that the idea 'has important strategic use precisely as a nonsubstantial and open-ended category', 'holding out the possibility for a convergence of cultural horizons' (1999: xvii).

Women's reactions to skepticism or fragmentation was usually negative.[22] For instance, in opposition to an outlook that wants to avoid an ontological

21. See the 'Introduction' in Foucault 1976a.
22. For Haraway's and Dorothy Smith's responses, see above, 5.4.

commitment, the pragmatist philosopher Sandra Rosenthal argued that 'historical rootedness is at once ontological rootedness' (1986: 172). Gilligan expressed the desire 'to move the discussion of differences away from [skeptical] relativism to relationship' (1993: xviii). Grosz voiced the opinion that 'I do not believe that the phenomenon of [this kind of] postmodernism...has anything to offer feminism' (1997: 74).

These rejections were often based on ethics. Haber observed that 'if 'good' is equivalent to whatever one adopts, then justice (as well as morality) becomes a matter of dominance of the strongest voice' (1994: 31). According to Linda Alcoff, skepticism 'has an unfortunately useful application in postmodern capitalism to disarm indiscriminately all theories of liberation' (1997: 24).

Nevertheless, a few feminists did move toward accepting skepticism. Among these was Jane Flax. It is true, early on she had argued that 'all concepts must be relational and contextual' (1983: 271). However, in subsequent works she sought to incorporate semiskeptical insights. She was still suspicious of the '[nominalist] postmodernist critique of subjectivity', which came at the time when 'women have just begun to remember their selves' (1990: 216, 222). Yet she sufficiently accepted skepticism to say that there can be justice independently of questions of truth (1992: 459).

An opposite path (toward less skepticism) was taken by Barbara Herrnstein Smith. In 1988, with appreciation for Derrida and Foucault but without much express involvement in feminism, she argued for moderate skepticism.[23] Subsequently, she made clear that she favored a more positive interactional view, according to which beliefs are modified or maintained by the consequences of acts that are based on those beliefs (1997: 45).

For some women, in fact, participation in a skeptical line implied caution toward feminist enthusiasm. For instance, Ann Game sympathetically described a deconstructive sociology which emphasizes 'particularity', 'multiplicity', and 'sexual indeterminacy'; she accordingly disavowed seeking 'a 'feminist' revolution' (1991: 189-90). Along this line, Anna Yeatman said that 'feminist theory has matured to the point where it is able to subject its own premises to an ironical skeptical and critical mode of analysis' (1994: 49).

However, positive relational views remained predominant. As skepticism receded in at least some male thinking (see above, 7.5), Susan Friedman welcomed 'the return of history and the "Real" to theory' (1998: 12, 182). Similarly enthusiastic was Charlene Spretnak, part of a broad movement by members of both sexes that linked internal and social transformation. She

23. In this work, she emphasized a market model for society; in contrast, a relational conception—while it can have room for a market—would not make it a central principle of organization.

contrasted two different kinds of 'postmodernism', labeling the second—
which she obviously preferred—'ecological' (1999: 73), as follows:

World:	An aggregate of fragments	A community of subjects
Primary truth:	The particular	The particular-in-context
Science:	It's only a narrative!	Complexity

5. *Summing Up*

Perhaps since the term 'postmodern' remains extremely unclear, women's
thinking has sometimes been confusingly placed together with the nominalist version, which on the whole opposed the women's movement. It is
more accurate to see that women favored, for the most part, the transmodern
relational view of form, contributing much to its emergence near the year
1900 CE.

Women writers were rarely skeptical and were ambivalent toward the
mixed nominalist/relational perspectives of Foucault and Derrida. They
could tie in with pragmatism (Sandra Rosenthal, Benhabib) or, in part at
least, with the dialogical tradition (Butler, Oliver), but they could also
express in other ways the larger relational ethos, which recognized connectivity together with a degree of separation. To be sure, their thought was not
uniform, and some women leaned toward essentialism or, less often, toward
nominalism.

Most women writers favored interactive freedom. Socially, they supported a variety of relations, both positive and negative—often favoring
cooperation but allowing for individuality. Personally, they frequently
valued both the body and an intuitive ('spiritual' or 'sacred') sense of reality
as a whole. To be sure, they differed in regard to specific policy questions.

Chapter 9

Intercultural Views

Given the increasing interaction between areas of the world and between cultures, an important twentieth-century phenomenon was the presence of a considerable number of thinkers who stood on the border between cultural spheres. Those represented in the present chapter are all non-Caucasian, although most of them have lived at least temporarily in the West, especially in the US. Since some of them are women, this group of writers overlaps with the one discussed in Chapter 8.

The outlook of these thinkers was predominantly relational. That is understandable, in part since they were deeply involved in interactions between groups and in part since the major alternative at the time—nominalism— was primarily a Western way of thinking.

1. *Disputes about Postmodernism*

For the most part, intercultural writers rejected the nominalist version of postmodernism, especially when some of its representatives claimed to speak for the rest of the world. For instance, one nominalist postmodern said that 'in a certain sense, the discourse of postmodernism—although it is a discourse established in the Eurocentric 'First' world—is the discourse *of* the periphery', which 'decenters the centre' (Docherty 1993: 445). That was a rather strange claim; it implied, first, that Europe was the center of discourse and, second, that the discourse of the periphery could be presented by members of such a center by employing 'ventriloquism', as Radhakrishnan called it (2000: 64).

Indeed, a charge leveled against nominalist/skeptical postmodernism (for instance, by Kumkum Sangari 1999: 25-26) was that it universalized itself and thereby avoided recognition of the significance of other cultures. Like others, Inderpal Grewal and Caren Kaplan pointed out that most writings of this kind ignored both postcolonial and gender issues (1994: 5-6). Attributing an imperialist orientation to such writings, Ziauddin Sardar said that 'now that the west itself doubts the validity of its own reality and truth, it seeks to maintain the status quo and continue unchecked on its trajectory of expansion and domination by undermining all criteria of reality and truth'

(1998: 15; cf. 291). Earlier, the African American Barbara Christian said of most nominalist postmodern writing that she was 'appalled by the sheer ugliness of its language, its lack of clarity [and] pleasurableness, its alienating quality'; it 'mystifies rather than clarifies...our condition, making it possible for a few people who know [this theory] to control the critical scene'. In fact, it 'surfaced, interestingly enough, just when the literature of peoples of color, of black women, of Latin Americans, of Africans began to move to the center' (1987: 56).[1]

Another charge against nominalist postmodernism was that it runs counter to desirable social movements. For instance, Maria Nzomo judged that a one-sided emphasis on separateness is 'not in harmony with the democratic ideals and strategies guiding women in their pursuit of gender-sensitive democratization in Kenya' (1995: 133). The Marxian Rajnarayan Chandavarkar thought that attention to 'the material world' was threatened by skepticism (1998: 21).

Nevertheless, a number of non-Caucasian assessments of this outlook were more favorable, at least for their own interests. Some averred that skeptical-postmodern themes could be used to destabilize the 'repressive European archive' (Tiffin 1991: x). Others saw in the rise of skepticism a sign that Western thought was becoming exhausted, so that its hegemony could be overcome by non-Western orientations (thus, Akbar Ahmed 1992: 28; Susantha Goonatilake 1998: 3).

Many of the critiques directed against radical nominalism were only partially applicable to the mixed nominalist/relational positions of Foucault and Derrida. In fact, appreciative use of some of their observations was made by Edward Said, Gayatri Spivak, Homi Bhabha, Chandra Mohanty, Rajagopalan Radhakrishnan, and Édouard Glissant, although on the whole they had more fully relational views, which are cited below.[2] Yet these writers did not accept Foucault's and Derrida's ideas uncritically. For instance, Said, who made use of Foucault's idea of 'discourse' in 1978, claimed a few years later that it was not a coincidence that skeptical textualism ('only the text is real') became popular in the 'free market' Reagan period, the culture of which he at least partially opposed (1983: 4). Spivak had reservations about Derrida's outlook regarding women's roles (1987: 84, 91) and later criticized Foucault's work prior to c. 1980

1. Cf. similar statements by Hartsock and S. Harding, both in 1987 (see above, 8.4), by the Native American Jace Weaver (1996: 166), and by those listed by Shohat and Stam (1994: 345).

2. E.g., Radhakrishnan could value poststructuralism, but not (skeptical) postmodernism (2000: 38). Partha Chatterjee's use of Foucault was partial (1993: 75). For some other positive, as well as negative, views of poststructuralism, see essays reprinted in Chaturvedi 2000: 94-95, 131-33, 179, 220-38, 276. Mostly negative views were reported by Neil Larsen (2000: 155).

(she was aware that Foucault had a change in perspective thereafter; e.g. Spivak 1999: 121, 238, 253-58, 265, 278).

The term 'postmodern', in any case, is ambiguous. Marianne Marchand and Jane Parpart indicated that many writers—including contributors to the volume they edited—used the term to designate an outlook that sees not just fragmentation, but 'unity in diversity' (1995: 131). Similarly, Arif Dirlik and Xudong Zhang thought that 'postmodernism'—in contrast to 'modern' Marxism—'has heuristic uses for dealing with a situation of simultaneous unity and dispersal' (2000: 4, 17). In such uses, the word becomes synonymous with 'transmodern'. This term, then, was used by a number of Western observers to describe intercultural developments (e.g. Luyckx 1999; Venn 2000: 2, 236; Turnbull 2000: 1).

2. *Major Intercultural Themes*

Relationality vs. Sheer Otherness
During the latter half of the twentieth century, many Caucasian writers believed (or supposedly believed) that there was a sharp difference between cultures, so that communication between cultures is impossible or at least inadvisable. To be sure, it is not easy to find a thoughtful version of such a belief, for, although there were many references to such a view, individual thinkers who might have held it are rarely cited. In any case, non-Caucasians did not ordinarily hold such a non-communicational outlook.

Rather, the idea of sheer otherness was seen as a problem. For instance, in 1978, Said described 'Orientalism' as a Western outlook that inappropriately envisioned the Orient (specifically, Islam) as a unified 'other' inferior to the 'West'.[3] In 1993, he again argued that European imperialism presupposed an emphasis on stereotypical differences (58). In opposition to taking a separate stance, he said that 'we face...the deep, profoundly perturbed and perturbing questions of our relationship to others'; we cannot step outside of these relations to an independent vantage point, for we are 'of the connections, not outside or beyond them' (55). This statement accepted relativity, but it also implied that it is not wise to withdraw from involvement with the rest of the world in order to give attention to 'local' issues (20-21, *pace* Foucault and Lyotard; cf. 41, 278). He favored proceeding through the UN in the Gulf crisis (1991).

In a somewhat similar way, T. Minh-ha Trinh advocated a recognition of 'difference' without 'separation' or 'division'. Especially, she rejected the

---

3. Unfortunately, Said's conception of 'Orientalism' was itself not free of the essentialism he deplored. It would have been better if he has simply said that most European scholars of Islam had a derogatory view.

188 *The Concept of Form in the Twentieth Century*

assumption that every group has a distinct point of view which each of its members can represent (1989: 80, 82).

Bhabha contrasted an engaged 'difference' with an 'ethical relativism' of 'distance', which, he said, treats 'diversity' as an object of contemplation (1990: 208-209; 1994: 34-36). He emphasized that cultures are not isolated but interrelated, so that hybrids are formed, as others had already noted (1990: 211; 1994: 35-36). His vision of 'difference' should therefore not be confused with 'differentiation', with which he said colonialists justified the conquest of supposedly inferior 'others' (1994: 70, 111).[4]

Edouard Glissant, a major Caribbean-French writer, contributed important theoretical reflections. He made 'Relation' (capitalized) his central notion. With striking assonance, he defined relation as 'the possibility for everyone to be, in every moment, solidary and solitary' (1990: 145 [ch. 4, *précis*]). In other words, relationality involves both connection and disconnection—presumably each partial. The relative independence of every entity (person, text, and so on) is guarded by its 'opacity', that is, by the fact that it cannot be 'grasped' or (fully) understood.[5] This represents 'freedom', but not 'autism' (1990: 204).

Interaction vs. Pure Localism

In a number of works, it became clear that local cultures have never been isolated and that the so-called 'West', too, has never been independent of other cultures (e.g. Said 1993: 217). Arjun Appadurai accordingly described 'locality' not as independent but as 'relational' (1996: 178), as did Sangari (1999: xlviii). Gordana Jovanović averred that a purely particular point of view is an isolated, inaccessible one. Instead of an 'autistic' outlook, he favored a 'communicational' one (1998: 180-81).

Indeed, there was much interest in growth through interaction. Such growth could be viewed as anticolonialist. Frantz Fanon complained that colonial powers tried to keep the cultures over which they ruled from changing, so that they became 'mummified' (1964, ch. 2 [1956]). Instead, Fanon declared, 'what we want to do is go forward...in the company of all...to a different level than that which Europe has shown' (1961, Conclusion). His was not an isolated opinion. Rather, according to Claude Lévi-Strauss, local leaders in Africa and Asia were largely opposed to stand-pat relativism, which was popular among anthropologists (1958–73, 2.4 [1965]).

---

4. See above, 1.3. The African American Houston Baker, Jr., observed a dualistic 'self-and-other' in the Enlightenment (1986: 183). Albert Memmi, too, spoke of the 'antithesis hardened by the colonizer' (1966, Conclusion).

5. Cf. Celia Britton 1999 (with index), for this and other themes. Cf. also above, 4.1.

Among African figures, Amilcar Cabral urged the 'development...of a national culture...of a universal culture...of feelings of humanism, of solidarity, of respect' (1973: 55). Although he was strongly Afrocentric, Cheikh Diop, too, was transnational in 'forseeing...the blooming of an era of genuine humanity...without ethnic coordinates' (1981: 476-77). In 1985, Samir Amin called for a 'delinked', 'polycentric' world to counter global capitalism. This was not a separatist vision; rather, he hoped that it would 'lay the foundation for a renewal of internationalism of peoples and universalism' (1990: ix). To facilitate this, he urged a reconciliation of 'general interdependence' with 'a legitimate concern for autonomy' (1991: 90).

Speaking out of Indic tradition, J.L. Mehta eloquently expressed a vision of interaction in 1969:

> Can we simply turn our backs on our own past, just discard it, and appropriate the final fruits of Western self-understanding as *the* inner telos of [human beings] universally and as such, or shall we reject the spiritual-philosophical endeavor of the West altogether as of no consequence and seek to entrench ourselves into a specifically Indian philosophizing...or shall we begin to *understand* both in their mutual otherness, to learn the language of each and so to evolve ways of thinking and talking which will be truly appropriate to our membership of both worlds, striving in such fashion to transform it into one? (1985: 159 [1969]).

Spivak, whose home was India, hoped for mutually enriching exchanges as well (1999: 382-83). Both visionary and cautious in expression, she sought an 'internationality of ecological justice in that impossible, undivided world of which one must dream'. She believed that the way forward involves 'love', a process that is 'slow, attentive', and 'mindchanging on both sides'.

Generality vs. Different Kinds of Universality

A controversial issue was that of universality. Unfortunately, the word 'universalism' has several quite different meanings or applications. Thus, in the following they are considered in turn.

One kind of universalism, which can be called 'unitive', expresses the belief that human life is highly uniform. As a description of human life, it almost inevitably identifies the universal with a particular view. Labeled 'pseudo-universalism' (Ruether 1974: 233; Appiah 1992: 54), it 'inaccurately universalizes a particular perspective' (M. Farley 1993: 171). Indeed, as was explained above (1.1; 4.1), a strongly unitive universalism treats a whole as a large particular.

Quite differently, relational universalism envisions a net without bounds. Potentially, it has a positive regard for all human beings, whether their ideas agree with each other or not. Seyla Benhabib, who advocated 'universal moral respect', called this kind of universal 'interactive' (1990: 337; 1992: 152-53, 169). Pheng Cheah referred to it as a 'polymorphic universal', one that has room for many forms (1997: 180). Jodi Dean said that 'reflective solidarity provides spaces for difference because it upholds the possibility of a universal, communicative "we" ', with 'multiple, interconnecting discursive spheres' (1996: 8-9). Similarly, Radhakrishnan called for 'a universalism based not on dominance or representational violence but on relationality and dialogism based on multiple interlocking histories'. He said that one cannot 'honor multiplicity and heterogeneity without an understanding of the very terrain of connectedness that makes heterogeneity visible' (2000: 41, 58).

Ambiguous theoretically but important in practice is a 'strategic' form of universalism, which includes a 'legal' version (Benhabib 2002: 28).[6] Clarifying its intellectual sense, Longxi Zhang said that, for him, 'the word "universal" means "widely shared" or "common", rather than "totally identical" '. He indicated that its purpose is to counter 'Eurocentrism and racism', which 'have always depended on an emphasis on much-exaggerated racial, ethnic, and cultural differences' (1998: 12, 8). Practical universalism of this kind was probably intended by Kenan Malik when he declared that 'only a universalist conception of humanity can provide the political basis on which to build a struggle for equality' (1996: 8), as well as by Chilla Bulbeck when she observed that a 'humanist universalism has been a crucial element' in resisting racist colonialism (1998: 14).[7]

Beyond confronting colonialism, strategic universalism has been present in attempts to provide a concrete shape to wide-ranging concerns. In this way, it is embodied in UN policies, especially in the 1948 'Universal Declaration of Human Rights'. Although there are differences in interpreting those rights (as is legitimate), most countries in the world have endorsed them formally (Cassese 1999). In fact, it seems that most people have supported the rights, even though some of their leaders have expressed objections (Robertson 2000: 440).

It is true, there is a danger that the idea of 'universal rights' may seek to impose uniformity, for instance on the basis of specifically Western ideas. Accordingly, Gustavo Esteva and Madhu Prakash opposed that idea in the name of 'grassroots postmodernism' (1998: 110). Nevertheless, their objections were directed more toward the theory of universal rights with its possible implications for the future than toward actual practices by the UN, for

6. Cf. above, 8.4, for Judith Butler.
7. The same kind of outlook was held by Ihab Hassan, who had popularized a radically nominalist meaning for the word 'postmodern' but did not accept such an outlook himself (see above, 6.3). He said: 'Does a whisper of the universal...sound through our transcultural discourse? ...Clearly, we cannot abandon all hope of some planetary morality, ecological and pacific, and accept only force and deceit as arbiters of human conflicts' (1990: 5).

their own specific concerns were largely in harmony with UN policies.[8] As a matter of fact, the viewpoint of these two writers was neither isolationist nor skeptical. They rejected 'moral relativism' (130) and called for 'intercultural hospitality', which 'is impossible without a respectful and loving dialogue' (129).

In any case, within relational theory the complement to particularity is not strict universality, but 'generality'. This means that a given phenomenon may be shared, even if not by everyone.

Accordingly, Nancy Fraser and Linda Nicholson favored a process that is 'comparativist rather than universalizing' (1988: 114). In doing so, they were not alone. Sonya Michel observed a decade later that there was a 'comparative turn' in gender studies, one that engaged in 'broad cross-cultural and transhistorical comparisons' and pointed to 'pervasive' processes together with cultural variations (1998: 190). V.Y. Mudimbe had already characterized a 'transhistoric' view as follows: 'It enlarges...regional archives and brings them into contact with the analyst's mind, thus inventing in a dynamic manner both understanding and history' (1988: 199).[9]

Comparisons had to take account of the fact that given cultures are not monolithic wholes. In fact, this phenomenon itself had comparative significance. On the one hand, Paulin Hountondji pointed out that certain divergences within a given locality can also appear as divergences within world-wide culture, so that they are in that sense global (1977: 235); for instance, intellectuals in one society may have more in common with intellectuals in another society than with compatriots. On the other hand, Naeem Inayatullah and David Blaney (2004) noted that external differences often mirror tensions within a society in such a way that the other is contained within the collective self.

Comprehensive vs. Limited Views of History

Finally, one must address the issue of large-scale historical movements. Some writers already mentioned explicitly dealt with this issue.

Among them, Glissant did not accept a 'totality' that is 'at rest' (and thus is totalitarian), but he described relation (a 'movement') as an 'open' or 'virtual' totality. This 'totality in movement' incorporates both order and disorder (1990: 185-86, 147). Grewal and Kaplan had 'difficulty embracing Lyotard's ludic view', which has 'its own master narrative with its own exclusive, elitist rhetorics' (1994: 4-6).

---

8. Specifically, the right of parents to determine their children's education—for which Esteva and Prakash argued—is expressly supported by the UN declaration, and the UN was in the process of formulating rights for indigenous peoples, on whose behalf they spoke (cf. Anaya 1999: 155). They also disapproved of a number of local groups that had violated the UN declaration (1998: 126, 137).

9. For the use of the word 'transhistoric(al)', see also Patricia Collins, below.

Speaking not only for himself, Said pointed out that Lyotard's 1979 view of the death of grand narratives did not 'harmonize' with the attitudes of postcolonial writers. On the contrary, the theme of emancipation remains active:

> Whereas post-modernism [according to Lyotard]...stresses the disap-
> pearance of the grand narratives of emancipation and enlightenment, the
> emphasis behind much of the work done by the first generation of post-
> colonial artists and scholars is exactly the opposite: the grand-narratives
> remain, even though their implementation and realization are at present in
> abeyance, deferred, or circumvented (1994: 349).

Said continued by saying that in postcolonial work there has indeed been

> a great emphasis on the local, regional, and contingent...but it seems to me
> to be most interestingly connected in its general approach to a universal
> set of concerns, all having to do with emancipation, revisionist attitudes
> toward history and culture, and a widespread use of recurring theoretical
> models and styles (1994: 350).

Certainly, interactive freedom was a strong ideal in postcolonial efforts. In fact, contrary voices are difficult to find. Specific themes that have been mentioned so far—including various kinds of commonality and a large perspective—reappear also in the more narrowly focused surveys in the rest of the current chapter.

3. Inter-Group Relations within the US

A major sphere of concern occurs in the nature of relationships between Caucasians and others that were present in the US through conquest, importation as slaves, or immigration. Interaction without homogenization was a major interest for many of these groups.

At the beginning of the twentieth century, W.E.B. DuBois already saw a double consciousness, a 'two-ness' in African American life. He thought that neither the 'African' nor the 'American' aspect should be obliterated, as both have a contribution to make to the world. He said: 'The Negro would not Africanize America, for America has too much to teach the world and Africa. He would not bleach his Negro soul in a flood of white Americanism, for he knows that Negro blood has a message for the world (1903, part 1)'. Similarly, the philosopher Alain Locke valued the peculiarity of African American literature, art, drama, and music and called his view 'relativistic', although he eschewed 'ultra-relativism' (1989: 77, 83 [1944, 1945]). Along with variety, he supported a 'groping toward universal and spiritual principles and forces' in line with his Baha'i faith (1989: 131 [1933]). Later, Henry Gates gave extensive attention to the special characteristics of what he described as African American culture, but he also welcomed the return of 'an ethical universal' (1992: 193).

Speaking for Native American interests, David Moore rejected a conflict 'between conquered and conqueror, between absorption and resistance, winner and loser', typical of 'colonial hegemonies'. He looked instead for a 'postcolonial...nonoppositional and heteroglossic' approach, which is 'dialogic' (1994: 9-17).

Among minorities, women were perhaps especially inclined toward inclusiveness even as they recognized differences. According to Alice Walker, 'what is always needed in the appreciation of art, or life, is the larger perspective. Connections are made, or at least attempted, where none existed before...to encompass in one's glance at the varied world the common thread, the unifying theme through immense diversity' (1983: 5). Indebted to Walker, Jacquelyn Grant said that 'there is an implied universality which connects' African American women with others, along with differences that divide them: 'They share race suffering with Black men; with White women and other Third World women they are victims of sexism; and with poor Blacks and whites and other Third World peoples, especially women, they are disproportionately poor' (1989: 216-17). Also following Walker, Delores Williams said that the womanist 'is a universalist by temperament', whose 'universality includes loving men and women sexually or nonsexually' (1987: 66-70).

Similarly, Patricia Collins reported that, instead of 'competition and domination', 'Afrocentric models of community stress connection, caring, and personal accountability' (1990: 223).[10] She pointed to an 'empowerment that is distinct from existing models of power as domination' (1990: 224). She thus also criticized a scholarly outlook for which 'ethics and values are deemed inappropriate in the research process' and in which 'adversarial debates...become the preferred method of ascertaining truth: the arguments that can withstand the greatest assault and survive intact become the strongest truth' (205). Freely admitting that 'a Black woman's standpoint is only one angle of vision...a partial perspective' (234), Collins held that scholarly 'analysis must retain a creative tension between the specificity needed to study the workings of race, class, and gender in Black women's lives and generalizations about these systems created by cross-cultural and transhistorical research' (224).

Some writers valued the ability to draw on more than one tradition. For instance, Gloria Anzaldúa (with a Native American and Hispanic background) described a *mestiza* (mixed person) as follows: 'not only does she sustain contradictions, she turns ambivalence into something else'; she herself favored both social collaboration and 'paralogical' thinking, a kind of 'spiritual *mestizaje*' (1999: 45-46, 75; 1997: vii). John Brown Childs

---

10. This conception was an ideal one, of course, as Paul Gilroy noted (1993: 52, 232).

(combining a Native American with an African heritage) favored 'coordinated heterogeneity across 'identity lines',' including those of 'ethnicity', 'race', 'class', and 'gender' (2003: 21).

It is true, more or less strongly separatist points of view have also been voiced by minorities in the US. Among persons with an African heritage, a position along this line was advocated quite strongly by Marcus Garvey in the 1920s and 1930s. His group-particularism—understandable as it was— even exhibited affinities with European fascism (Gilroy 2000: 231-32). However, separation was not intended to be permanent but to serve as a temporary measure 'until each and every race by its own initiative lifts itself up to the common standard of humanity, as to compel the respect and the appreciation of all, and so make it possible for each one to stretch out the hand of welcome' (Garvey 1968–69, I: 26).

Later positions taken up by Malcolm X, Stokely Carmichael, and others were less strongly separatist, even while seeking independence (see Van Deburg 1997). They envisioned independence as a step toward an eventual interaction with others. For instance, Carmichael and Charles Hamilton, in describing 'the politics of liberation in America', said that 'before a group can enter the open society, it must first close ranks. By this we mean that group solidarity is necessary before a group can operate effectively from a bargaining position of strength in a pluralistic society' (1967: 44).

A concern for group solidarity, of course, raises the question to what extent 'racial' groups, or others like them, are internally unified. As an answer to this question, it was widely recognized (as is implied in a relational view) that there are internal differences together with connectivity. Responding to this recognition, W. Lawrence Hogue noted that if the theme of internal differentiation is taken one-sidedly, it is in line with 'modernity', which 'connotes the loss of metaphysical meaning, rampant individualism, nihilism, hedonism, alienation, fragmentation' (1996: 5). He did not altogether reject this 'modern' fragmentation and its continuation in nominalist 'postmodernity', but he thought that connectivity should also be recognized. Making a careful distinction, Stuart Hall, a Caribbean, asserted: 'I emphasize diversity rather than fragmentation' (1999: 214).

It is important, of course, to remember that relations are not always harmonious but often involve 'resistance' (e.g. Cornel West 1993: 291) or, more generally, 'struggle'. Such oppositions may be violent, although they do not always need to be so.

With an emphasis on nonviolence, Martin Luther King, Jr., championed in theory and in life the idea that 'love' is powerful, even as it engages in resistance (1958, 1963a). Of course, the idea that love is powerful may be wishful thinking by the downtrodden. Yet bell hooks pointed out that 'the civil rights movement had the power to transform society because the individuals who struggled alone and in community for freedom and justice wanted these gifts to be for all...the moment we choose to love we begin to move towards freedom, to act in ways that liberate ourselves and others' (1994: 249-50).

A confidence of this sort can be called 'faith', although it does not need to be formally religious. For instance, West was in favor of 'keeping faith', 'convinced by the prophetic...tradition' (1993, title, 134). Somewhat similarly, although sharply critical of organized religion, Anzaldúa held that 'spirituality'—which 'means to be aware of the interconnections between things'—is 'oppressed people's only weapon and means of protection' (2000: 9, 98).

4. *The International Women's Movement*

Besides relations between different groups within a single society, another major sphere of concern was interactions that reach across geographical areas. This is too vast a topic to be adequately covered. However, brief attention is given here to the international women's movement.

This movement observed both commonalities and differences in women's situations around the world. Appeals to common concerns had an important place, but there was also a reluctance simply to import recent 'Western' feminism and an interest in identifying 'indigenous alternatives' (Basu 1995: 18). In fact, it was recognized that efforts by women to defend and better their situations had gone on for a long time, both with and without transnational links (e.g. Alena Heitlinger 1999: 8-9). Many efforts continued to proceed in decentralized form (A. Miles 1996: 113), while at the same time international interchanges sometimes were taking place in more-or-less formal networks (Moghadam 2005).[11]

In introducing a volume by 'third world women', Mohanty noted that, although 'some of the essays call into question notions of a "third world" and of "universal sisterhood", a number of writers strongly assert their belief in international coalitions' (1991: 5). Speaking for herself, she saw an

> urgent need...to appreciate and understand the complex *relationality* that shapes our social and political lives. First and foremost this suggests relations of power, which anchor the 'common differences' between and among the feminist politics of different constituencies of women and men...not reducible to binary oppositions [but with] multiple, fluid structures of dominations which intersect (13).

Similarly, Carole Davies, drawing on black experience, called for a 'critical relationality' that allows for variety in both procedures and aims (1994: 56). Using approximately the same terminology, Susan Friedman concluded that

11. V. Spike Peterson and Ann Runyon went this far: 'Although the goals of particular struggles may vary, the most important point is that each struggle contributes to a global climate that nourishes equity and social justice' (1999: 238).

'a feminist multiculturalism that is global in its reach and configuration needs scripts of relational positionality' (1998: 49, 66).

5. *Prospects for Two-Way Interaction*

Interactions between societies—like interactions between groups within a society—raise important cultural issues, to be mentioned briefly. For such relations, there are three major alternatives: (1) a state of conflict in which one side may gain a victory over the other, which leads to the next possibility; (2) a uniformity in which differences are largely obliterated; or (3) a balance between particularity and an affirmation of common worth. (A fourth alternative, continual chaos, is not viable.)

An important variation of the third alternative is that groups learn from each other while retaining certain characteristic features. Such a process can be understood within a relational perspective, which does not envision a rigid demarcation of units. In line with this perspective, Annelise Riles suggested the 'network' as the appropriate 'form' of international practice (1999: 28-29). Such a form is, in fact, already largely in place, although with problems of its own (see Manuel Castells 2000).

For a long time, European ideas were forcefully thrust on other parts of the world. Thus, counter-measures that drew on Western culture were taken. For instance, as Xu Ben has noted, some Chinese thinkers drew on nominalist 'postmodern' theories to argue for 'Chinese exclusivity' (2001: 119). More positively, according to a report by Anindita Balslev, philosophers in India have given extensive attention to European and US ideas, not merely comparing them with their own, but attempting to see how their own thinking can gain from them (1991: 7-8).

Clearly, other cultures have learned from the West, but an important question arises: is the West similarly open to learning? For although Asian, African, and other traditions contributed to the development of relational orientations near the beginning of the twentieth century, subsequently most western philosophers did not deal seriously with those traditions.[12] This was true even though some of them, including Alasdair MacIntyre and Rorty, acknowledged that this failure to consider other traditions impoverished Western thinking (Balslev 1991: 64, 75).

Some writers voiced the scruple that receiving contributions from other societies is a form of conquest. Such a scruple may indeed be justified if non-Western forms are used simply to reinforce pre-existing Western ideas (cf. J. Clarke 2000: 54, 199). Insofar as that is not the case, however, learning implies respect.

---

12. One exception (not the only one) is Robert Neville, who identifies as a Confucian.

In any case, quite a few non-Europeans were ready to contribute not only in substance but also in procedure to a postmodernity that takes account of a variety of traditions in creative ways (Ashis Nandy 1987: xvii). For instance, according to Léopold Senghor (1993: 32 [1970]), *négritude* values community with 'dialogue and reciprocity' and accordingly permits 'black Africa to make its contribution to the "Civilization of the Universal" which is so necessary in our interdependent world of the second half of the twentieth century'.[13] Sardar contrasted the (post)modernism that 'celebrates egoism' with Muslim tradition, which emphasizes connectivity; he valued this Muslim outlook, although he also appreciated modernity's restraint of authoritarianism (1998: 273-76, 287). According to Carver Yu, Chinese traditional thinking can continue to stimulate relational thinking, in part since it saw a close connection between humanity and the nonhuman world (1987: xx, 116). Suggestive for a possible interchange is that, contra late-medieval and postmedieval Christian nominalists, 'in the Chinese worldview, order is not imposed from without but is inherent in the process of existence itself' (D. Hall and Ames 1995: 278).

The potential contribution of Buddhism is perhaps both skeptical and relational in character. It had already made an impact on Mach and others (Goonatilake 2001: 14-15). In many of its forms, Buddhism highlights fragmentation and speaks of illusion in such a way that it comes close to skepticism. Yet it does not represent pure skepticism or nihilism, for it provides mystical insight and grants ordinary knowledge at least the status of a lower truth. Its idea of 'co-arising' is relational.

Jain ontology is strongly affirmative. It can be a significant conversation partner for relational theory. Specifically, it has as a central theme 'identity-in-difference', according to which 'unity and diversity are relative aspects of every real thing' (Dravid 2001: 126). Socially, Jainism's strong emphasis on nonviolence has made a worldwide impact.

Insofar as a 'mutual transformation' of viewpoints (L. Gandhi 1998: 140) takes place, it represents a form of interactive freedom. The modern West's peculiar contribution to an interchange is its emphasis on external negative freedom for individuals and groups. The contribution of other cultures may lie more in a recognition of connectivity. As has been indicated in Chapter 3, international exchange was already active in the rise of formal relational theory; there is some evidence that a drawing together is also taking place in the larger culture (Nisbett 2003: 224-29).

If Western philosophy continues to open itself up to other traditions, a likely result will be a renewed interest in an internal freedom that includes a

---

13. Senghor did not originate the concept of *négritude*. It is, of course, too simple to equate this with all and only African life. (Senghor has been criticized by Tsenay Serequeberhan [1994: 47-52], among others, for implying that.)

transtemporal—spiritual or more-or-less mystical—dimension. The experiential revolution of the 1960s, which was often in touch with non-European traditions, indeed celebrated an interactive inner freedom in which 'flesh' and 'spirit' are joined.

6. *Concluding Reflections*

It is apparent that non-Eurocentric writers overwhelmingly accepted relationality or some other perspective that joins particularity and commonality. One may ask why this was the case. A possible answer is that an emphasis on connectivity has been strong in predominantly agricultural societies. This stands in tension with the particularist emphasis that arose in the 'modern' industrializing West. Aspects of both orientations can be incorporated in a relational view.

A major theme emerging from this discussion is the importance of a relational or interactive universal. This kind of universal allows for, and encourages, the flourishing of groups—however constituted—each with their own characteristics, but it welcomes communication between them for their mutual benefit. This principle applies also to subgroups and individuals within a group, so that groups of various sizes are each not monolithic.

In terms of freedom, many of those who were not Eurocentric were moved by interaction with the West to make increased room for negative freedom in the social realm, in other words, for individuality. Yet the positive form of social freedom continued to be desired, along with inner freedom, whether religious or otherwise.

Chapter 10

INFORMATION AS DYNAMIC FORM: A VIEW OF HISTORY

Is the rise of explicit relational theory a happenstance, or can one account for its rise together with that of radical nominalism? In answer to that question, one can draw on relational theory itself. In particular, information theory, which deals with dynamic relations (see above, 5.6), provides the following response: historical processes exhibit a pattern that is governed by probability; in other words, they are contingent but not completely arbitrary. In fact, both human and nonhuman history can be understood with the aid of the concept of information.

1. *Information and Entropy as Correlates*

Employed technically, the word 'information' is a dynamic term. It refers to the imparting of form to something, to having an impact. An entity does not 'have' information in itself; what it does have is a potential for information. This potential is always relative in the sense that it varies according to the framework within which it is considered. Specifically, in mental relationships, 'information' refers to how much new knowledge is gained in a communication process in contrast to what is already known.[1]

Information thus removes 'uncertainty'. With regard to mental matters, 'uncertainty' refers to a lack of knowledge. Lack of knowledge, however, is not equivalent to a psychological state of doubt; rather, receiving information that contradicts a previously settled belief may even create doubt. Instead, 'uncertainty' is synonymous with 'unpredictability', that is, the degree of surprise it can furnish.

The characterizations of information and uncertainty just outlined produce a very important paradox, which constitutes the heart of information theory.

---

1.   This dynamic meaning of 'information' (referring to an acquiring of knowledge) must be clearly distinguished from the common meaning that is synonymous with 'knowledge' or 'message' (which may or may not be new). The latter meaning occurs, for instance, in a statement that a book or the DNA of an organism 'contains information'; if one has the technical meaning in mind, one should say that the book or DNA contains potential information.

Since information is by definition an uncertainty that is removed, it follows that prior uncertainty is required in order for information to take place. More specifically, the potential amount of information in any given situation is equal to the recognizable uncertainty (the amount of surprise that is possible) in that situation.

In 1948, this insight led to the development of information theory as a theoretical framework for the transmission of messages by telephone. The principle that Claude Shannon set forth is as follows: the signals that are transmitted need to be highly unpredictable by the recipient, if much information is to be provided. The task of the telephone engineer, then, is to produce a channel that provides for a maximum amount of discernible unpredictability at a given economic cost. The word 'discernable' is important, since it indicates a relativity to the perceptual capacity of a recipient.

Shannon used the term 'entropy' as a synonym for uncertainty, since his mathematical formula corresponded to one that was used to measure thermodynamic entropy, the increasing uncertainty toward which thermodynamic processes move. In fact, information theorists have generalized the notion of entropy so that thermodynamic entropy represents only one possible kind of entropy.

2. *Entropy and Information as Aspects of Complexity*

In part under the influence of Shannon's analysis, conceptualizations for information and entropy were developed in mathematics from the 1960s on. Specifically, entropy came to be defined as the amount of algebraic information that is needed in order to describe a mathematical object or to solve a mathematical problem. In the pursuit of this topic, the word 'complexity' came to be used as a synonym for entropy.[2] We thus have a series of terms that are synonymous: uncertainty = entropy = unpredictability = (descriptive) complexity.

Descriptive (often called 'informational') complexity represents one side, but only one side, of what is best called 'organized complexity'. Organized complexity has two characteristics: on the one hand, it has high entropy in the sense of descriptive complexity (or unpredictability); on the other

---

2.   Since there are different ways of measuring the needed information, there can be different ways of indicating this complexity, but these differences are moderate. (See, for instance, Chaitin 1990: 29-58 [1974]; Li and Vitanyi 1990: 189; Cover and Thomas 1991: 3. Shannon's entropy and descriptive complexity are not precisely the same, but they are closely related; Shannon's entropy measures the capacity of a channel, while descriptive complexity measures an individual phenomenon.) In mathematics, common designations are 'algebraic complexity', 'informational complexity', and 'Kolmogorov complexity'. The designation 'descriptive complexity', however, is useful for communication across fields.

hand, there are many lines of connections ('communications') between its elements.[3] This combination is, in fact, what is usually meant by 'complexity' in ordinary English. Consequently, when the word 'complex' is used hereafter without a qualifier, it will refer to organized complexity.

Organized complexity such as in a tree or animal may be said to represent a relatively 'high level of order'. This is different from 'orderliness' or predictability, such as in an ice cube or larger block of ice.[4] Much confusion has been caused by a failure to distinguish between these two ways of speaking about order.

Unfortunately, there is no standard way to measure a degree of organized complexity, for there is no accepted standard for assessing the lines of communication within an object. Nevertheless, it is possible to make some general observations.

Organized complexity tends to increase with size. Size and complexity do not necessarily go together. However, an object that contains several components is necessarily more complex than any of them, since the complexity of the components is part of the complexity of the whole.

In fact, a high degree of organized complexity can usually be attained in practice only by combining several layers of organization. The reason for this situation is that direct communication between a large number of units overwhelms a system to such an extent that a system of some size requires subsystems in order to operate effectively (see above, 5.5). In this layered way, living organisms contain cells, which contain molecules, which contain atoms, which contain still smaller entities.

Such layering is often called 'hierarchical'. However, the arrangement has to a large extent not been imposed from above. Rather, in the evolution of the universe, the multiplicity of levels was produced predominantly from below, for there were atoms before molecules, unicellular organisms before multicellular ones, and so on. It is true, there can also be downward differentiation, so that a large whole produces divisions within itself, but that is a secondary development.

The phenomenon that layering arises from below implies that organized complexity appears only gradually. Each layer needs time for its formation. A certain minimum of entropy, or uncertainty, must be available on one level if the next step in communication, or organization, is to take place. For instance, it was not possible for atoms to form until the four basic forces of the universe (electromagnetism, gravity, and the two nuclear forces) separated. Similarly, animals and plants require a variety of inorganic compounds for their nourishment. The observable growth of organized complexity in the universe—subject to fluctuations—is thus due, not to any

---

3. Similarly, Mark Taylor 2001: 140.
4. For the distinction, see again Yockey 2005: 169, 185.

special drive, but to the fact that such greater complexity presupposes, as a rule, a somewhat less complex form as an antecedent.[5]

The growth of complexity does imply a certain ontological ground, as follows: a precondition for an increase in organized complexity is that the elements involved in an evolutionary process exhibit partial independence together with a partial readiness to be connected.[6] The reason for this principle is that at least partial independence is needed for an increase in entropy, which is one side of organized complexity, and that at least a partial readiness to be connected is required for communication, which represents organized complexity's other side.[7]

A private thought experiment can illustrate such a process. Imagine the repeated shuffling of a large number of cards. If the cards are all independent (they do not stick together), their random shuffling tends on the whole toward an increase in unpredictability, as is desired for card playing. If, however, the cards sometimes stick together, they will presumably join into ever bigger and—depending on the nature of the stickiness—ever more complex combinations, although one must allow for fluctuations. Such a pattern is exhibited by the evolution of the universe.

Independence plays an important role in thermodynamics. Thermodynamic entropy tends to increase continuously, for it involves a process in which units act freely in relation to each other (Atkins 1984: 58). To be sure, the thermodynamic trend represents a statistical tendency, not a rigid direction, but the number of units involved is so huge that thermodynamic entropy increases steadily in the universe. This steady increase is facilitated

5.   In fact, it is not necessary to explain the observable trend toward increased complexity in both inorganic and organic forms on the basis of an assumption that increased complexity regularly aids survival. Darwin did use that explanation from the third edition of his *Origin of the Species* in 1861 on (see Darwin 1959) in response to Herbert Spencer's observation about a rise in complexity. More recent observations have led to doubt about such a view. Dirk Schulze-Makuch and Louis Irwin (2004: 42), among others, even judge that in organic evolution instability tends to increase with complexity.

6.   Explanations of a rise in complexity along the general line presented here without an assumption that complexity aids survival (see n. 5) have already been set forth by P.T. Saunders and M.W. Ho (1976: 376), Jeffrey Wicken (1987: 77), Steen Rasmussen 1990, and Stuart Kauffman (most adequately in 2000: 172-75), among others. Wicken worked with the aid of information theory. Kauffman and Rasmussen employed computer modeling; specifically, Kauffman found that moderate (not heavy) interaction between parts leads to complexity.

7.   Similarly, Richard Solé and Brian Goodwin recognized that an entropy increase assumes 'separated entities', while organized complexity reflects 'links' (2000: 42), although they do not note expressly that separateness and connectivity can each be partial. Earlier, John Polkinghorne spoke of an 'interweaving of chaos and order' (1989: 46).

by the expansion of the universe; without that expansion, entropy would presumably have soon reached a maximum.[8]

Organized complexity, however, requires not only an increase in entropy but also communication. Communicative processes take place in several ways including the following.

One kind of communication, which operates in an elementary form on the physical level, is attraction, which includes gravity. This leads toward 'clumping'.

Another kind of effective communication, although less important, is negative. Some physical forces repel; these also provide a kind of order that is distinct from randomness. Similarly, 'hostile' rivalry can contribute to structuring, as computer models have shown (Sent 1998: 126).

More important—probably most important—for the creation of organized complexity is 'synergy' or 'cooperation', which operates on all levels of existence. Synergy includes 'resonance', 'sharing', and, for organisms, 'symbiosis'.[9] For instance, in a molecule, an electron can be 'shared', that is, serve double duty. Within organisms, many parts promote the functioning of the whole and in that sense support each other. In human culture, various features complement one another.

A frequently occurring kind of communication is 'incorporation'. Molecules incorporate atoms; organisms incorporate both organic and inorganic materials as food; empires swallow up smaller states. If such incorporation destroys a lower-level organization—as happens in the ingestion of organic food and usually in conquest—this process has a negative aspect, although non-conscious beings do not experience it as a problem.

8. The term 'entropy', which means 'transformation' (that is, evolution), was applied to the thermodynamic phenomenon by Rudolf Clausius in 1865 (Broda 1983: 79). Its interpretation as a statistical tendency toward disorder (unpredictability in detail) was presented by Ludwig Boltzmann soon thereafter. At one time, it was thought that this thermodynamic trend would eventually lead to a dead equilibrium. At the end of the nineteenth century, this belief supported a pessimistic view of history. Subsequently, however, the expansion of the universe was observed. As the universe increases in size, its elements can become increasingly unpredictable, since they have a large space in which to operate. If the expansion continues indefinitely, there will then never be a time when one can say that things are as unpredictable as they can get. This trend can be seen in an optimistic way. (The idea that the expansion of the universe allows for an expansion of entropy and thereby for biological complexity was stated already by K.G. Denbigh [1975: 84].)

9. This has been seen by, among others, Mikhail Vol'kenshtein (1970: 6, 9, 11, 140-41, 462 [1965]); Manfred Eigen and Ruthild Winkler (1975: 6); Hermann Haken (1977 and later); Werner Ebeling and Rainer Feistel, declaring that 'the formation of structure is a result of cooperation', as a general principle of physics (1982: 51); Richard Dawkins (1986: 170); Wicken (1987: 63-64); Grégoire Nicolis and Ilya Prigogine (1989: 3, 41, 212); Kauffman (1993: 183); Lynn Margulis (again 1998, with references); Peter Corning (again 1998, for all levels, with references).

The basic principles of evolution that have just been outlined operate on all levels of existence, so that there is no sharp difference between inorganic, organic, and cultural evolution. Specific interactions on different levels are varied and need to be investigated by empirical sciences, but their theoretical basis is the same on all levels: insofar as organized complexity increases, it takes place through a growth in entropy due to an (at least partial) independence together with (at least partial) communication.

As pointed out earlier (in Chapter 4), a combination of a degree of independence with a degree of connectivity is inherent in the notion of relationship. Relationality—when it is dynamic—then, provides the ontological ground for the emergence of complexity in history.

3. *The Interplay between Entropy and Information*

Since organized complexity involves both relatively high entropy and relatively elaborate communication, one can ask how these two aspects are related. It turns out that they grow together; in fact, they can enhance each other.

On the one hand, entropy, or uncertainty, provides an opportunity for information. This is a central insight owed to Shannon and has already been illustrated by the fact that biological evolution presupposes physical differentiation.

On the other hand, information tends to increase entropy, or uncertainty. That happens in several ways.

First of all, any process, including communication, has a tendency to increase thermodynamic entropy in a larger whole. In thermodynamics, there is no such thing as an 'antientropic' process. In fact, as stated by Sally Goerner, the formation of local order is an especially 'efficient producer of entropy' in the larger world (1993: 88).

Thermodynamic entropy, however, as has already been indicated, is only a special kind of entropy. More generally, communicative processes often lead to a growth in entropy in the sense of unpredictability in two ways. Internally, the structure of a complex object requires more information to describe it (and thus has higher 'entropy') than does any of its parts alone.[10] Externally, a complex object tends toward increased entropy (opportunities for surprise) within a larger sphere of observation, for a complex object has a greater variety of forms it can exhibit and greater unpredictability in behavior.

---

10. It is true, less information may be needed than the sum of the information that is required to describe each of its parts separately, for there can be some overlap. (For instance, for an automobile it is not necessary to describe each wheel anew.) In that sense, there is a decrease in internal entropy. However, the whole has greater 'uncertainty' than do its parts individually.

For instance, while all electrons are quite simple and are all exactly the same, atoms are not only internally more complex, but they also exhibit externally some unpredictability in kind and operation; that is, if one knows only that a given object is an atom, one is still 'uncertain' what kind of atom it is and therefore what it will do. The internal and the external mathematical entropies of molecules are greater, and the corresponding entropies of organismic systems are greater still. Richard Bird has accordingly said that life represents 'increasing disorder'—together with 'a management of disorder' (2003: 187, 192).[11] Human beings and their cultures exhibit still higher unpredictability, probably including fragility.

4. Entropy and Information in Human Existence

Awareness, or Internal Freedom
For most nonhuman levels of existence, the term 'information' is used metaphorically. On the human level, information involves a conscious, indeed self-conscious, awareness. Awareness enhances both entropy and communication and thus contributes to organized complexity. Human beings experience both aspects as inner freedom.

On the one hand, awareness increases entropy by supporting flexibility in perception and action. Reflective actions are more free (unpredictable) in responding to incoming stimuli than are more-or-less-fixed 'instincts'. Conscious reflection is thus especially useful in novel situations. For instance, it usually aids the learning of new procedures, although it may be a hindrance when one has become an expert in a given field (experts often lose awareness of their procedures).[12]

Furthermore, the flexibility (or 'entropy') made available by consciousness makes ethical self-critique possible as a negative aspect of internal freedom. As research has shown, human perceptions and decisions largely take place in an unconscious or semiconscious state, but reflexive (that includes reflective) consciousness permits one's decisional impulses to be placed under scrutiny (Nørretranders 1998: 210-43). Reflexive awareness also subjects one's prior thinking to reflection and thus further introduces unpredictability.[13]

On the other hand, awareness provides opportunities for information through connectivity beyond what is available in a non-conscious or

11. Accordingly, Daniel Brooks and E.O. Wiley (1988: 32, 48) and similarly Humberto Maturana and Francisco Varela (1987: 99) could treat biological evolution as an example of the growth of entropy in a generalized (not specifically thermodynamic) sense.

12. Thus, already, James 1890, I: 114.

13. Cf. what Foucault said in his last years (see above, 7.4). Whitehead said that 'consciousness is the feeling of negation' (1929: 245).

206 The Concept of Form in the Twentieth Century

semiconscious condition and thus speeds up learning (see Bayley *et al.* 2005). Often, several items of knowledge gained under a variety of different circumstances are placed into interaction with each other to create a new vision, which represents an internal-positive freedom. In fact, although human complexity does not appear to support an overall ability to survive, it does provide the basis for contemplating and speaking about reality.

A noteworthy feature of contemplating and speaking about reality is that through scientific endeavors it has been possible to show lines of connection in the world together with lines of difference. Physics furnishes the most obvious example. A large number of particles have been discovered. At the same time, it has been shown that these fall into one or more patterns. Four fundamental forces have been identified and 'unified' to a considerable extent, so that they can be seen in relation to each other. Presumably, the forces have long operated in approximately this way, but their operation has now entered into human awareness. A reasonable hunch is that physical theory will never be completely unified, but it is also clear that reality does not merely contain a jumble of unrelated items.[14]

To some extent, a similar process has taken place in philosophy. In this field, the relational theory described in this volume has gone far toward answering the old question of how general categories and particulars relate to each other. Aristotle accepted both dimensions but simply added them to each other. Differently, relational theory holds that generality and particularity are two aspects of relationality. Aristotle encumbered the dimension of generality with a problematic distinction between 'essential' and 'accidental' properties. Relational theory is able to dispense with this distinction, since it is more flexible and can allow for more gradations in regard to how important a given feature is for a particular object in a particular setting. If relational theory is at least approximately appropriate, the basic structures of reality which it formulates have become reflectively conscious.

Although unifications have provided certain theoretical simplicity, conceptual structures have also become more complex ('rich') because previous ideas are often not jettisoned when new ones arise. For example, the present study incorporates elements of the following nineteenth-century notions: Hegel's idea of a growth in consciousness, Marx's emphasis on the social conditioning of thought, Spencer's observation of a growth in complexity, Darwin's recognition that more or less random variation (in other words, entropy) plays an important role in evolution, and Peirce's idea that 'growth comes only from love' (if love is equated with communication).[15]

14. Smolin speculates that 'the universe indeed had free choice about a great many of the properties of the elementary particles' (1997: 72).

15. For instance, Spencer's observation of a movement from 'an incoherent homogeneity to a coherent heterogeneity' (1862, §127) points to growth in both entropy (heterogeneity) and communication (coherence). See also Peirce 1931–58, 6.289.

The optimistic outlook of these writers has been replaced here by an acceptance of contingency and (as will be seen) by a greater sense of tragedy. In
this way, older opinions are rejected, or at least modified. Nevertheless, a
recognition that parts of earlier views can be incorporated in subsequent
structures implies that human intellectual endeavors can make at least some
long-range contributions.

Outside science and philosophy—especially in literature—complexity
of awareness applies not only to a recognition of actuality but also to an
apprehension of possibility. As pointed out above (5.3), human signs point
not only to actual objects or events but also to possibilities. Within the realm
of imagined possibilities, conscious beings can create entropy and information, such as when a fictional narrative creates suspense ('uncertainty')
followed by a resolution. Even if individual narratives have not increased
in complexity, the total store of accessible narratives has grown, so that
cultural complexity as a whole has increased.

External (Social) Freedom
One side of social growth appears in the form of increasing social entropy.
This trend is by no means to be disparaged, as long as positive interaction
is also present. Specifically, as societies grow in size, there is on the whole
an increasing division of labor and a greater variety of tasks that can be
performed. The progress of the women's movement in recent times is an
important example of this trend. Earlier divisions of tasks into male and
female have become too simplistic, and there are now multiple roles that
cut across this contrast.

Together with this development, there has been a tendency toward
increased communication within the human world. This is due in part to a
growth in the sheer size of the human population and in part to an increasing range of human contact, both geographically and sometimes within a
particular society.

The range of human contact is aided by the means of communication
that are used. The use of writing, initially limited to scribal profession-
als (usually male), aided the rise of aristocracy (including kingship and
empires), which employed writing for the spread of power beyond a small
locale. The development of alphabetic script permitted wider literacy and
furthered the rise of an intelligentsia and of some forms of religion that in
part challenged the position of the politically powerful. As a next major
step, the use of print, which made written materials available to many, supported and was supported by the rise of a middle class.[16] From the end
of the nineteenth century on, newer media had an even wider scope and

16. For instance, print eliminated the need for tens of thousands of copyists for text-
books (Innis 1950: 169).

reached toward all socioeconomic levels and to all parts of the earth. The noteworthy movement from aristocratic to relatively egalitarian organization in Western society (at least) thus has a correlate in the means that have been employed to process information, although the correlation between informational means and social order is not rigid.[17]

5. *Interaction between Good and Evil*

According to one way of looking at them, information and entropy are neutral phenomena without a clear connection with values. Is it possible, however, to link them with issues of desirability.

One way to make such a linkage is to regard information and entropy as having positive and negative value, respectively. This kind of linkage is supported by the observation that in more-or-less conscious beings a dissolution of their structure (entropy) can be signaled by pain, while information-intake is normally pleasurable.[18] Together these two operations aid growth (see above, 5.5). An equation of entropy with negative value, however, is problematic, for, especially on the human level, entropy or unpredictability represents 'negative freedom', which can be valued for human, as well as for some nonhuman, beings.

A possible principle of ethics—one of several that may need to be taken into account—is that active consideration for another being is to be roughly proportional to the complexity of that being or of its type.[19] One side of organized complexity is entropy (as seen above). An appreciation for entropy is, then, a part of ethics if this consists in having respect for another being.

Entropy also plays a significant role in aesthetics, since it is presupposed by information. Experiments and informal observations show that enjoyment of what is seen or heard involves the absorption of as much 'information' as a conscious being can handle. This is equivalent to the 'uncertainty' that is removed; unpredictability is thus an important factor.[20] The standard expressed in the phrase 'how much one can handle' indicates that aesthetic

17. For instance, the connection between kingship and the use of writing is not a necessary one, as kingship in Africa outside of Egypt has shown.
18. Along this line, Juan Segundo too readily equated entropy and negentropy with evil and good, respectively, although he recognized the interplay of good with evil and of information with entropy (1988: 44, 71, 79, etc.; cf. Stefano 1992: 5-6, 85).
19. Nozick unduly emphasized unification as a standard (1981: 417; 1989: 164).
20. The association of complexity with uncertainty or entropy was accepted within aesthetics by contributors to D.E. Berlyne (1974: 94, 112-16, 310). Specifically, it has been shown that at least some poetry, especially 'good' poetry, is less predictable (has higher 'entropy') in comparison with other expressions, as long as it does have order (e.g. Fónagy 1961: 605; Lotman 1972, 1.5, 21). A similar situation holds true for art (Arnheim 1971: 15, 51: 'ordering increases entropy'). For music, see n. 21.

value is relative, not in the sense of arbitrary but in the sense of relational—namely, relative to persons with their individual capacities, backgrounds, and interests. For instance, an experienced musician may be able to perceive the complex structure of a given piece sufficiently to find the work enjoyable, while an amateur may be unable to find a pattern that binds together the many diverging impulses. Conversely, the professional musician may be bored by too simple a pattern in a work that pleases the amateur.[21]

The principle that applies in art holds true for various nonintellectual activities, such as sports. Their maximum pleasure (in-formation) usually involves as much challenge (entropy) as one can handle.

Is there progress? There is 'progress' insofar as it is true that entropy and communication both grow. Similarly, pain and pleasure both increase as beings become more conscious. The same may also hold true, in the ethical realm, for a growth in both other-enhancing and destructive activities. The twentieth century witnessed, for instance, not only a development of interactive freedom that appeared intellectually in the form of relational thought, but also unusually vicious outbursts of destructiveness that were connected with strife between groups. Radical nominalism, too, represents a problematic side insofar as it withdraws from a concern for human and other beings.

In fact, just as entropy and information feed into each other, so approved and disapproved processes frequently appear to provide opportunities for each other. A valued development can lead to problems, and a terrible event can have positive consequences.[22]

In terms of the conceptualization of Hayden White (1973), a historical view that recognizes a joint growth and even interplay of good and evil can be said to contain elements of both tragedy and comedy. The idea of such an interplay has been present in Jewish and Christian scriptures, as well as in Buddhism and perhaps in other traditions (Ziporyn 2000).[23] In

21. Both the present writer and a colleague of his in musicology have observed that in listening to music the next sound is more difficult to predict for 'high' compositions (the 'best' they can handle) than is true for pieces they consider to be of lesser worth, while productions without discernible connectivity do not strike one as musical.

22. Thus also William Thompson (1976: 79-80).

23. In the book of Genesis (chs. 1–3), disobedience ('evil') leads to moral maturity ('good'). In the narrative thereafter, a continuing history of transgression (violence, etc.) elicits as a counter-measure the election of Abraham, beginning a history with new directions (Genesis 12). In the Joseph story, a series of reprehensible or questionable actions eventuates in a useful outcome (Gen. 50.20). In the New Testament, Paul gives a specific formulation of this paradoxical pattern by saying that 'where sin increased, there grace increased even more' (Rom. 5.20). Examples of the reverse theme—that good can lead to evil—are less clear in biblical literature, but at least two examples can be given. In Hos. 13.6, God is represented as saying, 'As they were fed, they became

these religious traditions, the 'comic' (positive) side of history outshines the tragic side, although the comic aspect is in some sense transhistorical. As has been mentioned, the poet Hölderlin presented a secularized version of this orientation: 'Where danger grows, what saves also grows'. Heidegger and Baudrillard adopted this comic view, although they differed from each other in that Heidegger considered entropy to be danger while Baudrillard viewed it as salvation. Lyotard projected in his last years a 'complexifying process' that leads human beings to 'the best and the worst' (1993b: 93); such a sober meta-narrative balances comedy and tragedy.

6. Relational and Chaotic Perspectives as Correlates in the Present

The observation of an interplay between uncertainty and information sheds light on the social and intellectual situation at the present time. Nominalist postmodernism rightly points to an increase in unpredictability, in other words, to an increase in entropy. A relational response accepts this situation, but views it in part as an opportunity for communication.[24]

At the same time, a relational perspective will probably open up new uncertainties. In fact, it is likely that history will become ever more unpredictable. As was stated by Nicholas Rescher, 'increasing complexity...complicates the management of life' (1998: 201). One uncertainty is how long human culture will survive.

On a more moderate scale, the same uncertainty applies to the relational outlook that has been described. Perhaps it will decompose again into rival approaches, as happened to a large extent in the 1970s (see above, 6.1). Such a development would be in line with the observation that highly valued arrangements can be fragile. At the same time, it is also possible that a richer vision will arise.

A recognition of unpredictability should not lead one to despair and thus to passivity. On the contrary, ethical action would be undermined if a positive future were assured.

7. Summary

The concept of 'information', based on relational notions, represents a dynamic idea of form, for in-formation is a process in which something new happens. It presupposes a state of 'entropy', that is, unpredictability. Entropy thus presents an opportunity, not just a problem.

---

full...and lifted their hearts—therefore they forgot me'. David, greatly supported by God, commits adultery and, to cover this up, murder (2 Samuel 11). Buber was one who espoused the theme formally, holding that each spiral of history leads to 'greater ruin' and to 'a more fundamental return' (1923: 160).

24. Thus, earlier, Buss (1979: 13) and Philip Hefner (1984: 473, 475).

Growth in both entropy and communication leads to an increase in organized complexity. Entropy and communication have, in fact, grown interactively on all levels of existence, including both the inorganic and the organic. The reason is that entropy reflects (partial) independence and communication reflects (partial) connectivity, a combination that is recognized by relational theory.

Growth in awareness represents an increase in both entropy and communication. In awareness, entropy appears as negative freedom and communication as positive freedom. This duality holds true both internally and externally. Inner freedom includes, negatively, self-criticism and, positively, regard for another being for its own sake. External negative freedom supports social entropy, while external positive freedom furnishes social communication.

Although information is usually experienced as valuable, it requires entropy as a precondition. In fact, just as entropy and information can grow together and even provide opportunity for each other, so moral good and moral evil readily increase together, sometimes interactively.

In the history of human culture, a growth in both social and intellectual complexity appears to have taken place. Relational theory can be said to represent an intellectual advance, since it incorporates both particularity and generality. Radical nominalism provides a challenge to this development, yet it can also serve as an opportunity for further communication. As a relatively complex view, the relational perspective may be unstable.

On the basis of observations made here, the general form of history can be characterized as follows: it is probabilistic (contingent), interactive, and both comic and tragic. Such an open future provides for the possibility of meaningful action.

BIBLIOGRAPHY

Abbot, Francis Ellingwood. 1864. 'The Philosophy of Space and Time'. *The North American Review* 99: 64-116.
——1870. 'The Practical Work of Free Religion'. *The Index* 1, No. 6 (5 February): 2-3.
——1885. *Scientific Theism*. Boston: Little, Brown, & Co. German, 1893.
——1906. *The Syllogistic Philosophy*. Boston: Little, Brown, & Co.
Abrams, M.H. 1953. *The Mirror and the Lamp*. New York: Oxford University Press.
Abramson, Paul R., and Ronald Inglehart. 1995. *Value Change in Global Perspective*. Ann Arbor: University of Michigan Press.
Abse, Tobias. 1994. 'Italy: A New Agenda'. Pages 189-232 in *Mapping the West European Left*, ed. P. Anderson and P. Camiller. London: Verso.
Adams, Carol J. 1993. *Ecofeminism and the Sacred*. New York: Continuum.
——1994. *Neither Man nor Beast: Feminism and the Defense of Animals*. New York: Continuum.
Addams, Jane. 1902. *Democracy and Social Ethics*. New York: Macmillan.
——1907. *Newer Ideals of Peace*. New York: Macmillan.
Addison, J.W., et al. 1965. *The Theory of Models*. Amsterdam: North-Holland.
Adorno, Theodor W. 1956. *Zur Metakritik der Erkenntnistheorie*. Stuttgart: W. Kohlhammer. English, 1982.
Agazzi, Evandro. 1981. *Modern Logic—A Survey*. Dordrecht: D. Reidel.
Ahmed, Akbar S. 1992. *Postmodernism and Islam*. London: Routledge.
Akenside, Mark. 1794. *The Pleasures of Imagination*. Exeter, NH: Thomas Odiorne.
Alcoff, Linda Martin. 1997. 'The Politics of Postmodern Feminism Revisited'. *Cultural Critique* 36: 5-27.
Allen, Amy. 1999. *The Power of Feminist Theory*. Boulder, CO: Westview Press.
Allen, Henry. 2000. *What it Felt Like Living in the American Century*. New York: Pantheon Books.
Allen, Pamela. 1970. *Free Space*. New York: Times Change Press.
Allen, R.T. 1998. *Beyond Liberalism*. New Brunswick, NJ: Transaction Publishers.
Allwood, Gill. 1998. *French Feminisms*. London: UCL.
Althusser, Louis. 1970. 'Idéologie et appareils idéologiques d'état'. *La Pensée* 151: 3-38. English in *Lenin and Philosophy and Other Essays*, 1971.
Altman, Dennis. 1971. *Homosexual Oppression and Liberation*. New York: Avon.
Amin, Samir. 1985. *La déconnexion*. Paris: La Decouverte. English, 1990.
——1990. *Delinking*. London: Zed Books. English of 1985, with new preface.
——1991. *L'empire du chaos*. Paris: L'Harmattan. English, 1992.
Anaya, S. James. 1999. 'Indigenous Peoples and Their Demands within the Modern Human Rights Movement'. Pages 149-61 in *The Universal Declaration of Human Rights: Fifty Years and Beyond*, ed. Y. Danieli et al. Amityville, NY: Baywood.
Anderson, Judith. 1984. *Outspoken Women*. Dubuque, IA: Kendall/Hunt.

Anderson, Pamela Sue. 1998. *A Feminist Philosophy of Religion*. Oxford: Blackwell.

Anderson, Terry H. 1995. *The Movement and the Sixties*. Oxford: Oxford University Press.

Angelelli, Ignacio. 1967. *Studies on Gottlob Frege and Traditional Philosophy*. Dordrecht: D. Reidel.

Anscombe, G.E.M. 1957. *Intention*. Oxford: Blackwell.

Anzaldúa, Gloria. 1997. 'Foreword'. Pages vii-viii in R. Conner *et al.*, eds.

———1999. Interview. Pages 43-78 in G. Olson and L. Worsham. eds.

———2000. *Interviews/Entrevistas*, ed. A. Keating. London: Routledge.

Apel, Karl-Otto. 1968. 'Die erkenntnisanthropologische Funktion der Kommunikationsgesellschaft und die Grundlagen der Hermeneutik'. Pages 163-71 in *Information und Kommunikation*, ed. S. Moser. Munich: R. Oldenbourg.

———1973. *Transformation der Philosophie*. Frankfurt a.M: Suhrkamp. English, 1980.

———1988. *Diskurs und Verantwortung*. Frankfurt a.M.: Suhrkamp.

Appadurai, Arjun. 1996. *Modernity at Large*. Minneapolis: University of Minnesota Press.

Appel, Fredrick. 1999. *Nietzsche Contra Democracy*. Ithaca, NY: Cornell University Press.

Appelbaum, David. 1986. *Contact and Attention*. Washington: University Press of America.

Appiah, Kwame Anthony. 1992. *In My Father's House: Africa in the Philosophy of Culture*. Oxford: Oxford University Press.

Aquinas, St. Thomas. 1947. *Summa Theologica*. New York: Benzinger Brothers.

Arendt, Hannah. 1958. *The Human Condition*. Chicago: University of Chicago Press.

———1961. *Between Past and Future*. New York: Viking Press.

———1963. *On Revolution*. New York: Viking Press.

———1970. *On Violence*. New York: Harcourt, Brace, & World.

———2005. *The Promise of Politics*. New York: Schocken Books.

Arendt, Hannah, and Karl Jaspers. 1985. *Briefwechsel 1926–1969*. Munich: Piper.

Armstrong, D.M. 1978. *Nominalism and Realism*. Cambridge: Cambridge University Press.

———1986. 'The Nature of Possibility'. *Canadian Journal of Philosophy* 16: 575-94.

Arnheim, Rudolf. 1971. *Entropy and Art*. Berkeley: University of California Press.

Arntzenius, Frank. 1995. 'Indeterminism and the Direction of Time'. *Topoi* 14: 67-81.

Aschheim, Steven E. 1992. *The Nietzsche Legacy in Germany 1890–1990*. Berkeley: University of California Press.

Ashford, Douglas E. 1986. *The Emergence of the Welfare States*. Oxford: Blackwell.

Ashton-Jones, Evelyn, and Dene Kay Thomas. 1995. 'Composition, Collaboration, and Women's Ways of Knowing: A Conversation with Mary Belenky'. Pages 81-101 in G. Olson and E. Hirsh.

Atkins, P.W. 1984. *The Second Law*. New York: Scientific American Books.

Atkinson, Norma Pereira. 1984. *An Examination of the Life and Thought of Zina Fay Peirce, an American Reformer and Feminist*. Ann Arbor, MI: University Microfilms International.

Aune, Bruce. 1967. 'Possibility'. *The Encyclopedia of Philosophy*, VI: 419-24. New York: Macmillan.

Auyang, Sunny Y. 1998. *Foundations of Complex-System Theories in Economics, Evolutionary Biology, and Statistical Physics*. Cambridge: Cambridge University Press.

Bachelard, Gaston. 1934. *Le nouvel esprit scientifique*. Paris: Alcan. English, 1984.

Bachmann, Talis. 2000. *Microgenetic Approach to the Conscious Mind*. Amsterdam: John Benjamins.

Bacon, Francis. 1620. *Novum organum. Instauratio magna*. London: Joannem Billium.

Bacon, John. 1995. *Universals and Property Instances*. Oxford: Blackwell.

Badiou, Alain. 1988. *L'être et l'èvénement*. Paris: Éditions du Seuil. English, 2005.

——1993. *L'éthique*. Paris: Hatier. English, 2001.

——1997. *Saint Paul: La fondation de l'universalisme*. Paris: Presses Universitaires de France. English, 2003.

Bahm, Archie J. 1974. *Metaphysics*. New York: Barnes & Noble.

Bain, Alexander. 1870. *Logic*. London: Longmans, Green, Reader, & Dyer.

Baker, Houston A. Jr. 1986. 'Caliban's Triple Play'. *Critical Inquiry* 13: 182-96.

Bakhtin, Mikhail M. 1990. *Art and Answerability*. Austin: University of Texas Press.

——1993. *Toward a Philosophy of the Act*. Austin: University of Texas Press.

Bakunin, Mikhael. 1842. 'Die Reaktion in Deutschland'. Numbers 247-51 in *Deutsche Jahrbücher für Wissenschaft und Kunst*, ed. Arnold Ruge.

Baldwin, James Mark. 1915. *Genetic Theory of Reality*. New York: Putnam's Sons.

Balslev, Anindita Niyogi. 1991. *Cultural Otherness: Correspondence with Richard Rorty*. Shimla: Indian Institute of Advanced Study.

Bambach, Charles R. 1995. *Heidegger, Dilthey, and the Crisis of Historicism*. Ithaca, NY: Cornell University Press.

——2003. *Heidegger's Roots*. Ithaca, NY: Cornell University Press.

Bannet: see Tavor Bannet.

Barash, Jeffrey Andrew. 2003. *Martin Heidegger and the Problem of Historical Meaning*. New York: Fordham University Press.

Barcan Marcus, Ruth. 1993. *Modalities*. Oxford: Oxford University Press.

Barr, Stephen M. 2003. *Modern Physics and Ancient Faith*. Notre Dame, IN: University of Notre Dame Press.

Barrentine, Pat, ed. 1993. *When the Canary Stops Singing: Women's Perspective on Transforming Business*. San Francisco: Berrett-Koehler.

Barrett, Michèle. 1988. *Women's Oppression Today*. 2nd edn. London: Verso. 1st edn, 1980.

Barrow, John D., and Frank J. Tipler. 1986. *The Anthropic Cosmological Principle*. Oxford: Oxford University Press.

Barth, Karl. 1919. *Der Römerbrief*. Bern: Bäschlin.

——1922. *Der Römerbrief*, 2nd edn. Munich: Kaiser.

——1924. *Die Auferstehung der Toten*. Munich: Kaiser.

——1927. *Die Lehre vom Worte Gottes*. Vol. I of *Die christliche Dogmatik im Entwurf*. Munich: Kaiser.

——1932. *Die Lehre vom Wort Gottes*. Vol I/1 of *Die kirchliche Dogmatik*. Munich: Kaiser.

Barwise, Jon, and John Perry. 1999. *Situations and Attitudes*. 2nd edn. n.p.: CSLI Publications. Same as 1983 edn, plus new prefatory matters.

Bar-Yam, Yaneer. 1997. *Dynamics of Complex Systems*. Reading, MA: Addison-Wesley.

Basu, Amrita. 1995. *The Challenge of Local Feminisms: Women's Movements in Global Perspective*. Boulder, CO: Westview Press.

Bataille, Georges. 1970–88. *Oeuvres complètes*. Paris: Gallimard.

Batnitzky, Leora. 2000. *Idolatry and Representation*. Princeton, NJ: Princeton University Press.

Baudrillard, Jean. 1976. *L'échange symbolique et la mort*. Paris: Gallimard. English, 1993.

——1979. *De la séduction*. Paris: Denoël. English, 1990.

——1981. *Simulacres et simulation*. Paris: Galilée. English, 1994.

——1983. *Les stratégies fatales*. Paris: Grasset. English, 1990.

——1989. 'Anorexic Ruins'. Pages 29-45 in *Looking Back at the End of the World*, by J. Baudrillard, *et al*. New York: Semiotext[e].

——1990. *La transparence du mal*. Paris: Galilée. English, 1993.

——1995. *Le crime parfait*. Paris: Galilée. English, 1996.

——2000. *The Vital Illusion*. New York: Columbia University Press.

Bauman, Zygmunt. 1992. *Intimations of Postmodernity*. London: Routledge.

——1993. *Postmodern Ethics*. Oxford: Blackwell.

——2006. *Liquid Fear*. Cambridge: Polity Press.

Bayley, Peter J., *et al*. 2005. 'Robust Habit Learning in the Absence of Awareness and Independent of the Medial Temporal Lobe'. *Nature* 436 (28 July): 550-53.

Beauvoir, Simone de. 1947. *Pour une morale de l'ambiguïté*. Paris: Gallimard. English, 1948.

——1949. *Le deuxième sexe*. Paris: Gallimard. English, 1952.

——1984. 'France: Feminism—Alive, Well, and in Constant Danger'. Pages 229-35 in *Sisterhood is Global*, ed. R. Morgan. New York: Feminist Press.

Beecher, Catharine E. 1860. *An Appeal to the People in Behalf of their Rights as Authorized Interpreters of the Bible*. New York: Harper.

Beiser, Frederick C. 1996. *The Sovereignty of Reason*. Princeton, NJ: Princeton University Press.

Belenky, Mary Field, *et al*. 1986. *Women's Ways of Knowing*. New York: Basic Books.

Bell, Bernard Iddings. 1939. *Religion for Living: A Book for Postmodernists*. New York: Harper.

Bell, Daniel. 1988. *The End of Ideology: On the Exhaustion of Political Ideas in the Fifties*. 2nd edn. Cambridge, MA: Harvard University Press. 1st edn, 1960.

Bem, Sandra Lipsitz. 1993. *The Lenses of Gender*. New Haven: Yale University Press.

Ben-David, Joseph. 1990. *Scientific Growth*. Berkeley: University of California Press.

Bengel, John Albert. 1877. *Gnomon of the New Testament*. 7th edn. Edinburgh: T. & T. Clark.

Benhabib, Seyla. 1987. 'The Generalized and the Concrete Other'. Pages 154-77 in *Women and Moral Theory*, ed. E. Kittay and D. Meyers. Totowa, NJ: Rowman & Littlefield.

——1990. 'Afterword'. Pages 330-69 in *The Communicative Ethics Controversy*, ed. S. Benhabib and F. Dallmayr. Cambridge, MA: MIT Press.

——1992. *Situating the Self: Gender, Community and Postmodernism in Contemporary Ethics*. London: Routledge.

——2002. *The Claims of Culture: Equality and Diversity in the Global Era*. Princeton, NJ: Princeton University Press.

Benjamin, Jessica. 1988. *The Bonds of Love*. New York: Pantheon.

Bennet, Andy. 2000. *Popular Music and Youth Culture*. London: Macmillan.

Bentham, Jeremy. 1843. *Works*. Edinburgh: William Tait.

Bergson, Henri. 1934. *La pensée et le mouvant*. Paris: F. Alcan. English: *The Creative Mind*, 1946.

Berkovitz, Joseph, and Meir Hemmo. 2005. 'Model Interpretations of Quantum Mechanics and Relativity: A Reconsideration'. *Foundations of Physics* 35: 373-98.

Berlin, Isaiah. 1958. *Two Concepts of Liberty*. Oxford: Clarendon Press.
——1993. 'A Reply to David West'. *Political Studies* 41: 297-98.
Berlyne, D.E., ed. 1974. *Studies in the New Experimental Aesthetics*. New York: Wiley.
Berman, Morris. 1981. *The Reenchantment of the World*. Ithaca, NY: Cornell University Press.
Bernasconi, Robert. 2001. 'Who Invented the Concept of Race?' Pages 11-36 in *Race*, ed. R. Bernasconi. Oxford: Blackwell.
Bernauer, James, and David Rasmussen, eds. 1988. *The Final Foucault*. Cambridge, MA: MIT Press.
Bernet, Rudolf, *et al*. 1989. *Edmund Husserl*. Hamburg: F. Meiner.
Bernheim, Ernst. 1908. *Lehrbuch der historischen Methode und der Geschichtsphilosophie*. 5th edn. Leipzig: Duncker & Humblot.
Bernsmeier, Helmut. 1994. *Der Wandel um 1880*. Frankfurt a.M.: Peter Lang.
Bernstein, Richard J. 1983. *Beyond Objectivism and Relativism*. Philadelphia: University of Pennsylvania Press.
Bertalanffy, Ludwig von. 1968. *General System Theory*. New York: Braziller.
Bertens, Hans. 1995. *The Idea of the Postmodern*. London: Routledge.
Bérubé, Michael. 2000. 'The Return of Realism and the Future of Contingency'. Pages 137-56 in *What's Left of Theory?* ed. J. Butler *et al*. London: Routledge.
Bhabha, Homi K. 1990. 'The Third Space'. Pages 207-21 in *Identity, Community, Culture, Difference*, ed. J. Rutherford. London: Lawrence & Wishart.
——1994. *The Location of Culture*. London: Routledge.
Bird, Richard J. 2003. *Chaos and Life: Complexity and Order in Evolution and Thought*. New York: Columbia University Press.
Blackmore, John T. 1972. *Ernst Mach*. Berkeley: University of California Press.
Blair, Tony. 1998. *The Third Way*. London: The Fabian Society.
Blasche, Siegfried. 1995. 'Freiheit'. *Enzyklopädie, Philosophie und Wissenschaftstheorie*, I: 675-81. Stuttgart: Metzler.
Blau, Peter M. 1974. *On the Nature of Organizations*. New York: Wiley.
Bloch, Ernst. 1959. *Das Prinzip Hoffnung*. Frankfurt a.M.: Suhrkamp. English, 1986.
Bloor, David. 1999. 'Anti-Latour'. *Studies in the Philosophy and History of Science* 30: 81-112.
Blumenberg, Hans. 1966. *Die Legitimität der Neuzeit*. Frankfurt a.M.: Suhrkamp. English, 1983.
Blumenthal, David, *et al*. 2000. 'Dabru Emet: A Jewish Statement on Christians and Christianity'. *First Things* 107: 39-41.
Bly, Robert. 1990. *Iron John*. Reading, MA: Addison-Wesley.
Bocharov, Sergey. 1994. 'Conversations with Bakhtin'. *PMLA: Publications of the Modern Language Association of America* 109: 1009-24.
Bocheński, I.M. 1956. *Formale Logik*. Freiburg: K. Alber. English, 1961.
Böckenhoff, Josef. 1970. *Die Begegnungsphilosophie*. Freiburg: Karl Alber.
Boggs, Carl. 2000. *The End of Politics*. New York: Guilford Press.
Bohr, N. 1935. 'Can Quantum-Mechanical Description of Physical Reality be Considered Complete?' *Physical Review*, Second Series, 1948: 696-702.
Bologh, Roslyn Wallack. 1990. *Love or Greatness*. London: Unwin Hyman.
Bonnell, Victoria E., and Lynn Hunt, eds. 1999. *Beyond the Cultural Turn*. Berkeley: University of California Press.
Born, Max. 1968. *My Life and My Views*. New York: Scribner.
Boston Women's Health Book Collective. 1984. *The New Our Bodies, Ourselves*. New York: Simon & Schuster.

Boulding, Kenneth E. 1964. *The Meaning of the Twentieth Century*. New York: Harper & Row.

Bourdieu, Pierre. 1980. *Le sens pratique*. Paris: Minuit. English, 1990.

Boutroux, Émile. 1916. *The Contingency of the Laws of Nature*. Chicago: Open Court. French, 1874.

Bradley, F.H. 1893. *Appearance and Reality*. Oxford: Clarendon Press.

——1935. *Collected Essays*. Oxford: Clarendon Press.

Braidotti, Rosi. 1991. *Patterns of Dissonance*. London: Routledge. French not available.

——1997. 'Revisiting Male Thanatos: Response'. Pages 214-22 in *Feminism Meets Queer Theory*, ed. E. Weed and N. Schor. Bloomington: Indiana University Press.

Bramwell, Anna. 1989. *Ecology in the 20th Century*. New Haven: Yale University Press.

Brandom, Robert B. 1994. *Making It Explicit*. Cambridge, MA: Harvard University Press.

Brandt, Barbara. 1995. *Whole Life Economics*. Philadelphia: New Society Publishers.

Brenkert, George G. 1991. *Political Freedom*. London: Routledge.

Brent, Joseph. 1998. *Charles Sanders Peirce*. 2nd edn. Bloomington: Indiana University Press.

Brentano, Franz. 1926. *Die vier Phasen der Philosophie*. Leipzig: F. Meiner.

——1933. *Kategorienlehre*. Ed. A. Kastil. Leipzig: F. Meiner.

Britton, Celia M. 1999. *Edouard Glissant and Postcolonial Theory*. Charlottesville: University Press of Virginia.

Broda, Engelbert. 1983. *Ludwig Boltzmann*. Woodbridge, CT: Ox Bow Press. Revision of the German, 1955.

Brodribb, Somer. 1992. *Nothing Mat(t)ers: A Feminist Critique of Postmodernism*. North Melbourne: Spinifex Press.

Brooke, John Hedley. 1991. *Science and Religion*. Cambridge: Cambridge University Press.

Brooks, Daniel R., and E.O. Wiley. 1988. *Evolution as Entropy*. 2nd edn. Chicago: University of Chicago Press.

Brooks, David. 2000. *Bobos in Paradise*. New York: Simon & Schuster.

Brown, Norman O. 1966. *Love's Body*. New York: Random House.

Brush, Stephen G. 1983. *Statistical Physics and the Atomic Theory of Matter*. Princeton, NJ: Princeton University Press.

Buber, Martin. 1923. *Ich und Du*. Leipzig: Insel-Verlag. Cited with reference to page numbers in vol. I of *Werke*, 1962–, 79-170. English, 1937, 1970.

——1962–. *Werke*. Munich: Kosel-Verlag.

——1973. *Briefwechsel aus sieben Jahrzehnten*. Heidelberg: L. Schneider.

Buck-Morss, Susan. 2000. *Dreamworld and Catastrophe: The Passing of Mass Utopia in East and West*. Cambridge, MA: MIT Press.

Buhrkamp, Wilhelm. 1927. *Begriff und Beziehung*. Leipzig: F. Meiner.

Bulbeck, Chilla. 1998. *Re-Orienting Western Feminisms*. Cambridge: Cambridge University Press.

Bullert, Gary. 1983. *The Politics of John Dewey*. Buffalo, NY: Prometheus Books.

Bultmann, Rudolf. 1926. *Jesus*. Berlin: Deutsche Bibliothek. English, 1934.

——1933–58. *Glauben und Verstehen*. Tübingen: Mohr.

Burgard, Peter J. 1994. *Nietzsche and the Feminine*. Charlottsville: University Press of Virginia.

Buss, Martin J. 1979. 'Understanding Communication'. Pages 3-44 in *Encounter with the Text*, ed. M. Buss. Philadelphia: Fortress Press.
——1999. *Biblical Form Criticism in its Context*. Sheffield: Sheffield Academic Press.
——2002. 'Ideas of Life Situation and Interdisciplinary Relations'. http://www.religion. emory.edu/faculty/buss.html. (Scheduled to be printed.)
——2006. 'The Impact of Faith on Relational Thought'. *Consensus* 31, No. 2: 75-85.
——2007. 'Relational Form in Individual Disciplines'. http://www.religion.emory.edu/ faculty/buss.html. (Scheduled to be printed.)
Butler, Judith. 1990. *Gender Trouble*. London: Routledge. See also Butler 1999.
——1992. 'Contingent Foundations'. Pages 3-21 in J. Butler and J. Scott, eds.
——1993. *Bodies That Matter*. London: Routledge.
——1997. *The Psychic Life of Power*. Stanford, CA: Stanford University Press.
——1999. 'Preface (1999)'. Pages vii-xxvi in *Gender Trouble*. 2nd edn. London: Routledge.
——2004. *Undoing Gender*. London: Routledge.
Butler, Judith, and Joan Scott, eds. 1992. *Feminists Theorize the Political*. London: Routledge.
Cabral, Amilcar. 1973. *Return to the Source*. New York: Monthly Review Press.
Cahoone, Lawrence E., ed. 1996. *From Modernism to Postmodernism*. Oxford: Blackwell.
Calkins, Mary Whiton. 1908. *The Persistent Problems of Philosophy*. 2nd edn. New York: Macmillan. 1st edn, 1907; 5th edn, 1925.
Campbell, Karlyn Kohrs. 1989. *Man Cannot Speak for Her*. New York: Greenwood Press.
Camus, Albert. 1942. *Le mythe de Sisyphe*. Paris: Gallimard. English, 1952.
——1951. *L'homme révolté*. Paris: Gallimard. English, 1954.
Cannadine, David. 2001. *Ornamentalism: How the British Saw their Empire*. Oxford: Oxford University Press.
Cantor, Norman F. 1988. *Twentieth-Century Culture*. New York: P. Lang.
Caputo, John D. 1997. *Deconstruction in a Nutshell*. New York: Fordham University Press.
Carmichael, Stokely, and Charles V. Hamilton. 1967. *Black Power: The Politics of Liberation in America*. New York: Random House.
Carnap, Rudolf. 1928. *Der logische Aufbau der Welt*. Berlin: Weltkreis-Verlag.
——1937. *The Logical Syntax of Language*. London: K. Paul, Trench, Trübner & Co.
Carr, David. 1987. *Interpreting Husserl*. Dordrecht: M. Nijhoff.
Carson, Clayborne. 1981. *In Struggle: SNCC and the Black Awakening of the 1960s*. Cambridge, MA: Harvard University Press.
Cartwright, Nancy. 1989. *Nature's Capacities and their Measurement*. Oxford: Clarendon Press.
——1999. *The Dappled World*. Cambridge: Cambridge University Press.
Cassese, Antonio. 1999. 'Are Human Rights Truly Universal?' Pages 149-65 in *The Politics of Human Rights*, ed. O. Savic. London: Verso.
Cassirer, Ernst. 1910. *Substanzbegriff und Funktionsbegriff*. Berlin: B. Cassirer.
——1923-29. *Philosophie der symbolischen Formen*. Berlin: B. Cassirer. English, 1953-96.
——1942. *Zur Logik der Kulturwissenschaften*. Göteborg: Elanders boktryckeri aktiebolag. English, 1961.

Castells, Manuel. 2000. *The Information Age.* Vol I of *The Rise of the Network Society.* 2nd edn. Oxford: Blackwell.

Castoriadis, Cornelius. 1997. *World in Fragments.* Stanford, CA: Stanford University Press.

Caufield, Catherine. 1996. *Masters of Illusion.* New York: Henry Holt & Co.

Chafetz, Janet Saltzman, and Anthony Gary Dworkin. 1986. *Female Revolt.* Totowa, NJ: Roman & Allanheid.

Chaitin, Gregory J. 1990. *Information, Randomness, and Incompleteness.* 2nd edn. Singapore: World Scientific.

——1999. *The Unknowable.* Singapore: Springer.

Chalmers, David J. 1996. *The Conscious Mind.* Oxford: Oxford University Press.

——1997. 'Moving Forward on the Problem of Consciousness'. Pages 379-422 in *Explaining Consciousness,* ed. Jonathan Shear. Cambridge, MA: Harvard University Press.

Chambliss, William J. 1999. *Power, Politics and Crime.* Boulder, CO: Westview Press.

Chandavarkar, Rajnarayan. 1998. *Imperial Power and Popular Politics.* Cambridge: Cambridge University Press.

Chatterjee, Partha. 1993. *The Nation and its Fragments.* Princeton, NJ: Princeton University Press.

Chaturvedi, Vinayak, ed. 2000. *Mapping Subaltern Studies and the Postcolonial.* London: Verso.

Cheah, Pheng. 1997. 'Given Culture: Rethinking Cosmopolitical Freedom in Transnationalism'. *boundary 2* 24, No. 2: 157-97.

Cheney, Sheldon. 1924. *A Primer of Modern Art.* New York: Boni & Liveright.

Chihara, Charles S. 1998. *The Worlds of Possibility.* Oxford: Clarendon Press.

Childs, John Brown. 2003. *Transcommunality: From the Politics of Conversion to the Ethics of Respect.* Philadelphia: Temple University Press.

Chladenius, Johann Martin. 1742. *Einleitung zur richtigen Auslegung vernünfftiger Reden und Schriften.* Leipzig: Lanckisch.

Chodorow, Nancy. 1978. *The Reproduction of Mothering.* Berkeley: University of California Press.

Christian, Barbara. 1987. 'The Race for Theory'. *Cultural Critique* 6: 51-63.

Christie, Francis Albert. 1927. 'Abbot, Francis Ellingwood'. *Dictionary of American Biography,* I: 11-12.

Church, Alonzo. 1936. 'A Bibliography of Symbolic Logic'. *Journal of Symbolic Logic* 1: 121-216.

Churchland, Patricia S. 1998. 'Feeling Reasons'. Pages 239-54 in *On the Contrary,* ed. P. Churchland and P. Churchland. Cambridge, MA: MIT Press.

Cioran, E.M. 1949. *Précis de decomposition.* Paris: Gallimard. English, 1975.

Cixous, Hélène. 1975. 'Sorties'. Pages 114-246 in *La jeune née,* ed. H. Cixous and C. Clement. Paris: Union generale d'editions. English, 1986.

——1993. *Three Steps on the Ladder of Writing.* New York: Columbia University Press.

Clark, Katerina, and Michael Holquist. 1984. *Mikhail Bakhtin.* Cambridge, MA: Belknap Press.

Clarke, Eric O. 1999. 'The Citizen's Sexual Shadow'. *boundary 2* 26, No. 2: 163-91.

Clarke, J.J. 2000. *The Tao of the West.* London: Routledge.

Code, Lorraine. 1991. *What Can She Know?* Ithaca, NY: Cornell University Press.

Cohen, Hermann. 1904. *Ethik des reinen Willens.* Berlin: B. Cassirer.

——1912. *Ästhetik des reinen Gefühls*. Berlin: B. Cassirer.
——1919. *Die Religion der Vernunft aus den Quellen des Judentums*. Leipzig: G. Fock.
Cohn-Bendit, Daniel, and Gabriel Cohn-Bendit. 1968. *Le gauchisme*. Paris: Éditions du Seuil. Roughly equivalent English translation, 1968.
Cole, Bruce, and Adelheid Gealt. 1989. *Art of the Western World*. New York: Summit Books.
Colish, Marcia L. 1985. *The Stoic Tradition*. Leiden: E.J. Brill.
Collins, Anthony. 1713. *A Discourse of Free-thinking Occasion'd by the Rise and Growth of a Sect Call'd Free-thinkers*. London: n.p.
Collins, Patricia Hill. 1990. *Black Feminist Thought*. Boston: Unwin Hyman. 2nd edn. London: Routledge, 2000.
Collins, Randall. 1998. *The Sociology of Philosophies*. Cambridge, MA: Harvard University Press.
Conner, Randy P., *et al.*, eds. 1997. *Cassell's Encyclopedia of Queer Myth, Symbol, and Spirit*. London: Cassell.
Copleston, Frederick. 1946–63. *A History of Philosophy*. Westminster, MD: Newman Press.
Coreth, Emerich. 1985. *Vom Sinn der Freiheit*. Innsbruck: Tyrolia-Verlag.
Coriando, Paolo-Ludovica. 1998. *Der letzte Gott als Anfang*. Munich: Fink.
Cornell, Drucilla. 1991. *Beyond Accommodation*. London: Routledge. 2nd edn, 1999.
——1998. *At the Heart of Freedom*. Princeton, NJ: Princeton University Press.
Corning, Peter A. 1998. 'The Synergism Hypothesis'. *Journal of Social and Evolutionary Systems* 21: 133-72.
Cotterill, Rodney. 1998. *Enchanted Looms*. Cambridge: Cambridge University Press.
Covell, Charles. 1992. *The Defence of Natural Law*. New York: St. Martin's Press.
Cover, Thomas M., and Joy A. Thomas. 1991. *Elements of Information Theory*. New York: Wiley.
Crane, R.S. 1953. *The Languages of Criticism and the Structure of Poetry*. Toronto: University of Toronto Press.
Cravens, Hamilton. 1987. 'Recent Controversy in Human Development: A Historical View'. *Human Development* 30: 325-35.
Crisafulli, Chuck. 2000. *The Doors*. New York: Thunder's Mouth Press.
Critchley, Simon. 1992. *The Ethics of Deconstruction*. Oxford: Blackwell.
Crosby, Donald A. 1988. *The Specter of the Absurd*. Albany: State University of New York Press.
Culver, John C., and John Hyde. 2000. *American Dreamer: The Life and Times of Henry A. Wallace*. New York: Norton.
Cunningham, Conor. 2002. *Genealogy of Nihilism*. London: Routledge.
Cushing, James T. 1994. *Quantum Mechanics: Historical Contingency and the Copenhagen Hegemony*. Chicago: University of Chicago Press.
DaCosta, Newton C., and Walter A. Carnielli. 1986. 'On Paraconsistent Deontic Logic'. *Philosophia* 16: 293-305.
Dahrendorf, Rolf. 1975. *The New Liberty*. Stanford, CA: Stanford University Press.
Dainton, Barry. 2001. *Time and Space*. Montreal: McGill-Queen's University Press.
Dallmayr, Fred R. 1984. *Language and Politics*. Notre Dame, IN: University of Notre Dame Press.
——1993. 'Modernity and Postmodernity'. Pages 105-20 in *Dialectic and Narrative*, ed. T. Flynn and D. Judovitz. Albany: State University of New York Press.
Daly, Mary. 1998. *Quintessence*. Boston: Beacon.

Danziger, Sheldon, and Peter Gottschalk, eds. 1993. *Uneven Tides*. New York: Russell Sage Foundation.

Darwin, Charles. 1871. *The Descent of Man and Selection in Relation to Sex*. London: J. Murray. A concordance to this was published in 1987.

——1959. *The Origin of Species*. Ed. M. Peckham. Philadelphia: University of Pennsylvania Press. This edition presents all variations from 1859 to 1878.

Davidson, Donald. 1984. *Inquiries into Truth and Interpretation*. Oxford: Clarendon Press.

——1990. 'The Structure and Context of Truth'. *Journal of Philosophy* 87: 279-328.

Davies, Carole Boyce. 1994. *Black Women, Writing and Identity*. London: Routledge.

Davis, David Brion. 1975. *The Problem of Slavery in the Age of Revolution 1770–1823*. Ithaca, NY: Cornell University Press.

——2001. *In the Image of God*. New Haven: Yale University Press.

Dawkins, Richard. 1986. *The Blind Watchmaker*. New York: Norton.

Dean, Jodi. 1996. *Solidarity of Strangers*. Berkeley: University of California Press.

Dean, Mitchel. 1994. *Critical and Effective Histories*. London: Routledge.

DeAngelis, D.L., *et al*. 1986. *Positive Feedback in Natural Systems*. Berlin: Springer-Verlag.

Dearborn, Mary V. 1988. *Love in the Promised Land*. New York: Free Press.

Dedekind, Richard. 1888. *Was sind und sollen die Zahlen?* Braunschweig: F. Vieweg.

Deely, John. 1994. *New Beginnings*. Toronto: University of Toronto Press.

Deely, John, *et al*., eds. 1986. *Frontiers in Semiotics*. Bloomington: Indiana University Press.

Delacampagne, Christian. 1999. *A History of Philosophy in the Twentieth Century*. Baltimore: The Johns Hopkins University Press. Revised from the French, 1995.

Deleuze, Gilles. 1968. *Différence et répétition*. Paris: Presses Universitaires de France.

Deleuze, Gilles, and Félix Guattari. 1980. *Mille Plateaux*. Paris: Minuit. English, 1987.

Deliège, Robert. 2004. *Lévi-Strauss Today*. Oxford: Berg. French, 2001.

De Morgan, Augustus. 1966. *On Syllogism and Other Logical Writings*. London: Routledge & Kegan Paul.

Denbigh, K.G. 1975. *An Inventive Universe*. London: Hutchinson.

Denkel, Arda. 1996. *Object and Property*. Cambridge: Cambridge University Press.

Derrida, Jacques. 1967a. *L'écriture et la différence*. Paris: Éditions du Seuil. English, 1978.

——1967b. *La voix et la phénomène*. Paris: Presses universitaires de France. English, 1973.

——1967c. *De la grammatologie*. Paris: Editions de Minuit. English, 1974.

——1972a. *Marges de la philosophie*. Paris: Editions de Minuit. English, 1982.

——1972b. *La dissemination*. Paris: Éditions du Seuil. English, 1981.

——1982. *L'oreille de l'autre*. Montreal: VLB. English, 1985.

——1984. 'Deconstruction and the Other'. Pages 107-26 in *Dialogues with Contemporary Continental Thinkers*, ed. R. Kearney. Manchester: Manchester University Press.

——1985. 'Deconstruction in America'. *Critical Exchange* 17: 1-33.

——1988. *Limited Inc*. Evanston, IL: Northwestern University Press.

——1990. 'Force of Law: The "Mystical Foundation of Authority"'. English with facing French. *Cardozo Law Review* 11: 919-1045.

——1991. 'Circonfession'. Pages 7-291 in *Jacques Derrida*, ed. G. Bennington and J. Derrida. Paris: Galilée. English, 1993.

——1992. *Donner la mort*. Paris: Metailié-Transition. Followed by a discussion. English, 1995.

——1994. *Politiques de l'amitié*. Paris: Galilée. English, 1997.

——1996a. *Le monolinguisme de l'autre*. Paris: Galilée. English, 1998.

——1996b. 'Remarks on Deconstruction and Pragmatism'. Pages 77-88 in *Deconstruction and Pragmatism*, ed. C. Mouffe. London: Routledge.

——1996c. 'Foi et savoir'. Pages 9-86 in *La Religion*, ed. J. Derrida and G. Vattimo. Paris: Éditions du Seuil. English, 1998.

——2001. *Acts of Religion*. London: Routledge.

Derrida, Jacques, and Elisabeth Roudinesco. 2001. *Le Quoi Demain...* Paris: Arthème Fayard. English, 2004.

Des Pres, Terrence. 1976. *The Survivor*. Oxford: Oxford University Press.

Detlefsen, Michael. 1996. 'Philosophy of Mathematics in the Twentieth Century'. Pages 50-123 in *Philosophy of Science, Logic and Mathematics in the Twentieth Century*, ed. S. Shanker. London: Routledge.

Dewey, John. 1916. *Democracy and Education*. New York: Macmillan.

——1922. *Human Nature and Conduct*. New York: Carlton House.

——1925. *Experience and Nature*. Chicago: Open Court.

——1929. *The Quest for Certainty*. New York: Minton, Balch.

——1934. *Art as Experience*. New York: Minton, Balch & Company.

——1938. *Logic*. New York: H. Holt & Company.

——1963. *Experience and Education*. New York: Macmillan.

Dews, Peter. 1979. 'The *Nouvelle Philosophie* and Foucault'. *Economy and Society* 8: 127-71.

——1987. *Logics of Disintegration*. London: Verso.

Dey, Eric L., *et al.* 1991. *The American Freshman: Twenty-Five Year Trends, 1966–1990*. Los Angeles: Higher Education Research Institute, UCLA.

Diener, Ed, and Eunkook M. Suh, eds. 2000. *Culture and Subjective Well-Being*. Cambridge, Mass: MIT Press.

Diggins, John Patrick. 1994. *The Promise of Pragmatism*. Chicago: University of Chicago Press.

Dilthey, Wilhelm. 1921–. *Gesammelte Schriften*. Leipzig: Teubner.

Dimand, Mary Ann, *et al.*, eds. 1995. *Women of Value*. Aldershot: E. Elgar.

Diop, Cheikh Anta. 1981. *Civilisation ou barbarie*. Paris: Presence africaine. English, 1990.

Dirlik, Arif, and Zhang Xudong. 2000. 'Introduction: Postmodernism in China'. *boundary 2* 24, No. 3: 1-18.

Docherty, Thomas, ed. 1993. *Postmodernism: A Reader*. New York: Columbia University Press.

Doležel, Luomír. 1998. *Heterocosmica: Fiction and Possible Worlds*. Baltimore: The Johns Hopkins University Press.

Doll, Peter. 1985. *Menschenschöpfung und Weltschöpfung in der alttestamentlichen Weisheit*. Stuttgart: Verlag Katholisches Bibelwerk.

Donovan, Josephine. 1993. *Feminist Theory*. 2nd edn. New York: F. Ungar.

——1996. 'Attention to Suffering'. Pages 147-69 in *Beyond Animal Rights*, ed. J. Donovan and C. Adams. New York: Continuum.

Dosse, François. 1991–92. *Histoire du structuralisme*. Paris: La Découverte. English, 1997.

Doty, William G. 1998. 'Imagining the Future-Possible'. Pages 104-21 in T. Pippin and G. Aichele.

Dravid, Raja Ram. 2001. *The Problem of Universals in Indian Philosophy*. Delhi: Motilal Banarsidass.

DuBois, W.E.B. 1903. *The Souls of Black Folk*. Chicago: A.C. McClurg.

Duchen, Claire. 1986. *Feminism in France*. London: Routledge & Kegan Paul.

Duhem, P. 1906. *La théorie physique: Son objet et son structure*. Paris: Chevalier & Riviere. English, 1954.

Dumitriu, Anton. 1977. *History of Logic*. Tunbridge Wells, Kent: Abacus Press. Romanian, 1975.

Dumitriu, Petru. 1965. *Die Transmoderne*. Frankfurt a.M.: Fischer.

Dummett, Michael. 1978. *Truth and Other Enigmas*. Cambridge, MA: Harvard University Press.

Duns Scotus, John. 1975. *God and Creatures*. Ed. F. Alluntis and A. Wolter. Princeton, NJ: Princeton University Press.

Dupré, Louis. 1993. *Passage to Modernity*. New Haven: Yale University Press.

——2004. *The Enlightenment and the Intellectual Foundations of Modern Culture*. New Haven: Yale University Press.

Duran, Jane. 1991. *Toward a Feminist Epistemology*. Savage, MD: Rowman & Littlefield.

Dussel, Enrique. 1995. *The Invention of the Americas*. New York: Continuum. Spanish: *1492: El encubrimiento del otro*, 1993. 3rd Spanish edn, without *1492* in the title, 1994.

Eagleton, Terry. 1966. *The New Left Church*. Baltimore: Helicon.

——1970. *The Body as Language: Outline of a 'New Left' Theology*. London: Sheed & Ward.

——1996. *The Illusions of Postmodernism*. Cambridge: Cambridge University Press.

Eaton, Heather. 1998. 'The Edge of the Sea: The Colonization of Ecofeminist Religious Perspectives'. *Critical Review of Books in Religion* 11: 57-82.

Ebeling, Werner, and Rainer Feistel. 1982. *Physik der Selbstorganisation und Evolution*. Berlin: Akademie-Verlag.

Ebner, Ferdinand. 1963–65. *Schriften*. Munich: Kösel. English of his key 1921 work in: *The Word and Spiritual Realities*, by Harold J. Green. Ann Arbor, MI: University Microfilms International, 1981.

Echols, Alice. 1989. *Daring to Be Bad: Radical Feminism in America 1967–1975*. Minneapolis: University of Minnesota Press.

Eddington, Arthur. 1939. *The Philosophy of Physical Science*. New York: Macmillan.

Edwards, Tim. 1994. *Erotics and Politics*. London: Routledge.

Ehrt, Adolf. 1933. *Totale Krise?—Totale Revolution?* Berlin: Eckart-Verlag.

Eichrodt, Walter. 1933–39. *Theologie des alten Testaments*. Leipzig: J.C. Hinrichs. English, 1961–67.

Eigen, Manfred, and Ruthild Winkler. 1975. *Das Spiel*. Munich: Piper. English, 1981.

Einstein, Albert. 1949. 'Aubiographisches/Autobiographical Notes'. Pages 2-95 in *Albert Einstein: Philosopher-Scientist*, ed. P. Schilpp. Evanston, IL: Library of Living Philosophers.

Eisler, Riane. 1995. *Sacred Pleasure*. San Francisco: HarperSanFrancisco.

Eisler, Rudolf. 1922. *Handwörterbuch der Philosophie*. 2nd edn. Berlin: E.S. Mittler.

Elam, Diane. 1992. *Romancing the Postmodern*. London: Routledge.

——1994. *Feminism and Deconstruction*. London: Routledge.

Eller, Cynthia. 1993. *Living in the Lap of the Goddess*. New York: Crossroads.

Ellwood, Robert S. 1994. *The Sixties Spiritual Awakening*. New Brunswick, NJ: Rutgers University Press.

Elshtain, Jean Bethke. 1995. *Democracy on Trial*. New York: Basic Books.
——1997. *Real Politics*. Baltimore: The Johns Hopkins University Press.
Emerson, Ralph Waldo. 1841–44. *Essays*. Boston: J. Munroe & Company.
Emmet, Dorothy. 1953. 'The Concept of Power'. *Proceedings of the Aristotelian Society*, n.s. 54: 1-26.
Engel, J. Ronald. 1983. *Sacred Sands*. Middletown, CT: Wesleyan University Press.
Engell, James. 1981. *The Creative Imagination*. Cambridge, MA: Harvard University Press.
Ericksen, Robert P. 1985. *Theologians Under Hitler*. New Haven: Yale University Press.
Ermarth, Michael. 1978. *Wilhelm Dilthey: The Critique of Historical Reason*. Chicago: University of Chicago Press.
Ernest, Paul. 1998. *Social Constructivism as a Philosophy of Mathematics*. Albany: State University of New York Press.
Escoffier, Jeffrey. 1998. *American Homo: Community and Perversity*. Berkeley: University of California Press.
Esteva, Gustavo, and Madhu Suri Prakash. 1998. *Grassroots Post-Modernism*. London: Zed Books.
Ettinger, Elzbieta. 1995. *Hannah Arendt, Martin Heidegger*. New Haven: Yale University Press.
Etzioni, Amitai. 1968. *The Active Society*. New York: Free Press.
——1988. *The Moral Dimension: Toward a New Economics*. New York: Macmillan.
Everdell, William R. 1997. *The First Moderns*. Chicago: University of Chicago Press.
Eze, E., ed. 1997. *Postcolonial African Philosophy*. Oxford: Blackwell.
Fang, J. 1970. *Bourbaki*. Hauppauge, NY: Paideia.
Fanon, Frantz. 1961. *Les damnés de la terre*. Paris: F. Maspero. English, 1967.
——1964. *Pour la révolution africaine: écrits politiques*. Paris: F. Maspero.
Farganis, Sondra. 1977. 'Liberty: Two Perspectives on the Women's Movement'. *Ethics* 88: 62-73.
Farley, Edward. 1990. *Good and Evil*. Minneapolis: Fortress Press.
Farley, Margaret A. 1993. 'Feminism and Universal Morality'. Pages 170-90 in *Prospects for a Common Morality*, ed. G. Outka and J. Reeder, Jr. Princeton, NJ: Princeton University Press.
Fauconnier, Gilles, and Mark Turner. 2002. *The Way We Think*. New York: Basic Books.
Faust, Gerald W., Richard I. Lyles, and Will Phillips. 1998. *Responsible Managers Get Results*. New York: AMACON.
[Fay] Peirce, Melusina. 1884. *Co-operative Housekeeping*. Boston: Osgood.
——1918. *New York: A Symphonic Study*. New York: Neale.
Faye, Emmanuel. 2005. *Heidegger: L'introduction du nazisme dans la philosophie*. Paris: Albin Michel.
Feder, Ellen K., and Emily Zakin. 1997. 'Flirting with the Truth'. Pages 21-51 in *Derrida and Feminism*, ed. E. Feder *et al*. London: Routledge.
Feffer, Andrew. 1993. *The Chicago Pragmatists and American Progressivism*. Ithaca, NY: Cornell University Press.
Felken, Detlef. 1988. *Oswald Spengler*. Munich: Beck.
Ferré, Frederick. 1996. *Being and Value*. Albany: State University of New York Press.
——1998. *Knowing and Value*. Albany: State University of New York Press.
Ferry, Luc. 1990. *Homo aestheticus*. Paris: B. Grasset.
——1992. *Le nouvel ordre écologique*. Paris: B. Grasset. English, 1995.

Ferry, Luc, and Alain Renault. 1997. *Why We Are Not Nietzscheans*. Chicago: University of Chicago Press. French, 1991.

Feyerabend, Paul. 1978. *Science in a Free Society*. London: NLB.

Ffrench, Patrick. 1995. *The Time of Theory*. Oxford: Clarendon Press.

Fichte, Johann Gottlieb. 1797. *Zweite Einleitung in die Wissenschaftslehre*. Hamburg: F. Meiner.

——1806. *Die Anweisung zum seeligen Leben*. Berlin: Realschulbuchhandlung.

——1808. *Reden an die deutsche Nation*. Berlin: Realschulbuchhandlung. English, 1922.

Field, Harty H. 1980. *Science Without Numbers*. Princeton, NJ: Princeton University Press.

Findlay, James F., Jr. 1993. *Church People in Struggle*. New York: Oxford University Press.

Finkielkraut, Alain. 1982. *L'avenir d'une negation*. Paris: Éditions du Seuil. English, 1998.

——1984. *La sagesse de l'amour*. Paris: Gallimard. English, 1997.

——1996. *L'humanité perdue*. Paris: Éditions du Seuil. English: *In the Name of Humanity*, 2000.

Finkielkraut, Alain, et al. 1991. 'Une guerre requise'. *Libération* 3034, 21 February: 12.

Fisch, Max H. 1982. 'Introduction'. Pages xv-xxxv in vol. I of Peirce 1982-.

Fitzgerald, P.F. 1882. *An Essay on the Philosophy of Self-Consciousness*. London: Trubner.

Flax, Jane. 1983. 'Political Philosophy and the Patriarchal Unconscious'. Pages 245-81 in *Discovering Reality*, ed. S. Harding and M. Hintikka. Dordrecht: D. Reidel.

——1990. *Thinking Fragments*. Berkeley: University of California Press.

——1992. 'The End of Innocence'. Pages 445-63 in *Feminists Theorize the Political*, ed. J. Butler and J. Scott. London: Routledge.

Flood, Patrick James. 1998. *The Effectiveness of UN Human Rights Institutions*. Westport, CT: Praeger.

Flora, Peter, and Arnold J. Heidenheimer, eds. 1981. *The Development of Welfare States in Europe and America*. New Brunswick, NJ: Transaction Books.

Flynn, Thomas R. 1997–2005. *Sartre, Foucault, and Historical Reason*. Chicago: University of Chicago Press.

Fogel, Robert William. 2000. *The Fourth Great Awakening*. Chicago: University of Chicago Press.

Fónagy, Ivan. 1961. 'Informationsgehalt von Wort und Laut in der Dichtung'. Pages 591-605 in *Poetics*. Polska Akademia Nauk, Instytut Badan Literackich. Warsaw: Panstwowe Wydawnictwo Naukowe.

Forman, Paul. 1971. 'Weimar Culture, Causality and Quantum Theory, 1918–1927'. Pages 1-115 in *Historical Studies in the Physical Sciences*, vol. III, ed. R. McCormmach. Philadelphia: University of Pennsylvania Press.

Foucault, Michel. 1963a. *Naissance de la clinique*. Paris: Presses universitaires de France. English, 1973.

——1963b. 'Préface à la transgression'. *Critique* 19: 751-69. English in vol. II of *Essential Works*, 1998: 69-87.

——1966. *Les mots et les choses*. Paris: Gallimard. English: *The Order of Things*, 1970.

——1967. 'Deuxième entretien'. With Raymond Bellour. *Les lettres françaises* 1187, June 15: 6-9. English in Foucault 1989.

——1968. 'Réponse à une question'. *Esprit* 371: 850-74. English in *The Foucault Effect*, 1991.

——1969. *L'archéologie du savoir*. Paris: Gallimard. English, 1972.

——1971. 'Par delà le bien et le mal'. *Actuel* 14, November: 42-47.

——1975. *Surveiller et punir: Naissance de la prison*. Paris: Gallimard. English, 1979.

——1976a. *La volonté de savoir*. Vol. I of *Histoire de la sexualité*. Paris: Gallimard. English, 1980.

——1976b. 'La fonction politique de l'intellectuel'. *Politique hebdo* 247, 26 November: 31-33. English in Foucault 1980.

——1977a. 'Vérité et pouvoir'. *L'Arc* 70: 16-26. English in Foucault 1980.

——1977b. 'Pouvoirs et strategies'. *Les révoltes logiques* 4: 89-97. English in Foucault 1980.

——1980. *Power/Knowledge*. New York: Pantheon Books.

——1981a. 'Questions of Method'. *Ideology and Consciousness* 8: 3-14.

——1981b. 'Est-il donc important de penser?' *Libération* 30–31 May: 21. English in vol. III of *Essential Works*, 2000: 454-58.

——1982. 'The Subject and Power'. Pages 208-26 in *Michel Foucault*, ed. H. Dreyfus and P. Rabinow. Chicago: University of Chicago Press. Reprinted in vol. III of *Essential Works*, 2000: 326-48.

——1983a. 'On the Genealogy of Ethics'. Pages 229-52 in *Michel Foucault*, ed. H. Dreyfus and P. Rabinow. Chicago: University of Chicago Press. Reprinted in vol. I of *Essential Works*, 1997: 253-80.

——1983b. 'Un system fini à une demande infini'. Pages 39-63 in *Sécurité sociale: l'enjeu*. Paris: Syros. English in vol. III of *Essential Works*, 2000: 365-81.

——1984a. 'L'éthique du souci de soi comme pratique de liberté'. *Concordia* 6: 99-116. English in vol. I of *Essential Works*, 1997: 281-301.

——1984b. *L'usage des plaisirs*. Vol. II of *Histoire de la sexualité*. Paris: Gallimard. English, 1985.

——1984c. 'Le souci de la vérité'. *Magazine littéraire* 207, May: 18-23. English in vol. I of *Essential Works*, 1997: 87-92.

——1984d. 'Le retour de la morale'. *Les Nouvelles* 2937, June 28–July 5: 36-41. English in Foucault 1989.

——1988. 'Truth, Power, Self', and 'Technologies of the Self'. Pages 9-49 in *Technologies of the Self*, ed. L. Martin. Amherst: University of Massachusetts Press. 'Technologies of the Self' reprinted in vol. I of *Essential Works*, 1997: 223-51.

——1989. *Foucault Live (Interviews, 1966–84)*. New York: Semiotext(e).

——1991. *Remarks on Marx*. New York: Semiotext(e).

Fraenkel, Abraham A., and Yehoshua Bar-Hillel. 1958. *Foundations of Set Theory*. Amsterdam: North-Holland.

Fraser, Nancy, and Linda Nicholson. 1988. 'Social Criticism Without Philosophy: An Encounter Between Feminism and Postmodernism'. *Theory, Culture and Society* 5: 373-94. Reprinted in Nicholson 1999.

Frege, Gottlob. 1879. *Begriffsschrift*. Halle: L. Nebert.

——1891. *Funktion und Begriff*. Jena: H. Pohle.

Freire, Paulo. 1993. *Pedagogy of the Oppressed*. New York: Continuum. 1st edn, 1970.

Fricker, Miranda. 1994. 'Knowledge as Construct'. Pages 95-109 in *Knowing the Difference*, ed. K. Lennon and M. Whitford. London: Routledge.

——2000. 'Feminism in Epistemology: Pluralism Without Postmodernism'. Pages 146-65 in *The Cambridge Companion to Feminism in Philosophy*, by M. Fricker and J. Hornsby. Cambridge: Cambridge University Press.

Friedan, Betty. 1981. *The Second Stage*. New York: Summit Books.

Friedman, Marilyn. 2006. 'Nancy J. Hirschmann on the Social Construction of Women's Freedom'. *Hypatia* 21: 182-91.

Friedman, Susan Stanford. 1998. *Mappings*. Princeton, NJ: Princeton University Press.

Friedmann, Hermann. 1930. *Die Welt der Formen*. Munich: Beck.

Friedrich, Carl J. 1958. *The Philosophy of Law in Historical Perspective*. Chicago: University of Chicago Press. Revised from the German of 1955.

Frijda, Nico H. 1986. *The Emotions*. Cambridge: Cambridge University Press.

Frisina, Warren G. 2002. *The Unity of Knowledge and Action*. Albany: State University of New York Press.

Fromm, Erich. 1956. *The Art of Loving*. New York: Harper & Brothers.

Frye, Marilyn. 1983. *The Politics of Reality*. Trumansburg, NY: Crossing.

Fuller, Steve. 1988. *Social Epistemology*. Bloomington: Indiana University Press.

Fürstenberg, Friedrich. 1994. 'Säkularisierung'. *Wörterbuch der Religionssoziologie*, 279-87. Gütersloh: Gütersloher Verlagshaus.

Gadamer, Hans-Georg. 1960. *Wahrheit und Methode*. Tübingen: J.C.B. Mohr. 3rd edn, 1972. English, 1975.

——1984. 'Text und Interpretation'. Pages 24-55 in *Text und Interpretation*, ed. P. Forget. Munich: Fink.

Gallop, Jane. 1988. *Thinking Through the Body*. New York: Columbia University Press.

Gallup, George, Jr., and D. Michael Lindsay. 1999. *Surveying the Religious Landscape*. Harrisburg, PA: Morehouse.

Game, Ann. 1991. *Undoing the Social*. Toronto: University of Toronto Press.

Gandhi, Leela. 1998. *Postcolonial Theory*. New York: Columbia University Press.

Garland, Ronald. 1990. *Working and Managing in a New Age*. Atlanta: Humanics New Age.

Garvey, Marcus. 1968–69. *Philosophy and Opinions*. New York: Arno Press.

Gasché, Rodolphe. 1999. *Of Minimal Things: Studies on the Notion of Relation*. Stanford, CA: Stanford University Press.

Gates, Henry Louis, Jr. 1992. *Loose Canons*. Oxford: Oxford University Press.

Gay, Peter. 1968. *Weimar Culture*. New York: Harper & Row.

Gebser, Jean. 1985. *The Ever-Present Origin*. Athens, OH: Ohio University Press. German 1st edn, 1949–53.

Gellert, Michael. 2001. *The Fate of America*. Washington: Brassey's.

Gendler, Tamar Szabó, and John Hawthorne, eds. 2002. *Conceivability and Possibility*. Oxford: Clarendon Press.

George, Robert P., ed. 1992. *Natural Law Theory*. Oxford: Clarendon Press.

Gerstle, Gary. 2001. *American Crucible*. Princeton, NJ: Princeton University Press.

Gibbs, Robert. 2000. *Why Ethics?* Princeton, NJ: Princeton University Press.

Giddens, Anthony. 1991. *Modernity and Self-Identity*. Stanford, CA: Stanford University Press.

Gier, Nicholas F. 1981. *Wittgenstein and Phenomenology*. Albany: State University of New York Press.

Gilead, Amihud. 1999. *Saving Possibilities: A Study in Philosophical Psychology*. Amsterdam: Rodopi.

Giles, Miles. 2006. 'Social Constructivism and Sexual Desire'. *Journal for the Theory of Social Behaviour* 36: 225-38.

Gilligan, Carol. 1982. *In a Different Voice*. Cambridge, MA: Harvard University Press.

——1993. 2nd edn of Gilligan 1982.

228   *The Concept of Form in the Twentieth Century*

Gilman, Charlotte Perkins. 1914. *The Man-Made World*. 3rd edn. New York: Charlton.
Gilroy, Paul. 1993. *The Black Atlantic: Modernity and Double Consciousness*. Cambridge, MA: Harvard University Press.
——2000. *Against Race*. Cambridge, MA: Harvard University Press. Identical to *Between Camps*, 2000.
Glissant, Édouard. 1990. *Poétique de la Relation*. Paris: Gallimard. English, 1997.
Glover, Jonathan. 1999. *Humanity: A Moral History of the Twentieth Century*. New Haven: Yale University Press.
Gödel, Kurt. 1940. *The Consistency of the Axiom of Choice and the Generalized Continuum-Hypothesis With the Axioms of Set Theory*. Princeton, NJ: Princeton University Press.
Godwin, Nicola, *et al.*, eds. 1996. *Assaults on Convention*. London: Cassell.
Goedeckemeyer, Albert. 1941. *Die Stoa*. Stuttgart: Fromman.
Goerner, Sally J. 1993. *Chaos and the Evolving Ecological Universe*. Langhorne, PA: Gordon and Breach.
Goguen, J.A. 1969. 'The Logic of Inexact Concepts'. *Synthese* 19: 325-73.
Goldfarb, Jeffrey C. 1991. *The Cynical Society*. Chicago: University of Chicago Press.
Goodman, Nelson. 1978. *Ways of Worldmaking*. Indianapolis: Hackett.
——1996. 'Comments'. Pages 203-13 in *Starmaking*, ed. P. McCormick. Cambridge, MA: MIT Press.
Goodman, Russell B. 2002. *Wittgenstein and William James*. Cambridge: Cambridge University Press.
Goodwin, Brian. 1994. *How the Leopard Changed its Spots*. New York: Scribner.
Goonatilake, Susantha. 1998. *Toward a Global Science*. Bloomington: Indiana University Press.
——2001. *Anthropologizing Sri Lanka*. Bloomington: Indiana University Press.
Gordon, David M. 1996. *Fat and Mean*. New York: Free Press.
Gordon, Linda. 1989. *Heroes of Their Own Lives*. New York: Viking.
Goss, Robert E., and Amy Adams Squire Strongheart. 1997. *Our Families, Our Values: Snapsnots of Queer Kinship*. New York: Haworth.
Gossett, Thomas F. 1963. *Race*. Dallas: Southern Methodist University Press.
Gotthelf, Allan. 2000. *On Ayn Rand*. Belmont, CA: Wadsworth.
Gould, Carol G. 1978. *Marx's Social Ontology*. Cambridge, MA: MIT Press.
Gower, Barry. 1996. *Scientific Method*. London: Routledge.
Grant, Jacquelyn. 1989. *White Women's Christ and Black Women's Jesus*. Atlanta: Scholars Press.
Grassman, Robert. 1872. *Die Formenlehre oder Mathematik*. Stetten: R. Grassman.
Green, Karen. 1995. *The Woman of Reason*. New York: Continuum.
Green, Thomas Hill. 1883. *Prolegomena to Ethics*. Ed. A.C. Bradley. Oxford: Clarendon Press.
——1885–88. *Works*. London: Longmans, Green.
Greene, Brian. 1999. *The Elegant Universe*. New York: Norton.
Greimas, A.J. 1966. *Sémantique structurale*. Paris: Larousse. English, 1983.
Grewal, Inderpal, and Caren Kaplan, eds. 1994. *Scattered Hegemonies*. Minneapolis: University of Minnesota Press.
Griffin, David Ray, ed. 1988. *The Reenchantment of Science*. Albany: State University of New York Press.
——2000. *Religion and Scientific Naturalism*. Albany: State University of New York Press.

Griffin, David Ray, *et al.* 1993. *Founders of Constructive Postmodern Philosophy.* Albany: State University of New York Press.

Griffiths, Norwenna. 1995. *Feminisms and the Self: The Web of Identity.* London: Routledge.

Grigsby, Jim, and David Stevens. 2000. *Neurodynamics of Personality.* New York: Guilford Press.

Grosskurth, Phyllis. 1980. *Havelock Ellis: A Biography.* New York: Knopf.

Grosz, Elizabeth. 1994. *Volatile Bodies.* Bloomington: Indiana University Press.

——1997. 'Ontology and Equivocation'. Pages 73-101 in N.J. Holland, ed.

Grotius, Hugo. 1995. *De iure praedae commentarius.* Buffalo, NY: Hein.

Gutting, Gary. 2001. *French Philosophy in the Twentieth Century.* Cambridge: Cambridge University Press.

Haack, Susan. 1998. *Manifesto of a Passionate Moderate.* Chicago: University of Chicago Press.

Haakonssen, Knud. 1996. *Natural Law and Moral Philosophy.* Cambridge: Cambridge University Press.

Haber, Honi Fern. 1994. *Beyond Postmodern Politics.* London: Routledge.

Habermas, Jürgen. 1968a. *Technik und Wissenschaft als 'Ideologie'.* Frankfurt a.M.: Suhrkamp.

——1968b. *Erkenntnis und Interesse.* Frankfurt a.M.: Suhrkamp. English, 1971, which includes the last part of 1968a. 2nd edn, 1973, with 'Nachwort'.

——1970. *Zur Logik der Sozialwissenschaften.* Frankfurt a.M.: Suhrkamp. English, 1988.

——1981. *Theorie des kommunikativen Handelns.* Frankfurt a.M.: Suhrkamp. English, 1984–87.

——1983. *Moralbewusstsein und kommunikatives Handeln.* Frankfurt a.M.: Suhrkamp. English, 1990.

——1985. *Der philosophische Diskurs der Moderne.* Frankfurt a.M.: Suhrkamp. English, 1987.

Hacking, Ian. 1999. *The Social Construction of What?* Cambridge, MA: Harvard University Press.

Haken, Hermann. 1977. *Synergetics.* Berlin: Springer.

Hall, David L., and Roger T. Ames. 1995. *Anticipating China.* Albany: State University of New York Press.

Hall, Stuart. 1999. Interview. Pages 205-39 in G. Olson and L. Worsham, eds.

Hamann, Johann Georg. 1949–57. *Sämtliche Werke.* Vienna: Thomas-Morus-Presse.

Hanson, Norwood Russell. 1958. *Patterns of Discovery.* Cambridge: Cambridge University Press.

Haraway, Donna. 1988. 'Situated Knowledges'. *Feminist Studies* 14: 575-99.

——1989. *Primate Visions: Gender, Race and Nature in the World of Modern Science.* London: Routledge.

——1990. 'A Manifesto for Cyborgs'. Pages 190-233 in *Feminism/Postmodernism*, ed. L. Nicholson. London: Routledge.

——1992. 'Ecce Homo, Ain't (Ar'n't) I a Woman, and Inappropriate/d Others: The Human in a Post-Humanist Landscape'. Pages 86-100 in J. Butler and J. Scott, eds.

——1997. *Modest_Witness@Second_Millennium.* London: Routledge.

——1999. *How Like a Leaf.* London: Routledge.

Harding, M. Esther. 1935. *Woman's Mysteries.* London: Longmans, Green & Co.

230   *The Concept of Form in the Twentieth Century*

Harding, Sandra. 1986. *The Science Question in Feminism*. Ithaca, NY: Cornell University Press.

——1987. 'Introduction: Is There a Feminist Method?' Pages 1-14 in *Feminism and Methodology*, ed. S. Harding. Bloomington: Indiana University Press.

——1991. *Whose Science? Whose Knowledge? Thinking from Women's Lives*. Ithaca, NY: Cornell University Press.

——1998. *Is Science Multicultural?* Bloomington: Indiana University Press.

Hare-Mustin, Rachel T., and Jeanne Marecek, eds. 1990. *Making a Difference: Psychology and the Construction of Gender*. New Haven: Yale University Press.

Harmann, Willis. 1998. *Global Mind Change*. San Francisco: Berret-Koehler.

Harrington, Anne. 1996. *Reenchanted Science*. Princeton, NJ: Princeton University Press.

Harris, Errol E. 1991. *Cosmos and Anthropos*. Atlantic Heights, NJ: Humanities Press International.

Harrison, Peter. 1990. *'Religion' and the Religious in the English Enlightenment*. Cambridge: Cambridge University Press.

Hartmann, Nicolai. 1949. *Der Aufbau der realen Welt*. 2nd edn. Meisenheim: A. Hain.

Hartshorne, Charles. 1983. *Insights and Oversights of Great Thinkers*. Albany: State University of New York Press.

Hartsock, Nancy C.M. 1983. *Money, Sex, and Power*. New York: Longman.

——1990. 'Foucault on Power: A Theory for Women?' Pages 157-75 in *Feminism/Postmodernism*, ed. L. Nicholson. London: Routledge.

——1998. *The Feminist Standpoint Revisited and Other Essays*. Boulder, CO: Westview.

Hassan, Ihab. 1975. *Paracriticisms*. Urbana: University of Illinois Press.

——1987. *The Postmodern Turn*. Columbus: Ohio State University Press.

——1990. 'The Burden of Mutual Perceptions: Japan and the United States'. *International House of Japan Bulletin* 10, No. 1: 1-6.

Hatab, Lawrence. 2005. *Nietzsche's Life Sentence*. London: Routledge.

Hayles, N. Katherine. 1993. 'Constrained Constructivism'. Pages 27-43 in *Realism and Representation*, ed. G. Levin. Madison: University of Wisconsin Press.

Healey, Richard. 1995. 'Dissipating the Quantum Measurement Problem'. *Topoi* 14: 55-65.

Heath, Deborah. 1997. Review of *Ecologies of Knowledge*, edited by S. Star. *American Anthropologist* 97: 144.

Hefner, Philip. 1984. 'God and Chaos: The Demiurge Versus the Ungrund'. *Zygon* 19: 469-85.

Hegarty, Paul. 2004. *Jean Baudrillard: Live Theory*. London: Continuum.

Hegel, Georg W.F. 1812–16. *Wissenschaft der Logik*. Nürnberg: J.L. Schrag.

——1821. *Grundlinien des Philosophie des Rechts*. Berlin: Nicolaische Buchhandlung.

——1969–. *Werke*. Frankfurt a.M.: Suhrkamp.

Heidegger, Martin. 1919/20. 'Grundprobleme der Phänomenologie (1919/20)'. In Heidegger 1976–, vol. LVIII.

——1920/21. 'Einleitung in die Phänomenologie der Religion'. In Heidegger 1976–, LX: 1-159.

——1927. *Sein und Zeit*. Available in Heidegger 1976–, vol. II. English, 1962, 1996.

——1928. 'Metaphysische Anfangsgründe der Logik im Ausgang von Leibniz'. In Heidegger 1976–, vol. XXVI.

——1929. 'Was ist Metaphysik?' Cited according to Heidegger 1976–, IX: 103-22.

——1933. 'Die Selbstbehauptung der deutschen Universität'. In Heidegger 1976–, XVI: 107-17.

——1934a. 'Zur Eröffnung der Schulungskurse'. In Heidegger 1976–, IX: 232-37.

——1934b. 'Logik als die Frage nach dem Wesen der Sprache'. In Heidegger 1976–, vol. XXXVIII.

——1934/35. 'Hölderlins Hymnen "Germanien" und "der Rhein" '. In Heidegger 1976–, vol. XXXIX.

——1935. *Einführung in die Metaphysik*. Cited according to Heidegger 1976–, vol. XL. English, 1959.

——1936/37. 'Beiträge zur Philosophie (Vom Ereignis)'. In Heidegger 1976–, LXV: 1-417. English, 1999.

——1938. 'Das Seyn'. In Heidegger 1976–, LXV: 421-510.

——1938/39. 'Besinnung'. Cited according to Heidegger 1976–, vol. LXVI.

——1938/40. 'Die Geschichte des Seyns'. In Heidegger 1976–, LXIX: 1-173.

——1943. 'Vom Wesen der Wahrheit'. In Heidegger 1976–, IX: 177-202.

——1946. 'Brief über den "Humanismus" '. Cited according to Heidegger 1976–, IX: 313-64.

——1949. 'Die Kehre'. Cited according to Heidegger 1976–, LXXIX: 68-77.

——1950. *Holzwege*. Frankfurt a.M.: Klostermann. The pagination of this edition is given in the margin of Heidegger 1976–, vol. V. English, 2002.

——1954a. *Vorträge und Aufsätze*. Pfullingen: Neske. Cited according to Heidegger 1976–, VII.

——1954b. 'Was heisst Denken?' In Heidegger 1976–, vol. VIII.

——1957. *Identität und Differenz*. Pfullingen: Neske. English, 1969.

——1959a. *Unterwegs zur Sprache*. Pfullingen: Neske. The pagination of this edition is given in the margin of Heidegger 1976–, vol. XII. English, 1971.

——1959b. *Gelassenheit*. Pfullingen: Neske. English: *Discourse on Thinking*, 1966.

——1976–. *Gesamtaussage*. Frankfurt a.M.: Klostermann.

Heidelberger, Michael. 1993. *Die innere Seite der Natur*. Frankfurt a.M.: Klostermann.

Heisenberg, Werner. 1958. *Physics and Philosophy*. New York: Harper & Brothers. German, 1959.

——1969. *Der Teil und das Ganze*. Munich: R. Piper. English: *Physics and Beyond*, 1971.

Heitlinger, Alena. 1999. *Émigré Feminism: Transnational Perspectives*. Toronto: University of Toronto Press.

Hekman, Susan J. 1996. *Feminist Interpretations of Michel Foucault*. University Park: Pennsylvania State University Press.

Held, Virginia. 1993. *Feminist Morality*. Chicago: University of Chicago Press.

Hellman, Geoffrey. 1989. *Mathematics without Numbers*. Oxford: Clarendon Press.

Helmholtz, Hermann von. 1879. *Die Thatsachen in der Wahrnehmung*. Berlin: A. Hirschwald.

Henckmann, Wolfhart. 1998. *Max Scheler*. Munich: Beck.

Henninger, Mark G. 1989. *Relations: Medieval Theories 1250–1325*. Oxford: Clarendon Press.

Herberg, Will. 1976. *Faith Enacted as History*. Philadelphia: Westminster Press.

Herbert, Nick. 1985. *Quantum Reality*. Garden City, NY: Anchor Press/Doubleday.

Herbert of Cherbury. 1937. *De veritate*. Bristol: Arrowsmith. 1st edn, 1624.

Herman, Jonathan R. 1996. *I and Tao: Martin Buber's Encounter with Chuang Tzu*. Albany: State University of New York Press.

Hesse, Mary. 1980. *Revolutions and Reconstructions in the Philosophy of Science*. Bloomington: Indiana University Press.

Heyes, Cressida J. 2000. *Line Drawings*. Ithaca, NY: Cornell University Press.

Heyward, Isabel Carter. 1982. *The Redemption of God*. Lanham, MD: University Press of America.

Hildebrandt, Stefan, and Anthony Tromba. 1996. *The Parsimonious Universe*. New York: Springer.

Himmelfarb, Gertrude. 1995. *The De-Moralization of Society*. New York: Knopf.

Hinrichs, J. 1995. 'Dialog, dialogisch'. *Historisches Wörterbuch der Philosophie*, II: 226-29. Basel: Schurabe.

Hirschmann, Nancy J. 1992. *Rethinking Obligation: A Feminist Method for Political Theory*. Ithaca, NY: Cornell University Press.

——2003. *The Subject of Liberty: Toward a Feminist Theory of Freedom*. Princeton, NJ: Princeton University Press.

Hirsh, Arthur. 1981. *The French New Left*. Boston: South End Press.

Hirsh, Elizabeth, and Gary A. Olson. 1995. 'Starting from Marginalized Lives: A Conversation with Sandra Harding'. Pages 3-42 in G. Olson and E. Hirsh, eds.

Hirshman, Linda R., and Jane E. Larson. 1998. *Hard Bargains: The Politics of Sex*. Oxford: Oxford University Press.

Hitler[, Adolf]. 1980. *Sämtliche Aufzeichnungen, 1905-1924*, ed. Eberhard Jäckel. Stuttgart: Deutsche Verlags-Anstalt.

Hobbes, Thomas. 1651. *Leviathan*. Cambridge: Cambridge University Press.

——1656. *Elements of Philosophy*. London: R. & W. Leybourn. Latin, 1655.

——1840. *The English Works of Thomas Hobbes of Malmesbury*. London: J. Bohn.

Hodges, Wilfred. 1993. *Model Theory*. Cambridge: Cambridge University Press.

Höffding, Harald. 1901. *Religionsphilosophie*. Leipzig: O.R. Reisland.

Hogue, W. Lawrence. 1996. *Race, Modernity, Postmodernity*. Albany: State University of New York Press.

Holland, Gail. 1998. *A Call for Connection*. Novato, CA: New World Library.

Holland, Nancy J., ed. 1997. *Feminist Interpretations of Jacques Derrida*. University Park: Pennsylvania State University Press.

Hood, Pamela M. 2004. *Aristotle on the Category of Relation*. Lanham, MD: University Press of America.

hooks, bell. 1990. *Yearning: Race, Gender, and Cultural Politics*. Boston: South End Press.

——1994. *Outlaw Culture*. London: Routledge.

Hookway, Christopher. 1985. *Peirce*. London: Routledge & Kegan Paul.

Hopkins, Michael. 1999. *The Planetary Bargain: Corporate Social Responsibility Comes of Age*. London: Macmillan.

Horkheimer, Max, and Theodor W. Adorno. 1944. *Dialektik der Aufklärung*. New York: Social Studies Association. English, 1972.

Horstmann, Rolf-Peter. 1984. *Ontologie und Relationen*. Königstein: Hain.

Horwitz, Rivka. 1988. *Buber's Way to 'I and Thou'*. Philadelphia: Jewish Publication Society.

Hountondji, Paulin J. 1977. *Sur la 'philosophie africaine'*. Paris: Maspero. English, 1983.

Howson, Colin, and Peter Urbach. 1993. *Scientific Reasoning: The Bayesian Approach*. 2nd edn. Chicago: Open Court.

Hübner, Kurt. 1978. *Kritik der wissenschaftlichen Vernunft*. Munich: Alber. English, 1983.

Hudelson, Richard. 1990. *Marxism and Philosophy in the Twentieth Century*. New York: Praeger.

Hughes, H. Stuart. 1958. *Consciousness and Society*. New York: Knopf.

Hull, Margaret Betz. 2002. *The Hidden Philosophy of Hannah Arendt*. London: RoutledgeCurzon.

Humboldt, Wilhelm von. 1903–36. *Gesammelte Schriften*. Berlin: B. Behr.

Hume, David. 1739. *A Treatise of Human Nature*. London: J. Noon.

Hunt, Alan. 1978. *The Sociological Movement in Law*. Philadelphia: Temple University Press.

Hunt, Lynn. 1990. 'History Beyond Social Theory'. Pages 95-111 in *The States of 'Theory'*, ed. D. Carroll. New York: Columbia University Press.

Husserl, Edmund. 1950–. *Husserliana*. The Hague: Nijhoft.

——1981. *Shorter Works*. Notre Dame, IN: University of Notre Dame Press.

——1994. *Briefwechsel*. Dordrecht: Kluwer.

Hutcheon, Linda. 1988. *A Poetics of Postmodernism*. London: Routledge.

Ihde, Don. 1999. *Expanding Hermeneutics*. Evanston, IL: Northwestern University Press.

Inayatullah, Naeem, and David L. Blaney. 2004. *International Relations and the Problem of Difference*. London: Routledge.

Inglehart, Ronald. 1990. *Culture Shift in Advanced Industrial Society*. Princeton, NJ: Princeton University Press.

——1997. *Modernization and Postmodernization*. Princeton, NJ: Princeton University Press.

Inglehart, Ronald, *et al*. 1998. *Human Values and Beliefs*. Ann Arbor: University of Michigan Press.

Innis, H.A. 1950. *Empire and Communications*. Oxford: Clarendon Press.

Irigaray, Luce. 1984. *Éthique de la différence sexuelle*. Paris: Minuit. English, 1993.

——1987. *Sexes et parentés*. Paris: Editions de Minuit. English, 1993.

——1990. 'Questions à Emmanuel Lévinas'. *Critique* 46: 911-20. English in *The Irigaray Reader*, 1991.

——1992. *J'aime à toi*. Paris: B. Grasset. English, 1996.

Ironside, Philip. 1996. *The Social and Political Thought of Bertrand Russell*. Cambridge: Cambridge University Press.

Irvine, A.D. 1996. 'Philosophy of Logic'. Pages 9-49 in *Philosophy of Science, Logic and Mathematics in the Twentieth Century*, ed. S. Shankar. London: Routledge.

Jackson, Cecile. 1995. 'Radical Environmental Myths'. *New Left Review* 210: 124-40.

Jaggar, Alison M. 1989. 'Love and Knowledge'. *Inquiry* 32: 151-76.

Jakobsen, Janet R. 1998. *Working Alliances and the Politics of Difference*. Bloomington: Indiana University Press.

James, William. 1890. *The Principles of Psychology*. New York: H. Holt & Company.

——1897. *The Will to Believe*. New York: Longmans, Green, & Co.

——1907. *Pragmatism*. New York: Longmans, Green, & Co.

——1909a. *The Meaning of Truth*. New York: Longmans, Green, & Co.

——1909b. *A Pluralistic Universe*. New York: Longmans, Green, & Co.

——1920. *The Letters of William James*. Boston: Atlantic Monthly Press.

Jameson, Fredric. 1991. *Postmodernism*. Durham, NC: Duke University Press.

Jammer, Max. 1966. *The Conceptual Development of Quantum Mechanics*. New York: McGraw-Hill.

——1973. 'Indeterminacy in Physics'. *Dictionary of the History of Ideas*, II: 586-94. New York: Charles Scribner's Sons.

Janich, Peter. 1996. *Konstruktivismus und Naturerkenntnis*. Frankfurt a.M.: Suhrkamp.

Jappe, Anselm. 1999. *Guy Debord*. Berkeley: University of California Press. With a new afterword for the English. French, 1955.

Jardine, Alice A. 1985. *Gynesis*. Ithaca, NY: Cornell University Press.

Jaspers, Karl. 1932. *Philosophie*. Berlin: J. Springer. English, 1969–71.

——1935. *Vernunft und Existenz*. Groningen: J.B. Wolters. English, 1955.

——1948. *Der philosophische Glaube*. Munich: R. Piper. English, 1949.

——1958. *Die Atombombe und die Zukunft des Menschen*. Munich: R. Piper. English, 1961.

Jeffreys, Sheila. 1993. *The Lesbian Heresy*. London: The Women's Press.

Jencks, Charles. 1977. *The Language of Post-Modern Architecture*. London: Academy Editions.

——1987a. *The Language of Post-Modern Architecture*. 5th edn. London: Academy Editions.

——1987b. *Post-Modernism: The New Classicism in Art and Architecture*. London: Academy Editions.

——1997. *The Architecture of the Jumping Universe*. 2nd edn. London: Academy Editions. 1st edn, 1995.

Jenkins, Keith. 2000. 'A Postmodern Reply to Perez Zagorin'. *History and Theory* 39: 181-200.

——ed. 1997. *The Postmodern History Reader*. London: Routledge.

Jensen, Pamela Grande, ed. 1996. *Finding a New Feminism*. Lanham, MD: Rowman & Littlefield.

Jenson, June. 1996. 'Representations of Difference: The Varieties of French Feminism'. Pages 73-114 in *Mapping the Women's Movement*, ed. M. Threlfall. London: Verso.

Jevons, W. Stanley. 1874. *The Principles of Science*. London: Macmillan. 2nd edn, 1877.

Johnson, Pauline. 1994. *Feminism and Radical Humanism*. Boulder, CO: Westview Press.

Jónasdóttir, Anna G., and Drude von der Fehr. 1998. 'Introduction'. Pages 1-18 in *Is There a Nordic Feminism?* ed. D. Fehr *et al*. London: UCL Press.

Joravsky, David. 1970. *The Lysenko Affair*. Cambridge, MA: Harvard University Press.

Jovanović, Gordana. 1998. 'Towards a Communicative Feminist Psychology'. Pages 159-83 in *Deconstructing Feminist Psychology*, ed. E. Burman. London: Sage.

Kalupahana, David J. 1976. *Buddhist Philosophy*. Honolulu: University Press of Hawaii.

Kamber, Richard. 2000. *On Sartre*. Belmont, CA: Wadsworth.

Kamlah, Andreas. 1983. 'Probability as a Quasi-Theoretical Concept'. *Erkenntnis* 19: 239-51.

Kamm, Josephine. 1977. *John Stuart Mill in Love*. London: Gordon & Cremonesi.

Kant, Immanuel. 1787. *Kritik der reinen Vernunft*. 2nd edn. Riga: Hartknoch. 1st edn, 1781.

——1788. *Kritik der praktischen Vernunft*. Riga: Hartknoch.

——1910–. *Gesammelte Schriften*. Berlin: Reimer.

——1961. *Frühschriften*. Berlin: Akademie-Verlag.

Kanter, Donald L., and Philip H. Mirvis. 1989. *The Cynical Americans*. San Francisco: Jossey-Bass.

Karanakis, Alexander. 1969. *Tillers of a Myth*. Madison: University of Wisconsin Press.

Katsenelinboigen, Aron. 1997. *The Concept of Indeterminism and its Applications: Economics, Social Systems, Ethics, Artificial Intelligence, and Aesthetics.* Westport, CT: Praeger.

Katz, Stephen T. 1994. *The Holocaust in Historical Context.* New York: Oxford University Press.

Kauffman, Stuart A. 1993. *The Origins of Order.* Oxford: Oxford University Press.

——2000. *Investigations.* Oxford: Oxford University Press.

Kaufmann, Walter. 1980. *Nietzsche, Heidegger, and Buber.* New York: McGraw-Hill.

Kean, Hilda. 1998. *Animal Rights.* London: Reaktion Books.

Kearney, Richard. 1993. 'Derrida's Ethical Re-Turn'. Pages 28-50 in *Working Through Derrida*, ed. G. Madison. Evanston, IL: Northwestern University Press.

——2001. *The God Who May Be.* Bloomington: Indiana University Press.

Keating, Ana Louise. 1996. *Women Reading Women Writing.* Philadelphia: Temple University Press.

Keller, Evelyn Fox. 1985. *Reflections on Gender and Science.* New Haven: Yale University Press.

——1992. *Secrets of Life, Secrets of Death.* London: Routledge.

Keller, Jean. 1997. 'Autonomy, Relationality, and Feminist Ethics'. *Hypatia* 12: 152-64.

Kellogg, Charles Flint. 1967. *NAACP.* Baltimore: The Johns Hopkins University Press.

Kenner, Hugh. 1968. *The Counterfeiters.* Bloomington: Indiana University Press.

Kepes, Gyorgy, ed. 1965. *Structure in Art and Science.* New York: George Braziller.

Ketner, Kenneth Laine. 1998. *His Glassy Essence.* Nashville: Vanderbilt University Press.

Key, Ellen. 1909. *The Century of the Child.* New York: Putnam's Sons. Swedish, 1902.

Kienzler, Wolfgang. 1997. *Wittgensteins Wende zu seiner Spätphilosophie 1930–1932.* Frankfurt a.M.: Suhrkamp.

King, Martin Luther, Jr. 1958. *Stride Toward Freedom.* New York: Harper & Brothers.

——1963a. *Strength to Love.* New York: Harper & Row.

——1963b. *Letter from Birmingham City Jail.* Philadelphia: American Friends Service Committee.

Kirk, G.S., *et al.* 1983. *The Presocratic Philosophers.* 2nd edn. Cambridge: Cambridge University Press.

Kisiel, Theodore. 2002. *Heidegger's Way of Thought.* London: Continuum.

Kittay, Eva Feder. 1999. *Love's Labor: Essays on Women, Equality, and Dependency.* London: Routledge.

Klir, George J., and Mark J. Wierman. 1999. *Uncertainty-Based Information.* 2nd edn. Heidelberg: Physica.

Kneale, William, and Martha Kneale. 1962. *The Development of Logic.* Oxford: Clarendon Press.

Knuuttila, Simo. 1993. *Modalities in Medieval Philosophy.* London: Routledge.

Koffka, K. 1935. *Principles of Gestalt Psychology.* New York: Harcourt, Brace & Company.

Köhler, Manfred. 2000. *Das unheimliche Jahrhundert: Aspekte einer politischen Philosophie im Zeitalter des Nihilismus.* Marburg: Tectum.

Koven, Seth, and Sonya Michel, eds. 1993. *Mothers of the New World.* London: Routledge.

Kren, George M., and Leon Rappoport. 1994. *The Holocaust and the Crisis of Human Behavior.* 2nd edn. New York: Holmes & Meier.

Kripke, Saul A. 1959. 'A Completeness Theorem in Model Logic'. *Journal of Symbolic Logic* 24: 1-14.
——1980. *Naming and Necessity*. Oxford: Basil Blackwell.
Kristeva, Julia. 1974a. *La révolution du langage poétique*. Paris: Éditions du Seuil; partial English, 1984.
——1974b. 'La femme, ce n'est jamais ça'. *Tel Quel* 59: 19-25. English in E. Marks and I. de Courtivron, eds.
——1979. 'Le temps des femmes'. *33/44: Cahiers de recherches de science des textes et documents* 5, Winter: 5-19. English in *The Kristeva Reader*, 1986.
——1985. *Au commencement était l'amour*. Paris: Hachette. English, 1987.
——1996. *Interviews*. New York: Columbia University Press.
——1998a. *Contre la dépression nationale*. Paris: Les éditions Textuel. English: *Revolt, She Said*, 2002.
——1998b. 'L'Europe divisée: politique, éthique, religion'. *L'Infini* 63: 38-62. English in *The Crisis of the European* [sic] *Subject*, 2000.
Kroker, Arthur, and David Cook. 1988. *The Postmodern Scene*. 2nd edn. New York: St. Martin's Press. 1st edn, 1986.
Kroker, Arthur, and Marilouise Kroker, eds. 1993. *The Last Sex*. New York: St. Martin's Press.
Kropotkin, P. 1902. *Mutual Aid*. New York: McClure, Phillips & Co.
Krüger, Lorenz, *et al.*, eds. 1987. *The Probabilistic Revolution*. Cambridge, MA: MIT Press.
Kuhn, Thomas S. 1962. *The Structure of Scientific Revolutions*. Chicago: University of Chicago Press.
LaBarbera, Priscilla A., and Zeynep Gürhan. 1997. 'The Role of Materialism, Religiosity, and Demographics in Subjective Well-Being'. *Psychology and Marketing* 14: 71-97.
Laclau, Ernesto, and Chantal Mouffe. 1985. *Hegemony and Socialist Strategy*. London: Verso.
Lakatos, Imre. 1978. *The Methodology of Scientific Research Programmes*. Cambridge: Cambridge University Press.
Lakoff, George. 1987. *Women, Fire, and Dangerous Things*. Chicago: University of Chicago Press.
Lakoff, George, and Mark Johnson. 1999. *Philosophy in the Flesh*. New York: Basic Books.
Lane, Richard J. 2000. *Jean Baudrillard*. London: Routledge.
Langer, Susanne K. 1937. *An Introduction to Symbolic Logic*. Boston: Houghton Mifflin.
——1942. *Philosophy in a New Key*. Cambridge, MA: Harvard University Press.
——1953. *Feeling and Form*. New York: Charles Scribner's Sons.
——1967–82. *Mind: An Essay on Human Feeling*. Baltimore: The Johns Hopkins University Press.
Larsen, Neil. 2000. 'DetermiNation: Postcolonialism, Poststructuralism, and the Problem of Ideology'. Pages 140-56 in *The Pre-occupation of Postcolonial Studies*, ed. F. Afzal-Khan and K. Seshadri-Crooks. Durham, NC: Duke University Press.
Lasch, Christopher. 1991. *The True and Only Heaven: Progress and its Cities*. New York: Norton.
Lash, Scott. 1990. *Sociology of Postmodernism*. London: Routledge.
Laszlo, Ervin. 1972. *The Systems View of the World*. New York: Braziller.

Latour, Bruno. 1987. *Science in Action*. Cambridge, MA: Harvard University Press.
——1993. *We Have Never Been Modern*. New York: Harvester Wheatsheaf. Revised from the French of 1991.
——1999. *Pandora's Hope*. Cambridge, MA: Harvard University Press.
Laudan, Larry. 1981. *Science and Hypothesis*. Dordrecht: D. Reidel.
——1984. *Science and Values*. Berkeley: University of California Press.
Laumann, Edward O., *et al*. 1994. *The Social Organization of Sexuality*. Chicago: University of Chicago Press.
Lauretis, Teresa de. 1994. *The Practice of Love*. Bloomington: Indiana University Press.
Lavers, Annette. 1982. *Roland Barthes: Structuralism and After*. London: Methuen.
Lawson, Hilary. 1985. *Reflexivity—The Postmodern Experiment*. London: Hutchinson.
——1989. 'Introduction'. Pages xi-xxviii in *Dismantling Truth*, ed. H. Lawson and L. Appignanesi. London: Weidenfeld and Nicolson.
Leclerc, Ivor. 1986. *The Philosophy of Nature*. Washington: Catholic University of America Press.
Le Doeuff, Michèle. 1989. *Des femmes, de la philosophie, etc.* Paris: Éditions du Seuil. English: *Hipparchia's Choice*, 1991.
——1990. 'Women, Reason, Etc'. *Differences* 2: 1-13.
——1998. *Le sexe du savoir*. Paris: Aubier. English, 2003.
Lee, Dorothy. 1959. *Freedom and Culture*. Englewood Cliffs, NJ: Prentice-Hall.
Leibniz, Gottfried Wilhelm. 1765. *Nouveaux essais sur l'entendment humain*. Amsterdam, Leipzig: Schreuder.
——1879-90. *Die philosophischen Schriften von Gottfried Wilhelm Leibniz*. Berlin: Weidmann.
——1965. *Kleine Schriften zur Metaphysik*. Frankfurt a.M.: Insel-Verlag.
Leisegang, Dieter. 1969. *Die drei Potenzen der Relation*. Frankfurt a.M.: Heiderhoff.
Lenin, Vladimir Ilich. 1929. *What Is to Be Done?* New York: International Publishers.
Lenz, Elinor, and Barbara Myerhoff. 1985. *The Feminization of America*. Los Angeles: J.P. Tarcher.
Leonard, Peter. 1997. *Postmodern Welfare*. London: Sage.
Lerner, Gerda. 1993. *The Creation of Feminist Consciousness*. Oxford: Oxford University Press.
Lerner, Michael. 1996. *The Politics of Meaning*. Reading, MA: Addison-Wesley.
Levinas, Emmanuel. 1947. *De l'existence à l'existant*. 2nd edn. Paris: Fontaine. English, 1978.
——1951. 'L'ontologie est-elle fondamentale?' *Revue de métaphysique et de morale* 56: 88-98.
——1957. 'La philosophie et l'idée de l'Infini'. *Revue de métaphysique et de morale* 62: 241-53.
——1961. *Totalité et infini*. La Haye: Martinus Nijhoff. English, 1969.
——1963. *Difficile liberté*. Paris: Michel. English, 1990.
——1967. 'Martin Buber and the Theory of Knowledge'. Pages 133-50 in Schilpp and Friedman. French in *Noms propres*, 1976.
——1974. *Autrement qu'être ou au-delà de l'essence*. Dordrecht: Kluwer. English, 1981.
——1982. *Éthique et infini*. [Paris]: Fayard. English, 1985.
——1985. 'Totalité et totalisation'. *Encyclopaedia Universalis*, XVIII: 102-104. Reprinted in *Altérité et transcendence*, 1995. English, 1999.

——1986. *Dieu qui vient a l'id*ée. 2nd edn. Paris: J. Vrin. English, 1998.

——1995. *Altérité et transcendence*. St. Clement: Fata Morgana. English, 1999.

Levine, Peter. 1995. *Nietzsche and the Modern Crisis of the Humanities*. Albany: State University of New York Press.

Lévi-Strauss, Claude. 1955. *Tristes tropiques*. Paris: Plon. Partial English, 1961; complete English, 1973.

——1958–73. *Anthropologie structurale*. Paris: Plon. English, 1963–76.

Lewis, Clarence Irving. 1970. *Collected Papers*. Stanford, CA: Stanford University Press.

Lewis, David K. 1986. *On the Plurality of Worlds*. Oxford: Basil Blackwell.

Li, Ming, and Paul M.B. Vitányi. 1990. 'Kolmogorov Complexity and its Applications'. Pages 187-254 in vol. I of *Algorithms and Complexity*, ed. J. van Leeuwen. Amsterdam: Elsevier.

Lichtheim, George. 1972. *Europe in the Twentieth Century*. London: Weidenfeld & Nicolson.

Lindley, David. 1993. *The End of Physics*. New York: Basic Books.

Lisska, Anthony J. 1996. *Aquinas's Theory of Natural Law*. Oxford: Clarendon Press.

Litt, Theodor. 1924. *Individuum und Gemeinschaft*. 2nd edn. Leipzig: Teubner.

——1938. *Der deutsche Geist und das Christentum*. Leipzig: Klotz.

Lloyd, Genevieve. 1984. *The Man of Reason*. Minneapolis: University of Minnesota Press. 2nd edn, 1993, with new introduction.

[Locke, Alain]. 1989. *The Philosophy of Alain Locke*. Ed. Leonard Harris. Philadelphia: Temple University Press.

Locke, John. 1690. *An Essay Concerning Human Understanding*. London: Basset.

Long, Douglas G. 1977. *Bentham on Liberty*. Toronto: University of Toronto Press.

Longino, Helen E. 1990. *Science as Social Knowledge*. Princeton, NJ: Princeton University Press.

Lorenzen, Paul. 1987. *Constructive Philosophy*. Amherst: University of Massachusetts Press.

Losee, John. 1972. *A Historical Introduction to the Philosophy of Science*. Oxford: Oxford University Press.

Lotman, Jurij. 1972. *Analiz poeticheskogo teksta*. Leningrad: 'Prosveshchenie', Leningr. Otd-nie. English, 1975.

Lotze, Hermann. 1884–88. *Mikrokosmus*. 4th edn. Leipzig: S. Hirzel. 1st edn, 1864.

Lovejoy, Arthur O. 1930. *The Revolt Against Dualism*. Chicago: Open Court.

Lowe, Donald M. 1982. *A History of Bourgeois Perception*. Chicago: University of Chicago Press.

Lowry, Richard. 1982. *The Evolution of Psychological Theory*. New York: Aldine.

Lukács, György. 1953. *Die Zerstörung der Vernunft*. Berlin: Aufbau.

Lüpke, Johannes von. 1992. 'Theologie als "Grammatik zur Sprache der heiligen Schrift"'. *Neue Zeitschrift für systematische Theologie* 34: 227-50.

Luther, Martin. 1883–. *Werke*. Weimar: Böhlaus Nachfolger.

Luyckx, Marc. 1999. 'The Transmodern Hypothesis, Towards a Dialogue of Cultures'. *Futures* 31: 971-82.

Lyotard, Jean-François. 1973. *Dérive à partir de Marx et Freud*. Paris: Union générale d'éditions. English of pp. 305-16 in Lyotard 1993a.

——1974. *Économie libidinale*. Paris: Editions de Minuit. English, 1993.

——1977. *Rudiments païens: genre dissertatif*. Paris: Union générale d'éditions. English of pp. 157-212 in *Toward the Postmodern*, 1993; of pp. 213-32 in *The Lyotard Reader*, 1989.

——1979a. *La condition postmoderne*. Paris: Editions de Minuit. English, 1984.

——1979b. *Au juste*. Paris: C. Bourgois. English: *Just Gaming*, 1985.

——1982. 'Réponse à la question: quèst-ce que le postmoderne?' *Critique* 419 (April): 357-67. English: appendix to the *Postmodern Condition*, 1984.

——1983. *Le différend*. Paris: Editions de Minuit. English, 1988.

——1985. 'Histoire universelle et différences culturelles'. *Critique* 41: 559-68. English in *The Lyotard Reader*, 1989.

——1986. *Le postmoderne expliqué aux enfants*. Paris: Galilée. English, 1993.

——1988a. *L'inhumain*. Paris: Galilée. English, 1991.

——1988b. 'Réécrire la modernité'. *Les Cahiers de Philosophie* 5: 193-203. English in *The Inhuman*, 1991.

——1992. 'D'un trait d'union'. *Rue Descartes* 4: 47-60. English in *The Hyphen*, 1999, ch. 2.

——1993a. *Political Writings*. Minneapolis: University of Minnesota Press.

——1993b. *Moralités postmodernes*. Paris: Galilée. English: *Postmodern Fables*, 1997.

——1993c. 'The Other's Rights'. Pages 135-47 in *On Human Rights*, ed. S. Shute and S. Hurley. New York: Basic Books.

——1995. Responses to questions. Pages 172-92 in G. Olson and E. Hirsh, eds.

——1998. *La Confession d'Augustin*. Paris: Galilée. English, 2000.

——2004. 'Before the Law, After the Law'. Pages 104-21 in *Questioning Judaism*, ed. Elisabeth Weber. Stanford: Stanford University Press.

MacCallum, Gerald C., Jr. 1967. 'Negative and Positive Freedom'. *The Philosophical Review* 76: 312-34.

Macdonald, Cynthia. 1998. 'Tropes and Other Things'. Pages 329-50 in *Contemporary Readings in the Foundation of Metaphysics*, ed. S. Laurence and C. Macdonald. Oxford: Blackwell.

Macey, David. 1993. *The Lives of Michel Foucault*. London: Hutchinson.

Mach, Ernst. 1886. *Beiträge zur Analyse der Empfindungen*. Jena: G. Fischer.

Machiavelli, Niccolò. 1997. *Discourses on Livy*. Oxford: Oxford University Press. Italian, 1551.

MacIntyre, Alasdair. 1985. *After Virtue*. 2nd edn. Notre Dame, IN: University of Notre Dame Press.

Mackay, D.S. 1930. 'An Historical Sketch of the Problem of Relations'. Pages 1-34 in *Studies in the Problem of Relations*, ed. University of California Philosophical Union. Berkeley: University of California Press.

Maihofer, Andrea. 1998. 'Care'. Pages 383-92 in *A Companion to Feminist Philosophy*, ed. A. Jaggar and I. Young. Oxford: Blackwell.

Maihofer, Werner, ed. 1962. *Naturrecht oder Rechtspositivismus?* Bad Homburg von der Höhe: H. Geutner.

Majoor, Bart. 1998. 'Drug Policy in the Netherlands'. Pages 129-64 in *How to Legalize Drugs*, ed. Jefferson Fish. Northvale, NJ: Aronson.

Makarushka, Irena S.M. 1994. *Religious Imagination and Language in Emerson and Nietzsche*. London: Macmillan.

Makkreel, Rudolf A. 1975. *Dilthey*. Princeton, NJ: Princeton University Press.

Malik, Kenan. 1996. *The Meaning of Race*. London: Macmillan.

Mann, Paul. 1999. *Masocriticism*. New York: New York University Press.

Mannheim, Karl. 1929. *Ideologie und Utopie*. Bonn: F. Cohen. English, somewhat modified, in Mannheim 1936, chs. 2–4.

——1931. 'Wissenssoziologie'. Pages 659-80 in *Handwörterbuch der Soziologie*, ed. A. Vierkandt. Stuttgart: Enke. English: Mannheim 1936, ch. 5.

——1936. *Ideology and Utopia*. London: Routledge & Kegan Paul.

Manning, Rita C. 1992. *Speaking from the Heart: A Feminist Perspective on Ethics*. Lanham, MD: Rowman & Littlefield.

Mansbridge, Jane. 1996. 'Using Power/Fighting Power: The Polity'. Pages 46-66 in *Democracy and Difference*, ed. S. Benhabib. Princeton, NJ: Princeton University Press.

Mantegazza, Paolo. 1935. *The Sexual Relations of Mankind*. New York: Eugenics. Italian, 1892.

Marable, Manning. 1986. 'Black Studies'. Pages 35-66 in vol. III of *The Left Academy*, ed. B. Ohman and E. Vernoft. New York: Praeger.

Marcel, Gabriel. 1927. *Journal métaphysique*. Paris: Gallimard. English, 1952.

Marchand, Marianne, and Jane Parpart, eds. 1995. *Feminism/Postmodernism/Development*. London: Routledge.

Marcus, Ruth Barcan: see Barcan Marcus, Ruth.

Marcuse, Herbert. 1955. *Eros and Civilization*. Boston: Beacon Press.

——1964. *One-Dimensional Man*. Boston: Beacon Press.

Margulis, Lynn. 1998. *The Symbiotic Planet: A New Look at Evolution*. London: Weidenfeld & Nicolson.

Marion, Russ. 1999. *The Edge of Organization*. Thousand Oaks, CA: Sage.

Marks, Elaine, and Isabella de Courtivron. 1980. *New French Feminisms*. Amherst: University of Massachusetts Press.

Marks, Gary N. 1997. 'The Formation of Materialist and Postmaterialist Values'. *Social Science Research* 26: 52-68.

Martin, Jay. 2002. *The Education of John Dewey*. New York: Columbia University Press.

Marwick, Arthur. 1998. *The Sixties: Cultural Revolution in Britain, France, Italy, and the United States, c. 1958–c. 1974*. Oxford: Oxford University Press.

Marx, Karl, and Friedrich Engels. 1957–. *Werke*. Berlin: Dietz.

Mathews, Freya. 1991. *The Ecological Self*. London: Routledge.

Maturana, Humberto R., and Francisco J. Varela. 1987. *The Tree of Knowledge*. Boston: Shambhala.

Maxwell, Nicholas. 1998. *The Comprehensibility of the Universe*. Oxford: Clarendon Press.

May, Henry F. 1940. *Protestant Churches and Industrial America*. New York: Octagon Books.

Mayr, Ernst. 1974. 'Teleological and Teleonomic, A New Analysis'. Pages 91-117 in *Methodological and Historical Essays in the Natural and Social Sciences*, ed. R. Cohen and M. Wartofsky. Boston: D. Reidel.

McAdam, Doug. 1988. *Freedom Summer*. Oxford: Oxford University Press.

McAlister, Linda. 1982. *The Development of Franz Brentano's Ethics*. Amsterdam: Rodopi.

McCall, Storrs. 1994. *A Model of the Universe*. Oxford: Clarendon Press.

McGilvary, Evander Bradley. 1956. *Toward a Perspective Realism*. La Salle, IL: Open Court.

McGowan, John. 1991. *Postmodernism and its Critics*. Ithaca, NY: Cornell University Press.

McHale, Brian. 1987. *Postmodernist Fiction*. New York: Methuen.

McLaren, Margaret A. 2002. *Feminism, Foucault, and Embodied Subjectivity*. Albany: State University of New York Press.

McLeod, Stephen K. 2001. *Modality and Anti-Metaphysics*. Aldershot: Ashgate.

McWhorter, Ladelle. 1999. *Bodies and Pleasures*. Bloomington: Indiana University Press.

Mead, George H. 1934. *Mind, Self, and Society*. Chicago: University of Chicago Press.

Megill, Allan. 1985. *Prophets of Extremity*. Berkeley: University of California Press.

Mehta, J.L. 1985. *India and the West*. Chico, CA: Scholars Press.

Mellor, Mary. 1997. *Feminism and Ecology*. Washington Square: New York University Press.

Memmi, Albert. 1966. *Portrait du colonisé*. Paris: Pauvert. English, 1967.

Mensching, Günther. 1992. *Das Allgemeine und das Besondere*. Stuttgart: Metzler.

Merchant, Carolyn. 1996. *Earthcare*. London: Routledge.

Merleau-Ponty, Maurice. 1945. *Phénomenologie de la perception*. Paris: Gallimard. English, 1962.

——1949. *La structure du comportement*. 2nd edn. Paris: Presses universitaires de France. English, 1963.

Merton, Robert K. 1949. *Social Theory and Social Structure*. Glencoe, IL: Free Press.

Michel, Sonya. 1998. 'The Comparative Turn'. *Journal of Women's History* 10: 189-97.

Mies, Maria, and Vandana Shiva. 1993. *Ecofeminism*. Halifax, Nova Scotia: Zed Books.

Miles, Angela. 1996. *Integrative Feminisms: Building Global Visions, 1960s–1990s*. London: Routledge.

Mill, John Stuart. 1859. *On Liberty*. London: J.W. Parker & Son.

——1865. *An Examination of Sir William Hamilton's Philosophy*. London: Longman, Roberts, & Green.

Miller, James. 1993. *The Passion of Michel Foucault*. New York: Simon & Schuster.

Miller, Jean Baker. 1986. *Toward a New Psychology of Women*. Boston: Beacon Press.

Miller, Jean Baker, and Janet L. Surrey. 1997. 'Rethinking Women's Anger'. Pages 199-216 in *Women's Growth in Diversity*, ed. J. Jordan. New York: Guilford Press.

Miller, Jerome G. 1996. *Search and Destroy*. Cambridge: Cambridge University Press.

Miller, Timothy. 1991. *The Hippies and American Values*. Knoxville: University of Tennessee Press.

Minow, Martha. 1990. *Making All the Difference*. Ithaca, NY: Cornell University Press.

Miringoff, Marc, and Marque-Luisa Miringoff. 1999. *The Social Health of the Nation*. Oxford: Oxford University Press.

Misner, Paul. 1991. *Social Catholicism in Europe*. New York: Crossroad.

Mittelstrass, Jürgen. 1995. 'Perspektivismus'. *Enzyklopädie, Philosophie und Wissenschaftstheorie*, III: 96-97. Stuttgart: Metzler.

Moghadam, Valentine M. 2005. *Globalizing Women: Transnational Feminist Networks*. Baltimore: The Johns Hopkins University Press.

Mohanty, Chandra Talpade. 1987. 'Feminist Encounters'. *Copyright* 1: 30-44.

Mohanty, Chandra Talpade, *et al.*, eds. 1991. *Third World Women and the Politics of Feminism*. Bloomington: Indiana University Press.

Monk, Ray. 1996. *Bertrand Russell*. London: Jonathan Cape.

Montague, Richard. 1974. *Formal Philosophy*. New Haven: Yale University Press.

Montaigne, Michel de. 1992. *Les essais*. Paris: Arléa.

Moody-Adams, Michelle M. 1998. 'Self/Other'. Pages 255-62 in *A Companion to Feminist Philosophy*, ed. A. Jaggar and I. Young. Oxford: Blackwell.

Moore, David L. 1994. 'Decolonizing Criticism'. *Studies in American Indian Literatures* 6, No. 4: 7-35.

Moore, G.E. 1922. *Philosophical Studies*. New York: Harcourt, Brace, & Co.

Moran, Dermot. 2005. *Edmund Husserl*. Malden, MA: Polity Press.

Morgan, Robin. 1982. *The Anatomy of Freedom: Feminism, Physics, and Global Politics*. Garden City, NY: Doubleday.

Morris, Meaghan. 1988. *The Pirate's Fiancée: Feminism, Reading, Postmodernism*. London: Verso.

Morris, Randall C. 1991. *Process Philosophy and Political Ideology*. Albany: State University of New York Press.

Morris, Richard. 1987. *The Nature of Reality*. New York: McGraw-Hill.

Moser, Mary Theresa. 1985. *The Evolution of the Option for the Poor in France 1880–1965*. Lanham, MD: University Press of America.

Mott, Stephen, and Ronald J. Sider. 1999. 'Economic Justice: A Biblical Paradigm'. Pages 15-45 in *Toward a Just and Caring Society*, ed. D. Gushee. Grand Rapids, MI: Baker Books.

Mouffe, Chantal. 1996. 'Democracy, Power, and the Political'. Pages 245-56 in *Democracy and Difference*, ed. S. Benhabib. Princeton, NJ: Princeton University Press.

——1999. Interview. Pages 165-201 in G. Olson and L. Worsham, eds.

Moyne, Samuel. 2005. *Origins of the Other*. Ithaca, NY: Cornell University Press.

Mudimbe, V.Y. 1988. *The Invention of Africa*. Bloomington: Indiana University Press.

Müller, Günther. 1968. *Morphologische Poetik: Gesammelte Aufsätze*. Darmstadt: Wissenschaftliche Buchgesellschaft.

Munt, Sally. 1998. *Heroic Desire*. London: Cassell.

Murdoch, Iris. 1971. *The Sovereignty of Good*. New York: Schocken Books.

Murphey, Murray G. 1961. *The Development of Peirce's Philosophy*. Cambridge, MA: Harvard University Press.

Murphy, Arthur E. 1963. *Reason and the Common Good*. Englewood Cliffs, NJ: Prentice-Hall.

Murphy, Nancey. 1997. *Anglo-American Postmodernity*. Boulder, CO: Westview.

Murray, David J. 1995. *Gestalt Psychology and the Cognitive Revolution*. London: Harvester Wheatsheaf.

Murrmann-Kahl, Michael. 1992. *Die entzauberte Heilsgeschichte*. Gütersloh: Gütersloher Verlagshaus G. Mohn.

Murti, T.R.V. 1955. *The Central Philosophy of Buddhism*. London: George Allen & Unwin.

Mussolini, Benito. 1924. *Diuturna*. Milan: Casa Editrice Imperia.

Myrdal, Gunnar. 1960. *Beyond the Welfare State*. New Haven: Yale University Press.

Nagel, Ernest. 1961. *The Structure of Science*. New York: Harcourt, Brace & World.

Naisbitt, John. 1985. *Reinventing the Corporation*. New York: Warner.

Nancy, Jean-Luc. 1985. 'Des lieux divins'. Pages 539-87 in *Qu'est-ce que Dieu?* ed. Facultés Universitaires Saint-Louis. Brussels: Facultés Universitaires Saint-Louis. English in *The Inoperative Community*, 1991, ed. Peter Connor.

——1988. *L'expérience de la liberté*. Paris: Galilée. English, 1993.

——1993. *Le sens du monde*. Paris: Galilée. English, 1997.

Nandy, Ashis. 1987. *Traditions, Tyranny and Utopias*. New Delhi: Oxford University Press.

Needham, Joseph. 1954–2004. *Science and Civilization in China*. Cambridge: Cambridge University Press.

Nelson, Lynn Hankinson. 1990. *Who Knows*. Philadelphia: Temple University Press.

Neville, Robert C. 1974. *The Cosmology of Freedom*. New Haven: Yale University Press.

Newman, Fred, and Lois Holzman. 1997. *The End of Knowing*. London: Routledge.

Nichols, Shaun, and Stephen Stich. 2003. 'How to Read Your Own Mind'. Pages 157-200 in *Consciousness*, ed. Q. Smith and A. Jokic. Oxford: Clarendon Press.

Nicholson, Linda. 1999. *The Play of Reason*. Ithaca, NY: Cornell University Press.

Nicolaisen, Carsten. 1966. *Die Auseinandersetzungen um das Alte Testament im Kirchenkampf 1933–1945*. Diss. Hamburg.

Nicolis, Grégoire, and Ilya Prigogine. 1989. *Exploring Complexity*. New York: W.H. Freeman.

Niebuhr, Reinhold. 1957. *Love and Justice*. Philadelphia: Westminster Press.

Nietzsche, Friedrich. 1967–. *Werke*. Ed. G. Colli and M. Montinari. Berlin: W. de Gruyter.

Nisbett, Richard E. 2003. *The Geography of Thought*. New York: Free Press.

Nissen, Lowell. 1997. *Teleological Language in the Life Sciences*. Lanham, MD: Rowman & Littlefield.

Noddings, Nel. 1984. *Caring*. Berkeley: University of California Press.

——1989. *Women and Evil*. Berkeley: University of California Press.

Nørretranders, Tor. 1998. *The User Illusion*. New York: Viking. Danish, 1991.

Novick, Peter. 1988. *That Noble Dream*. Cambridge: Cambridge University Press.

Nozick, Robert. 1981. *Philosophical Explanations*. Cambridge, MA: Harvard University Press.

——1989. *The Examined Life*. New York: Simon & Schuster.

Nubiola, Jaime. 1996. 'Scholarship on the Relations between Wittgenstein and Charles S. Peirce'. Pages 281-94 in *Studies in the History of Logic*, ed. I. Angelelli and M. Cerezo. Berlin: W. de Gruyter.

Nussbaum, Martha C. 1989. 'A Reply'. *Soundings* 72: 725-81.

——1990. *Love's Knowledge*. Oxford: Oxford University Press.

——1995. *Poetic Justice*. Boston: Beacon Press.

——1999. *Sex and Social Justice*. Oxford: Oxford University Press.

Nzomo, Maria. 1995. 'Women and Democratization Struggles in Africa'. Pages 131-58 in M. Marchand and J. Parpart.

Oakeshott, Michael. 1996. *The Politics of Faith and the Politics of Scepticism*. New Haven: Yale University Press.

Oakley, Ann. 2000. *Experiments in Knowing*. Cambridge: Polity Press.

O'Brien, Lucy. 1995. *She Bop: The Definitive History of Women in Rock, Pop and Soul*. London: Penguin.

Ochs, Peter. 1998. *Peirce, Pragmatism and the Logic of Scripture*. Cambridge: Cambridge University Press.

Oden, Thomas C. 1995. *Corrective Love*. St. Louis, MO: Concordia.

Ogden, C.K., and I.A. Richards. 1923. *The Meaning of Meaning*. New York: Harcourt, Brace & World.

Okin, Susan Moller. 1989. *Justice, Gender, and the Family*. New York: Basic Books.

Ollman, Bertell. 1976. *Alienation*. 2nd edn. Cambridge: Cambridge University Press.

Oliver, Kelly. 1997. *Family Values: Subjects Between Nature and Culture*. London: Routledge.

——1998. *Subjectivity Without Subjects: From Abject Fathers to Desiring Mothers*. Lanham, MD: Rowman & Littlefield.

——2001. *Witnessing: Beyond Recognition.* Minneapolis: University of Minnesota Press.

Oliver, Kelly, and Marilyn Pearsall, eds. 1998. *Feminist Interpretations of Friedrich Nietzsche.* University Park: Pennsylvania State University Press.

Olson, Gary A., and Elizabeth Hirsh, eds. 1995. *Women Writing Culture.* Albany: State University of New York Press.

Omnés, Roland. 1999. *Understanding Quantum Mechanics.* Princeton, NJ: Princeton University Press.

O'Neill, William L., ed. 1969. *The Woman Movement.* London: George Allen & Unwin.

Ortega y Gasset, José. 1914. *Meditaciones del Quijote.* Madrid: [Imprenta Clásica Española]. English, 1961.

——1916–21. *El espectador.* Madrid: Mayo. German, 1934.

——1923. *El tema de nuestro tiempo.* Madrid: Calpe. German, 1931.

Ott, Hugo. 1988. *Martin Heidegger: Unterwegs zu seiner Biographie.* Frankfurt: Campus Verlag.

Paci, Enzo. 1972. *The Function of the Sciences and the Meaning of Man.* Evanston, IL: Northwestern University Press. Italian, 1963.

Padel, Ruth. 2000. *I'm a Man: Sex, Gods and Rock'n'Roll.* London: Faber & Faber.

Pagden, Anthony. 1995. *Lords of all the World.* New Haven: Yale University Press.

Page, George. 1999. *Inside the Animal Mind.* New York: Doubleday.

Paine, Thomas. 1794. *The Age of Reason.* Paris: Barrois.

Panofsky, Erwin. 1991. *Perspective as Symbolic Form.* New York: Zone Books. German, 1924/25.

Panzer, Joel S. 1996. *The Popes and Slavery.* New York: Allen House.

Parent, William A. 1983. 'Recent Work on the Concept of Liberty'. Pages 247-75 in *Recent Work in Philosophy,* ed. K.G. Lucey and T.R. Machan. Totowa, NJ: Rowman & Allanheld.

Parker, Florence E. 1956. *The First 125 Years: A History of Distributive and Service Cooperation in the United States, 1829–1954.* Superior, WI: Cooperative Publishing Association.

Pavel, Thomas G. 1989. 'The Present Debate: News from France'. *Diacritics* 19, No. 1: 17-32.

Pearl, Judea. 2000. *Causality.* Cambridge: Cambridge University Press.

Pearson, Karl. 1892. *The Grammar of Science.* London: Walter Scott. 2nd edn, 1900.

Pedrycz, Witold, and Fernando Gomide. 1998. *An Introduction to Fuzzy Sets.* Cambridge, MA: MIT Press.

Peirce, Charles S. 1931–58. *Collected Papers.* Cambridge, MA: Harvard University Press.

——1976. *The New Elements of Mathematics.* The Hague: Mouton.

——1982–. *Writings.* Bloomington: Indiana University Press.

Peirce, Melusina Fay: see [Fay] Peirce, Melusina.

Pepper, Stephen C. 1942. *World Hypotheses.* Berkeley: University of California Press.

Perelman, Chaïm, and Lucie Olbrechts-Tyteca. 1958. *Traité de l'argumentation: La nouvelle rhétorique.* Paris: Presses universitaires de France. English, 1971.

Perlman, James S. 1995. *Science Without Limits: Toward a Theory of Interaction Between Nature and Knowledge.* Amhurst, NY: Prometheus.

Persons, Stow. 1947. *Free Religion: An American Faith.* New Haven: Yale University Press.

Peters, John Durham. 1999. *Speaking into the Air*. Chicago: University of Chicago Press.

Peters, Michael A. 2001. *Poststructuralism, Marxism, and Neoliberalism*. Lanham, MD: Rowman & Littlefield.

Peterson, V. Spike, and Ann Sisson Runyan. 1999. *Global Gender Issues*. Boulder, CO: Westview.

Pettigrew, David E. 1995. 'Peirce and Derrida'. Pages 365-78 in *Peirce's Doctrine of Signs*, ed. V. Colapietro and T. Olshewsky. Berlin: W. de Gruyter.

Phelan, Shane. 1994. *Getting Specific: Postmodern Lesbian Politics*. Minneapolis: University of Minnesota Press.

Philipse, Herman. 1998. *Heidegger's Philosophy of Being*. Princeton, NJ: Princeton University Press.

Phillips, Anne. 1993. *Democracy and Difference*. University Park: Pennsylvania State University Press.

Piaget, Jean. 1945. *La formation du symbole*. Nueuchatel: Delachaux & Niestlé. English: *Play, Dreams and Imitation in Childhood*, 1951.

——1968. *Le structuralisme*. Paris: Presses universitaires de France. English, 1970.

Piaget, Jean, and Rolando Garcia. 1983. *Psychogenèse et histoire des sciences*. Paris: Flammarion. English, 1989.

Pippin, Tina, and George Aichele, eds. 1998. *Violence, Utopia and the Kingdom of God: Fantasy and Ideology in the Bible*. London: Routledge.

Planck, Max. 1949. *Vorträge und Erinnerungen*. 5th edn. Stuttgart: S. Hirzel. Partial English, 1949.

Plantinga, Theodore. 1980. *Historical Understanding in the Thought of Wilhelm Dilthey*. Toronto: University of Toronto Press.

Pohlenz, Max. 1948–49. *Die Stoa*. Göttingen: Vandenhoeck & Ruprecht.

Poincaré, H. 1903. *La Science et l'hypothèse*. Paris: E. Flammarion. English, 1952.

Pole, David. 1983. *Aesthetics, Form and Emotion*. New York: St. Martin's Press.

Polkinghorne, John. 1989. *Science and Creation*. Boston: New Science Library.

Polt, Richard. 2005. 'Ereignis'. Pages 375-91 in *A Companion to Heidegger*, ed. Hubert L. Dreyfus and Mark A. Wrathall. Oxford: Blackwell.

Pope, Whitney. 1999. *The Search for Freedom*. Columbus: Ohio State University Press.

Popkin, Richard H. 1987. *Isaac La Peyrère*. Leiden: E.J. Brill.

Popper, Karl R. 1945. *The Open Society and its Enemies*. London: Routledge & Kegan Paul.

——1982. *Quantum Theory and the Schism in Physics*. Totowa, NJ: Rowan & Littlefield.

Preuss, Ulrich K. 1979. 'Politische Ordnungskonzepte für die Massengesellschaft'. Pages 340-77 in vol. I of *Stichworte zur 'Geistigen Situation der Zeit'*, ed. J. Habermas. Frankfurt a.M.: Suhrkamp. English, 1984.

Priest, Graham. 1987. *In Contradiction*. Dordrecht: M. Nijhoff. 2nd edn, 2006.

Priestley, Joseph. 1777. *Disquisitions Relating to Matter and Spirit*. London: J. Johnson.

Prigogine, Ilya, and Isabelle Stengers. 1984. *Order out of Chaos*. Boulder, CO: New Science Library.

Pujol, Michèle A. 1992. *Feminism and Anti-Feminism in Early Economic Thought*. Hants: Elgar.

Putnam, Hilary. 1971. *Philosophy of Logic*. New York: Harper & Row.

——1975. *Mind, Language and Reality*. Cambridge: Cambridge University Press.

——1979. *Mathematics, Matter and Method.* 2nd edn. Cambridge: Cambridge University Press. 1st edn, 1975.
——1981. *Reason, Truth and History.* Cambridge: Cambridge University Press.
——1987. *The Many Faces of Realism.* La Salle, IL: Open Court.
——2002. *The Collapse of the Fact/Value Dichotomy and Other Essays.* Cambridge, MA: Harvard University Press.
Quine, Willard Van Orman. 1960. *Word and Object.* Cambridge, MA: MIT Press.
——1963. *Set Theory and its Logic.* Cambridge, MA: Harvard University Press.
——1985. *The Time of My Life.* Cambridge, MA: MIT Press.
Rabinow, Paul, ed. 1984. *The Foucault Reader.* New York: Pantheon.
Radden, Jennifer. 1996. 'Relational Individualism in Feminist Therapy'. *Hypatia* 11, No. 3: 71-96.
Radhakrishnan, R. 2000. 'Postmodernism and the Rest of the World'. Pages 37-70 in *The Pre-occupation of Postcolonial Studies,* ed. F. Afzal-Khan and K. Seshadri-Crooks. Durham, NC: Duke University Press.
Rand, Ayn. 1943. *The Fountainhead.* Indianapolis: Bobbs Merrill.
——1990. *Introduction to Objectivist Epistemology.* 2nd edn. New York: Penguin Books.
Randall, John Herman, Jr. 1944. 'Epilogue: The Nature of Naturalism'. Pages 354-82 in *Naturalism and the Human Spirit,* ed. Y. Krikorian. New York: Columbia University Press.
Rapaport, David. 1974. *The History of the Concept of the Association of Ideas.* New York: International Universities Press.
Rasmussen, Steen. 1990. 'The Core-World: Emergence and Evolution of Cooperative Structures in a Computational Chemistry'. *Physica* D 42: 111-34.
Ratzinger, Joseph. 1968. *Einführung in das Christentum.* Munich: Kösel.
Rausching, Hermann. 1940. *Gespräche mit Hitler.* Zürich: Europa Verlag. 2nd expanded, edn, 1988.
Ray, Paul H. 1997. 'The Emerging Culture'. *American Demographics* 19, No. 2: 28-34, 56.
Ray, Paul H., and Sherry Ruth Anderson. 2000. *The Cultural Creative.* New York: Harmony Books.
Reader, Keith A. 1987. *Intellectuals and the Left in France Since 1968.* London: Macmillan.
Reagan, Charles E. 1996. *Paul Ricoeur: His Life and His Work.* Chicago: University of Chicago Press.
Reeves, Thomas C. 2000. *Twentieth-Century America.* Oxford: Oxford University Press.
Reich, Charles A. 1970. *The Greening of America.* New York: Random House.
Reich, Wilhelm. 1945. *The Sexual Revolution.* New York: Orgone Institute.
Reid, Thomas. 1764. *An Inquiry into the Human Mind, on the Principles of Common Sense.* Dublin: A. Ewing.
Reiss, Timothy J. 1982. *The Discourse of Modernism.* Ithaca, NY: Cornell University Press.
Renouvier, Charles. 1854–64. *Essais de critique générale.* Paris: [n.p.].
Rescher, Nicholas. 1993. *Pluralism.* Oxford: Clarendon Press.
——1998. *Complexity.* New Brunswick: Transaction Publishers.
——2000. *Realistic Pragmatism.* Albany: State University of New York Press.
Rescher, Nicholas, and Robert Brandom. 1979. *The Logic of Inconsistency.* Totowa, NJ: Rowman & Littlefield.

Restall, Greg. 2000. *An Introduction to Substructural Logics*. London: Routledge.

Reynolds, Morgan O. 1995. *Crime and Punishment in America*. Dallas: National Center for Policy Analysis.

Rich, Adrienne. 1986. *Blood, Bread and Poetry*. New York: Norton.

Richins, Marston L., and Floya W. Rudmin. 1994. 'Materialism and Economic Psychology'. *Journal of Economic Psychology* 15: 217-31.

Richlin, Amy. 1998. 'Foucault's *History of Sexuality*: A Useful Theory for Women?' Pages 138-70 in *Rethinking Sexuality*, ed. D. Larmour *et al*. Princeton, NJ: Princeton University Press.

Ricoeur, Paul. 1961. 'Le socialisme aujourd'hui'. *Le Christianisme social* 69: 451-60. English in *Political and Social Essays*, 1974.

——1983–85. *Temp et récit*. Paris: Éditions du Seuil. English, 1984–88.

——1990. *Soi-même comme un autre*. Paris: Éditions du Seuil. English, 1992.

——1991. 'Love and Justice'. Pages 187-202 in *Pluralism and Truth*, ed. W. Jeanrond and J. Rike. New York: Crossroad.

Riesman, David, *et al*. 1950. *The Lonely Crowd*. New Haven: Yale University Press.

Riles, Annelise. 1999. 'Global Designs'. *Proceedings of the Annual Meeting of the American Society of International Law* 93: 28-34.

Robertson, Geoffrey. 2000. *Crimes Against Humanity*. New York: New Press.

Rombach, Heinrich. 1965–66. *Substanz, System, Struktur*. Freiburg: K. Alber.

Rome, Sydney, and Beatrice Rome, eds. 1964. *Philosophical Interrogations*. New York: Holt, Rinehart & Winston.

Rommen, Heinrich A. 1947. *The Natural Law*. St. Louis: B. Herder. Enlarged from the German of 1936.

Ronen, Ruth. 1994. *Possible Worlds in Literary Theory*. Cambridge: Cambridge University Press.

Rorty, Richard. 1967a. 'Introduction'. Pages 1-39 in *The Linguistic Turn*. Chicago: University of Chicago Press.

——1967b. 'Relations, Internal and External'. *The Encyclopedia of Philosophy*, VII: 125-33. New York: Macmillan.

——1979. *Philosophy and the Mirror of Nature*. Princeton, NJ: Princeton University Press.

——1982. *Consequences of Pragmatism*. Minneapolis: University of Minnesota Press.

——1983. 'Postmodernist Bourgeois Liberalism'. *Journal of Philosophy* 80: 583-89.

——1989. *Contingency, Irony, and Solidarity*. Cambridge: Cambridge University Press.

——1990. 'Pragmatism as Anti-Representationalism'. Pages 1-6 in *Pragmatism*, ed. J. Murphy. Boulder, CO: Westview.

——1991. *Objectivity, Relativism, and Truth*. Cambridge: Cambridge University Press.

——1997. 'Post-Modernism'. *New York Times*, 1 November: B13.

——1998a. *Truth and Progress*. Cambridge: Cambridge University Press.

——1998b. *Achieving Our Country*. Cambridge, MA: Harvard University Press.

Rose, Hilary. 1994. *Love, Power, and Knowledge*. Bloomington: Indiana University Press.

Rose, Margaret A. 1991. *The Post-Modern and the Post-Industrial*. Cambridge: Cambridge University Press.

Rose, Nikolas. 1999. *Powers of Freedom: Reframing Political Thought*. Cambridge: Cambridge University Press.

Rosenau, Pauline Marie. 1992. *Post-Modernism and the Social Sciences*. Princeton, NJ: Princeton University Press.
Rosenberg, Rosalind. 1982. *Beyond Separate Spheres: Intellectual Roots of Modern Feminism*. New Haven: Yale University Press.
Rosenblueth, Arturo, Norbert Wiener, and Julian Bigelow. 1943. 'Behavior, Purpose and Teleology'. *Philosophy of Science* 10: 18-24.
Rosenthal, Bernice Glatzer. 1975. *Dmitri Sergeevich Merezhkovsky and the Silver Age*. The Hague: Martinus Nijhoff.
Rosenthal, Sandra B. 1986. *Speculative Pragmatism*. Amherst: University of Massachusetts Press.
Rosenzweig, Franz. 1937. *Kleinere Schriften*. Berlin: Schocken. English: *Scripture and Tradition*, 1994.
Rosmini, Antonio. 1837. *La società ed il suo fine*. Milan: Pogliani. English, 1995.
Ross, Kristin. 2002. *May 1968 and its Afterlives*. Chicago: University of Chicago Press.
Rousseau, G.S., ed. 1972. *Organic Form: The Life of an Idea*. London: Routledge & Kegan Paul.
Rowlands, Mark. 1999. *The Body in Mind*. Cambridge: Cambridge University Press.
Royce, Josiah. 1898. *Studies of Good and Evil*. New York: D. Appleton.
——1908. *Race Questions, Provincialism, and Other American Problems*. New York: Macmillan.
——1913. *The Problem of Christianity*. New York: Macmillan.
Rue, Loyal. 1994. *By the Grace of Guile*. Oxford: Oxford University Press.
Ruether, Rosemary Radford. 1974. *Faith and Fratricide: The Theological Roots of Anti-Semitism*. New York: Seabury.
——1998. *Women and Redemption*. Minneapolis: Fortress.
Russell, Bertrand. 1897. *An Essay on the Foundations of Geometry*. Cambridge: Cambridge University Press.
——1903. *The Principles of Mathematics*. Cambridge: Cambridge University Press.
——1921. *The Analysis of Mind*. London: G. Allen & Unwin.
——1935. *Religion and Science*. London: Thornton Butterworth.
——1937. *The Principles of Mathematics*. 2nd edn. London: G. Allen & Unwin.
——1940. *An Inquiry into Meaning and Truth*. New York: Norton.
——1945. *A History of Western Philosophy*. New York: Simon & Schuster.
——1946. *Ideas That Have Helped Mankind*. Girard, KS: Haldeman-Julius. Reprinted in Russell, *Atheism*, 1972.
——1956. *Logic and Knowledge*. London: G. Allen & Unwin.
——1957. *Why I am not a Christian and Other Essays on Religion and Related Subjects*. New York: Simon & Schuster.
——1967–69. *Autobiography*. London: G. Allen & Unwin.
——2002. *Yours Faithfully, Bertrand Russell: A Lifelong Fight for Peace, Justice, and Truth in Letters to the Editor*. Chicago: Open Court.
Ryan, Marie-Laure. 2001. *Narrative as Virtual Reality*. Baltimore: The Johns Hopkins University Press.
Saatkamp, Harold J., ed. 1995. *Rorty and Pragmatism*. Nashville: Vanderbilt University Press.
Safranski, Rüdiger. 1998. *Martin Heidegger*. Cambridge, MA: Harvard University Press. German, 1994.
Said, Edward W. 1978. *Orientalism*. New York: Pantheon Books. 2nd edn, see 1994.

——1983. *The World, the Text, and the Critic*. Cambridge, MA: Harvard University Press.

——1991. 'A Tragic Convergence'. *New York Times*, 11 January: A29.

——1993. *Culture and Imperialism*. New York: A.A. Knopf.

——1994. *Orientalism*. 2nd edn. New York: Vintage Books. Equals 1978 edn plus afterword.

Salmon, Wesley C. 1998. *Causality and Interpretation*. Oxford: Oxford University Press.

Sangari, Kumkum. 1999. *Politics of the Possible*. New Delhi: Tulika.

Santayana, George. 1927. *The Realm of Essence*. New York: Charles Scribner's Sons.

Sardar, Ziauddin. 1998. *Postmodernism and the Other*. London: Pluto Press.

Sartre, Jean-Paul. 1943. *L'être et le néant*. Paris: Gallimard. English, 1956.

——1945. *Huis clos*. Paris: Gallimard. First production, 1944. English: *No Exit*, 1946.

Saunders, P.T., and M.W. Ho. 1976. 'On the Increase in Complexity in Evolution'. *Journal of Theoretical Biology* 63: 375-84.

Saussure, Ferdinand de. 1916. *Cours de linguistique générale*. Paris: Payot.

Sawicki, Jana. 1991. *Disciplining Foucault*. London: Routledge.

Schaaf, Julius Jakob. 1965. 'Beziehung und Idee: Eine platonische Besinnung'. Pages 3-20 in *Parusia: Festgabe für Johannes Hirschberger*, ed. K. Flasch. Frankfurt a.M.: Minerva.

——1977. 'Letztbegründung als Theorie-Praxis-Vermittlung'. *Studia Philosophica* 37: 157-75.

Scheler, Max. 1913. *Zur Phänomenologie und Theorie der Sympathiegefühle und von Liebe und Haß*. Halle: Max Niemeyer. 2nd edn, 1923; English of 2nd edn, 1954.

Schilpp, Paul Arthur, and Maurice Friedman, eds. 1967. *The Philosophy of Martin Buber*. La Salle, IL: Open Court. German, 1963.

Schiralli, Martin. 1999. *Constructive Postmodernism: Toward Renewal in Cultural and Literary Studies*. Westport, CT: Bergin & Garvey.

Schleifer, Ronald. 2000. *Modernism and Time*. Cambridge: Cambridge University Press.

Schmiedeler, Edgar. 1941. *Cooperation: A Christian Mode of Industry*. Ozone Park, NY: Catholic Literary Guild.

Schmitz, H. Walter. 1985. 'Victoria Lady Welby's Significs'. Pages ix-ccxxxv in *Significs and Language*, by Victoria, Lady Welby. Amsterdam: J. Benjamins.

Schneewind, J.B. 1998. *The Invention of Autonomy*. Cambridge: Cambridge University Press.

Schneider, Joseph. 2005. *Donna Haraway: Live Theory*. New York: Continuum.

Schrag, Calvin O. 1992. *The Resources of Rationality*. Bloomington: Indiana University Press.

Schrift, Alan D. 2006. *Twentieth-Century French Philosophy*. Oxford: Blackwell.

Schröder, Ernst. 1880. Review of *Begriffsschrift*, by G. Frege. *Zeitschrift für Mathematik und Physik* 25: 81-94.

Schrödinger, E. 1924. 'Bohrs neue Strahlungshypothese und der Energiesatz'. *Die Naturwissenschaften* 12: 720-24.

Schulze-Makuch, Dirk, and Louis N. Irwin. 2004. *Life in the Universe*. Berlin: Springer.

Sciabarra, Chris Matthew. 2000. *Total Freedom*. University Park: Pennsylvania State University Press.

Scott, Clifford H. 1976. *Lester Frank Ward*. Boston: Twayne Publishers.

Scott, Fred N. 1922. 'English Composition as a Mode of Behavior'. *English Journal* 11: 463-73.

Scott, Joan Wallach. 1988. *Gender and the Politics of History.* New York: Columbia University Press. 2nd edn, with an added chapter, 1999.

Sedgwick, Eve Kosofsky. 1990. *Epistemology of the Closet.* Berkeley: University of California Press.

——1993. *Tendencies.* Durham, NC: Duke University Press.

Segundo, Juan Luis. 1988. *An Evolutionary Approach to Jesus of Nazareth.* Maryknoll, NY: Orbis Books. Spanish, 1982.

Seibert, M. Therese, *et al.* 1997. 'Trends in Male-Female Status Inequality, 1940–1990'. *Social Research* 26: 1-24.

Seidel, George J. 1999. 'Heidegger's Last God and the Schelling Connection'. *Laval théologique et philosophique* 55: 86-89.

——2001. 'Musing with Kierkegaard, Heidegger's *Besinnung*'. *Continental Philosophy Review* 34: 403-18.

——2002. 'The Last Heidegger'. *Idealistic Studies* 32: 63-71.

Seigfried, Charlene Haddock. 1996. *Pragmatism and Feminism.* Chicago: University of Chicago Press.

——ed. 2002. *Feminist Interpretations of John Dewey.* University Park: Pennsylvania State University Press.

Sellars, Roy Wood. 1922. *Evolutionary Naturalism.* Chicago: Open Court.

——1932. *The Philosophy of Physical Realism.* New York: Macmillan.

Sellers, Susan, ed. 1994. *The Hélène Cixous Reader.* London: Routledge.

Sen, Amartya K. 1985. 'Well-Being, Agency and Freedom'. *Journal of Philosophy* 82: 169-221.

——1999. *Development as Freedom.* New York: Knopf.

——2002. *Rationality and Freedom.* Cambridge, MA: Harvard University Press.

Senghor, Léopold Sédar. 1993. 'Negritude: A Humanism of the Twentieth Century'. Pages 27-35 in *Colonial Discourse and Post-Colonial Theory*, ed. P. Williams and L. Chrisman. New York: Harvester Wheatsheaf.

Sent, Esther-Mirjam. 1998. *The Evolving Rationality of Rational Expectation.* Cambridge: Cambridge University Press.

Serequeberhan, Tsenay. 1994. *The Hermeneutics of African Philosophy.* London: Routledge.

Serres, Michel. 1990. *Le contrat naturel.* Paris: Bourin. English, 1995.

——1992. *Eclaircissements.* Paris: Bourin. English: *Conversations on Science, Culture, and Time*, 1995.

Shannon, Claude E. 1948. 'The Mathematical Theory of Communication'. *Bell System Technical Journal* 27: 379-423, 623-56. Reprinted in C. Shannon and W. Weaver, *The Mathematical Theory of Communication*, 1949.

Shapiro, Stewart. 1997. *Philosophy of Mathematics.* Oxford: Oxford University Press.

Shepherd, Linda Jean. 1993. *Lifting the Veil.* Boston: Shambhala.

Sherman, Howard J. 1995. *Reinventing Marxism.* Baltimore: The Johns Hopkins University Press.

Sherwood, Yvonne, and Kevin Hart. 2005. *Derrida and Religion.* London: Routledge.

Shohat, Ella, and Robert Stam. 1994. *Unthinking Eurocentrism.* London: Routledge.

Short, T.L. 2004. 'The Development of Peirce's Theory of Signs'. Pages 214-40 in *The Cambridge Companion to Peirce*, ed. C. Misak. Cambridge: Cambridge University Press.

Sigwart, Christoph. 1873–78. *Logik.* Freiburg i.B.: J.C.B. Mohr.

Simon, Herbert A. 1962. 'The Architecture of Complexity'. *Proceedings of the American Philosophical Society* 106: 467-82.

Simon, Linda. 1998. *Genuine Reality: A Life of William James.* New York: Harcourt Brace & Co.

Sinaga, Anicetus B. 1981. *The Toba-Batak High God.* St. Augustine: Anthropos Institut.

Singer, Peter. 2000. *A Darwinian Left.* New Haven: Yale University Press.

Skinner, Quentin. 1978. *The Foundations of Modern Political Thought.* Cambridge: Cambridge University Press.

——1998. *Liberty Before Liberalism.* Cambridge: Cambridge University Press.

——2003. 'States and the Freedom of Citizens'. Pages 11-27 in *States and Citizens,* ed. B. Stråth and Q. Skinner. Cambridge: Cambridge University Press.

Skyttner, Lars. 1996. *General Systems Theory: An Introduction.* London: Macmillan.

Sloterdijk, Peter. 1983. *Kritik der zynischen Vernunft.* Frankfurt a.M.: Suhrkamp. English, 1987.

Sluga, Hans. 1993. *Heidegger's Crisis.* Cambridge, MA: Harvard University Press.

——1996. 'Whose House is That? Wittgenstein on the Self'. Pages 320-53 in *The Cambridge Companion to Wittgenstein,* ed. H. Sluga and D. Stern. Cambridge: Cambridge University Press.

Smith, Adam. 1759. *The Theory of Moral Sentiments.* London: Millar. Cited according to divisions in the sixth and later editions.

——1776. *An Inquiry into the Nature and Causes of the Wealth of Nations.* London: Strahan & Cadell.

——1978. *Lectures on Jurisprudence.* Oxford: Clarendon Press.

Smith, Barbara, ed. 1983. *Home Girls.* New York: Kitchen Table—Women of Color Press.

Smith, Barbara Herrnstein. 1988. *Contingencies of Value.* Cambridge, MA: Harvard University Press.

——1997. *Belief and Resistance.* Cambridge, MA: Harvard University Press.

Smith, Dorothy E. 1990. *The Conceptual Practices of Power.* Boston: Northeastern University Press.

——1997. 'Comment on Hekman's "Truth and Method: Feminist Standpoint Theory Revisited" '. *Signs* 22: 392-98.

——1999. *Writing the Social.* Toronto: University of Toronto Press.

Smith, Wilfred Cantwell. 1962. *The Meaning and End of Religion.* San Francisco: Harper & Row.

Smolin, Lee. 1997. *The Life of the Cosmos.* Oxford: Oxford University Press.

Sneed, Joseph D. 1971. *The Logical Structure of Mathematical Physics.* Dordrecht: Reidel.

Soames, Scott. 2003. *Philosophical Analysis in the Twentieth Century.* Princeton, NJ: Princeton University Press.

Sober, Elliott, and David Sloan Wilson. 1998. *Unto Others: The Evolution and Psychology of Unselfish Behavior.* Cambridge, MA: Harvard University Press.

Solé, Richard, and Brian Goodwin. 2000. *Signs of Life.* New York: Basic Books.

Sollers, Philippe. 1983. 'Éditorial'. *L'Infini* 1: 3-6.

Somers, Robert H. 1965. 'The Mainspring of the Rebellion'. Pages 530-57 in *The Berkeley Student Revolt,* ed. S.M. Lipset and S. Wolin. Garden City, NY: Doubleday & Co.

Sorrell, Kory Spencer. 2004. *Representative Practices: Peirce, Pragmatism, and Feminist Epistomology*. New York: Fordham University Press.

Spaeman, R. 1972. 'Freiheit, IV'. *Historisches Wörterbuch der Philosophie*, II: 1087-98. Basel: Schwabe.

Spangler, David. 1976. *Revelation: The Birth of a New Age*. Elgin, IL: Lorian Press.

Spencer, Herbert. 1855. *Principles of Psychology*. London: Longman, Brown, Green, & Longmans. 3rd edn, 1880.

——1862. *First Principles*. New York: D. Appleton.

Spencer-Brown, G. 1979. *Laws of Form*. New York: Bantam Books.

Spengler, Oswald. 1918–22. *Untergang des Abendlandes*. Munich: C.H. Beck. English, 1939.

Spiegelberg, Herbert. 1965. *The Phenomenological Movement*. 2nd edn. The Hague: Nijhoff.

——1981. *The Context of the Phenomenological Movement*. The Hague: Nijhoff.

Spinoza, Benedict de. 1985–. *The Collected Works*. Ed. Edwin Curley. Princeton, NJ: Princeton University Press.

Spivak, Gayatri Chakravorty. 1987. *In Other Worlds*. London: Routledge.

——1990. *The Post-Colonial Critic*. London: Routledge.

——1993. *Outside in the Teaching Machine*. London: Routledge.

——1999. *A Critique of Postcolonial Reason*. Cambridge, MA: Harvard University Press.

Spretnak, Charlene. 1991. *States of Grace*. San Francisco: Harper.

——1999. *The Resurgence of the Real*. London: Routledge.

——ed. 1982. *The Politics of Women's Spirituality*. Garden City, NY: Doubleday.

Stachowiak, Herbert. 1986–95. *Pragmatik*. Hamburg: F. Meiner.

Starhawk. 1987. *Truth or Dare: Encounters with Power, Authority, and Mystery*. San Francisco: Harper & Row.

——1988. *Dreaming the Dark: Magic, Sex, Politics*. 2nd edn. Boston: Beacon Press.

Stark, Rodney. 2003. *For the Glory of God*. Princeton, NJ: Princeton University Press.

Steele, Meili. 1997. *Theorizing Textual Subjects*. Cambridge: Cambridge University Press.

Stefano, Frances. 1992. *The Absolute Value of Human Action in the Theology of Juan Luis Segundo*. Lanham, MD: University Press of America.

Stein, Edith. 1917. *Zum Problem der Einfühlung*. Munich: Verlagsgesellschaft Gerhard Kaffke. English, 1970.

Steinem, Gloria. 1992. *Revolution from Within*. Boston: Little, Brown and Company.

Stengers, Isabelle. 1997. *Power and Invention: Situating Science*. Minneapolis: University of Minnesota Press.

Stern, Fritz. 1999. *Einstein's German World*. Princeton, NJ: Princeton University Press.

Stern, Philip D. 1991. *The Biblical Herem*. Atlanta: Scholars Press.

Stevens, Ramón. 1988. *Whatever Happened to Divine Grace?* Walpole, NH: Stillpoint.

Stevenson, W. Taylor. 1963. 'I-Thou and I-It: An Attempted Clarification of their Relationship'. *Journal of Religion* 43: 193-209.

Stigler, Stephen M. 1986. *The History of Statistics*. Cambridge, MA: Harvard University Press.

Stikkers, Kenneth W. 1980. 'Introduction'. Pages 1-30 in *Problems of a Sociology of Knowledge*, by M. Scheler. London: Routledge & Kegan Paul.

Stivers, Richard. 1994. *The Culture of Cynicism*. Oxford: Blackwell.

Stout, G.F. 1930. *Studies in Philosophy and Psychology*. London: Macmillan & Co.

Strange, Steven K., and Jack Zupko, eds. 2004. *Stoicism: Traditions and Transformations*. Cambridge: Cambridge University Press.

Strauss, Leo. 1953. *Natural Right and History*. Chicago: University of Chicago Press.

——1979. 'The Mutual Influence of Theology and Philosophy'. *Independent Journal of Philosophy* 3: 111-18.

Strauss, William, and Neil Howe. 1997. *The Fourth Turning*. New York: Broadway Books.

Strömholm, Stig. 1985. *A Short History of Legal Thinking in the West*. Stockholm: Norstedts.

Sugden, Robert. 2002. 'Beyond Sympathy and Empathy: Adam Smith's Concept of Fellow-Feeling'. *Economics and Philosophy* 18: 63-87.

Tavor Bannet, Eve. 1993. *Postcultural Theory*. New York: Paragon House.

Taylor, Charles. 1964. *The Explanation of Behaviour*. London: Routledge.

——1989. *Sources of the Self*. Cambridge, MA: Harvard University Press.

——1992. *Multiculturalism and the Politics of 'Recognition'*. Princeton, NJ: Princeton University Press.

Taylor, Dianna, and Karen Vintges, eds. 2004. *Feminism and the Final Foucault*. Urbana: University of Illinois Press.

Taylor, Humphrey. 1997. 'Harris Alienation Index'. *The Harris Poll*, December 31: 5-7.

Taylor, Marjorie, and Stephanie M. Carlson. 2000. 'The Influence of Religious Beliefs on Parental Attitudes About Children's Fantasy Behavior'. Pages 247-68 in *Imagining the Impossible*, ed. K. Rosengren *et al.* Cambridge: Cambridge University Press.

Taylor, Mark C. 2001. *The Moment of Complexity*. Chicago: University of Chicago Press.

Teichmüller, Gustav. 1882. *Die wirkliche und die scheinbare Welt*. Breslau: W. Koebner.

Tepe, Peter. 1992. *Postmoderne/Poststrukturalismus*. Vienna: Passagen.

Thom, René. 1972. *Stabilité structurelle et morphogenèse*. Reading, MA: W.A. Benjamin. English, 1975.

——1980. *Modèles mathematiques de la morphogenèse*. 2nd edn. Paris: Bourgois. English, 1983.

Thompson, William. 1976. *Evil and World Order*. New York: Harper & Row.

Tierney, Brian. 1997. *The Idea of Natural Rights*. Atlanta: Scholars Press.

Tierney, William G. 1997. *Academic Outlaws*. Thousand Oaks, CA: Sage.

Tiffin, Helen. 1991. 'Introduction'. Pages vii-xv in *Past the Last Post*, ed. I. Adam and H. Tiffin. London: Harvester Wheatsheaf.

Tindal, Matthew. 1730. *Christianity as Old as the Creation*. London: n.p.

Toffler, Alvin. 1980. *The Third Wave*. New York: Morrow.

Toland, John. 1696. *Christianity not Mysterious*. London: S. Buckley.

Touraine, Alain. 1971. *The May Movement*. New York: Random House. Updated from the French of 1968.

Toynbee, Arnold. 1934–61. *A Study of History*. London: Oxford University Press.

——1947–57. *A Study of History: Abridgment of Volumes I-X* by D.C. Somervell. New York: Oxford University Press.

Traina, Christina L.H. 1999. *Feminist Ethics and Natural Law*. Washington: Georgetown University Press.

Trinh, T. Minh-ha. 1989. *Woman, Nature, Other*. Bloomington: Indiana University Press.

Turnbull, David. 2000. *Masons, Tricksters and Cartographers: Comparative Studies in the Sociology of Scientific and Indigenous Knowledge*. Amsterdam: Harwood Academic Publishers.

Tweyman, Stanley, ed. 1995. *David Hume: Critical Assessments*. London: Routledge.

Ueding, Gert, and Bernd Steinbrink. 1986. *Grundriss der Rhetorik*. 2nd edn. Stuttgart: Metzler.

Unger, Peter. 1975. *Ignorance: A Case for Universal Scepticism*. Oxford: Clarendon Press.

Van DeBurg, William L., ed. 1997. *Modern Black Nationalism*. New York: New York University Press.

Vattimo, Gianni. 1992. *The Transparent Society*. Baltimore: The Johns Hopkins University Press. Considerably expanded from the Italian of 1989.

——1993. *The Adventure of Difference*. Baltimore: The Johns Hopkins University Press. Italian, 1980.

——1997. *Beyond Interpretation*. Stanford, CA: Stanford University Press. Italian, 1994.

——1998. 'The Trace of the Trace'. Pages 79-94 in *Religion*, ed. J. Derrida and G. Vattimo. Stanford, CA: Stanford University Press.

——1999. *Belief*. Stanford, CA: Stanford University Press. Italian, 1996.

——2001. 'The Generalized Communication Society'. Pages 230-33 in *Keys to the 21st Century*, ed. J. Bindé. Paris: UNESCO.

——2004. *Nihilism and Emancipation*. New York: Columbia University Press. Italian, 2003.

Ve, Hildur. 1998. 'Rationality and Identity in Norwegian Feminism'. Pages 325-43 in *Is There a Nordic Feminism?* ed. D. Fehr, *et al*. London: UCL Press.

Veenhoven, Ruut. 1993. *Happiness in Nations: Subjective Appreciation of Life in 56 Nations, 1946–1992*. Rotterdam: RISBO.

Venn, Couze. 2000. *Occidentalism*. London: Sage.

Vitz, Paul C. 1998. 'The Future of the University: From Postmodern to Tramsmodern'. Pages 105-16 in *Rethinking the Future of the University*, ed. D. Jeffrey and D. Manganiello. Ottawa: University of Ottawa Press.

Vol'kenshtein [=Volkenstein], Mikhail V. 1970. *Molecules and Life*. New York: Plenum. Russian, 1965.

Voltaire. 1879. *Oeuvres complètes*, XIX: *Dictionnaire philosophique*, vol. III. Paris: Garnier Frères.

Vries, Hent de. 1999. *Philosophy and the Turn to Religion*. Baltimore: The Johns Hopkins University Press.

Wahl, Jean. 1949. *A Short History of Existentialism*. New York: Philosophical Library. French, 1947, 1950.

——1959. *Les philosophies de l'existence*. Paris: Colin.

Waithe, Mary Ellen, ed. 1987–95. *A History of Women Philosophers*. Dordrecht: Kluwer.

Wajcman, Judy. 1998. *Managing Like a Man*. University Park: Pennsylvania State University Press.

Waldenfels, Bernhard. 1971. *Das Zwischenreich des Dialogs*. The Hague: Martinus Nijhoff.

——1987. *Ordnung im Zwielicht*. Frankfurt a.M.: Suhrkamp. English, 1996.

——1997. *Topographie des Fremden*. Frankfurt a.M.: Suhrkamp.

Walker, Alice. 1983. *In Search of Our Mother's Gardens*. San Diego: Harcourt Brace Jovanovich.

Walker, Margaret. 1997. *On Being Female, Black, and Free*. Knoxville: University of Tennessee Press.

Wall, Kevin. 1983. *Relation in Hegel*. Washington: University Press of America.

Walther, Elisabeth. 1989. *Charles Sanders Peirce*. Baden-Baden: Agis.

Ward, Graham. 1995. *Barth, Derrida and the Language of Theology*. Cambridge: Cambridge University Press.

Warner, Michael. 1999. *The Trouble with Normal: Sex, Politics, and the Ethics of Queer Life*. New York: Free Press.

Warnock, Mary. 1976. *Imagination*. Berkeley: University of California Press.

——2000. *A Memoir*. Oxford: Oxford University Press.

Warren, Scott. 1984. *The Emergence of Dialectical Theory*. Chicago: University of Chicago Press.

Wassermann, Christof, *et al.*, eds. 1992. *The Science and Theology of Information*. Geneva: Labor et Fides.

Watzlawick, Paul. 1984. *The Invented Reality*. New York: Norton.

Weaver, Jace. 1996. 'From I-Hermeneutics to We-Hermeneutics: Native Americans and the Post-Colonial'. *Semeia* 75: 153-76.

Weber, Eugen. 1999. *Apocalypses*. Cambridge, MA: Harvard University Press.

Weber, Max. 1920–21. *Gesammelte Aufsätze zur Religionssoziologie*. Tübingen: Mohr.

Wedberg, Anders. 1982–84. *A History of Philosophy*. Oxford: Clarendon Press. Swedish, 1970.

Weeks, Kathi. 1998. *Constituting Feminist Subjects*. Ithaca, NY: Cornell University Press.

Weil, Simone. 1962. *Pensées sans ordre concernant l'amour de Dieu*. Paris: Gallimard. English of parts cited: *Science, Necessity, and the Love of God*, 1968.

Weinberg, Martin S., *et al.* 1994. *Dual Attraction*. New York: Oxford University Press.

Weinberg, Steven. 1993. *The First Three Minutes*. 2nd edn. New York: Basic Books.

Weinfeld, Moshe. 1992. *The Promise of the Land*. Berkeley: University of California Press.

Weininger, Otto. 1903. *Geschlecht und Charakter*. Vienna: W. Braumüller. English, 1906.

Weissman, David. 2000. *A Social Ontology*. New Haven: Yale University Press

Welby, Victoria, Lady. 1896. 'Sense, Meaning and Interpretation'. *Mind* 5: 24-37, 186-202.

Wellmer, Albrecht. 1998. *Endgames*. Cambridge, MA: MIT Press.

Welsch, Wolfgang. 1993. *Unsere Postmoderne Moderne*. 4th edn. Berlin: Akademie Verlag.

West, Cornel. 1989. *The American Evasion of Philosophy*. Madison: University of Wisconsin Press.

——1993. *Keeping Faith*. London: Routledge.

Wheeler, John Archibald. 1994. *At Home in the Universe*. Woodbury, NY: American Institute of Physics Press.

Whewell, William. 1847. *The Philosophy of the Inductive Sciences*. 2nd edn. London: J.W. Parker.

Whitaker, J.K., ed. 1975. *The Early Economic Writings of Alfred Marshall, 1867–1890*. New York: Free Press.

Whitbeck, Caroline. 1984. 'A Different Reality: Feminist Ontology'. Pages 64-88 in *Beyond Domination*, ed. C. Gould. Totowa, NJ: Rowman & Allanheld.

White, Alan R. 1990. *The Language of the Imagination*. Oxford: Blackwell.

White, Hayden. 1973. *Metahistory*. Baltimore: The Johns Hopkins University Press.

Whitehead, Alfred North. 1925. *Science and the Modern World*. New York: Macmillan.

——1926. *Religion in the Making*. New York: Macmillan.

——1929. *Process and Reality*. New York: Free Press.

——1941. 'Mathematics and the Good'. Pages 666-81 in *The Philosophy of Alfred North Whitehead*, ed. P. Schilpp. Evanston, IL: Northwestern University Press.

Whitehead, Alfred North, and Bertrand Russell. 1925–27. *Principia Mathematica*. 2nd edn. Cambridge: Cambridge University Press. 1st edn, 1910–13.

Whiteley, Sheila. 2000. *Women and Popular Music*. London: Routledge.

Whitney, Ruth. 1998. *Feminism and Love*. Notre Dame, IN: Cross Road Books.

Whyte, Lancelot Law. 1954. *Accent on Form*. New York: Harper.

——ed. 1951. *Aspects of Form*. Bloomington: Indiana University Press.

Wicken, Jeffrey S. 1987. *Evolution, Thermodynamics, and Information*. Oxford: Oxford University Press.

Wiener, Norbert. 1948. *Cybernetics*. New York: MIT Press.

Wigger, J. Bradley. 1998. *The Texture of Mystery*. Lewisburg, PA: Bucknell University Press.

Wilber, Ken. 1998. *The Marriage of Sense and Soul*. New York: Random House.

Williams, Delores S. 1987. 'Womanist Theology: Black Women's Voices'. *Christianity and Crisis* 47: 66-70.

Williams, James. 2000. *Lyotard and the Political*. London: Routledge.

Williamson, Marianne. 1992. *A Return to Love*. New York: HarperCollins.

——1995. *Illuminata*. Riverhead, NY: Riverhead Books.

——1997. *The Healing of America*. New York: Simon & Schuster.

Wilson, Angelia R. 1997. 'Somewhere Over the Rainbow: Queer Translating'. Pages 91-111 in *Playing with Fire*, ed. S. Phelan. London: Routledge.

Wilson, James Q. 1993. *The Moral Sense*. New York: Free Press.

Winders, James A. 2001. *European Culture Since 1848*. New York: Palgrave.

Winter, Jay. 2006. *Dreams of Peace and Freedom*. New Haven: Yale University Press.

Wittgenstein, Ludwig. 1922. *Tractatus logico-philosophicus*. London: K. Paul, Trench, Trubner & Co. Original, 1921.

——1956. *Bemerkungen über die Grundlagen der Mathematik/Remarks on the Foundations of Mathematics*. Oxford: Blackwell.

——1958. *Preliminary Studies for the 'Philosophical Investigations', Generally Known as the Blue and Brown Books*. New York: Harper & Row.

——1979. *Wittgenstein's Lectures, Cambridge, 1932–1935*. Ed. A. Ambrose. Totowa, NJ: Rowman & Littlefield.

——1980. *Wittgenstein's Lectures, Cambridge, 1930–1932*. Ed. D. Lee. Totowa, NJ: Rowman & Littlefield.

——1984. *Schriften*. Frankfurt: Suhrkamp.

——1993. *Philosophical Occasions, 1912–1951*. Ed. J. Klagge and A. Nordmann. Indianapolis: Hackett.

——1994. *Wiener Ausgabe*. Vienna: Springer.

——1998. *Vermischte Bemerkungen/Culture and Value*. 2nd edn. Oxford: Blackwell.

——2001. *Philosophical Investigations*. Oxford: Blackwell. With German text.

——2003. *Ludwig Wittgenstein: Public and Private Occasions*. Ed. J. Klagge and A. Nordmann. Lanham, MD: Rowman & Littlefield. Partial German: *Denkbewegungen*, 1997.

Wollheim, Richard. 1959. *F.H. Bradley*. Baltimore: Penguin Books.

Woozley, A.D. 1949. *Theory of Knowledge*. London: Hutchinson & Co.

Wright, G.H. von. 1974. *Causality and Determinism*. New York: Columbia University Press.

——1986. 'Truth, Negation and Contradiction'. *Synthese* 66: 3-14.

Wundt, Wilhelm. 1908–11. *Grundzüge der physiologischen Psychologie*. 6th edn. Leipzig: W. Engelmann. English, 1910.

Wuthnow, Robert. 1978. *Experimentation in American Religion*. Berkeley: University of California Press.

——1998. *After Heaven: Spirituality in America Since the 1950's*. Berkeley: University of California Press.

Xu Ben. 2001. 'Postmodern-Postcolonial Criticism and Pro-Democracy Enlightenment'. *Modern China* 27: 117-47.

Yanal, Robert J. 1999. *Paradoxes of Emotion and Fiction*. University Park: Pennsylvania State University Press.

Yeatman, Anna. 1994. *Postmodern Revisionings of the Political*. London: Routledge.

Yeo, Eileen Janes. 1996. *The Contest for Social Science*. London: Rivers Oram Press.

Yockey, Hubert P. 2005. *Information Theory, Evolution, and the Origin of Life*. Cambridge: Cambridge University Press.

Young, Ian. 1995. *The Stonewall Experiment*. London: Cassell.

Young, Iris Marion. 1990. *Justice and the Politics of Difference*. Princeton, NJ: Princeton University Press.

Yu, Carver T. 1987. *Being and Relation: A Theological Critique of Western Dualism and Individualism*. Edinburgh: Scottish Academic Press.

Zadeh, Lofti A. 1965. 'Fuzzy Sets'. *Information and Control* 8: 338-53.

Zagzebski, Linda Trinkaus. 1996. *Virtues of the Mind*. Cambridge: Cambridge University Press.

Zhang, Longxi. 1998. *Mighty Opposites: From Dichotomies to Differences in the Comparative Study of China*. Stanford, CA: Stanford University Press.

Zillmer, Eric A., *et al*. 1995. *The Quest for the Nazi Personality*. Hillsdale, NJ: Lawrence Erlbaum.

Ziporyn, Brook. 2000. *Evil and/or/as the Good*. Cambridge, MA: Harvard University Press.

Žižek, Slavoj. 2003. *The Puppet and the Dwarf: The Perverse Core of Christianity*. Cambridge, MA: MIT Press.

Zurbrugg, Nicholas. 1993. *The Parameters of Postmodernism*. Carbondale: Southern Illinois University Press.

INDEX OF NAMES

Feistel, R., 203
Felken, D., 132
Ferré, F., 64, 98, 124
Ferry, L., 97, 122, 131
Feuerbach, L., 52
Feyerabend, P., 76
Ffrench, P., 163
Fichte, J.G., 52, 53, 137, 138, 139
Field, H.H., 123
Findlay, J.F., 37
Finkielkraut, A., 152, 163, 164, 168
Fisch, M.H., 48
Fitzgerald, P.F., 46
Flax, J., 183
Flood, P.J., 18
Flora, P., 27
Flynn, T.R., 145, 153
Foerster, H. von, 92
Fogel, R.W., 26, 28, 118
Fónagy, I., 208
Forman, P., 133
Foucault, M., 14, 35, 122, 126, 130, 147, 152, 153, 154, 155, 156, 161, 162, 163, 167, 168, 179, 180, 181, 182, 183, 184, 186, 187, 205
Fouque, A., 157, 158, 181
Fraenkel, A.A., 69
Fraser, N., 179, 191
Frege, G., 55, 67, 81
Freire, P., 36, 41
Freud, S., 95, 103
Fricker, M., 180
Friedan, B., 174
Friedman, Marilyn, 92
Friedman, Maurice, 65
Friedman, S.S., 183, 195
Friedmann, H., 94
Friedrich, C.J., 11, 52, 107, 127, 140
Frijda, N.H., 99, 106
Frisina, W.G., 106
Fromm, E., 34
Frye, M., 173, 174
Fuller, S., 71
Fürstenberg, F., 40

Gadamer, H.-G., 9, 59, 104
Gallop, J., 31
Gallup, G., 40
Game, A., 183
Gandhi, L., 38, 197
Garcia, R., 45
Garland, R., 29
Garvey, M., 194
Gasché, R., 65
Gassendi, P., 44, 71
Gates, H.L., 192
Gay, P., 133, 136
Gealt, A., 124
Gebser, J., 86
Gellert, M., 40
Gendler, T.S., 81
George, R.P., 107
Gerstle, G., 37
Gibbs, R., 49, 54, 60, 104, 166, 167
Giddens, A., 29
Gier, N.F., 55
Gilead, A., 81
Giles, M., 92
Gilligan, C., 65, 171, 172, 183
Gilman, C.P., 169, 170
Gilroy, P., 193, 194
Glasersfeld, E. von, 92
Glissant, É., 65, 66, 186, 188, 191
Glover, J., 115
Gödel, K., 69
Godwin, N., 118
Goedeckemeyer, A., 11
Goerner, S.J., 204
Goguen, J.A., 68
Goldfarb, J.C., 117
Gomide, F., 68
Goodman, N., 134
Goodman, R.B., 56
Goodwin, B., 96, 202
Goonatilake, S., 88, 186, 197
Gordon, D., 30, 119
Gordon, L., 36
Goss, R.E., 35
Gossett, T.F., 8
Gotthelf, A., 171
Gottschalk, P., 118
Gould, C.G., 45
Gower, B., 75
Gramsci, A., 165
Grant, J., 193
Green, C., 32
Green, K., 109
Green, T.H., 22, 32, 46, 48, 58, 59, 64, 107

Greene, B., 70
Greimas, A.J., 145
Grewal, I., 185, 191
Griffin, D.R., 7, 25, 122, 124, 126
Griffiths, N., 172
Grigsby, J., 14, 81
Grosskurth, P., 22
Grosz, E., 92, 180, 183
Grotius, H., 17, 19
Guattari, F., 35, 161, 162
Gürhan, Z., 29
Gutting, G., 144, 155

Haack, S., 177
Haakonssen, K., 107
Haber, H.F., 156, 180, 183
Habermas, J., 33, 49, 90, 103, 104, 105, 107, 161, 165, 167, 172
Hacking, I., 92
Haken, H., 203
Hall, D.L., 197
Hall, S., 194
Hamann, J.G., 57
Hamilton, C.V., 194
Hänsel, L., 57, 58
Hanson, N.R., 76
Haraway, D., 91, 179, 181, 182
Harding, M.E., 171
Harding, S., 109, 178, 179, 181, 186
Hare-Mustin, R.T., 31
Harmann, W., 41
Harrington, A., 97
Harris, E.E., 64, 118
Harrison, P., 8
Hart, K., 160
Hartmann, n., 46, 64
Hartshorne, C., 65
Hartsock, N.C.M., 178, 181, 182, 186
Hassan, I., 124, 126, 127, 190
Hatab, L., 131
Hawthorne, J., 81
Hayles, N.K., 91, 92
Healey, R., 88
Heath, D., 90
Hefner, P., 210
Hegarty, P., 141
Hegel, G.W.F., 5, 8, 21, 22, 45, 47, 61, 63, 64, 68, 83, 105, 127, 138, 139, 144, 206

Heidegger, M., 49, 51, 60, 81, 82, 130, 133, 136, 137, 138, 139, 140, 141, 142, 143, 144, 145, 147, 167, 168, 210
Heidelberger, M., 70
Heidenheimer, A.J., 27
Heisenberg, W., 87, 88, 96
Heitlinger, A., 195
Hekman, S.J., 180
Held, V., 33
Hellman, G., 82
Helmholtz, H. von, 101, 160
Hemmo, M., 84
Henckmann, W., 51
Henninger, M.G., 44
Heraclitus, 43
Herberg, W., 108
Herbert of Cherbury, 8, 18
Herbert, N., 87
Herder, J., 8
Herman, J.R., 54
Hertz, H., 101
Heschel, A., 43
Hesiod, 43
Hesse, M., 60, 65, 76, 91, 109, 171, 175
Heyes, C.J., 177
Heyward, I.C., 171
Hilbert, D., 102
Hildebrandt, S., 96
Himmelfarb, G., 120
Hinrichs, J., 52
Hirschmann, N.J., 13, 23, 33, 172, 174
Hirsh, A., 28, 157
Hirsh, E., 179
Hirshman, L.R., 33
Hitler, A., 91, 115, 132, 133, 137, 139
Ho, M.W., 202
Hobbes, T., 6, 19, 20, 44, 74, 78, 79, 109
Hodges, W., 73
Höffding, H., 87
Hogue, W.L., 194
Holland, G., 175
Holland, N.J., 180
Holquist, M., 52
Holzman, L., 136
Hood, P.M., 44
hooks, b., 178, 181, 194
Hookway, C., 47
Hopkins, M., 30